SAT® Subject Test: World History 2007–2008 Edition

Related Titles for College-Bound Students

AP Biology
AP Calculus AB/BC
AP Chemistry
AP English Language & Composition
AP English Literature & Composition
AP Environmental Science
AP European History
AP Macroeconomics/Microeconomics
AP Physics B & C
AP Psychology
AP Statistics
AP U.S. Government & Politics
AP U.S. History
AP World History

SAT Comprehensive Program 2007
SAT Premier Program 2007
12 Practice Tests for the SAT, 2007 Edition
SAT Strategies for Super Busy Students, 2007 Edition
Inside the SAT, 2007 Edition
SAT 2400, 2007 Edition
SAT Critical Reading Workbook, Second Edition
SAT Math Workbook, Second Edition
SAT Writing Workbook, Second Edition
SAT Vocabulary Flashcards Flip-O-Matic, Third Edition
Extreme SAT Vocabulary Flashcards Flip-O-Matic, Second Edition
The Ring of McAllister: A Score-Raising Mystery Featuring 1,046 Must-Know SAT Vocabulary Words, Third Edition
Frankenstein: A Kaplan SAT Score-Raising Classic
The Tales of Edgar Allan Poe: A Kaplan SAT Score-Raising Classic
Dr. Jekyll and Mr. Hyde: A Kaplan SAT Score-Raising Classic
The War of the Worlds: A Kaplan SAT Score Raising Classic
Wuthering Heights: A Kaplan SAT Score-Raising Classic
Domina El SAT: Prepárate para Tomar el Examen para Ingresar a la Universidad

SAT Subject Test: Biology E/M
SAT Subject Test: Chemistry
SAT Subject Test: Literature
SAT Subject Test: Mathematics Level 1
SAT Subject Test: Mathematics Level 2
SAT Subject Test: Physics
SAT Subject Test: Spanish
SAT Subject Test: U.S. History

SAT® Subject Test: World History

2007–2008 Edition

Peggy J. Martin

KAPLAN

PUBLISHING

New York • Chicago

Contributing Editors: Mark Ward, Annette Riffle, Brandon Jones
Editorial Director: Jennifer Farthing
Project Editor: Anne Kemper
Production Editor: Caitlin Ostrow
Production Artist: Virginia Byrne
Cover Designer: Carly Schnur

Colosseum photograph and Pantheon photograph by Lynn Baginski. Used with permission.
Population cartoon, Liberia cartoon, and Iran cartoon by Paresh Nath, internationalcartoons.com. Used with permission.
Tiananmen Square photograph and Buddhas photograph by Esther Portz. Used with permission.
Arabic buildings photograph by Rita Descheneaux. Used with permission.
Yugoslavia cartoon and Africa cartoon by Abigail Martin. Used with permission.
Stonehenge photograph by Marie Owen. Used with permission.
Delft Vase photograph, courtesy of Pately Bridge Antiques (earlyoak.co.uk). Used with permission.

Published Kaplan Publishing
888 Seventh Ave.
New York, NY 10106

Manufactured in the United States of America.
Published simultaneously in Canada.

March 2007
10 9 8 7 6 5 4 3 2 1

ISBN-13: 978-1-4195-5107-9
ISBN-10: 1-4195-5107-8

For information about ordering Kaplan Publishing books at special quantity discounts, please call 1-800-KAP-ITEM or write to Kaplan Publishing, 888 Seventh Ave., 22nd Floor, New York, NY 10106.

TABLE OF CONTENTS

Section Four: Practice Tests

ABOUT THE AUTHOR

Peggy J. Martin makes her home in Del Rio, Texas, where she teaches high school social studies. A graduate of Illinois State University with a major in Spanish and a minor in history, she also holds a Master of Education degree from Sul Ross State University. As a consultant in Advanced Placement World History, she has presented workshops in Texas and New Mexico. Outside the classroom, she spends her time reading, traveling, and keeping up with her husband, Gary, their three grown daughters, and their son, Jonathan.

AVAILABLE ONLINE

FOR ANY TEST CHANGES OR LATE-BREAKING DEVELOPMENTS

kaptest.com/publishing

The material in this book is up-to-date at the time of publication. However, the College Board and Educational Testing Service (ETS) may have instituted changes in the test after this book was published. Be sure to carefully read the materials you receive when you register for the test. If there are any important late-breaking developments—or any changes or corrections to the Kaplan test preparation materials in this book—we will post that information online at **kaptest.com/publishing**.

FEEDBACK AND COMMENTS

kaplansurveys.com/books

We'd love to hear your comments and suggestions about this book. We invite you to fill out our online survey form at **kaplansurveys.com/books**. Your feedback is extremely helpful as we continue to develop high-quality resources to meet your needs.

Section One

THE BASICS

CHAPTER 1

About the SAT Subject Tests

- Frequently Asked Questions
- SAT Subject Test Mastery

You're serious about going to the college of your choice. You wouldn't have opened this book otherwise. You've made a wise decision, because this book can help you achieve your college admissions goal. It'll show you how to score your best on the SAT Subject Test: World History. Before you begin to prepare for the World History test, however, you need some general information about the SAT Subject Tests and how this book will help you prepare. That's what this chapter is about.

FREQUENTLY ASKED QUESTIONS

Before you dive into the specifics of the content of the SAT Subject Test: World History, check out the following FAQs (frequently asked questions) about SAT Subject Tests in general. The information here is accurate at the time of publication, but it is a good idea to check the test information on the College Board website at collegeboard.com.

What Are the SAT Subject Tests?

Previously known as the College Board Achievement Tests and then as the SAT IIs, the SAT Subject Tests focus on specific disciplines: Literature, U.S. History, World History, Mathematics Levels 1 and 2, Physics, Chemistry, Biology, and many foreign languages. Each Subject Test lasts one hour and consists almost entirely of multiple-choice questions.

How Do the SAT Subject Tests Differ from the SAT?

The SAT is largely a test of verbal and math skills. True, you need to know some vocabulary and some formulas for the SAT, but it's designed to measure how well you read and think rather than what you know. SAT Subject Tests are very different. They're designed to measure what you know about specific disciplines. Sure, critical reading and thinking skills play a part on these tests, but their main purpose is to determine exactly what you know about mathematics, history, chemistry, and so on.

How Are the SAT Subject Tests Scored?

Like the SAT, SAT Subject Tests are scored on a 200–800 scale.

What Should I Bring to the SAT Subject Tests?

It's a good idea to get your test materials together the day before the test. You'll need an admission ticket; a form of identification (check the Registration Bulletin to find out what is and what is not permissible); a few sharpened No. 2 pencils; a good eraser; and a calculator (for Math Levels 1 and 2). If you'll be registering as a standby, collect the appropriate forms beforehand. Also, make sure that you have good directions to the test center. (We even recommend that you do a dry run getting to the site prior to Test Day—it can save you the grief of getting lost!)

SAT SUBJECT TEST MASTERY

Now that you know a little about the SAT Subject Tests, it's time to let you in on a few basic test-taking skills and strategies that can improve your scoring performance. You should practice these skills and strategies as you prepare for your SAT Subject Tests.

Use the Test Structure to Your Advantage

The SAT Subject Tests are different from the tests that you're used to taking. On your high school exams, you probably go through the questions in order. You probably spend more time on hard questions than on easy ones, since hard questions are generally worth more points. And you often show your work since your teachers tell you how you approach questions is as important as getting the right answers.

Well, forget all that! None of this applies to the SAT Subject Tests. You can benefit from moving around within the tests, hard questions are worth the same points as easy ones, and it doesn't matter how you answer the questions or what work you did to get there—only what your answers are.

The SAT Subject Tests are highly predictable. Because the format and directions of the SAT Subject Tests remain unchanged from test to test, you can learn how the tests are set up in advance. On test day, the various question types on the test shouldn't be new to you.

One of the easiest things you can do to help your performance on the SAT Subject Tests is to understand the directions before taking the test. Since the instructions are always the same, there's no reason to waste a lot of time on test day reading them. Learn them beforehand, as you work through this book and study the College Board publications.

Many SAT Subject Test questions are arranged by order of difficulty. Not all of the questions on the SAT Subject Test are equally difficult. The questions often get harder as you work through different parts of the test. This pattern can work to your benefit. As you work, you should always be aware of where you are in the test.

When working on more basic problems, you can generally trust your first impulse-the obvious answer is likely to be correct. As you get to the end of a test section, you need to be a bit more suspicious. Now the answers probably won't come as quickly and easily. If they do, look again because the obvious answers may be wrong. Watch our for answers that just "look right." They may be distracters—wrong answer choices deliberately meant to entice you.

You don't need to answer the questions in order. You're allowed to skip around on the SAT Subject Tests. High scorers know this fact. They move through the tests efficiently. They don't dwell on any one question, even a hard one, until they've tried every question at least once.

When you run into questions that look tough, circle them in your test booklet and skip them for the time being. Go back and try again after you've answered the more basic ones, if you've got time. On a second look, troublesome questions can turn out to be remarkably simple.

If you've started to answer a question but get confused, quit and go on to the next question. Persistence may pay off in high school, but it usually hurts your SAT Subject Test scores. Don't spend so much time answering one hard question that you use up three or four questions' worth of time. That'll cost you points, especially if you don't even get the hard question right.

The SAT Subject Tests have a "guessing penalty" that can actually work in your favor. The College Board likes to talk about the guessing penalty on the SAT Subject Tests. That's a misnomer: It's really a wrong answer penalty. If you guess wrong, you get penalized one quarter of a point. If you guess right, you're in great shape.

The fact is, if you can eliminate one or more answer choices as definitely wrong, you'll turn the odds in your favor and actually come out ahead by guessing. The fractional points that you lose are meant to offset the points you might get "accidentally" by guessing the correct answer. With practice, however, you'll see that it's often easy to eliminate several answer choices on some of the questions.

The SAT Subject Test answer grid has no heart. It sounds simple, but it's extremely important: Don't make mistakes filling out your answer grid. When time is short, it's easy to get confused going back and forth between your test booklet and your grid. If you know the answers, but misgrid, you won't get the points. Here's how to avoid mistakes.

Always circle the questions you skip. Put a big circle in your test booklet around any question numbers that you skip. When you go back, these questions will be easy to relocate. Also, if you accidentally skip a box on the grid, you can check your grid against your booklet to see where you went wrong.

Always circle the answers you choose. Circling your answers in the test booklet makes it easier to check your grid against your booklet.

Grid five or more answers at once. Don't transfer your answers to the grid after every question. Transfer them after every five questions. That way, you won't keep breaking your concentration to mark the grid. You'll save time and gain accuracy.

A Strategic Approach to SAT Subject Test Questions

Apart from knowing the setup of the SAT Subject Tests you'll be taking, you've got to have a system for attacking the questions. You wouldn't travel around an unfamiliar city without a map, and you shouldn't approach the SAT Subject Tests without a plan. What follows is the best method for approaching SAT Subject Test questions systematically.

Think about the questions before you look at the answers. The College Board loves to put distracters among the answer choices. Distracters are answers that look like they're correct, but aren't. If you jump right into the answer choices without thinking first about what you're looking for, you're much more likely to fall for one of these traps.

Guess—when you can eliminate at least one answer choice. You already know that the "guessing penalty" can work in your favor. Don't simply skip questions that you can't answer. Spend some time with them in order to see whether you can eliminate any of the answer choices. If you can, it pays for you to guess.

Pace yourself. The SAT Subject Tests give you a lot of questions in a short period of time. To get through the tests, you can't spend too much time on any single question. Keep moving through the tests at a good speed. If you run into a hard question, circle it in your test booklet, skip it, and come back to it later if you have time.

You don't have to spend the same amount of time on every question. Ideally, you should be able to work through the more basic questions at a brisk, steady clip, and use a little more time on the harder questions. One word of caution: Don't rush through easier questions just to save time for the harder ones. The basic questions are points in your pocket, and you're better off not getting to some harder questions if it means losing easy points because of careless mistakes. Remember, you don't get extra credit for answering hard questions.

Locate quick points if you're running out of time. Some questions can be done more quickly than others because they require less work or because choices can be eliminated more easily. If you start to run out of time, locate and answer any of the quick points that remain.

CHAPTER 2

Getting Ready for the SAT Subject Test: World History

- The Format of the SAT Subject Test: World History
- Preparing for the SAT Subject Test: World History
- Special Question Types
- Stress Management
- Countdown to the Test

Now that you're familiar with the basics of the SAT Subject Tests in general, it's time to focus on the World History test in particular. The SAT Subject Test: World History assesses your knowledge and understanding of the development of major global cultures and your capability to use historical skills such as making generalizations and interpretations and analyzing evidence. The test measures the application of historical understanding in all historical fields: political, social, economic, and intellectual and cultural.

THE FORMAT OF THE SAT SUBJECT TEST: WORLD HISTORY

The World History test is a one-hour test consisting of 95 questions. Each question has five possible answer choices. Many of the questions follow the recent increased emphasis on global topics and trends studied in high school world history courses. Among the skills tested are:

- Knowledge of historical terminology
- Comprehension of cause-and-effect relationships
- Knowledge of historical geography
- Familiarity with major historical developments
- Ability to utilize concepts necessary to historical analysis

- Capacity to use historical knowledge to interpret data in maps, graphs, charts, or cartoons
- Ability to interpret paintings or other artistic materials
- Ability to use historical knowledge to interpret quotations within the context of the period addressed

Breakdown of Topics

According to the College Board, the material covered on the SAT Subject Test: World History can be broken down both chronologically and geographically as follows:

Chronological Material	Approximate Percentage of Test
Prehistory and civilizations to the year 500 CE*	25
500–1500 CE	20
1500–1900 CE	25
Post-1900 CE	20
Cross-chronological	10

*The SAT Subject Test: World History uses the designations BCE (*before the common era*) and CE (*common era*) to reflect current usage in many world history textbooks. These designations correspond to B.C. (*before Christ*) and A.D. (*anno Domini*), which are used in some other world history textbooks.

Geographical Material	Approximate Percentage of Test
Europe	25
Africa	10
Southwest Asia	10
South and Southeast Asia	10
East Asia	10
The Americas (excluding the United States)	10
Global	25

PREPARING FOR THE SAT SUBJECT TEST: WORLD HISTORY

How to Use This Book

This book is intended to offer you a summary of the key concepts, trends, terminology, and events that may be covered on the SAT Subject Test: World History. It also gives you the opportunity to practice answering sample test questions similar to those you will encounter on the actual test.

Take the diagnostic test prior to reading the World History Review chapters in this book. This will give you an idea of where your strengths and weaknesses lie before beginning your review.

You will notice that each chapter in the World History Review begins with a timeline of events covered in that chapter, followed by a list of significant terms and names. The timeline will help you improve your understanding of periodization, or the common global characteristics of a given period of historical time. This understanding will assist you in making comparisons of diverse cultures and processes within the same historical time frame. The terms and names will help you focus on the key players within the historical narrative and acquaint you with the terminology required to respond successfully to the test questions.

After reviewing the World History Review chapters, assess your knowledge and understanding by taking Practice Test 1. Create a testing atmosphere close to that of the real test by finding a quiet, well-lit area in which to take the practice tests. Time the test so that you are allowed 60 minutes to complete the 95 test questions. Score your test by reviewing the answer key and explanations following each practice test. Then take Practice Test 2 and repeat the test-taking and scoring procedures.

Additional Academic Preparation

The SAT Subject Test: World History is not based on a specific textbook, but rather emphasizes the essential knowledge and themes that are generally presented in a standard high school world history course. Your academic preparation for the test may include a year-long high school course in global or world history or a course concentrating on the examination of world cultures or area studies. Reviewing the material found in your world history or world area studies textbook will assist you in identifying your areas of weakness. Supplemental readings from both primary and secondary sources can also be helpful; you can find these in classroom world history readers or in handouts you have received from your teacher during the course of your world history studies.

Kaplan's World History Study Tips

There are certain topics and approaches in the study of world history that are of particular importance to the understanding of the subject. Concentrating your study around these themes will assist you in organizing your knowledge and understanding of world history. Included among them are:

- Gender studies
- Comparisons among civilizations and societies
- Trade patterns
- Migratory patterns
- The spread of languages
- The teachings and diffusion of the world's major religions
- Global connections in the modern world

Remember that the SAT Subject Test: World History contains only a few questions that measure factual knowledge of a single geographical area or historical trend. Most questions are analytical in nature, assessing your understanding of connections between cultural or geographical regions. Also, keep in mind that the test questions often emphasize trends or processes that have a bearing on the modern world.

SPECIAL QUESTION TYPES

Some questions on the SAT Subject Test: World History refer to maps or political cartoons. These require some special approaches. Questions with political cartoons often ask you to interpret the cartoonist's message and point of view. Examine the images and pay special attention to any text or dates in the cartoon. For example, the image of Uncle Sam in a top hat is widely recognized as a symbol of the United States. Words and dates also function as clues regarding the issue that the cartoon is addressing.

Which of the following is true of the above cartoon, published in 2003?

(A) It suggests the United States gives too much aid to developing nations.

(B) It advocates American involvement in war-torn regions around the world.

(C) It portrays America's hesitation to intervene in Southeast Asia after the Vietnam War.

(D) It represents two Cold War-era examples of American global intervention.

(E) It depicts America's caution in aiding one African nation after losses in another.

The correct answer is (E). This cartoon represents the American response to two contemporary crises in African nations. Answer (C) is wrong because the cartoon does not refer to Southeast Asia, and (D) is wrong because the conflicts in question are not from the Cold War era. The cartoon does not take a position on whether or not the United States should intervene in the affairs of other nations, as (A) and (B) suggest. It depicts a cautious-looking Uncle Sam sticking his toe into a body of water labeled "Liberia," while remembering being bitten by a crocodile in a similar body of water marked "Somalia." Under the circumstances, his hesitation makes sense.

Here's another political cartoon question.

The above cartoon depicts

(A) advances toward democracy in the Middle East.

(B) the rocky road to democracy in a former Soviet republic.

(C) a Middle Eastern country's repression of democratic reform.

(D) a free and transparent election process.

(E) a communist government's repression of democratic reform.

The correct answer is (C). The cartoon shows the government of Iran as literally standing on pro-democracy campaigners while claiming to have free elections. Choices (A) and (D) are wrong. Iran is a Middle Eastern nation, not a former Soviet republic (B). Its government is not communist (D).

Questions with maps frequently test your knowledge of geography and chronology. Check the question for an indication of the time period. Distracters may refer to the right geographic location but the wrong period, and vice versa.

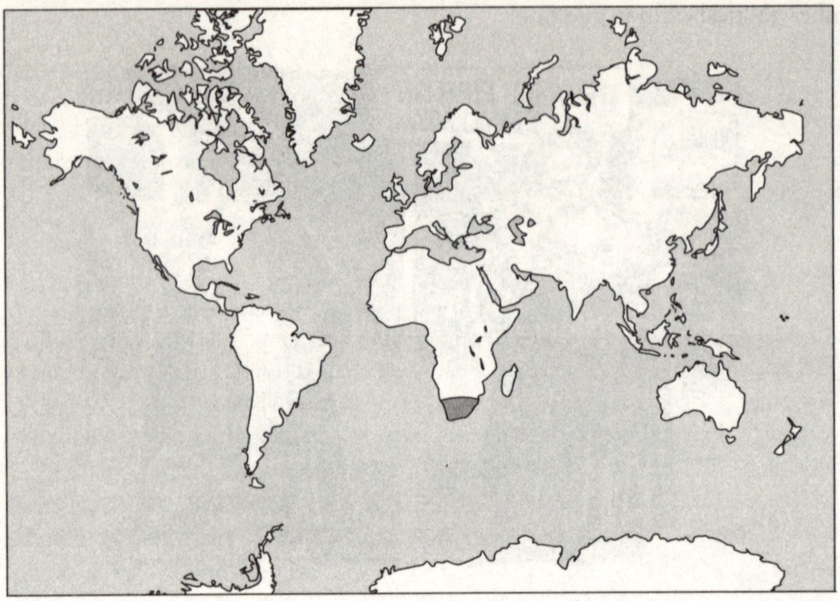

In 1760, which nation controlled the shaded region on the map above?

(A) Spain
(B) France
(C) England
(D) Netherlands
(E) Portugal

The correct answer is (D). Cape Town (modern South Africa) and the surrounding area was a Dutch colony in 1760. After parts of the colony declared their independence from the central administration, Great Britain took control of the region in 1795.

STRESS MANAGEMENT

Remember, a little stress is good. Anxiety is a motivation to study. The adrenaline that gets pumped into your bloodstream when you're stressed helps you stay alert and think more clearly. But if you feel that the tension is so great that it's preventing you from using your study time effectively, here are some things you can do to get it under control.

Take Control

Lack of control is a prime cause of stress. Research shows that if you don't have a sense of control over what's happening in your life, you can easily end up feeling helpless and hopeless. Try to identify the sources of the stress you feel. Which ones of these can you do something about? Can you find ways to reduce the stress you're feeling about any of these sources?

Focus on Your Strengths

Make a list of areas of strength you have that will help you do well on the test. We all have strengths, and recognizing your own is like having reserves of solid gold at Fort Knox. You'll be able to draw on your reserves as you need them, helping you solve difficult questions, maintain confidence, and keep test stress and anxiety at a distance. And every time you recognize a new area of strength, solve a challenging problem, or score well on a practice test, you'll increase your reserves.

Imagine Yourself Succeeding

Close your eyes and imagine yourself in a relaxing situation. Breathe easily and naturally. Now, think of a real-life situation in which you scored well on a test or did well on an assignment. Focus on this success. Now turn your thoughts to the World History test, and keep your thoughts and feelings in line with that successful experience. Don't make comparisons between them; just imagine yourself taking the upcoming test with the same feelings of confidence and relaxed control.

Set Realistic Goals

Facing your problem areas gives you some distinct advantages. What do you want to accomplish in the time remaining? Make a list of realistic goals. You can't help feeling more confident when you know you're actively improving your chances of earning a higher test score.

Exercise Your Frustrations Away

Whether it's jogging, biking, pushups, or a pickup basketball game, physical exercise will stimulate your mind and body, and improve your ability to think and concentrate. A surprising number of students fall out of the habit of regular exercise, ironically because they're spending so much time prepping for exams. A little physical exertion will help to keep your mind and body in sync and help you sleep better at night.

Eat Well

Good nutrition will help you focus and think clearly. Eat plenty of fruits and vegetables, low-fat protein such as fish, skinless poultry, beans, and legumes, and whole grains such as brown rice, whole wheat bread, and pastas. Don't eat a lot of sugar and high-fat snacks, or salty foods.

Work at Your Own Pace

Don't be thrown if other test takers seem to be working more furiously than you. Continue to spend your time patiently thinking through your answers; it is going to lead to better results. Don't mistake other people's sheer activity as signs of progress or higher scores.

Keep Breathing

Conscious attention to breathing is an excellent way to manage stress while you're taking the test. Most of the people who get into trouble during tests take shallow breaths: They breathe using only their upper chests and shoulder muscles, and may even hold their breath for long periods of time. Conversely, those test takers who breathe deeply in a slow, relaxed manner are likely to be in better control during the session.

Stretch

If you find yourself getting spaced out or burned out as you're taking the test, stop for a brief moment and stretch. Even though you'll be pausing on the test for a moment, it's a moment well spent. Stretching will help to refresh you and refocus your thoughts.

"Managing Stress" adapted from "The Kaplan Advantage Stress Management System" by Dr. Ed Newman and Bob Verini, copyright 1996 by Kaplan, Inc.

COUNTDOWN TO THE TEST

Three Days Before the Test

It's almost over. Eat an energy bar, drink some soda—do whatever it takes to keep going. Here are Kaplan's strategies for the three days leading up to the test.

Take a full-length practice test under timed conditions. Use the techniques and strategies you've learned in this book. Approach the test strategically, actively, and confidently.

WARNING: DO NOT take a full-length practice test if you have fewer than 48 hours left before the test. Doing so will probably exhaust you and hurt your score on the actual test. You wouldn't run a marathon the day before the real thing.

Two Days Before the Test

Go over the results of your practice test. Don't worry too much about your score, or about whether you got a specific question right or wrong. The practice test doesn't count. But do examine your performance on specific questions with an eye to how you might get through each one faster and better on the test to come.

The Night Before the Test

DO NOT STUDY. Get together an "SAT Subject Test: World History Kit" containing the following items:

- A watch
- A few No. 2 pencils (pencils with slightly dull points fill the ovals better)
- Erasers
- Photo ID card
- Your admission ticket from ETS

Know exactly where you're going, exactly how you're getting there, and exactly how long it takes to get there. It's probably a good idea to visit your test center sometime before the day of the test, so that you know what to expect—what the rooms are like, how the desks are set up, and so on.

Relax the night before the test. Read a good book, take a long hot shower. Get a good night's sleep. Go to bed early and leave yourself extra time in the morning.

The Morning of the Test

First, wake up. After that:

- Eat breakfast. Make it something substantial, but not anything too heavy or greasy.
- Don't drink a lot of coffee if you're not used to it, Bathroom breaks cut into your time, and too much caffeine is a bad idea.
- Dress in layers so that you can adjust to the temperature of the test room.
- Read something. Warm up your brain with a newspaper or a magazine. You shouldn't let the exam be the first thing you read that day.
- Be sure to get there early. Allow yourself extra time for traffic, mass transit delays, and/or detours.

During the Test

Don't be shaken. If you find your confidence slipping, remind yourself how well you've prepared. You know the structure of the test; you know the instructions; you've had practice with—and have learned strategies for—every question type.

If something goes really wrong, don't panic. If the test booklet is defective—two pages are stuck together or the ink has run—raise your hand and tell the proctor you need a new book. If you accidentally misgrid your answer page or put the answers in the wrong section, raise your hand and tell the proctor. He or she might be able to arrange for you to regrid your test after it's over, when it won't cost you any time.

After the Test

You might walk out of the exam thinking that you blew it. This is a normal reaction. Lots of people—even the highest scorers—feel that way. You tend to remember the questions that stumped you, not the ones that you knew. We're positive that you will have performed well and scored your best on the exam because you followed the Kaplan strategies outlined in this section.

Now, continue your exam prep by taking the diagnostic test that follows this chapter. After the diagnostic test you'll find answers with detailed explanations. Be sure to read these explanations carefully, even when you got the question right, as you can pick up bits of knowledge from them. Use your score to learn which topics you need to review more carefully.

Section Two

DIAGNOSTIC TEST

HOW TO TAKE THE DIAGNOSTIC TEST

Before taking this diagnostic test, find a quiet room where you can work uninterrupted for one hour. Make sure you have several No. 2 pencils with erasers.

Use the answer grid provided to record your answers. Guidelines for scoring your test appear on the reverse side of the answer grid. Time yourself. Spend no more than one hour on the 95 questions. Once you start the diagnostic test, don't stop until you've reached the one-hour time limit. You'll find an answer key and complete answer explanations following the test. Be sure to read the explanations for all questions, even those you answered correctly. Finally, you'll learn how the diagnostic test can help you in your review of world history.

Good luck!

HOW TO CALCULATE YOUR SCORE

Step 1: Figure out your raw score. Use the answer key to count the number of questions you answered correctly and the number of questions you answered incorrectly. (Do not count any questions you left blank.) Multiply the number wrong by 0.25 and subtract the result from the number correct. Round the result to the nearest whole number. This is your raw score.

SAT Subject Test: World History Diagnostic Test

Number right		Number wrong		Raw score
$\square$	$-$	$(0.25 \times \square)$	$=$	$\square$

Step 2: Find your scaled score. In the Score Conversion Table below, find your raw score (rounded to the nearest whole number) in one of the columns to the left. The score directly to the right of that number will be your scaled score.

A note on your practice test scores: Don't take these scores too literally. Practice test conditions cannot precisely mirror real test conditions. Your actual SAT Subject Test: World History score will almost certainly vary from your diagnostic and practice test scores. However, your scores on the diagnostic and practice tests will give you a rough idea of your range on the actual exam.

Conversion Table

Raw	Scaled	Raw	Scaled	Raw	Scaled	Raw	Scaled	Raw	Scaled	Raw	Scaled
95	800	75	760	55	650	35	530	15	420	–5	300
94	800	74	760	54	640	34	530	14	410	–6	290
93	800	73	750	53	640	33	520	13	410	–7	280
92	800	72	740	52	630	32	520	12	400	–8	280
91	800	71	740	51	630	31	510	11	400	–9	270
90	800	70	730	50	620	30	500	10	390	–10	260
89	800	69	730	49	620	29	500	9	380	–11	260
88	800	68	720	48	610	28	490	8	380	–12	250
87	800	67	720	47	600	27	490	7	370	–13	250
86	800	66	710	46	600	26	480	6	370	–14	240
85	800	65	700	45	590	25	480	5	360	–15	240
84	800	64	700	44	590	24	470	4	360	–16	230
83	800	63	690	43	580	23	460	3	350	–17	220
82	800	62	690	42	580	22	460	2	340	–18	220
81	800	61	680	41	570	21	450	1	340	–19	210
80	800	60	680	40	560	20	450	0	330	–20	210
79	790	59	670	39	560	19	440	–1	320	–21	200
78	780	58	670	38	550	18	440	–2	320	–22	200
77	780	57	660	37	550	17	430	–3	310	–23	200
76	770	56	660	36	540	16	420	–4	300	–24	200

Answer Grid
Diagnostic Test

1. (A) (B) (C) (D) (E)
2. (A) (B) (C) (D) (E)
3. (A) (B) (C) (D) (E)
4. (A) (B) (C) (D) (E)
5. (A) (B) (C) (D) (E)
6. (A) (B) (C) (D) (E)
7. (A) (B) (C) (D) (E)
8. (A) (B) (C) (D) (E)
9. (A) (B) (C) (D) (E)
10. (A) (B) (C) (D) (E)
11. (A) (B) (C) (D) (E)
12. (A) (B) (C) (D) (E)
13. (A) (B) (C) (D) (E)
14. (A) (B) (C) (D) (E)
15. (A) (B) (C) (D) (E)
16. (A) (B) (C) (D) (E)
17. (A) (B) (C) (D) (E)
18. (A) (B) (C) (D) (E)
19. (A) (B) (C) (D) (E)
20. (A) (B) (C) (D) (E)
21. (A) (B) (C) (D) (E)
22. (A) (B) (C) (D) (E)
23. (A) (B) (C) (D) (E)
24. (A) (B) (C) (D) (E)
25. (A) (B) (C) (D) (E)
26. (A) (B) (C) (D) (E)
27. (A) (B) (C) (D) (E)
28. (A) (B) (C) (D) (E)
29. (A) (B) (C) (D) (E)
30. (A) (B) (C) (D) (E)
31. (A) (B) (C) (D) (E)
32. (A) (B) (C) (D) (E)
33. (A) (B) (C) (D) (E)
34. (A) (B) (C) (D) (E)
35. (A) (B) (C) (D) (E)
36. (A) (B) (C) (D) (E)
37. (A) (B) (C) (D) (E)
38. (A) (B) (C) (D) (E)
39. (A) (B) (C) (D) (E)
40. (A) (B) (C) (D) (E)
41. (A) (B) (C) (D) (E)
42. (A) (B) (C) (D) (E)
43. (A) (B) (C) (D) (E)
44. (A) (B) (C) (D) (E)
45. (A) (B) (C) (D) (E)
46. (A) (B) (C) (D) (E)
47. (A) (B) (C) (D) (E)
48. (A) (B) (C) (D) (E)
49. (A) (B) (C) (D) (E)
50. (A) (B) (C) (D) (E)
51. (A) (B) (C) (D) (E)
52. (A) (B) (C) (D) (E)
53. (A) (B) (C) (D) (E)
54. (A) (B) (C) (D) (E)
55. (A) (B) (C) (D) (E)
56. (A) (B) (C) (D) (E)
57. (A) (B) (C) (D) (E)
58. (A) (B) (C) (D) (E)
59. (A) (B) (C) (D) (E)
60. (A) (B) (C) (D) (E)
61. (A) (B) (C) (D) (E)
62. (A) (B) (C) (D) (E)
63. (A) (B) (C) (D) (E)
64. (A) (B) (C) (D) (E)
65. (A) (B) (C) (D) (E)
66. (A) (B) (C) (D) (E)
67. (A) (B) (C) (D) (E)
68. (A) (B) (C) (D) (E)
69. (A) (B) (C) (D) (E)
70. (A) (B) (C) (D) (E)
71. (A) (B) (C) (D) (E)
72. (A) (B) (C) (D) (E)
73. (A) (B) (C) (D) (E)
74. (A) (B) (C) (D) (E)
75. (A) (B) (C) (D) (E)
76. (A) (B) (C) (D) (E)
77. (A) (B) (C) (D) (E)
78. (A) (B) (C) (D) (E)
79. (A) (B) (C) (D) (E)
80. (A) (B) (C) (D) (E)
81. (A) (B) (C) (D) (E)
82. (A) (B) (C) (D) (E)
83. (A) (B) (C) (D) (E)
84. (A) (B) (C) (D) (E)
85. (A) (B) (C) (D) (E)
86. (A) (B) (C) (D) (E)
87. (A) (B) (C) (D) (E)
88. (A) (B) (C) (D) (E)
89. (A) (B) (C) (D) (E)
90. (A) (B) (C) (D) (E)
91. (A) (B) (C) (D) (E)
92. (A) (B) (C) (D) (E)
93. (A) (B) (C) (D) (E)
94. (A) (B) (C) (D) (E)
95. (A) (B) (C) (D) (E)

Diagnostic Test

Directions: Each question or incomplete statement is followed by five suggested answers or completions. Select the best answer and fill in the corresponding oval on the answer sheet.

1. In which of the following eighteenth-century societies were agricultural laborers most likely to be men and women free from the bonds of servitude?

   (A) Jamaica
   (B) The Ottoman Empire
   (C) Brazil
   (D) Russia
   (E) Haiti

2. Which of the following manufactures is paired with its country of origin?

   (A) cotton—India
   (B) celadon pottery—Spain
   (C) porcelain—Korea
   (D) ironwork—Persia
   (E) carpets—China

3. Indian Ocean trade in the sixteenth century

   (A) was controlled by Portugal.
   (B) was dominated by Muslim merchants.
   (C) was dominated by Chinese merchants.
   (D) was an active commercial area for the French.
   (E) was a key commercial area for Australian aborigines.

4. In which of the following regions did native peoples NOT develop agriculture?

   (A) South Asia
   (B) Australia
   (C) Southwest Asia
   (D) North Africa
   (E) Andean highlands

5. Which is the correct sequence of the following revolutions?

   (A) French, Haitian, American, Chinese, Mexican
   (B) American, Haitian, French, Chinese, Mexican
   (C) French, American, Haitian, Mexican, Chinese
   (D) Haitian, American, French, Chinese, Mexican
   (E) American, French, Haitian, Mexican, Chinese

6. The Mayas and the people of Gupta India had in common the knowledge of

   (A) navigational techniques.
   (B) the cultivation of maize.
   (C) the concept of the zero.
   (D) the practice of inoculation.
   (E) cosmetic surgery.

GO ON TO THE NEXT PAGE

7. "If a man has knocked out the eye of a member of the aristocracy, his eye shall be knocked out… If he has knocked out the eye of a commoner… he shall pay one mina of silver."

   The above quotation is from
   (A) *The Epic of Gilgamesh.*
   (B) *The Popol Vuh.*
   (C) *The Rigveda.*
   (D) *The Upanishads.*
   (E) *The Code of Hammurabi.*

8. Which of the following is NOT true concerning the laws mentioned in the quotation in question 7?
   (A) They upheld the concept that punishment should be appropriate to the crime.
   (B) They reflected an egalitarian society.
   (C) They made government responsible for punishing the crimes of society.
   (D) Some social classes were deemed of greater importance than others.
   (E) Their provisions were more lenient than those of the Hittites.

9. Which of the following statements would be the most difficult to prove or disprove through research?
   (A) Phoenician trade made a greater impact upon the Mediterranean world than Minoan trade.
   (B) Similarities in beliefs and customs indicate cultural borrowing among early Mesoamerican peoples.
   (C) The Mongol Peace was a period of increased trade and interaction between Europe and Asia.
   (D) Buddhist practices changed as the religion spread from India to China.
   (E) Indo-European migrations resulted in the diffusion of language.

10. Of the following, which country emerged prosperous after World War I?
   (A) Great Britain
   (B) France
   (C) Japan
   (D) China
   (E) Russia

11. The Inca system of roads was most similar to those of the
   (A) Persians.
   (B) Indians.
   (C) Mongols.
   (D) Aztecs.
   (E) Mauryans.

12. The civilization portrayed in the photograph above
   (A) did not permit slavery.
   (B) strongly influenced the Greek civilization.
   (C) restricted its army to its citizens.
   (D) expanded its empire to include India.
   (E) constructed a system of roads that connected with Silk Road trade.

GO ON TO THE NEXT PAGE

13. Which of the following areas did not experience a social system based on feudalism?
    (A) Russia
    (B) Great Britain
    (C) Germany
    (D) Spain
    (E) Japan

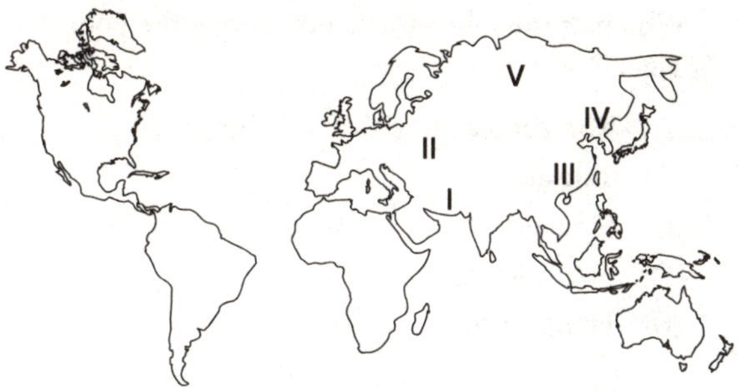

Questions 14–15 are based on the map above.

14. Areas I–V were all included in the
    (A) Islamic empire.
    (B) Hellenistic empire.
    (C) Mongol empire.
    (D) Ottoman empire.
    (E) Roman empire.

15. The empire portrayed in the map was known for
    (A) its conversion to Christianity.
    (B) its promotion of trade.
    (C) its appreciation for Western European Renaissance culture.
    (D) the efficiency of its agricultural techniques.
    (E) its efficient administrators.

16. The classical empires of Rome, India, and Han China shared in common
    (A) a strong centralized government throughout their history.
    (B) a state religion.
    (C) a resistance to long-distance trade.
    (D) centuries of bountiful harvests.
    (E) the threat of foreign peoples along their borders.

17. Polynesian society prior to 1600
    (A) had an advanced knowledge of metallurgy.
    (B) engaged widely in long-distance trade.
    (C) suffered from weak political leadership.
    (D) lived in an egalitarian society.
    (E) was polytheistic.

18. Which religion spread primarily through the efforts of traders?
    (A) Shintoism
    (B) Zoroastrianism
    (C) Judaism
    (D) Jainism
    (E) Buddhism

19. Linguists would be most apt to trace all of the following EXCEPT
    (A) the route of the Manila galleons.
    (B) Indo-European migrations.
    (C) the Bantu migrations.
    (D) the path of the Malay sailors.
    (E) Phoenician trade connections.

20. Trans-Saharan trade was especially active in which two commodities?
    (A) amber and silver
    (B) gold and salt
    (C) ivory and animal skins
    (D) ebony and cowrie shells
    (E) jade and exotic woods

21. "The Third Estate is the People and the People is the foundation of the State; it is in fact the State itself; the other orders are merely political categories while by the immutable laws of nature the People is everything."

    The above quotation was written by a contemporary of which revolution?
    (A) American
    (B) Mexican
    (C) Haitian
    (D) French
    (E) Chinese

GO ON TO THE NEXT PAGE

22. "I must enlighten my people, cultivate their manners and morals, and make them as happy as human beings can be, or as happy as the means at my disposal permit."

(Frederick II of Prussia)

These words were spoken by a ruler whose style of leadership can best be described as

(A) absolute monarchism.
(B) enlightened despotism.
(C) constitutional monarchism.
(D) divine monarchism.
(E) fascism.

23. The cartoon pictured above takes the opinion that

(A) Asians and Pacific Islanders are the region's greatest resources.
(B) The technological world has the responsibility of supplying the needs of Asians.
(C) Asians should support China's one-child policy.
(D) The limited resources of Asia and the Pacific are insufficient to meet the needs of its growing population.
(E) The Asian and Pacific populations can hope to have their needs satisfied eventually.

24. The region pictured above has seen the implementation of

(A) human cloning.
(B) stem cell research.
(C) the green revolution.
(D) guest workers.
(E) détente.

25. Which of the following is not among the Four Tigers?

(A) The People's Republic of China
(B) Taiwan
(C) Singapore
(D) South Korea
(E) Hong Kong

26. "The great questions of the day will not be settled by speeches or majority votes… but by blood and iron." (Otto von Bismarck)

The above words were spoken

(A) before the South American wars for independence.
(B) before World War I.
(C) after the Korean Conflict.
(D) after World War II.
(E) before the French Revolution.

27. All the pre-Columbian peoples of the Americas

(A) were polytheistic.
(B) integrated various ethnic groups into their societies.
(C) had a system of writing.
(D) limited their trade to regional networks.
(E) were noted as skilled administrators.

28. Which of the following empires was most global in its extent?

(A) Hellenistic
(B) Incan
(C) Moche
(D) Han
(E) Aztec

GO ON TO THE NEXT PAGE

29. Bartolomeu Dias was to the Atlantic Ocean as Zheng He was to the
    (A) Mediterranean Sea.
    (B) Indian Ocean.
    (C) Baltic Sea.
    (D) Pacific Ocean.
    (E) Caribbean Sea.

30. Examples of external migration in the twentieth century include all of the following EXCEPT
    (A) the flight of refugees from Kosovo.
    (B) the resettlement of Egyptian villagers in the environs of Cairo.
    (C) the flight of Hindus from Pakistan after the partition of the Indian subcontinent.
    (D) the arrival of Turkish guest workers in Western Europe.
    (E) the movement of the Nationalist Chinese to Taiwan.

31. The knowledge of agriculture
    (A) was usually passed from one culture to another.
    (B) diffused throughout the eastern hemisphere only.
    (C) showed the result of human planning.
    (D) arose in different areas of the world about the same time.
    (E) was confined to river valley civilizations.

32. Which of the following products was introduced from the Americas to the eastern hemisphere through the Columbian Exchange, then introduced to North America from Europe?
    (A) potato
    (B) corn
    (C) cassava
    (D) wheat
    (E) barley

33. Which of the following was an example of the U.S./Soviet policy of brinkmanship?
    (A) the Soviet invasion of Afghanistan
    (B) the Cuban Missile Crisis
    (C) glasnost
    (D) the Soviet repression of the Chechnyan rebellion
    (E) the docking of Apollo and Soyuz

34. All of the following served to spread Christianity EXCEPT
    (A) the unity of the Mediterranean basin in the first century.
    (B) the missionary efforts of Paul of Tarsus.
    (C) trade along the Silk Roads.
    (D) the Roman roads of the Pax Romana.
    (E) its acceptance as the official religion of Rome in the first century.

35. The Franco-Prussian War was significant in that it
    (A) prompted southern Germany to unite with northern Germany.
    (B) promoted the unification of France.
    (C) delayed the unification of Italy.
    (D) ended with France as the dominant power in Europe.
    (E) demonstrated the weaknesses of the Prussian government.

36. Women in Neolithic society
    (A) often accompanied men on hunting expeditions.
    (B) saw their status increase as agriculture became more commonplace.
    (C) were probably the first farmers.
    (D) were expected to devote themselves solely to childcare rather than to the procurement of food.
    (E) were usually the leaders of their clan.

GO ON TO THE NEXT PAGE

37. The industrial revolution experienced in several parts of the world throughout the nineteenth and twentieth centuries depended upon all of the following EXCEPT
    (A) *laissez faire* capitalism.
    (B) entrepreneurship.
    (C) capital investment and equipment.
    (D) an adequate supply of workers.
    (E) raw materials.

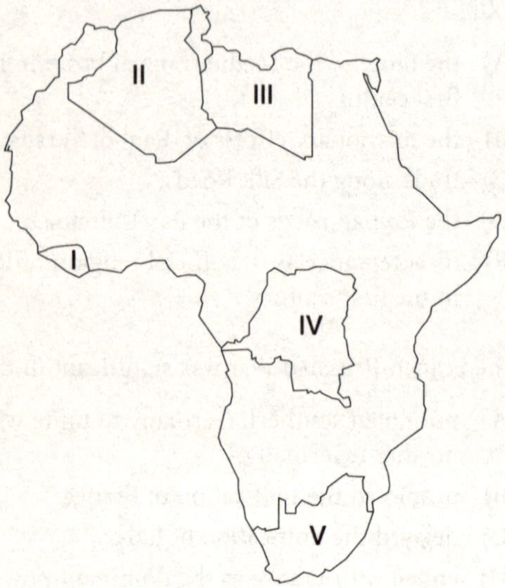

Questions 38–39 are based on the above map.

38. A nineteenth-century conflict between Europeans and native Africans occurred in which area?
    (A) I
    (B) II
    (C) III
    (D) IV
    (E) V

39. The only African country never controlled by a European nation is indicated by the numeral
    (A) I.
    (B) II.
    (C) III.
    (D) IV.
    (E) V.

40. All of the following have been emphasized by followers of Confucian philosophy EXCEPT
    (A) education.
    (B) efficient government.
    (C) a patriarchal family.
    (D) reverence for ancestors.
    (E) individualism.

41. Both Muslims and Jews deny
    (A) the importance of prayer.
    (B) the worship of one god.
    (C) the covenant relationship between God and man.
    (D) the divinity of Jesus.
    (E) the prophetic teachings of the Old Testament.

LITERACY RATES C. 1999
(Source: *CIA: The World Factbook*, 1999.)

Country	Men	Women
Afghanistan	47%	15%
China	90%	73%
France	99%	99%
India	66%	38%
Peru	95%	83%
Uganda	74%	38%

42. Which of the following is supported by the information in the chart above?
    (A) Men and women in developing nations have approximately equal access to educational opportunities.
    (B) Nations of the technological world offer equal educational opportunities for men and women.
    (C) Democratic nations provide equal educational opportunities.
    (D) Developing nations tend to offer more educational opportunities to men than to women.
    (E) Women in developing nations show low literacy rates.

GO ON TO THE NEXT PAGE

43. "By what principle of reason... should these foreigners send in return a poisonous drug, which involves in destruction those very natives of China?"

    The above quotation involves a criticism of which country?

    (A) Germany
    (B) Vietnam
    (C) The United States
    (D) France
    (E) Great Britain

44. The columns illustrated in the photograph above are characteristic of the architecture of which culture?

    (A) Indian
    (B) Greek
    (C) Persian
    (D) Russian
    (E) Arabic

45. Japanese modernization in the late nineteenth and early twentieth centuries was made possible by

    (A) the support of its national government.
    (B) its abundant supply of raw materials.
    (C) its industrial tradition.
    (D) its position as a leading world power.
    (E) its vast land resources.

46. The interest in the procurement of African slaves in the trans-Atlantic trade was caused primarily by the need for

    (A) workers on the Brazilian and Caribbean sugar plantations.
    (B) labor in the cotton fields of the British North American colonies.
    (C) servants in the households of Europe.
    (D) labor in the silver mines of Mexico.
    (E) laborers in the farms of the northern colonies of British North America.

47. The Mongols failed twice to conquer

    (A) Korea.
    (B) India.
    (C) Japan.
    (D) Russia.
    (E) Persia.

48. The Mexican independence movement from Spain was initiated by which class?

    (A) merchants
    (B) elites
    (C) mestizos
    (D) creoles
    (E) peninsulares

49. The Berlin Conference of 1884–1885 was noted for

    (A) its establishment of representative democracies for Africa.
    (B) the absence of representatives from African nations.
    (C) its consideration of African culture and ethnic groups.
    (D) its role in the unification of Germany.
    (E) Metternich's efforts in establishing peace and stability in Western Europe.

GO ON TO THE NEXT PAGE

50. The concept behind the establishment of the new Iranian government in 1980 was

(A) religious fundamentalism.
(B) parliamentary democracy.
(C) dynastic rule.
(D) Marxist socialism.
(E) absolute monarchy.

51. Which of the following characterized the rule of Peter the Great and Catherine the Great of Russia?

(A) Both granted increasing freedoms to the serfs.
(B) Both were interested in the modernization of Russia.
(C) Both sought heightened participation of their subjects in the political process.
(D) Both brought the Enlightenment culture of western Europe to Russia.
(E) Their liberal sentiments caused both to reject warfare to expand their empire.

52. Which of the following countries could not be found on a map drawn in 1800?

(A) Persia
(B) Japan
(C) Austria
(D) Poland
(E) Prussia

53. Greek culture was spread through all of the following EXCEPT

(A) the Hellenistic empire.
(B) colonization.
(C) the culture of Islamic Spain.
(D) the Byzantine empire.
(E) the empire of Mali.

54. The origins of Hinduism can be found in the literature of the

(A) Aryans.
(B) Sikhs.
(C) Tamils.
(D) Jainists.
(E) Dravidians.

55. Which of the following cultures merits the nickname "The Greeks of America"?

(A) Incan
(B) Mayan
(C) Aztec
(D) Olmec
(E) Toltec

56. "Men are born and remain free and equal in rights; social distinctions may be based only upon general usefulness."

Which of the following philosophers would most readily agree with the above words from the *Declaration of the Rights of Man and the Citizen*?

(A) Voltaire
(B) Locke
(C) Rousseau
(D) Hobbes
(E) Montesquieu

57. "The history of all hitherto existing society is the history of class struggles."

The author of this statement is responding to what movement in world history?

(A) the scientific revolution
(B) Social Darwinism
(C) the industrial revolution
(D) the commercial revolution
(E) the agricultural revolution

58. The Congress of Vienna of 1815

(A) prevented the unification of Italy.
(B) returned representative democracy to Europe.
(C) disrupted the balance of power in Europe.
(D) restored legitimate rulers to the thrones of Europe.
(E) created the instability that led to World War I.

GO ON TO THE NEXT PAGE

59. Which of the following was NOT included in Wilson's Fourteen Points?

    (A) provision for a peacekeeping organization
    (B) military reductions for Germany
    (C) the principle of self-determination
    (D) free trade
    (E) an end to secret treaties

60. Twentieth-century Central Africa and the Balkans have in common

    (A) incidences of ethnic cleansing.
    (B) the tradition of representative democracy.
    (C) a history of imperialism.
    (D) religious harmony.
    (E) linguistic unity.

61. The Negritude movement arose in the period

    (A) of the trans-Atlantic slave trade.
    (B) before European imperialism in Africa.
    (C) before the creation of new African states.
    (D) after the civil war in the Congo.
    (E) during the Zulu Wars.

62. "Nothing shall be done which may prejudice the civil and religious rights of existing non-Jewish communities in Palestine."

    The above is a clause from the

    (A) Balfour Declaration.
    (B) Camp David Accords.
    (C) Declaration of Principles.
    (D) Treaty of Versailles.
    (E) Palestine Liberation Organization.

63. The dominant language of the mass culture of the twenty-first century is

    (A) French.
    (B) Spanish.
    (C) Mandarin Chinese.
    (D) English.
    (E) Russian.

64. The fastest-growing religion of the twentieth century was

    (A) Hinduism.
    (B) Islam.
    (C) Christianity.
    (D) Buddhism.
    (E) Daoism.

65. The square pictured above was the scene of the 1989

    (A) Cultural Revolution.
    (B) conflict between Chinese troops and student protestors.
    (C) transfer of Hong Kong.
    (D) state visit of President Nixon.
    (E) Four Modernizations.

66. The year 2002 saw the introduction of

    (A) a common currency for Europe.
    (B) free trade in North America.
    (C) multinational corporations.
    (D) the European Union.
    (E) GATT.

67. Which of the following is NOT associated with the rule of Mikhail Gorbachev?

    (A) perestroika
    (B) glasnost
    (C) democratization
    (D) independence movements in the Baltic states
    (E) economic prosperity

GO ON TO THE NEXT PAGE

68. German reunification
    (A) has prevented Germany from joining in UN peacekeeping activities.
    (B) was widely anticipated by other world nations.
    (C) did not produce economic improvement by the close of the twentieth century.
    (D) produced a pledge from the German government that the unified country was committed to human rights and democracy.
    (E) was spearheaded by the economic prosperity of East Germany.

69. During the months preceding World War II, the response of European nations and Russia to Hitler can best be described as one of
    (A) deterrence.
    (B) containment.
    (C) appeasement.
    (D) reversal of the Versailles Treaty.
    (E) aggression.

70. The experience of colonial troops during World War I caused them to
    (A) take greater pride in their colonial powers governing them.
    (B) expect independence.
    (C) improve their national infrastructure.
    (D) retreat into isolationism.
    (E) establish representative democracies.

71. The Hittites and Assyrians had in common
    (A) great libraries.
    (B) liberal legal codes.
    (C) the assimilation of conquered peoples into their empires.
    (D) fair taxes.
    (E) iron metallurgy.

72. Throughout most of the twentieth century, Latin America witnessed
    (A) the dominance of stable governments on the continent.
    (B) steady economic growth.
    (C) heavy investments by foreign nations.
    (D) strong domestic industries.
    (E) the decline of foreign interest in its raw materials.

73. The Silk Roads
    (A) were land routes only.
    (B) stopped to the east of Mediterranean trade routes.
    (C) connected land routes to Indian Ocean trade.
    (D) had nothing to do with the transport of silk.
    (E) were protected throughout their length by pastoral nomads.

74. Key to the prosperity and longevity of Constantinople was its location on the
    (A) Caspian Sea.
    (B) Red Sea.
    (C) Bosporus Strait.
    (D) Adriatic Sea.
    (E) Baltic Sea.

75. "I believe it must be the policy of the United States to support free people who are resisting attempted subjugation by armed minorities or by outside pressures."

    The above words were spoken as part of the
    (A) Truman Doctrine.
    (B) Marshall Plan.
    (C) Yalta Conference.
    (D) Atlantic Charter.
    (E) Potsdam Conference.

GO ON TO THE NEXT PAGE

76. Contrary to what Marx and Engels had predicted, communism took hold in

    (A) industrialized nations.
    (B) developing nations.
    (C) countries with a democratic tradition.
    (D) countries already enjoying economic prosperity.
    (E) the post-industrialized world.

77. What is true of Athenian democracy?

    (A) Court trials were held without the use of juries.
    (B) All those who could reach the age of eighteen could vote.
    (C) It had a single executive.
    (D) Unfavorable decisions could not be appealed to a higher court.
    (E) It was a direct democracy.

78. All of the following are religions of salvation EXCEPT

    (A) Christianity.
    (B) Judaism.
    (C) Shintoism.
    (D) Zoroastrianism.
    (E) Islam.

79. "The unexamined life is not worth living" is a sentiment expressed by

    (A) Plato.
    (B) Aristotle.
    (C) Solon.
    (D) Cleisthenes.
    (E) Socrates.

80. From the Zhou dynasty through the twentieth century, Chinese rulers would

    (A) provide China with a decentralized government.
    (B) prevent foreign rulers from occupying the throne of China.
    (C) neglect to construct necessary dams and irrigation systems.
    (D) invoke the mandate of heaven to justify their rule.
    (E) insure equality of gender roles.

81. From Vietnam, the Tang dynasty of China became acquainted with

    (A) block printing.
    (B) tea.
    (C) porcelain.
    (D) bananas.
    (E) coffee.

82. "The *brahmin* was his mouth, of both his arms was the *kshatriya* made.
    His thighs became the *vaishya*, from his feet the *shudra* was produced."

    This passage from the *Rigveda* deals with the origin of

    (A) monarchical rule.
    (B) slavery.
    (C) the caste system.
    (D) humankind.
    (E) the earth.

GO ON TO THE NEXT PAGE

83. "For six days and six nights the winds blew, torrent and tempest and flood overwhelmed the world, tempest and flood raged together like warring hosts. When the seventh day dawned the storm from the south subsided, the sea grew calm, the flood was stilled."

The above words are from the

(A) *Popol Vuh.*
(B) *Rubaiyyat.*
(C) Egyptian *Book of the Dead.*
(D) *Vedas.*
(E) *Epic of Gilgamesh.*

84. The Lascaux cave paintings could be used as a primary source in a study of

(A) the highlands of New Guinea.
(B) ancient Austronesian peoples.
(C) the Nok culture.
(D) paleolithic humans.
(E) neolithic humans.

85. A key factor that allowed the Egyptian culture the opportunity to develop independently was

(A) its superior military force.
(B) being surrounded by natural geographical barriers.
(C) the animosity of its neighbors.
(D) the leadership of the pharaohs.
(E) being uninterested in long-distance trade.

86. All of the following are true of the Ming dynasty EXCEPT:

(A) It ended forever the threat of the Mongols to China.
(B) It produced fine porcelain vases.
(C) It sent out a massive expedition to explore the Indian Ocean.
(D) It established a trade route with East Africa.
(E) It focused on the reaffirmation of Chinese culture.

87. "A few years ago I discovered in the heavens many particulars which had been invisible until our time. Because of their novelty, and because of some consequences deriving from them which contradict certain physical propositions commonly accepted in philosophical schools, they roused against me no small number of such professors, as if I had placed these things in heaven with my hands in order to confound nature and the sciences."

These words were written by

(A) Kepler, in defense of his views of elliptical planetary orbits.
(B) Ptolemy, in defense of the geocentric theory.
(C) Copernicus, in defense of the geocentric theory.
(D) Galileo, in defense of the heliocentric theory.
(E) Aristotle, in defense of the heliocentric theory.

88. The Vikings

(A) established permanent colonies in North America.
(B) were part of the wave of barbarian invasions of the 400s.
(C) had no interest in establishing permanent settlements in Europe.
(D) failed to create permanent connections between the eastern and western hemispheres.
(E) failed to establish desired trade relationships with the Russians.

89. The English Bill of Rights provided for all of the following EXCEPT

(A) no suspension of the laws of Parliament.
(B) no levying of taxes without the specific consent of Parliament.
(C) no limits on royal power.
(D) no interference with freedom of speech in Parliament.
(E) the right for a citizen to petition the monarch concerning grievances.

GO ON TO THE NEXT PAGE

90. Which of the following is true concerning OPEC?
    - (A) Its member nations are confined to countries in Southwest Asia.
    - (B) It has used its power to oppose U.S. support for Israel.
    - (C) Its power increased after the Iran-Iraq War and the Gulf War.
    - (D) Its control of petroleum prices contributed to the global prosperity of the 1970s.
    - (E) It displayed its concern for the environment during the Gulf War.

91. All of the following were contributing factors to the fall of communism in the Soviet Union EXCEPT
    - (A) the Star Wars program initiated by Ronald Reagan.
    - (B) Soviet economic prosperity in the 1980s.
    - (C) Gorbachev's program of democratization.
    - (D) glasnost.
    - (E) perestroika.

92. Which of the following political units was the least culturally diverse in the nineteenth century?
    - (A) Tokugawa Japan
    - (B) Qing China
    - (C) Russia
    - (D) the Ottoman empire
    - (E) Brazil

93. The last country to abolish slavery was
    - (A) the United States.
    - (B) France.
    - (C) Great Britain.
    - (D) Brazil.
    - (E) Haiti.

94. Industrialization
    - (A) alleviated poverty in less-developed nations.
    - (B) was a direct contributor to imperialism.
    - (C) led to fewer opportunities for citizens to participate in the democratic process.
    - (D) was confined to Great Britain and the United States until the twentieth century.
    - (E) led to the decline in power of the middle class.

95. During the nineteenth century
    - (A) women in the United States and Great Britain won the right to vote.
    - (B) liberal movements resulted in the decline of anti-Semitism.
    - (C) famine resulted in the emigration of over a million Irish to other countries.
    - (D) Manifest Destiny led to greater cooperation between the United States and Mexico.
    - (E) political stability came to France.

STOP!

If you finish before time is up, you may check your work.

Answer Key
Diagnostic Test

1. B
2. A
3. B
4. B
5. E
6. C
7. E
8. B
9. A
10. C
11. A
12. E
13. D
14. C
15. B
16. E
17. E
18. E
19. A
20. B
21. D
22. B
23. A
24. C
25. A
26. B
27. A
28. A
29. B
30. B
31. D
32. A
33. B
34. E
35. A
36. C
37. A
38. E
39. A
40. E
41. D
42. E
43. E
44. B
45. A
46. A
47. C
48. C
49. B
50. A
51. B
52. D
53. E
54. A
55. B
56. C
57. C
58. D
59. B
60. A
61. C
62. A
63. D
64. B
65. B
66. A
67. E
68. D
69. C
70. B
71. E
72. C
73. C
74. C
75. A
76. B
77. E
78. C
79. E
80. D
81. B
82. C
83. E
84. D
85. B
86. A
87. D
88. D
89. C
90. B
91. B
92. A
93. D
94. B
95. C

ANSWERS AND EXPLANATIONS

1. **(B)** While the Ottomans widely used slave labor in their military, most of their agricultural workers were free peasants. Jamaica (A), Brazil (C), and Haiti (E) widely used slave labor. Russian serfs, while not slaves, remained bound to the land and to the landowner (D).

2. **(A)** The cotton textile industry was key to the economic prosperity of India. Celadon pottery (B) was a product of Korea, porcelain (C) of China, ironwork (D) of Spain, and carpets (E) of Persia.

3. **(B)** Although the Portuguese had a strong interest in Indian Ocean trade, Muslim merchants still dominated the area. The Chinese were not active in Indian Ocean trade in this time period (C), and neither the French (D) nor the Australians (E) had an active interest in trade in the Indian Ocean at that time.

4. **(B)** Not until the arrival of Europeans did Australians engage in agriculture. The Indus Valley in South Asia (A), Sumer in Southwest Asia (C), and Egypt in North Africa (D) were among the earliest agricultural civilizations. The Andean highlands were a key area of the cultivation of the potato (E).

5. **(E)** The beginning dates for the revolutions are: American (1775), French (1789), Haitian (1791), Mexican (1910), Chinese (1911).

6. **(C)** Both understood the concept of the zero as a place holder. Choice (B) was typical of the Mayas, while the other responses pertain to the Gupta.

7. **(E)** The *Code of Hammurabi* is one of the earliest known legal codifications. *The Epic of Gilgamesh* contains a creation account from Sumer, while *The Popol Vuh* is a Mayan creation story. The *Rig Veda* was a collection of hymns to Aryan gods, while the *Upanishads* were dialogues that explored the Vedas.

8. **(B)** The use of the words *aristocracy* and *commoner* does not indicate an egalitarian society, but rather one where some social classes had more privileges than others (D). The remaining choices are characteristics of the code. The provisions of the *Code of Hammurabi* were stricter than the more forgiving laws of the Hittites.

9. **(A)** Statement A is an opinion; it would be difficult to use research to make what amounts to a value judgment on the merits of the two respective trade systems. The remaining answer choices can be proven or disproved by researching the facts of each situation.

10. **(C)** Japan emerged from the war as a strong nation, while the other countries listed had suffered economic or physical devastation during the war. Both Great Britain (A) and France (B), committed to total war, bore the economic burden of the Great War and did not rebound rapidly after its conclusion. World War I also weakened the hold of Great Britain and France over their colonies. China (D), whose troops joined those of the Allies, was subjected to economic demands imposed on it by both the Japanese during World War I and also as a provision of the treaties ending the war. Russia (E), weakened by both tsarist economic and political parties and the staggering cost of the war, was forced to withdraw from the war in 1917.

11. **(A)** Both the Incas and the Persians had an efficient system of roads with way stations for travelers. The Indians, Aztecs, and Mauryans (B, D, E) were not especially noted for their efficient roads. While the Mongols influenced trade along the Silk Roads (C), they were not responsible for establishing those roads.

12. **(E)** The Colosseum is a ruin of ancient Rome. Roman roads connected the eastern Mediterranean with the Silk Roads. The Roman civilization widely used slavery (A). It was influenced by Greek civilization (B). Tribes along its borders were allowed to join the Roman army (C). India was not a part of the Roman empire (D).

13. **(D)** Part of the Islamic empire, Spain did not see the governmental disintegration that prompted the rise of feudalism. Serfs in Russia (A) were tied to the land of nobles, the tsar, or monasteries, and were not emancipated until 1861. After the Norman invasion of 1066, Great Britain (B) was placed under a feudal system in which all vassals owed their allegiance to the monarch. Feudalism in the area which is now Germany (C) followed the pattern common throughout most of Western Europe, in which a vassal received a benefice from a lord in exchange for military or another form of service. Japan (E) developed a feudal political system during its medieval period from the twelfth to the

sixteenth centuries. Japanese feudalism, with its code of *bushido* and its military, the *samurai*, bore some similarities to feudalism in western Europe.

14. **(C)** The areas indicated were all located within the boundaries of the Mongol empire. The Mongol empire, one of the largest in world history, included China, central Asia, Russia, Persia, and the Crimea. In contrast, the Islamic empire (A) included Spain and North Africa, but did not extend to Russia, Central Asia, or China. The Hellenistic empire (B) covered portions of Greece, Anatolia, Egypt, and Southwest Asia. The Ottoman empire (D) was confined to a narrow fringe of North Africa, the Balkans, Anatolia, and portions of Southwest Asia. The Roman empire (E) stretched from Britain to continental Western Europe to Anatolia, the eastern Mediterranean, and North Africa.

15. **(B)** Trade was especially protected during the Mongol Peace. The Mongols were not noted for large-scale conversion to Christianity (A). They attempted to keep the territories they dominated, especially Russia, from coming into contact with Renaissance learning (C). The Mongols were pastoral nomads, not farmers (D), and were noted for being inefficient administrators (E).

16. **(E)** The Huns were a threat to the northern borders of both China and India, and were the cause behind the movement of other barbarian tribes into the borders of Rome. All three governments weakened before they were overrun by barbarian tribes (A). Only one, Rome, had a state religion (Christianity) during part of its duration (B). All three empires engaged in long-distance trade (C). Rome and Han China experienced poor harvests in the closing years of their empire (D).

17. **(E)** The Polynesians worshipped a number of gods of nature. They did not have a knowledge of metallurgy (A) and traded primarily with local islands (B). They generally enjoyed strong political leadership within their tribes (C) and had a stratified social structure (D).

18. **(E)** Buddhism was spread primarily by traders, while Shintoism, Jainism, and Zoroastrianism remained confined primarily to Japan, India, and Persia respectively. Judaism spread through the various Diasporas.

19. **(A)** The Manila galleons were involved in the trade of silver from Mexico to China. Linguists, who study the history and science of languages, would be interested in the remaining choices. The Indo-European migrations spread language (B), as did the Bantu migrations in Africa (C). The Malay sailors carried their language to Madagascar (D), while the Pheonicians spread the alphabet (E).

20. **(B)** Salt was as valuable as gold in trans-Saharan trade. Amber is a trade product of Russia, and silver of Southwest and East Asia (A). Trade in ivory and animal skins (C) was especially active in the central and eastern regions of Sub-Saharan Africa and Indian Ocean trade. Ebony was also associated with trade from central and eastern Africa to the Indian Ocean network, while cowrie shells were used as currency along the Mediterranean and also in Indian Ocean trade (D). Jade is associated with trade involving such distant locations as China and Mesoamerica, while exotic woods were common items from central and eastern Africa (E).

21. **(D)** The Third Estate refers to the majority of the French population before the revolution. It is not a term found in any of the other societies mentioned.

22. **(B)** Enlightened despots felt a responsibility toward their subjects. Absolute monarchs ruled according to the divine right of kings (A), constitutional monarchs were limited by a constitution (C), divine monarchism is not a term used to describe any particular style of monarchy (D), and fascism is an authoritarian style that promoted nationalism (E).

23. **(A)** The vast population of Asia is emerging from the shelter marked RESOURCES IN THE ASIA AND PACIFIC REGION.

24. **(C)** The green revolution was implemented in Asia to increase food production. Human cloning (A) and stem cell research (B) are recent procedures not associated with the Asian/Pacific regions, guest workers (D) are associated with North Africans and Southwest Asians who have migrated to Europe for employment, and détente (E) is a term describing the development of understanding among the superpowers.

25. **(A)** China is not among the Four Tigers, or four economic giants of the Pacific Rim. The other four choices are.

26. **(B)** Bismarck uttered these words before World War I to indicate his lack of reliance on diplomacy to accomplish the goals of Prussia. Rather, warfare would best realize its goals.

27. **(A)** All worshipped gods of nature. The Aztecs were an example of a society that did not integrate others into its society (B). The Incas had no system of writing (C). The Toltecs carried on long-distance trade with the Anasazi (D), and only the Incas were particularly noted for their adminstrative ability (E).

28. **(A)** The Hellenistic empire of Alexander, extending from Greece to Egypt and northern India, united the cultures of East and West. The Incan empire (B), which included the Andes Mountains of present Ecuador, Peru, and Bolivia, was more regional in nature. The Moche empire (C), centered in northern Peru, was also regional in scope. The Han (D) built a regional empire in China which was culturally homogeneous. The Valley of Mexico saw the rise of the Aztec empire (E), which is also best classified as regional.

29. **(B)** As Dias explored the Atlantic, so Zheng He explored the Indian Ocean.

30. **(B)** The movement of people from rural to urban areas is an example of internal migration. External migration, or movement across longer distances, is exemplified in the other answer choices.

31. **(D)** Beginning about 7,000 BCE, agricultural settlements arose throughout East Asia, Southwest Asia, and Africa, for example. From the large distances separating early agricultural communities, it is apparent that agriculture probably developed independently (A) without human planning (C). Although agriculture was developed later in the western hemisphere, it was diffused through Mesoamerica and South America (B). Some of the earliest agricultural communities, such as Çatal Hüyük and Jericho, were not located in river valleys.

32. **(A)** The potato was introduced from South America to Ireland, then was carried to North America as a result of Scotch-Irish immigration. Corn (B) and cassava (C) were introduced from the Americas to the eastern hemisphere. Wheat (D) and barley (E) were products introduced to the Americas from the eastern hemisphere.

33. **(B)** Brinkmanship involved remaining on the brink of war; the Cuban Missile Crisis involved impending war between the superpowers. The Soviet invasion of Afghanistan (A) and the Chechnyan (D) crisis were armed conflicts. Glasnost (C) was the policy of open communication created in the Soviet Union under Gorbachev. The docking of the two spacecraft was a symbol of cooperation between the superpowers (E).

34. **(E)** Christianity was not the official religion of Rome until the fourth century. The missionary journeys of Paul (B) capitalized upon the unity of the Mediterranean basin in the first century (A). The facility of trade along the Roman roads (D) and the Silk Roads (C) served to spread Christianity.

35. **(A)** The southern states rallied to the support of unification after battling against a common enemy. France was already unified (B) as was Italy (C). The Prussians were the victors in the conflict (D, E).

36. **(C)** Women are believed to be the first farmers since men were usually preoccupied with hunting. Women, therefore, seldom accompanied men on hunting expeditions (A). The status of women decreased as agriculture developed into a task that involved equipment that was difficult for women to handle; more difficult tasks were considered more important and contributed to the status of men (B). Therefore, women rarely became clan leaders (E), although they were to carry out both the duties of childcare and food procurement (D).

37. **(A)** The other responses describe the factors of production, all of which were necessary to industrialization. Choice (A) is not a necessary component of industrialization.

38. **(E)** South Africa was the scene of conflicts between the Boers and Zulus. Country I is Liberia, II is Algeria, III

is Libya, IV is the Democratic Republic of Congo, and V is South Africa.

39. **(A)** Liberia was settled by freed slaves from the United States and was not controlled by a European nation. The remaining answer choices were colonial holdings of the following European countries: Algeria (B) of France, Libya (C) of Italy, Congo (D) of Belgium, and South Africa (E) of Great Britain.

40. **(E)** Family and groups were seen as more important than the individual. All of the other choices were important to Confucian thought.

41. **(D)** The Jews deny Christ as the promised Messiah, while the Muslims base their faith around the worship of Allah. Choice (C) is a key concept to Judaism, while choices (A), (B), and (E) are accepted by both Judaism and Islam.

42. **(E)** Most of the developing, or non-technological, nations (Afghanistan, India, Peru, and Uganda) included on the chart show low literacy rates for women. The exception is China, which is developing at a faster rate than the other choices indicated. Choice (A) is incorrect because there is insufficient information in the chart to determine the causes of the disparity in literacy rates. Choice (B) is likewise incorrect because of the inclusion of only one technological nation, France, in the chart. Choice (C) is incorrect because there is insufficient information to assess educational opportunity in the two democratic nations listed, France and India. Choice (D) is incorrect since the chart does not offer information to determine whether low literacy rates among women in developing nations are a result of fewer educational opportunities or of other cultural factors.

43. **(E)** The passage refers to the opium trade between China and Great Britain. In the late nineteenth century, Great Britain traded its manufactured products for tea from China. The Chinese, however, displayed only limited interest in British products, producing a trade imbalance between the two countries. To counteract the imbalance, the British, who colonized India, began trading Indian opium to China. Indian opium, which was of a higher quality than that of China, was readily accepted in exchange for Chinese tea. As a result, a significant number of Chinese, particularly among the elite classes, became addicted to opium. This addiction prompted the writing of the letter to Queen Victoria, which is excerpted in the quotation.

44. **(B)** The ornate Corinthian columns of the Pantheon in Rome, illustrated in the photograph, were introduced by the Greeks and adopted by the Romans in their architectural structures. The most ornate of the orders of Greek architecture (which also included the Doric and Ionic orders), the Corinthian featured a capital adorned with leaf carvings. Classical Indian architecture (A) utilized post-and-lintel construction and capitals decorated with animals such as lions. Persian architecture (C) was characterized by fluted shafts of vertical channels (possibly a Greek influence) and capitals decorated with flowers, palms, or creatures positioned back-to-back. Russian architecture (D) was characterized by the use of arches and domed spires. Islamic architecture (E) featured pointed spires and columns that supported arches.

45. **(A)** The Japanese government was behind its modernization efforts. Japan does not have an abundance of raw materials (B) nor vast land resources (E). Prior to the nineteenth century, Japan did not have an industrial tradition (C). During this time period Japan was just beginning to take the steps that would lead to her emergence as a world power.

46. **(A)** The sugar plantations, requiring a huge labor force because of the worldwide demand for sugar, were the major area of need for forced labor. African slaves on the sugar plantations in Brazil and the Caribbean experienced a high death rate resulting from the harsh working conditions in those areas. Choices (B) and (E) are incorrect since only about five percent of slaves crossing the Atlantic were ultimately destined for British North America. While some African slaves were used as household servants in Europe (C) and as laborers in Mexico's silver mines (D), these two areas also utilized only a small percentage of Africans in bondage.

47. **(C)** In 1274 and 1281, the *kamikaze* wind prevented a successful Mongol invasion.

48. **(C)** The mestizo class, under the leadership of Padre Hidalgo, were the initiators of the independence movement against Spain. The mestizos, a blend of

indigenous peoples and Europeans, were one of the classes in the social hierarchy of colonial Mexico. The creoles (D), some of whom were merchants (A), at first opposed the actions of Hidalgo, but later joined in the independence effort. The peninsulares (E), who were born in Spain and, along with the creoles, constituted the elites (B) in colonial Mexican society, did not seek independence from Spain.

49. **(B)** None of the African nations was invited to participate in the Berlin Conference, whose purpose was to divide Africa among the European nations. Choice (A) is incorrect since the conference did not concern itself with training Africans in self-rule. At the conference Africa was divided among European colonial powers without regard for ethnic or cultural groups (C). Choice (D) is incorrect because Germany had already been unified in 1871. Metternich's role in the establishment of European peace and stability was initiated at the Congress of Vienna in 1815 (E).

50. **(A)** The reaction to the abuses of the shah's government was a return to fundamental Islam under the leadership of the Ayatollah Khomeini.

51. **(B)** Peter the Great was concerned with westernizing and industrializing Russia, while Catherine continued his interest in industrialization. Neither was concerned with freeing the serfs (A), nor were they interested in the political participation of their subjects (C). Catherine alone was interested in Enlightenment culture (D). While Peter expanded the empire through war with Sweden, Catherine won control of the northern portion of the Black Sea through war with the Ottomans (E).

52. **(D)** In the eighteenth century, Poland had been partitioned three times between Russia, Prussia, and Austria, eliminating Poland from the map of Europe. Poland would be restored as a nation as a result of the peace treaties ending World War I. Austria (C) would continue as a significant presence in the struggles against Napoleonic France, while Prussia (E) would eventually become the nucleus of a unified Germany. Persia would not be renamed Iran until 1935 (A), and Japan in 1800 continued under the rule of the Tokugawa Shogunate (B).

53. **(E)** The African empire of Mali had no impact on the spread of Greek culture. The Hellenistic empire (A) spread Greek and Eastern cultures, as did that of Islamic Spain (C) and Byzantium (D). Greek colonization also spread its culture throughout the Mediterranean world (B).

54. **(A)** The Aryan *Rigveda* speaks of the origin of the caste system. Initially an oral tradition only, it was later written down. The Dravidians (E) were the original inhabitants of India who were conquered by the Aryans. The Jainists (D) are a branch of Hinduism whose members show reverence to all forms of life. The Sikhs (B) are a religious group whose beliefs are a blend of Hinduism, Buddhism, and Sufism. The Tamils (C) of southern India are followers of Hinduism contemporary to the era of Mauryan rule, centuries after the invasion of the Aryans.

55. **(B)** Mayan knowledge was as versatile as that of the Greeks. The other cultures mentioned did not have the level of advancement overall as did the Mayas.

56. **(C)** Rousseau, whose philosophy was based around the concept of the social contract, also spoke out against the use of social titles. Voltaire (A) championed the right of free speech, while Locke (B) spoke of the natural rights of "life, liberty, and property." Hobbes (D) favored an authoritarian monarchy to maintain order. The political philosophy of Montesquieu (E) included the concepts of the separation of powers and of checks and balances.

57. **(C)** The author of the statement is Karl Marx. Marxism was a reaction to the disparity of the workers and employers of industry.

58. **(D)** The principle of legitimacy was one of the guiding principles behind the Congress. It did nothing to hinder the unification of Italy (A), nor did it return representative government to Europe (B). The Congress restored the balance of power to Europe (C) and created stability until the years preceding World War I (E).

59. **(B)** Military reductions for Germany were included in the Treaty of Versailles, but not in Wilson's Fourteen Points. The other provisions mentioned were parts of the Fourteen Points.

60. **(A)** Rwanda and the incidences in Bosnia and Kosovo are examples of ethnic cleansing. Choices (B), (D), and (E) are not true of either area. Africa was subjected to European imperialism (C).

61. **(C)** Negritude was a black-pride movement in the early twentieth century. The Congo civil war occurred in the 1950s (D). The Zulu Wars occurred in the nineteenth century (E).

62. **(A)** The Balfour Declaration, issued in 1917, protected the existing rights of non-Jews in Palestine before the establishment of Israel in 1948. The Camp David Accords (B), signed in 1979, recognized the legitimacy of the state of Israel and provided for the return of the Sinai Peninsula to Egypt. The Declaration of Principles (C) was a 1993 agreement which allowed Palestinians self-rule in the West Bank and the Gaza Strip. The Treaty of Versailles (D), which ended World War I between Germany and the Allies, did not address Palestinian issues. Led by Yasir Arafat, the Palestine Liberation Organization (E) executes military actions against the state of Israel.

63. **(D)** Although Mandarin Chinese is the more widely spoken, English has become the language of international commerce.

64. **(B)** Islam has shown greater growth in the twentieth century than any other world religion.

65. **(B)** The picture portrays Tiananmen Square, which was the scene of the 1989 incident between student protestors for democracy and Chinese troops. The Cultural Revolution (A), which closed Chinese universities and attempted to establish equality for Chinese workers and peasants, took place from 1966 to 1976. The transfer of Hong Kong (C) from Great Britain to the People's Republic of China occurred in 1997. U.S. President Nixon's state visit to the People's Republic (D) took place in 1972. The Four Modernizations (E) was the set of goals of Chinese leader Deng Xiaoping in the 1980s.

66. **(A)** The euro was introduced in January 2002. The other responses were twentieth-century events.

67. **(E)** Gorbachev's regime was associated with economic decline. Perestroika, glasnost, and democratization were all parts of his programs for the Soviet Union, while during the end of his regime the Baltic states of Latvia, Lithuania, and Estonia declared their independence.

68. **(D)** Prior to unification, Germany publicly announced its commitment to democracy in order to set aside concerns of other nations that Germany would again attempt to dominate Europe. Germany is a member of the United Nations (A). Its unification and potential power were feared by some of the European nations (B).

69. **(C)** Policies such as that of the Munich Conference appeased Hitler rather than confront his aggressive actions. Containment (B) was the policy of the United States toward world communism during the Cold War.

70. **(B)** Many colonists firmly believed that their war efforts would win them independence. Therefore, they did not take pride in the powers that governed them (A), nor did they improve their infrastructure (C) or take steps toward democracy (E).

71. **(E)** The Hittites initiated iron smelting, while both they and the Assyrians widely used iron tools and weapons. Choices (A) and (C) pertain to the Assyrians, and (B) to the Hittites.

72. **(C)** Great Britain and the United States were key investors, preventing the Latin Americans from developing their own industries (D). Foreign powers continued to show interest in the raw materials of the continent (E). Because of the foreign influence, steady economic growth was not a reality (B), nor was there a pattern of stable governments in Latin America (A).

73. **(C)** The Silk Roads established both land and water routes in Eurasia (A). They carried silk and other goods as far as the Roman empire (B, D). In some areas they were protected by pastoral nomads (E).

74. **(C)** Location on the Bosporus placed Constantinople at a junction for trade routes from a number of societies and civilizations.

75. **(A)** The selection is a quote from U.S. President Truman. The Truman Doctrine was issued to support the efforts of Greece and Turkey to resist communism. The Marshall Plan (B) was a program of relief for European nations after World War II, while Yalta (C) and Potsdam (E) dealt with plans for the postwar world. The Atlantic Charter (D) dealt with free trade and self-determination.

76. **(B)** Communism took hold in those countries who were not highly industrialized. Marx and Engels thought that communism would take hold as a reaction to industrialization (A) and to economic prosperity resulting from industrialization (D). The post-industrial world is that which is characterized by a high percentage of employees in service industries (E). Since their focus was on economic theory, Marx and Engels did not address political status (C).

77. **(E)** Athenian citizens voted directly on all issues before the city-state. The Athenian courts used juries (A) with judges whose decisions were subject to appeals (D). Only free males over 20 who had served in the army were considered citizens (B). Athens did not have an executive, but rather an assembly (C).

78. **(C)** Shintoism is centered around the reverence of ancestors rather than a life in the hereafter. Judaism, Zoroastrianism, and Islam offer the hope of an afterlife for those who follow the beliefs of the faith and lead moral lives on earth. Christianity offers salvation to those who believe that Jesus Christ is the Son of God and Savior (A).

79. **(E)** Socrates believed in acquiring knowledge by questioning. Plato's philosophies (A) concerned themselves primarily with government, while Aristotle was fascinated by a broad range of knowledge (B). Both Solon (C) and Cleisthenes (D) were reformers in early Athens.

80. **(D)** The mandate of heaven was used to explain the decline of one dynasty and the takeover by another. Chinese dynasties provided centralized government (A); among their chief concerns was often the construction and maintenance of dams and irrigation systems vital to Chinese welfare (C). Chinese rulers and society tended to keep women in a subordinate position (E).

81. **(B)** Tea was originally imported from Vietnam. Block printing and porcelain were of Chinese origin, while bananas originated in Southeast Asia and spread throughout the Indian Ocean to Madagascar and then to Africa. Coffee is believed to have possibly originated in the Ethiopian highlands.

82. **(C)** The classifications mentioned in the passage are terms for the various Hindu castes.

83. **(E)** *The Epic of Gilgamesh* contains a Sumerian account of the flood nearly identical to that of the *Genesis* account of the Hebrews. *The Popol Vuh* of the Mayas (A) features a creation account. The poetry of *The Rubaiyyat* of Omar Khayyam (B) is a Persian literary work from the Abbasid dynasty. The Egyptian *Book of the Dead* (C) is a collection of texts from ancient Egypt that contain spells, prayers, and hymns to guide the departed soul through the afterlife. The *Vedas* (D) are the sacred literature of the Aryans. They contain spells, prayers, and instructions for carrying out religious rituals.

84. **(D)** Dated by archeologists to the Paleolithic Era, the Lascaux cave paintings of France reflected the culture of paleolithic man through the nature of the animal paintings found at the site.

85. **(B)** Deserts, mountains, and seas prevented the easy penetration of Egypt by foreign invaders (C) more than did its military (A) or the might of its pharaohs (D). Egypt engaged in long-distance trade with the Mediterranean world and kingdoms to its south (E).

86. **(A)** The Mongols continued to be a threat along China's northwestern borders. For this reason the Ming dynasty retreated from its Indian Ocean explorations under Zheng He (C) to reaffirm Chinese culture (E). The Ming were known for their porcelain vases (B) and had traded with East Africa in its early years (D).

87. **(D)** The passage suggests that the speaker has discovered information which contradicts traditional thought concerning the universe. It also implies that he has been called to task by intellectuals regarding his new findings. Both these circumstances describe the life of Galileo, who developed the heliocentric theory and, for this reason, was called before the Church and forced to publicly recant his findings.

88. **(D)** The Vikings explored and settled North America for perhaps 100 (A) years beginning in 1000, but they did not remain to establish trading networks that might have connected the eastern and western hemispheres. They did, however, trade with Kievan Rus c. 900 (E). A part of a wave of invaders in the 800s (B), by 1000 the Vikings had established some settlements in areas such as Normandy in northern France (C).

89. **(C)** The English Bill of Rights strengthened the authority of Parliament, putting limits on the power of the monarchy. It also guaranteed citizens the right of petition (E).

90. **(B)** In 1973 the OPEC nations imposed an oil embargo on the United States in response to its support of Israel in its war with the Arabs. Among OPEC nations not located in Southwest Asia are Nigeria and Venezuela (A). After the Iran-Iraq War and the Gulf War, the influence of OPEC declined as developed nations were able to find new fuel sources (C). Its control of oil prices caused a global economic crisis in the 1970s (D). Disregarding the environment during the Gulf War, the OPEC nation of Iraq set fire to the oil fields of Kuwait and dumped oil into the Persian Gulf (E).

91. **(B)** The Soviet economy was depressed prior to the fall of communism. Gorbachev's programs of democratization, *glasnost,* and *perestroika* (C, D, E) opened the way for some freedom of expression and restructuring of the Soviet economy. Reagan's Star Wars program showcased the technological capability of the United States to take the initiative in defending its interests over that of the Soviet Union (A).

92. **(A)** Tokugawa Japan remained isolated, especially from the western world. Qing China blended the Chinese with the Manchu (B). Russia embraced peoples of Mongol, Slavic, Viking, and Byzantine heritage (C), while the Ottoman empire ruled a diverse population (D). Brazil was inhabited by Europeans, Indians, and African slaves (E).

93. **(D)** Abolition was realized in Brazil in 1888. Dates for the other choices are the United States (1865), French colonies (1814), British colonies (1833), and Haiti (1804).

94. **(B)** The need for raw materials and markets on the part of industrialized nations prompted their quest for colonies. Industrialization often led to the exploitation of developing nations by industrialized nations (A). It led to reform movements, some of which broadened participation in the democratic process (C). Industrialization quickly spread to Germany, France, Belgium, and other areas of Europe (D), and led to greater economic prosperity which promoted the strength of the middle class (E).

95. **(C)** The Irish potato famine produced massive migration from Ireland in the mid-1800s. Women in the United States and Great Britain would not win the vote until the 1900s (A). Zionist movements arose in the wake of increased anti-Semitism (B). Manifest Destiny led to two conflicts with Mexico over Texas and the southern U.S. boundary (D). France underwent a number of political upheavals before the declaration of the Third Republic in 1875 (E).

HOW TO USE THE RESULTS OF YOUR DIAGNOSTIC TEST IN YOUR REVIEW

After taking the diagnostic test, you should have an idea of what subjects you are strong in and what topics you need to study more. You can use this information to tailor your approach to the following review chapters. If your time to prepare for the test is limited, skip right to the chapters covering the aspects of world history that you need to review most.

Section Three

WORLD HISTORY REVIEW

CHAPTER 3

Human Origins

TIMELINE

6,000,000 years ago	Appearance of the first humans
3.2 million years ago	Beginning of the Paleolithic Age *Australopithecenes*
2.5 million years ago	*Homo habilis*
1.4 million years ago	*Homo erectus*
100,000 years ago	*Homo sapiens*
8000–3000 BCE	Neolithic Age
8000 BCE	Founding of Jericho
7000 BCE	Worldwide development of agriculture Founding of Çatal Hüyük
4000 BCE	Domestication of animals

IMPORTANT PEOPLE, PLACES, EVENTS, AND CONCEPTS

anthropology*
archeology*
artifact*
paleontologist*
radiocarbon dating*
thermoluminescent dating*
tree-ring dating*
DNA dating*
Paleolithic Age*
Neolithic Age*
Donald Johanson
*Australopithecenes**
Mary Leakey
Louis Leakey
Richard Leakey
Java Man
Peking Man
hominid*
*Homo sapiens**
Cro-Magnon Man
Neanderthal Man
Neolithic Revolution*
pastoral nomadism*
specialization of labor*
Jericho
Çatal Hüyük

Note: Terms marked with an asterisk appear in the Glossary.

THE DAWN OF HUMANKIND

Scientists believe that humans have existed on the earth for perhaps as long as six million years. The study of ancient humans belongs to the field of **anthropology**, the study of humans as a species, and to **archeology**, the study of cultures through the examination of **artifacts**, or objects shaped by humans. In addition, **paleontologists** complete the picture by studying fossilized remains; these investigations can reveal the nature of a particular society's culture, or its way of life.

Scientists use several methods to determine the age of fossils and artifacts. **Radiocarbon dating** (also called the carbon 14 method) measures the amount of radiocarbon remaining in a fossil skeleton, thus revealing its age. **Thermoluminescent dating** measures radioactivity released from electrons in heated flint and clay, allowing for dating of objects made from these two materials. **Tree-ring dating**, or dendrochronology, notes the chronological sequence of the annual growth rings in trees. **DNA dating** involves obtaining samples of the genetic material DNA from living donors and comparing it with the DNA from other persons or from animals; computers are then used to determine the rate of change in the DNA.

THE PALEOLITHIC AGE

Scientists divide prehistory into two eras: the **Paleolithic Age** and the **Neolithic Age**. The Paleolithic Age, or Old Stone Age, extended from the time the first **hominids** appeared until about 8000 BCE (A hominid is a humanlike creature that walks upright.)

The oldest known hominid is "Lucy," a female whose fossilized skeleton was discovered by **Donald Johanson** in Ethiopia in 1974. Lucy was estimated to have lived about 3.2 million years ago. She was an example of ***Australopithecenes***, a hominid close in appearance to modern humans. In 1977, **Mary Leakey** found a striking example in Tanzania of the footprints of two australopithecenes walking side by side.

The first species to be classified in the same *Homo* species as modern humans was *Homo habilis*, discovered by **Louis Leakey** in the early 1960s in the Olduvai Gorge in Tanzania. Assumed to have appeared about 2.5 million years ago, *Homo habilis* ("handy man") was found with tools he had fashioned for hunting and butchering animals.

About one million years ago, *Homo habilis* was replaced by an upright hominid, *Homo erectus*. Presumed to have existed almost 1.4 million years ago, a skeleton of *Homo erectus* was found by Richard Leakey in Kenya in 1984. The skulls of **Java Man** and **Peking Man**, found in Indonesia and China, respectively, are examples of *Homo erectus*. Artifacts found near *Homo erectus* include a hand ax and tools used for butchering large animals.

About 100,000 years ago, a new human appeared, ***Homo sapiens*** ("wise human"). Characterized by a greater capacity for speech than his predecessors, *Homo sapiens* knew how to use fire for warmth and cooking and to ward off animals. He developed burial rituals as well as beautiful artwork and utilized stone quartzite tools.

African Origins

An examination of the emergence of *Homo sapiens* has given rise to two theories explaining the diffusion of humans. Most archeologists agree that *Homo erectus* evolved first in Africa, spreading from that continent to Asia and to Europe about one million years ago. At this point, however, two different avenues of thought emerge:

- The multiregional model maintains that in each region of subsequent migration, *Homo erectus* evolved into *Homo sapiens.*
- The other model, termed by some historians the "out of Africa" scheme, argues that *Homo erectus* evolved into *Homo sapiens* only in Africa.

According to this second theory, which is currently the more widely accepted, modern humans *Homo sapiens sapiens,* or **Cro-Magnon** man, displaced older humans such as **Neanderthal man** (*Homo sapiens*) in Europe. By about 90,000 BCE, he also diffused throughout the Americas, Australia, the Arctic, and the landbridge between the mainland of Asia and Japan.

The "out of Africa" model presents the emergence of race as a relatively recent phenomenon compared to that of the multiregional model: Perhaps as recently as 5,000 years ago, differences in skin pigmentation occurred as an adaptation to various environments.

Paleolithic Culture

To survive as a hunter, Paleolithic man needed to be able to observe the migratory habits of game animals as well as organize with other members of his clan or tribe to plan the various strategies of the hunt. This ability to coordinate his efforts with his fellow man was greatly facilitated by the development of language. Paleolithic woman's major responsibility was bearing and rearing children as well as tending the fire; their dwellings were caves and simple lean-to shelters. Both men and women in Paleolithic culture needed to acquire knowledge of their environment in order to supplement their diet by gathering seeds, nuts, and berries.

Artwork originated in the late Paleolithic era, with some of the finest examples found in the Lascaux Caves of southern France and the Caves of Altamira in northern Spain. One branch of *Homo sapiens,* Neanderthal man, buried his dead and left evidence of funeral rituals and offerings left with the dead, possibly demonstrating a belief in an afterlife. Paleolithic men and women, with their ability to plan, communicate, construct necessary tools, and express their creativity, paved the way for an era which would revolutionize food production and population growth—the Neolithic Age.

THE NEOLITHIC AGE

Paleolithic man's reliance on hunting became precarious when protracted ice ages precipitated the environmental changes that led to the extinction of many varieties of big-game animals. When the last ice age ended (about 7000 BCE), hunting and herding no longer provided sufficient nutrients. Gradually men and women settled down to till the soil. The resulting **Neolithic, or Agricultural, Revolution** not only saw the beginnings of permanent settlement; the increasing variety of nutrients supplied by sowing and harvesting resulted in healthier bodies that produced an increasingly large population. Additionally, the development of agriculture heightened the importance of women, since they were probably the earliest farmers; clay fertility goddesses have been found among the artifacts of early agricultural villages.

Until recently, historians believed that agriculture developed first in Southwest Asia and from there spread to Africa and Asia. However, current scholars believe that around 7000 BCE, agriculture developed independently in several parts of the world at about the same time; Southwest Asia, China, Africa, and the Americas. Around 4000 BCE, the first animals were being domesticated throughout the world, giving rise to **pastoral nomadism**.

The Earliest Towns

Increased agricultural productivity fostered the **specialization of labor**. When not everyone needed to engage in agriculture to sustain the lives of early villagers, craftsmen and artisans emerged to enrich the lives of the inhabitants of early settlements. The specialization of labor encouraged the development of trade which, in turn, contributed to the rise of towns.

Two of the earliest towns were **Jericho** (in modern-day Palestine) and **Çatal Hüyük** (in present-day Turkey). Jericho, a community of about 2,000 inhabitants, relied on the cultivation of wheat and barley. Founded around 8000 BCE, it featured tall, thick city walls. Jericho became a trade center that connected places such as Anatolia and the area around the Red Sea. The most advanced community of the Neolithic Age was Çatal Hüyük, where life revolved around long-distance trade (including the Mediterranean region) and the labor of artisans. The dwellings in this community center were uniformly-built houses of mud-dried brick with entrance openings in their flat roofs.

The blend of agriculture and craftsmanship would lead to the further growth of towns. Areas of especially rich agricultural lands would contribute to further population growth and the rise of civilizations in four river valleys in Asia and Africa and also in valleys and highlands of the Americas.

THINGS TO REMEMBER

- Archeologists and paleontologists study early humans via artifacts and fossilized remains.
- Early hominids include *Homo habilis* and *Homo erectus*. *Homo sapiens* (Neanderthal Man) emerged about 100,000 years ago, probably in Africa. *Homo sapiens sapiens* (modern humans) later displaced older hominids throughout the world.
- Early humans showed an increasing ability to adapt to their environment and efforts to cooperate for the advancement of the clan or tribe. They utilized tools and spoken language.
- The Paleolithic era lasted from the time of the first human ancestors until about 8000 BCE
- The Neolithic Age began around 8000 BCE with the development of agriculture in several parts of the world.
- Agriculture led to the first permanent settlements, population growth, and specialization of labor.
- The status of women may have increased with the advent of agriculture, as women were the first farmers.

REVIEW QUESTIONS

1. Paleolithic humans

   (A) domesticated animals.
   (B) discovered agriculture.
   (C) were organized around a well-defined social hierarchy.
   (D) were a female-dominated society.
   (E) were foragers.

2. A common thread woven throughout the history of early humans in the Paleolithic Age was

   (A) the use of language.
   (B) the desire to control the environment.
   (C) the belief in an afterlife.
   (D) the creation of towns.
   (E) the lack of technology.

3. Agriculture during the Neolithic Age resulted in all of the following EXCEPT

   (A) the specialization of labor.
   (B) the rise of towns.
   (C) a decrease in population.
   (D) increased social contacts.
   (E) the development of trade.

4. An archeologist using DNA evidence as the basis of his research could link the DNA of modern humans with that of

   (A) *Homo habilis.*
   (B) *Homo erectus.*
   (C) *Australopithecus.*
   (D) *Homo sapiens sapiens* (Cro-Magnon Man).
   (E) *Homo sapiens* (Neanderthal Man).

5. The skeleton of Lucy is an early example of a humanlike being that

   (A) walked upright.
   (B) believed in an afterlife.
   (C) cultivated crops.
   (D) knew the use of the wheel.
   (E) domesticated animals.

ANSWERS AND EXPLANATIONS

1. (E)

Paleolithic humans were not settled peoples; therefore, they acquired their food supply through foraging, or hunting and gathering. Agriculture (B) and the domestication of animals (A) are both incorrect answers because they would not be discovered until the later Neolithic Age. Choice (D) is incorrect because Paleolithic society appeared to have treated men and women similarly, while (C) is not a correct response because the society seemed to be free of social classes.

2. (B)

Through their use of simple tools and fire, Paleolithic humans demonstrated their desire to manipulate their environment. Their use of tools is an example of early technology; therefore, (E) is incorrect. The use of language (A) did not develop until the emergence of *Homo erectus,* while the earliest evidence of belief in an afterlife (C) is attributed to the Neanderthal, who showed evidence of using rituals in the burial of their dead. Towns (D) did not emerge until the Neolithic Age.

3. (C)

The increased variety of nutrients provided by agriculture produced a general population increase worldwide. The other responses were the results of the transition to agriculture. Agricultural surplus resulted in a need for fewer farmers, making (A) incorrect. Choice (B) is incorrect because the increase in population and specialization of labor prompted people to settle in towns. Life in towns provided greater opportunities for social contact (D), while agricultural surpluses and the works of craftsmen prompted trade (E).

4. (D)

DNA studies show that *Homo sapiens sapiens* is the ancestor of modern humans. The DNA of modern humans has not been shown to match that of the earlier humans mentioned in the other responses.

5. (A)

Lucy is an example of *australopithecenes,* an early hominid, or being that walked upright. Choice (B) is characteristic of the later *Homo sapiens.* Choices (C) and (E) were developed during the Neolithic Age. The wheel (D) was developed by the Sumerian civilization.

CHAPTER 4

Early Agricultural Civilizations and Societies

TIMELINE

4000 BCE	Sumerians move into Mesopotamia Discovery of the wheel and bronze tools in Sumer Domestication of maize in central Mexico
3500 BCE	First cities in Mesopotamia
3100 BCE	Unification of Egypt; first Egyptian dynasty
3100–2200 BCE	The Old Kingdom
2300 BCE	Formation of the Akkadian empire
2100–1650 BCE	The Middle Kingdom
1792–1750 BCE	Reign of Hammurabi
1766–1122 BCE	Shang Dynasty
1650 BCE	Hyksos invasion of Egypt
1550–700 BCE	The New Kingdom
1500 BCE	Aryan invasion of the Indus Valley
500 BCE	Formation of Confucianism Formation of Daoism
350 BCE	Formation of Legalism
1000–300 BCE	Olmec civilization

800–400 BCE	Chavin culture
563–483 BCE	Siddhartha Gautama
551–479 BCE	Confucius
525 BCE	Persian conquest of Mesopotamia and Egypt

IMPORTANT PEOPLE, PLACES, EVENTS, AND CONCEPTS

civilization*
Mesopotamia
Sumer
Fertile Crescent
city-state*
ziggurat*
cuneiform*
polytheism*
Epic of Gilgamesh
Sargon the Great
Akkadians
Babylonians
Hammurabi
Code of Hammurabi*
Menes
pharaoh
theocracy*
Great Pyramid of Giza
Grand Canal
Hyksos
Akhnaton
hieroglyphics*
papyrus
Rosetta Stone
Jean François Champollion
Queen Ahhotep
Hatshepsut
Harappa
Mohenjo-Daro
Khyber Pass
Aryans
Vedas
brahmin*
caste*
pariah*
purdah*
sati*
Hinduism
Upanishads
karma*
dharma*
Shiva*
Jainism
Buddhism
Siddhartha Gautama
Four Noble Truths*
Eightfold Path*
nirvana*
Mahayana Buddhism
Shang
loess*
oracle bone*
yin and yang*
mandate of heaven*
Confucius
Daoism
Laozi
Legalism
Shang Yang
foraging*

THE RISE OF CIVILIZATION

Historians define a **civilization** as a culture with advanced cities, skilled workers, complex institutions, a system of writing or alternate form of recordkeeping, and advanced technology. Some of the earliest civilizations grew up in valleys whose rivers enriched the land alongside them with deposits of fertile silt. From villages and cities in the Fertile Crescent of Southwest Asia, the Nile Valley of Egypt, the Indus Valley of the Indian subcontinent, and the Yellow River Valley of China emerged civilizations whose contributions would shape global culture to the present day.

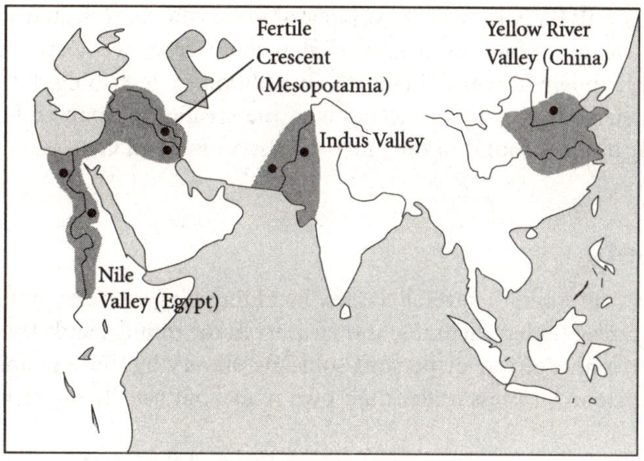

Early Civilizations, c. 1500 BCE

CIVILIZATION IN THE FERTILE CRESCENT

Around 4000 BCE, a group of people called the Sumerians moved from the east into the valley between the Tigris and Euphrates Rivers. The area, found today in Iraq, was called by the Greeks "**Mesopotamia**," or "land between the rivers." Its southernmost reaches, which border the Persian Gulf, featured a delta of fertile soil known as **Sumer**. Sumer was part of a larger belt of land between Mesopotamia and Egypt known as the **Fertile Crescent**. It is here that the earliest civilization in Southwest Asia began.

The flood waters of the Tigris and Euphrates were unpredictable and often violent. While devastating floods could frequently overrun the surrounding countryside, these same floodwaters would deposit a layer of silt to enrich the land. Although fertile agricultural territory, Mesopotamia was an area ripe for invasion. Flat and with few natural barriers, it became easy prey for invaders with an eye on the richness of the land. Here the Sumerians established a government of numerous **city-states**, which were comprised of a city and the land surrounding it.

Sumerian Achievements

The Sumerians increased the bounty of their land by the construction of irrigation systems to distribute the floodwaters. Irrigation projects required planning and cooperation. More advanced agricultural methods and the construction of city buildings were made possible by the discovery of the wheel and bronze tools about 4000 BCE. As farming surpluses mounted, population increased, giving rise to the first cities around 3500 BCE. The characteristic architectural form of the Sumerians was the **ziggurat**, a multitiered temple whose height was designed to bring glory to the gods and to its builders.

The most significant contribution of the Sumerians was their system of writing, called **cuneiform**, which was formed by pressing a wedge-shaped stylus into wet clay. Necessary for a people whose increasing trade required the keeping of accurate records, cuneiform consisted of pictographs to represent ideas, then later, sounds. Other major contributions were a lunar calendar and the development of principles of geometry and trigonometry. A number system based on 60 gave the world the time measurements of 60 seconds to a minute and 60 minutes per hour. Later Mesopotamian societies would expand the sixty-based number system to measure the circumference of a circle as 360 degrees.

Sumerian religion was **polytheistic**, with a panoply of gods who were feared for their control over nature. Much of what we know about Sumerian religion comes from accounts in the Sumerian ***Epic of Gilgamesh***, the first epic poem in world literature. In addition to describing the relationship between the Sumerians and their gods, it contains accounts of the creation of man and a Great Flood which were strikingly similar to those found in the Judeo-Christian Book of Genesis.

Sumerian Society

Sumerian society was composed of several classes, including kings, priests, nobles, and government officials in the upper ranks; traders, artisans, and farmers in the middle; and slaves in the lowest rank. Slaves were usually prisoners of war or persons sold into slavery by those unable to pay their debts. Women could participate in business under their own name, but usually under male supervision.

Trade, both local and long-distance, became an integral part of the Sumerian economy. Surplus food was traded, along with glass, a Sumerian invention, and pottery, originally produced by women on a potter's wheel, but later by men when its importance as a trade item was recognized. Sumerian trade reached to the shores of the Persian Gulf and the Mediterranean Sea as well as to the civilizations of the Indus River Valley.

Fall of Sumerian Society

About 2300 BCE, the Sumerian city-states were united by a Semitic invader known as **Sargon the Great**. The **Akkadian** empire (named after its capital, Akkad) endured less than 100 years but served to spread Sumerian culture throughout the Fertile Crescent. After the decline of the Akkadian empire, a number of other peoples such as the Babylonians, Hittites, Assyrians, and Chaldeans overran the fertile unprotected land of the ancient Sumerians.

Of particular significance were the **Babylonians**, whose emperor, **Hammurabi** (1792–1750 BCE), codified the laws of Mesopotamia, basing them in part on earlier Sumerian codes. The **Code of Hammurabi** dealt with issues of family, business, and criminal law. A key characteristic of the code was its concept of retaliatory punishment—"an eye for an eye." The wealthy, however, could satisfy the law by paying a fine as punishment. Women were also subjected to more severe punishments than men for the same code violations. Hammurabi's Code had a lasting impact because it conveyed the principle that government had a responsibility for regulating society.

The Decline of Mesopotamia

By the sixth century BCE the Persians had conquered the Chaldeans and had begun their domination of Mesopotamia. The advanced Persian culture did not assimilate into Mesopotamian culture. Overusage of the land may have led to its inability to provide for its people any longer. Mesopotamia would lessen in importance until it became a center for Islam in the ninth century CE.

CIVILIZATION ALONG THE NILE

To the west of Sumer, on the banks of the mighty Nile River, grew a civilization that would develop much more independently than the civilization of Sumer. Dependent upon the fertile silt deposited by the annual, predictable floodwaters of the Nile, the Egyptians established villages rather than cities along the riverbanks as early as 5000 BCE. Like the Mesopotamians, the Egyptians trapped the waters of the Nile in reservoirs that would carry moisture to outlying fields by means of connecting ditches. In addition to abundant water and fertile soil, Egypt enjoyed a better climate than that of the Sumerians. Egypt, unlike Mesopotamia, was surrounded by natural barriers that kept its civilization isolated and protected. The cataracts, or rapids, of the northerly-flowing Nile, the waters of the Mediterranean Sea, and the formidable deserts of the east and west protected Egypt from invaders.

By 3200 BCE, the farming villages along the Nile were united into two kingdoms: the northern Lower Egypt and the more southern Upper Egypt. About 3100 BCE, **Menes**, a king of Upper Egypt, united the two separate kingdoms. Considered the first **pharaoh**, or Egyptian ruler, Menes also established the first Egyptian dynasty. The Egyptians developed a **theocracy**, in which the pharaoh ruled as a god over religion as well as the government. Historians divide Egyptian history into three periods.

- **The Old Kingdom (3100–2200 BCE).** During this era the great pyramids were constructed. An example is the **Great Pyramid of Giza**.
- **The Middle Kingdom (2100–1650 BCE).** A period of strong pharaohs, it was during this time that the **Grand Canal** was dug from the Nile River to the Red Sea, promoting trade.
- **The New Kingdom (1550–700 BCE).** This era saw the construction of massive public buildings and great cities. It followed upon an invasion of the **Hyksos** (c. 1650) from across the Sinai Peninsula. The Hyksos rulers called themselves pharaohs and adopted Egyptian culture during their approximately century-long rule. The New Kingdom was followed by centuries of decline which culminated in the Persian conquest of Egypt in 525 BCE.

Egyptian Achievements

The early Egyptians were polytheistic, worshipping many gods of nature. Believing in an afterlife, the Egyptians thought their god Osiris would weigh each person's heart to determine the extent of his good deeds in this life. The Egyptians prepared the deceased body by mummification and buried it with objects for use in the afterlife. The pyramids of the pharaohs served as both tombs and samples of the magnificence of Egyptian architecture. Constructed without knowledge of the wheel or the pulley, the pyramids demonstrate not only the mechanical skills of the Egyptians but also their social skills with regard to their ability to plan and execute such massive projects. In the 1300s BCE, the Egyptian religion took on a new dimension as the pharaoh of that time, **Akhnaton**, attempted to introduce monotheism, or the worship of one god, whom he called Aton, to the Egyptians. This idea, which was radical for its time, failed due to lack of support from the Egyptian priesthood.

Knowledge of Egyptian history is derived from its system of writing, called **hieroglyphics**. Based on pictures of objects to represent ideas or sounds, hieroglyphics were written on **papyrus**, a thin parchment made from reeds along the banks of the Nile. The key to deciphering the meaning of hieroglyphics in the present day was the **Rosetta Stone**, found in 1798 CE by French soldiers serving under Napoleon in Egypt. The Rosetta Stone was carved with three different inscriptions, one in Greek, a second in a simple form of hieroglyphics known as Demotic, and a third in hieroglyphics. In the 1820s a French linguist, **Jean François Champollion**, used his knowledge of Greek to decipher the hieroglyphics.

Egyptian contributions in science and mathematics were not as advanced as those of the Mesopotamians. The Egyptians were knowledgeable about a number of medicines and, of course, their knowledge of the science of embalming was superb. Egyptian physicians knew how to set broken bones and sometimes used surgery for the treatment of certain conditions. The Egyptians also developed a solar calendar composed of twelve months of thirty days each and employed a simple form of geometry to survey land after the annual floods.

Egyptian Society

Egyptian society was stratified, with separate classes for the priests and nobles, peasants, and slaves. Slaves were often prisoners of war, serious criminals, or debtors. Women were probably more respected in Egypt than in Mesopotamia, but their major responsibility was the rearing of children. Some women had the opportunity to escape their traditional duties by working as scribes. Two Egyptian queens worthy of note: **Queen Ahhotep**, who helped drive out the Hyksos, and **Hatshepsut** (1472–1458 BCE), who declared herself queen because her stepson, the heir to the throne, was only a child. Hatshepsut was noted for her promotion of trade.

Egyptian trade was not so widespread as that of the Mesopotamians. During the New Kingdom, however, trade contacts were made with Sumer, the eastern end of the Mediterranean Sea, and Nubia to the south.

CIVILIZATION IN THE INDUS RIVER VALLEY

About the time that the Mesopotamians and the Egyptians were developing their great civilizations, another was arising in the river valley of the Indus, located in modern-day Pakistan. The two sites most extensively excavated by archeologists were the Indus River Valley cities of **Harappa** and **Mohenjo-Daro**, situated about 400 miles apart. Unique to both these cities was their precise layout. Their streets followed a precise grid in which the streets ran at right angles, showing evidence of extensive city planning. Both boasted a citadel with public buildings including temples and a community granary. Houses were almost identical, constructed of brick of uniform sizes, and often two or three stories high. Most unusual, however, was the indoor plumbing present in most houses. Residents evidently took showers by standing and pouring water over themselves; the waste water was then collected in sewage canals in the street to carry off household wastes of the community. In addition, Mohenjo-Daro contained a public bath, perhaps used for cleansing for religious purposes.

Since the language of the Indus Valley people found on clay seals has to this point proved undecipherable, much of our knowledge of their civilization comes from artifacts. Little is known of the status of women, although there are some signs that women were perhaps treated equally to men in the earliest days of the Indus Valley civilization. Harappa and Mohenjo-Daro relied on the irrigated, fertile farmland surrounding them for their food supply. Signs of long-distance trade have been discovered in the findings of artifacts from Mesopotamia, southern India, and Afghanistan.

Although archeological evidence suggests that the Indus Valley cities prospered, there is also indication of an abrupt decline about 1900 BCE. Perhaps the Indus River changed its course or disease weakened the population. Whatever the cause, the decline of the Indus Valley civilization made it an easy prey to invaders from the northwest, invaders who would radically alter the history of the Indian subcontinent.

The Aryan Invasion

The foreign peoples who invaded the Indus Valley about 1500 BCE were a nomadic people called the Aryans. Originally from the areas of present-day Iran and Afghanistan, these Indo-European invaders penetrated through the **Khyber Pass** of the Hindu Kush Mountains to enter the Indian subcontinent. Perceiving themselves as a superior race, they quickly subjugated the more advanced civilization of the Indus Valley peoples, which in their mind was an inferior one. The Aryans employed horse-drawn chariots and bronze weapons. A light-skinned people, they quickly dominated the dark-skinned inhabitants of the Indus Valley, but they did not conquer the southern portion of India, which retained a culture separate from the northern part of the subcontinent.

Information concerning the Aryans comes from the ***Vedas***, hymns and chants that later became part of the Hindu religion. The earliest example of the *Vedas* was the *Rigveda*, which was followed later by three other *Vedas* that included descriptions of religious ceremonies. After being passed down orally by the Aryans, the *Vedas* were later written down in Sanskrit.

The Aryan conquerors divided society into four different classes; from these the Hindu **caste** system would eventually emerge. The Aryan classes were based on skin color, with the three highest classes comprised of the light-skinned Aryans. At the top were the **brahmins**, or priests, followed by a second class of warriors. The third class included farmers, traders, and freemen, while the fourth was the serfs, who were under bondage. In time these classes became castes, fixed and determined by birth. In addition to the four castes was another category, the **pariahs**, or untouchables. The idea of the caste system remains among some traditional members of Indian society today.

Women in the Indus Valley

The status of women declined markedly with the arrival of the Aryans and even further with the implementation of the caste system. The practice of ***purdah*** (public isolation from non-family members) and ***sati*** (the suicide of widows) became prominent in Indian culture. The Laws of Manu, from Hindu India, stated that women were to be treated with respect. Some women distinguished themselves in the fields of education, literature, the arts, and music. They could not, however, own property and had to be obedient to the men in their family.

The Emergence of Hinduism

From the Aryan tradition emerged the teachings of the religion of **Hinduism**. Hindu philosophy is expressed in the teachings of the ancient works the ***Upanishads*** and the epics of the *Mahabharata* and the *Ramayana*.

Hinduism teaches that the tangible world is only an illusion. Upon death the soul is reincarnated, or reborn, according to its good or evil deeds, or ***karma***, in its previous life. Good karma might result in birth into a higher caste in the next life, while bad karma could sentence the guilty party to a lower caste in the next life or to life as an untouchable or, worse, an insect. Good karma could be realized by following the rules (***dharma***) of one's caste.

The principal gods worshipped by Hindus include *Brahman*; the life force. The individual self, or *atman*, has the responsibility to know Brahman. A person with such knowledge will, after death, unite with Brahman to achieve *moksha*, or liberation. The attainment of moksha will result in an end to the cycle of reincarnation. Other gods worshipped by the Hindus include ***Shiva***, both creator and destroyer of evil; and *Vishnu*, the preserver.

In the fifth century BCE, a new philosophy called **Jainism** evolved. Based on a belief in the sanctity of all life, Jainism remains today a religion followed by only a small minority of Indians.

The Rise of Buddhism

Of far greater impact on world civilization was the emergence of **Buddhism**, which had its beginnings as a rebellion against what some perceived as the empty rituals of Hinduism. The founder of Buddhism, **Siddhartha Gautama**, was born around 563 BCE in northern India. By the age of 29, he decided to go on a search to explain the presence of suffering in the world. After six years of futile pursuit of the answer to his question, while meditating beneath a tree, he was suddenly given the enlightenment that suffering was caused by man's desire. From this point onward he took the name Buddha, the Enlightened One.

The Buddha would spread his teachings until his death in 483 BCE. His teachings were based on what he termed the **Four Noble Truths**: (1) all human life is filled with sorrow and suffering; (2) suffering is caused by desire; (3) by rejecting desire, people progressing through a number of reincarnations can realize ***nirvana***, or a state of perfect peace; (4) *nirvana* is attained by following the **Eightfold Path**: right faith, right intention, right speech, right action, right living, right effort, right mindfulness, and right meditation. Buddhism also rejected the caste system.

As Buddhism spread out of India, it divided into two branches. The first, Theravada, accepted Buddha as a great spiritual leader but did not follow complex rituals. Rather, it emphasized a monastic life for both men and women and is prevalent today in Sri Lanka and Cambodia. The second branch, **Mahayana Buddhism**, spread to Vietnam, Korea, China, and Japan. There it is manifested in priests, temples, and elaborate rituals as well as in a belief in the deity of the Buddha.

EARLY CIVILIZATION IN CHINA

As Aryan invaders were penetrating the Indus Valley, agricultural villages along the Huang He (Yellow) River in China were organizing under the **Shang**, a people belonging to the Sino-Tibetan language group. The Shang, a nomadic people, fought on horseback and in chariots and used bronze weapons. The society of the Shang was stratified, with a monarch at the top rung, followed by warriors, artisans, traders, and peasants.

During the Shang dynasty, irrigation systems established by earlier inhabitants of the Huang He River valley were expanded. The floods of the Huang He have always been devastating, earning it the nickname "China's Sorrow." The Huang He River earned its name from a buildup of yellow silt, or **loess**, carried down the river from higher elevations by erosion. This loess would accumulate in the riverbanks until it reached a level almost as high as the riverbank. Dikes and channels were constructed to alleviate the prospect of severe flooding; still, throughout history, the Huang He's disastrous floods have killed millions.

The valley of the Huang He would become the cradle of Chinese civilization. Here wheat and millet would become staple crops contributing to a rapid rise in population. To the south, the Yangtze River, located in a warm, humid area, would become the central rice-producing area of China. Surrounded by a formidable desert, plateaus, and mountains, China would become far more isolated than the other river valley civilizations. Grasslands to the northwest served as outlets for migratory movement and trade.

Craftsmanship and Writing

Shang artisans were noted for their exquisite craftsmanship, especially in bronze. During the Shang Dynasty, silkworm cultivation began and silk was traded to India. Architects created pagoda-like structures found in forts and palaces built around the city of Anyang in the Huang He River valley.

Chinese writing was characterized by ideographs, or characters representing ideas. A person would need to memorize about 8,000 ideographs to be considered well-educated. Some of the earliest samples of Chinese writing have been found on **oracle bones**. In order to divine the will of the gods, the Chinese would write questions to the gods on animal bones or shells. The oracle, or soothsayer, would then heat these bones and read the patterns in the cracks on the bones, thereby divining the will of the gods.

The inscriptions found on the oracle bones suggest that Chinese writing evolved from pictographs. Later, several pictographs were combined to form an ideograph, or symbol which represents complex or abstract concepts. The ideographs were then further refined to form modern Chinese characters.

Gender Roles

The traditional Chinese concept of the family began to emerge under the Shang and Zhou dynasties. Ancestors and the elderly were objects of reverence and education was stressed as an avenue to the family's wealth and power. Fathers were in authority over women and children and carried the duty of arranging marriages for their children. From ancient times until the early twentieth century, it was not uncommon for daughters to be sold into slavery to alleviate financial pressures upon the family.

The differences between male and female roles is illustrated by the ancient Chinese concepts of ***yin*** (male) and ***yang*** (female), which were later embraced particularly by the Daoist philosophy. Male assertiveness and toughness were to be balanced by female submission and gentleness.

The Zhou Dynasty

By the twelfth century BCE, the Shang dynasty weakened and was conquered by the Zhou, a people from central Asia. The Zhou claimed that they possessed the "**mandate of heaven**," a concept granting them the authority to rule. This idea of the mandate of heaven would be adopted by succeeding Chinese dynasties as a rationalization for their assumption of power from a previous weakened dynasty.

Chinese dynastic history, which would endure from the time of the Shang to the 1912 overthrow of the Manzhou (Manchu) dynasty, can be visualized as a series of waves, with one dynasty coming to power, achieving prominence, weakening, declining, then finally falling to another dynasty. In 771 BCE, the declining Zhou empire was attacked by peoples from the north. Nomadic invaders capitalizing on the vulnerability of the weak Zhou penetrated the kingdom. For five hundred years a weaker Zhou kingdom would survive. Continuous warfare and chaos created a reaction among the Chinese scholars that would define the nature of Chinese civilization.

The Great Chinese Philosophies

The most influential person in Chinese cultural history, Kung Fu-tsu, or **Confucius** (551–479 BCE) gained prominence toward the end of the Zhou dynasty. The philosophy that he preached emphasized reverence for one's elders and ancestors, good government, and education. Confucius felt that order and harmony would materialize only if Chinese rulers relied on well-educated men. These concepts would remain the hallmark of Chinese culture until the twentieth century. A result of the Confucian emphasis on traditional values was often a resistance to necessary change.

As Confucianism spread throughout China, two rival philosophies arose: Daoism and Legalism. Perhaps founded by the philosopher **Laozi**, **Daoism** (Taoism) centered around nature and following Dao, or "the Way." Followers of Daoism sought a way of life in harmony with the natural world. Daoists viewed people as incapable of governing themselves and saw the least government as the best government.

Legalism, founded by **Shang Yang** about 350 BCE, also arose during the decline of the Zhou dynasty as a reaction to the chaos and lack of authority of the period. Central to its belief was the idea that a government that allowed its subjects freedom was promoting disorder; the basic objective of good rulers was to further the strength of the state. As a result, Legalism insisted on censorship, prohibition of independent thought, and controlled education separated by class. Between 500 and 350 BCE, therefore, the traditional Chinese concepts of the value of family, education, and government were already etched into the basic tenets of Chinese culture.

AGRARIAN SOCIETIES OF THE AMERICAS

Agriculture in the Americas developed gradually as dependence on hunting and gathering gave way to plant domestication. As in other areas of the world, women probably became the first farmers while the men continued to devote their attentions to hunting. About 7000 BCE, at the same time that the agricultural community of Çatal Hüyük was flourishing, Amerindians on the western edge of North and South America were developing agricultural societies. Agriculture was evident in some areas of the Peruvian highlands by 7000 BCE; by 5000 BCE, it had spread to many parts of the Americas. By about 4000 BCE, the domestication of maize, which would lead to tremendous population growth, became established in central Mexico. By 2000 BCE, maize joined the potato as a major crop in Peru, and eventually spread to the basins of the Amazon and Orinoco, where manioc, or cassava, was already under cultivation. In the same period, agriculture was firmly established in the southwestern portion of what is now the United States.

The earliest known civilization in the Americas is that of the Olmec (1000–300 BCE) in southern Mexico. Findings of Olmec pottery and ceramics as far away as Costa Rica and throughout Mexico indicate an active trade. Perhaps the most curious aspect of the Olmec civilization was their construction of huge heads of basalt standing up to nine feet in height. The Olmecs also constructed great pyramids and possessed a simple writing system, a number system, and a calendar.

During approximately the same period (800–400 BCE), the Chavin culture of the high valley of the Peruvian coast developed similarly to that of the Olmecs. In addition to sculptures in jade and clay, objects wrought in gold have also been found in archeological sites. The Chavin participated in an active vertical trade between low-lying coastal areas and high mountain regions, a trade which contributed to the early civilization of the Andes Mountains. While, for the most part, agriculture developed independently in various locations of the world, other societies, as the next chapter will address, were establishing a mutual dependence through trade.

AGRICULTURAL SOCIETIES OF OCEANIA

Trading contacts between Southeast Asia and New Guinea are evident from around 3000 BCE, with some traders settling in New Guinea and others spreading throughout the islands of the western Pacific. In nearby Australia, aboriginal peoples maintained a **foraging** society until the arrival of the European settlers in the nineteenth century. New Guinea, however, followed a different path; by 3000 BCE, inhabitants were cultivating yams and taro and domesticating pigs and chickens. The resulting population growth and specialization of labor produced skillfully crafted pottery and tools.

As the Pacific islands were further settled, large animals indigenous to the islands were quickly killed off before food crops were introduced. In addition to fish and seaweed from nearby ocean waters, settlers of the Pacific islands introduced taro, yams, breadfruit, bananas, pigs, chickens, and dogs from one island to another. As populations grew, the more venturesome islanders would build oceangoing canoes and sail to an uninhabited island of the Pacific. Throughout the Pacific islands societies ruled by strong chiefs emerged as the prominent form of political organization, especially in areas such as Tonga, Samoa, and Hawaii. Societal patterns in Oceania, therefore, progressed similarly to those in other agricultural societies, with surplus food leading to demographic growth, specialization of labor, and the rise of more complex institutions.

COMPARISON OF EARLY AGRICULTURAL SOCIETIES

	Geography	Crops	Trade	Religion	Writing	Technology
Sumer	Tigris-Euphrates, violent flooding, few natural barriers	wheat, barley	Indus, Egypt	polytheism	cuneiform	wheel, sailplow, arch, ziggurat, number system based on 60, irrigation
Egypt	Nile River, predictable floods, natural barriers	wheat, barley	Sumer, Nubia	polytheism	hieroglyphics	pyramid, irrigation, calendar
Indus	Indus River unpredictable floods, Himalayas, Hindu Kush	wheat, barley, cotton	Sumer, Persia	polytheism	writing based on hieroglyphics	sewage systems, indoor plumbing, irrigation
China	Huang He (Yellow) River, Yangtze, violent flooding, natural barriers	wheat, rice	Central and Southeast Asia	ancestral spirits	pictographs	bronze work irrigation
Americas	mountains, seas, rainforests	maize, potatoes	local peoples Southwest region of present-day United States	polytheism	glyphs (Mesoamerica)	calendar, work in jade and turquoise
New Guinea	Pacific Ocean	taro, yams	Southeast Asia, local islands	polytheism	none	pottery, tools, ocean canoes

THINGS TO REMEMBER

- Characteristics of a civilization include: cities, skilled laborers, social institutions, means of record keeping (such as writing), and advanced technology.
- Six early civilizations are:
  - Sumeria/Mesopotamia (circa 4000–500 BCE)
    - A location between the Tigris and Euphrates Rivers brought agricultural prosperity, which enabled trade and the growth of great cities.
    - Sumerian culture produced the world's first epic poem (Epic of Gilgamesh).
    - The vulnerable location of the Sumerian society led to its invasion by many peoples, including the Babylonians, who codified the legal system (Code of Hammurabi).
    - In the sixth century BCE this region became part of Persia.
  - Egypt (circa 3100–525 BCE)
    - Around 3100 BCE the kingdoms of Upper and Lower Egypt were united.
    - The ruler (pharaoh) was considered a god.
    - Geographic isolation saved Egypt from the threat of foreign invaders, until the Hyksos conquered Egypt and established the New Kingdom.
  - Indus River Valley
    - Remains of the advanced cities of Harappa and Mohenjo-Daro have been found in Pakistan. Artifacts indicate a writing system and technology with a decline in 900 BCE.
    - Aryans invaded around 1500 BCE and conquered north India, bringing the seeds of Hindu religion and the caste system.
    - Buddhism was founded by Siddhartha Gautama (563–483 BCE), who claimed that suffering comes from desire.
  - China
    - The Shang dynasty emerged in the Huang He (Yellow) River valley.
    - China was isolated by geography.
    - Women were subservient to men and the family took primacy over the individual.
    - The Zhou invaded around 1100 BCE and established a dynasty. After 771 BCE a period of civil wars began.

- Important Chinese philosophies from this chaotic period include:
    - Confucianism (reverence for ancestors, strong government, education, tradition)
    - Daoism (living in harmony with nature, least government is best)
    - Legalism (people must be controlled by strong government).
- Americas
    - Agriculture first developed in Peru by 7000 BCE. Potato and later maize were staples.
    - Olmec (1000–300 BCE) is earliest known civilization in Americas (southern Mexico).
    - Chavin culture (800–400 BCE) in Peruvian highlands led regional trade.
- Oceania
    - No agriculture in Australia until European contact.
    - New Guinea created agrarian culture with domesticated animals by 3000 BCE.
    - Settlers spread to other Pacific islands, bringing farming techniques, which led to population growth and further dispersal. Complex societies emerged in Samoa, Hawaii, and elsewhere.

REVIEW QUESTIONS

1. The following are true of the Hyksos EXCEPT

    (A) they ended Egypt's confidence in its natural barriers.
    (B) they ruled Egypt as pharaohs.
    (C) they were able to conquer Egypt because of power struggles among the pharaohs.
    (D) they created a new language that was a synthesis of the Hyksos and Egyptian tongues.
    (E) they introduced chariots to the Egyptians.

2. All of the earliest agricultural societies

    (A) were polytheistic.
    (B) engaged only in regional trade.
    (C) used pictographs as their form of writing.
    (D) grew up in river valleys.
    (E) developed unstratified social structures.

3. The following are true of the Shang dynasty EXCEPT that

    (A) it left bronze artifacts displaying detailed craftsmanship.
    (B) it was a socially stratified society.
    (C) it ruled the northeastern portion of China.
    (D) it was the first Chinese dynasty to leave written records.
    (E) it used the concept of the mandate of heaven to justify its rule.

4. Hinduism and Buddhism are similar in that they both

    (A) center their beliefs around a moral code.
    (B) uphold the caste system as a manifestation of one's virtue.
    (C) emphasize the joy that life holds for faithful followers.
    (D) are based upon a personal relationship with a deity.
    (E) offer salvation in the afterlife for believers.

5. With regard to the views of ancient Chinese philosophies concerning government,

    (A) Daoism would be confident of the efficiency of democratic government.
    (B) Confucianism would be supportive of revolutionary change.
    (C) Legalism would be likely to favor an autocratic ruler.
    (D) Daoism would favor a strong central government.
    (E) Legalism would support freedom of the press.

ANSWERS AND EXPLANATIONS

1. (D)

The Hyksos did not contribute to a new language blend. The ease with which the chariots (E) of the Hyksos entered Egypt across the Isthmus of Suez eroded Egyptian confidence in the impenetrability of their desert barrier (A). While on the throne of Egypt, the Hyksos rulers referred to themselves as "pharaoh" (B). They were able to conquer Egypt after a succession of power struggles between weak pharaohs and some nobles at the end of the Middle Kingdom (C).

2. (A)

All of the early agricultural societies worshipped many gods. Although societies of Oceania tended to trade only regionally, others such as the early Mesoamerican cultures, Sumer, and the Harappan civilization engaged in long-distance trade (B). While the majority of the early societies used pictographs, the farmers of New Guinea did not have a written language (C). The societies of New Guinea, Mesoamerica, South America, for example, did not emerge in river valley settings (D). The majority of early agrarian societies developed stratified societies (E) that had an elite class, often composed of priests.

3. (E)

The mandate of heaven concept originated with the Zhou dynasty to rationalize their overthrow of the Shang. The Shang left many finely-crafted items of bronze as well as bronze weapons. (A). Its society was deeply divided between peasants and nobles (B). Ruling the North China Plain (C), its rulers were the first Chinese dynasty to leave written records (D). Oracle bones also provided examples of Chinese writing under the Shang.

4. (A)

Hinduism contends that a person's karma, or good or evil deeds, determines the caste into which he would be reincarnated, while Buddhism concentrates on following the Eightfold Path of right living. Buddhism rejects the caste system (B) and concentrates on an answer to the pain and suffering in life (C). Neither religion is based on a personal relationship with a deity (D). Hinduism offers *moksha*, or the end of the cycle of reincarnation (E); also, some branches of Buddhism, such as the Salvation Land Sect, offer salvation to believers.

5. (C)

Legalism favored censorship (E) and restrictions on independent thought. Daoism views people as incapable of governing themselves (A) and favors the least government (D). Confucianism is resistant to change and would not support revolution (B).

ANSWERS AND EXPLANATIONS

1. (D)

CHAPTER 5

Interactions Among Early Empires and Societies

TIMELINE

2000 BCE	Arrival of the Hittites in Anatolia Beginning of Bantu migrations Abraham migrates to Canaan Phoenicians settle along the Mediterranean coast
1650 BCE	Hittite empire
1600–1450 BCE	Minoan civilization
1500 BCE	Hittite introduction of iron smelting Hebrews well established in Canaan
1450–1100 BCE	Mycenaean civilization
1000 BCE	Kingdom of Kush Hebrews establish a kingdom
722 BCE	Fall of the Kingdom of Israel to the Assyrians First Diaspora of the Jewish people
700–500 BCE	Large-scale Bantu migrations
612 BCE	Fall of Nineveh
586 BCE	Conquest of the Kingdom of Judah by Nebuchadnezzar
500 BCE–200 CE	Nok culture
330s BCE	Conquest of Persia by Alexander the Great
250 BCE–150 CE	Height of Meroë's power

IMPORTANT PEOPLE, PLACES, EVENTS, AND CONCEPTS

empire*	Saul	Yahweh*
terra cotta*	David	covenant*
Abraham	Solomon	Messiah*
Moses	diaspora*	Torah*
Exodus	Cyrus	Carthage
Ten Commandments	monotheism*	

THE DEVELOPMENT OF IRON METALLURGY

The Hittites

The wave of Indo-European migrations that brought the Aryans into the Indus Valley also brought the Hittites, a semi-nomadic group from central Asia, to Anatolia (present-day Turkey) about 2000 BCE. By 1650 BCE, they had formed an **empire** and occupied Babylon. To a large extent, they assimilated into Mesopotamian culture; the Hittites continued to use their own Indo-European language when addressing one another, but for trade and dealing with other peoples, they used the Akkadian language of Mesopotamia. They established a legal code in which punishment involved payment of damages—more lenient than the Hammurabi "eye for an eye" retribution.

The most noteworthy contribution of the Hittites was their introduction of iron smelting around 1500 BCE. The first society to use iron weapons, the Hittites also employed the three-man chariot in warfare, which allowed one of the chariot riders to hold up a shield for protection. Around 1200 BCE, the Hittites fell to an invasion of other Indo-Europeans from the north.

The Assyrians

The first group to widely use iron technology adopted from the Hittites was the Assyrians, who employed iron weapons in warfare to terrorize and subjugate Southwest Asia. Around 1000 BCE, the Assyrians established the first true empire (because of the extension of their territory and the diversity of the peoples over which they ruled). At its height, the Assyrian empire reached from Anatolia, Syria, Palestine, and Egypt, across Armenia and Mesopotamia, and into western Persia (modern-day Iran). Perhaps the most highly feared people in the ancient world, the Assyrians also fought from chariots and distinguished themselves as the first people to use the battering ram and the siege tower. Their conquest of Babylon involved another advanced tactic: tunneling under city walls.

To control those they conquered, the Assyrians frequently deported conquered peoples from their homelands and dispersed them throughout their empire. Conquered groups suffered a further loss of identity when the Assyrians settled their own citizens among the conquered. Still others were enslaved to work on public building projects. One of these projects was the great library in the Assyrian capital of Nineveh. Constructed by the last Assyrian king, Ashurbanipal (669–627 BCE), the library contained thousands of tablets, some of which are still preserved today.

Although they were skilled conquerors, the Assyrians were not capable administrators of their vast empire. They did, however, engage in long-distance trade in luxury items. Continuing in the Mesopotamian tradition, they accomplished achievements in mathematics and astronomy. Thus the Assyrians helped to preserve Mesopotamian culture. Weakened by the combined armies of the Babylonians, Arameans, Medes, and Scythians, the Assyrian empire continued to weaken, causing the fall of Nineveh in 612 BCE.

African Societies

The Bantu-Speaking People

The history of humankind has frequently been one of migration, or movement, from one location to another, either in search of improved economic conditions, release from political or religious oppression, or another reason. One of the most dramatic migrations in human history was undertaken by the Bantu-speaking people of Africa. Beginning around 2000 BCE, these farmers and herders from what is now Nigeria began to migrate south and east across the African continent. By 700–500 BCE, the initial trickle of migrations had become a large-scale movement across sub-Saharan Africa.

Following the Congo River through the rain forests, they farmed the land along the river and learned to apply their knowledge of raising sheep and goats to herding cattle. The Bantu used iron-tipped weapons to drive off foragers who challenged the Bantu's movement into their lands. Intermarrying with the people they encountered, the Bantu spread their customs and their language through southern and eastern Africa. Millions of Africans today speak a Bantu-related language.

The Kingdom of Kush

Historians are uncertain whether the Bantu-speaking people developed ironworking independently or borrowed the idea from another culture. Although the presence of rich iron deposits from Bantu homelands favors the idea of independent invention, the Bantu were not the only Africans who developed iron tools and weapons. To the south of Egypt near the Red Sea lay the kingdom of Kush, which arose around 1000 BCE and whose major city, Meroë, would become active in trade routes linking India, Arabia, and Africa. Situated in an area with abundant deposits of iron, Meroë would become a major center for iron-smelting and iron weapons and tools. Africans for miles around would rely on Meroë to trade jewelry, glass, and fine cotton in exchange for iron.

The kingdom of Kush demonstrated its appreciation for Egyptian culture by modeling its pharaohs and pyramids after the Egyptians. Prosperous between 250 BCE and 150 CE, Meroë's power declined in favor of a new power 400 miles to the south on the Red Sea. The kingdom of Aksum would now rule the former kingdom of Kush.

The Nok Culture

Another African culture which developed iron smelting was the Nok culture of West Africa (500 BCE–200 CE). The Nok, who were farmers from what is now Nigeria, used iron tools for farming and hunting. Their characteristic **terra cotta** sculptures of animal and human heads reveal much about the culture of the Nok people. A hairdo consisting of several topknots, which is seen among the Nigerian people today, is depicted in some of the terra cotta sculptures of the Nok.

THE HEBREWS

The Descendants of Abraham

One of the peoples who would fall to the Assyrians were the Hebrews. Around 2000 BCE, **Abraham**, who is considered the father of the Hebrews, migrated from Ur in Mesopotamia to the tiny area of Canaan along the eastern Mediterranean coast. By about 1500 BCE, the descendants of Abraham had become well established in the southern part of Palestine. Because of a great famine in Palestine during the period when the Hyksos ruled Egypt, the Hebrews migrated to Egypt, where food was still plentiful. Remaining in Egypt about 430 years, the Hebrews were forced to serve as slaves during the New Kingdom period of Egyptian history. Led out of slavery by **Moses**, a Hebrew who had been raised by the Egyptian royal family, the Hebrews returned to the land of Canaan. The flight from Egypt, known as the **Exodus**, was marked by the giving of the Hebrew moral law, or the **Ten Commandments**, from Mount Sinai on the Sinai Peninsula.

Before they could once again dominate Canaan, the Hebrews were forced to subdue tribes of Canaanites and Philistines who had settled in Canaan. Around 1000 BCE, the Hebrews had conquered these tribes sufficiently enough to establish their own kingdom under their first king, **Saul**. Saul's successor, **David**, became known through his victory over the Philistine giant Goliath. David also conquered Jerusalem, which became the capital of the Hebrew kingdom.

It was left to King David's son **Solomon** (970–935 BCE) to accomplish the construction of a magnificent temple in Jerusalem. During the reign of Solomon, the Hebrews briefly served as middlemen in the trade between Egypt and Mesopotamia. For the most part, however, the Hebrews did not widely engage in trade. As a result of his heavy expenditures, Solomon imposed oppressive taxes upon the Hebrew people. Upon his death, the kingdom was divided, with the northern ten tribes forming the Kingdom of Israel and the southern two tribes forming the Kingdom of Judah. In 722 BCE, the Kingdom of Israel fell to the Assyrians, who dispersed the Hebrew people throughout their own empire. The resulting **diaspora**, or scattering, of the northern ten tribes of Israel resulted in the loss of their cultural identity.

The kingdom of Judah remained intact until it, too, fell to invaders—the Chaldeans under King Nebuchadnezzar in 586 BCE. The Chaldean conquerors completely destroyed Solomon's temple. Carried off to Babylon, the people of Judah were held in captivity in Babylon for 70 years until King **Cyrus** of the Persians allowed them to return to Judah. With the construction of new city walls and a temple less wondrous than Solomon's, the Jews remained under Persian rule until the Persians were conquered by Alexander the Great in the 330s BCE. With Rome's rise to power, Palestine became a Roman province.

Monotheism and the Covenant

The influence of the Hebrews did not diminish with their captivity. They gave the world the concept of **monotheism**, or the worship of one god, whom they called **Yahweh**. The relationship established between the Jewish people and Yahweh was an intimate one based on a **covenant** in which Yahweh promised to be their God and they promised to be his people. Central to this covenant was the belief that, in time, God would send the Hebrews a promised **Messiah**, or anointed one, to save them from their sins. Later, while under Roman rule, some of the Jewish people came to hope that the Messiah would also set up an earthly kingdom. The Ten Commandments, or moral laws of the Hebrews, would become the basic moral code of the Judeo-Christian tradition. The Hebrew **Torah** not only chronicled the early history of the Jewish people but also became the first five books of the Old Testament of the Christian Bible.

MARITIME INTERACTIONS

The Phoenicians

One of the few societies with which the Hebrews traded was that of a group of Canaanites known as the Phoenicians. Around 2000 BCE, the Phoenicians settled along the Mediterranean coast in what is now Lebanon. Because they did not have enough land to support agriculture, they turned to the sea for their livelihood. The Phoenicians also manufactured glass for trade as well as a prized purple dye they obtained from the murex shell found along their shores. Also treasured were the famed cedars of Lebanon, which the Hebrews used to construct Solomon's temple.

In an effort to keep accurate records for their trade activity, the Phoenicians developed a 22-letter alphabet. Based on Sumerian cuneiform, the Phoenician alphabet was the byproduct of contact with the Sumerian culture through trade. The Phoenicians passed on their alphabet through trade to the Greeks, who would later introduce it to the Romans.

From their principal cities of Tyre and Sidon, the Phoenicians expanded their influence by setting up colonies throughout the Mediterranean world. A particularly prosperous colony was established at **Carthage** on the coast of North Africa. Carthage would later challenge Rome for control of the western Mediterranean. In the sixth century BCE, Assyrian invasions caused the Phoenician society to collapse.

The Minoans

By the time the Phoenician trade became active, another society, the Minoans, settled on the island of Crete (about 1600 BCE). The Minoans established a long-distance trade network that included Mesopotamia, Egypt, and the Greek mainland.

Our knowledge of the Minoans is restricted to archeological discoveries because their writing—called Linear A, an adaptation of Egyptian hieroglyphics—is presently undecipherable. What is known about the Minoan civilization from archeology indicates rule by a monarch; elaborate architectural forms including the enormous 800-room palace at the city of Knossos; bronze metallurgy; efficient record-keeping; and widespread prosperity among its inhabitants. The absence of fortifications suggests a society at peace with neighboring peoples. Statues of female deities indicate a high value placed on fertility. From pictures on Minoan vases, archeologists have determined that a popular Minoan activity was bull-jumping: either a sport or a religious celebration, bull-jumping involved athletes hurling themselves over the horns and backs of bulls.

The Mycenaeans

About 1450 BCE, the Minoan civilization was destroyed, presumably by the invasion of another group, the Mycenaeans. Historians speculate that the Minoan civilization was already in decline, perhaps as a result of a natural disaster such as a tsunami, volcanic eruption, or earthquake.

The Mycenaeans established a more stratified society with slaves in the lowest position. Their writing, known as Linear B, was derived from the Minoan Linear A, showing the assimilation of some aspects of the Minoan culture with that of the Mycenaeans. As a result of the collapse of trade brought about by the downfall of the Minoan culture, the Mycenaean trade network spread throughout the Aegean Sea, reaching Anatolia (Asia Minor), Cyprus, and Egypt. Among items traded were probably oil, wine, and pottery. Mycenaean culture prospered on the Greek mainland until the Mycenaean towns started battling each other. By 1100 BCE, the Mycenaean civilization had fallen.

THINGS TO REMEMBER

- Long-lasting influences on human society emerged in Africa, the Middle East, and the Mediterranean between 2000 BCE and 150 CE.
    - Migration
    - Iron-smelting technology
    - New religious ideas (monotheism, Judeo-Christian tradition)
- The Hittites
    - Brought an Indo-European language to Anatolia (Turkey).
    - Introduced iron smelting to many groups and used iron weapons.
- The Assyrians
    - Created the world's first true empire.
    - Deported conquered peoples, assimilating some and enslaving others.
    - Used iron weapons and were the first to employ battering rams, siege towers, and tunneling under enemy walls.
- Bantu People
    - Migrated south and east across Africa.
    - Spread their language throughout Africa.
    - Developed iron-smelting technology.
- Kush (North Africa)
    - Engaged in iron smelting and made their capital of Meroë a trade center for iron.
    - Imitated aspects of Egyptian culture (pharaohs, pyramids).
- Nok (West Africa)
    - Engaged in iron smelting.
    - Created terra cotta sculpture.
- The Hebrews
    - Introduced monotheism and made the Ten Commandments their moral code.
    - Left slavery in Egypt in the Exodus.
- The Phoenicians
    - Created an alphabet that influenced Greeks and Romans.
    - Traded purple dye, cedars of Lebanon, and other commodities.
    - Established colonies around the Mediterranean, including Carthage.

- The Minoans
    - Conducted long-distance trade.
    - Engaged in bronze metallurgy.
    - Used the Linear A writing system.
- The Mycenaeans
    - Conquered the Minoans and assimilated into Minoan civilization.
    - Conducted long-distance trade.
    - Used the Linear B writing system.
    - Destroyed their civilization in civil wars.

REVIEW QUESTIONS

1. All of the following are true of both the Hittites and Bantu EXCEPT

   (A) they were migrants.
   (B) they assimilated with the people they encountered.
   (C) they introduced their language to the area they conquered.
   (D) they knew the use of iron.
   (E) they were accomplished farmers.

2. The Assyrians

   (A) were noted for their leniency toward their conquered peoples.
   (B) were not interested in the transmission of knowledge.
   (C) were highly skilled administrators.
   (D) adopted the use of iron from Indo-European migrants.
   (E) destroyed the culture of the Sumerians.

3. The Hebrews

   (A) saw their influence diminish with their captivity at the hands of the Chaldeans.
   (B) were masters of long-distance trade.
   (C) anticipated a coming Messiah.
   (D) believed in a merciless, unforgiving god.
   (E) rejected the Ten Commandments.

4. Both the Minoan and Mycenaean civilizations

   (A) focused on overland trade.
   (B) influenced the later Greek civilization.
   (C) lacked a written language.
   (D) were warlike peoples.
   (E) failed to prosper economically.

5. All of the following are true of the Phoenicians EXCEPT
   (A) they influenced the development of the Roman alphabet.
   (B) they traded with the Hebrews.
   (C) they traded with peoples of the Fertile Crescent.
   (D) they adopted the monotheism of the Hebrews.
   (E) they contributed to the fashion habits of the elite classes.

ANSWERS AND EXPLANATIONS

1. (E)

Only the Bantu were accomplished farmers; the Hittites carried out a semi-nomadic lifestyle. The Hittites introduced iron smelting to central Asia, while the Bantu also knew of the process (D). The Hittites introduced their Indo-European tongue, while the Bantu blended their language with Arabic to form Swahili (C) as they both migrated through Asia and Africa, respectively (A). The Bantu learned agricultural techniques from other Africans, while the Hittites used the language of the people they conquered in their everyday activities (B).

2. (D)

The Assyrians adopted the use of iron from the Hittites. They were noted for their harsh policies against conquered peoples (A). They established a library at Nineveh (B) and acted as transmitters of the Sumerian culture throughout the ancient world (E). They were skilled conquerors, but inept administrators (C).

3. (C)

The Hebrews anticipated a coming Messiah. Their god, while powerful, was also merciful, caring, and forgiving (D). After the Chaldean captivity, the Hebrews returned to Palestine to rebuild and influence the area (A). They engaged in some regional trade, but very little long-distance trade (B). The Ten Commandments, or moral laws of the Hebrews, would become the basic moral code of the Judeo-Christian tradition (E).

4. (B)

The Mycenaeans adopted some of the aspects of the Minoan culture and, in turn, carried the traits of both civilizations to the Greek mainland. Both engaged in maritime trade (A), which produced economic prosperity for both (E). Both possessed a written language, although that of the Minoans remains undecipherable (C). Minoan artifacts show a lack of city walls or weapons of war (D).

5. (D)

Although they traded with the Hebrews, particularly in cedar (B), the Phoenicians did not adopt their monotheistic religion. They transmitted their alphabet to the Greeks, who later transmitted it to the Romans (A). They exported a purple dye that was popular among the elite classes (E).

CHAPTER 6

Persia, Greece, and the Hellenistic World

TIMELINE

1100–800 BCE	Dorians dominate Greece
776 BCE	First Olympic Games
600s BCE	Rule of tyrants in Greece Political reform in Greece
500 BCE	Rise of Sparta Public participation begins in several *poleis*
500–479 BCE	Persian Wars
500 BCE–500 CE	Persian Empire
495–429 BCE	Age of Pericles (Golden Age of Athens)
431–404 BCE	Peloponnesian War
336 BCE	Philip of Macedon conquers Greece
336–323 BCE	Rule of Alexander the Great
146 BCE	Roman conquest of Greece

IMPORTANT PEOPLE, PLACES, EVENTS, AND CONCEPTS

polis*
Homer
helot*
marathon*
Xerxes
Thermopylae
Parthenon
Acropolis
golden mean*

tyrant*
aristocracy*
Solon
Cleisthenes
direct democracy*
Cyrus
satrap*
King's Eyes and Ears
Zoroastrianism
Zarathustra
Darius
Royal Road*
Delian League
Peloponnesian League
Pericles
philosopher*
Socrates
Plato
Aristotle
Oracle at Delphi
Pythagorean theorem
tragedy*
comedy*
hubris*
patriarchal*
Philip of Macedon
Alexander the Great
Alexandria of Egypt
Hellenistic culture*
mystery religion*
Cynicism*
Epicureanism*
Stoicism*
Zeno
Euclid
Ptolemy

THE RISE OF CITY-STATES IN GREECE

The fall of the Mycenaean kingdoms brought to Greece a period of chaos and decline. A new people, the Dorians, dominated this era, from 1100 to 800 BCE. (Historians are not sure whether the Dorians invaded Greece or whether they merely rose to prominence after the decline of the Mycenaeans.) Even the knowledge of writing was wiped out under the Dorians; it is a wonder that the Greek culture did not die out completely during this period. As a result of the chaotic Dorian period, some Greeks left the mainland to settle in colonies in Crete and Asia Minor. These migrations further spread the Greek culture.

During the Dorian period, the Greeks developed the political unit which would characterize their classical age: the ***polis***, or city-state. Each *polis* consisted of a city and surrounding lands, both under the same government. Greek geography contributed to the rise of the *poleis*: A mountainous terrain dotted by valleys, it was an ideal environment for the development of small, isolated city-states. Gradually, Athens and Sparta emerged as the most prominent city-states.

Geography further determined the livelihood of the poleis. The jagged coastline of the Greek mainland left each polis only a few miles from the sea, which promoted trade in the Mediterranean and Black Seas. The Greeks took to the sea to trade their wine and olive oil in exchange for grains, timber, and luxury goods. The rugged terrain of Greece left little land suitable for cultivation; fishing supplemented the diet of the Greeks. Geography also provided limits on the amount of land capable of sustaining the burgeoning population of the Greek city-states. Because of these limitations, the Greeks crossed the Mediterranean to establish colonies in various locations on its shores and the shores of the Black Sea, especially in Anatolia, or Asia Minor (modern-day Turkey). The result of Greek colonization was the diffusion of Greek culture throughout the Mediterranean world.

In addition, trade brought the Greeks into contact with the Phoenicians, who had developed a 22-character alphabet. The Greeks adopted the Phoenician alphabet, added symbols for vowel sounds, and later transmitted their alphabet to the Roman world. The eighth century BCE also produced the written versions of two great epic poems, the *Iliad* and the *Odyssey*. Attributed to the poet **Homer**, the poems centered on the legendary Trojan Wars between the Myceneans and the people of Troy in Asia Minor. The real conflict was probably a raid around 1200 BCE against Troy, a rival trading city of the Myceneans. Homer's epic poems described the various Greek gods and the human characteristics attributed to them.

DIVERSITY IN GREECE: ATHENS AND SPARTA

As the more than 200 Greek city-states concentrated on trade and colonization, two of them, Athens and Sparta, rose to particular prominence and developed their own unique characteristics.

The Spartan Military

By 500 BCE, Sparta, an agricultural community situated on the Peloponnesian peninsula, had risen as a highly disciplined military state. The Spartans, who were descendants of the Dorians, constituted approximately one-fifth of Spartan society. The remaining four-fifths was comprised of the ***helots***, or agricultural laborers, who had been conquered in the 700s BCE from neighboring Messenia. Governed by an assembly elected by all citizens, Sparta was in effect led by five elected *ephors* who ran the government. A dual monarchy provided ceremonial leadership. Constant fear of rebellion from the helot majority prompted the Spartans to maintain very rigid discipline of its citizens. The ephors forbade citizens from traveling outside Sparta and refused to allow visits from foreigners. In order to prevent Spartan over-reliance on money, the use of gold and silver was prohibited; Spartan money was made of cumbersome iron bars.

In Spartan society, all activity was focused on the strengthening of the state. Male children resided in military barracks from the age of seven and were required to serve in the military between the ages of twenty and sixty. Schooling was minimal for both men and women. The primary goal of the Spartan woman was to produce healthy babies; rigorous physical training promoted that goal. Spartan society featured an efficient government and an army that was almost undefeatable. To maintain their military state, however, the Spartans sacrificed individual freedom and produced little in the arts, literature, science, and philosophy.

Athenian Democracy

Eighty miles from Sparta stood the polis of Athens, which would become the cradle of democracy. Located near the Aegean coast, Athens depended on the sea for her livelihood, building up a sizeable fleet that was financed by proceeds from her silver mines. Early government in Athens was rule by landowning **aristocrats**. An assembly elected *archons*, who appointed officials and made all laws. In the seventh century BCE, as aristocrats were fighting among themselves, **tyrants** arose to seize power by force and rule with total authority. While some tyrants were harsh and unjust, others ended the aristocratic power struggles, encouraged trade, and passed fair laws. Still, the idea of authoritarian rule rankled the citizens of Athens, giving rise to reform movements within Athens.

One of the early reformers was **Solon**. Early in the sixth century, he established laws that prohibited enslavement for debt and allowed most citizens (defined as male descendants of citizens) to vote. Another reformer, Draco, wrote down laws that were so strict that today a very rigid law is termed a *draconian law*. Pisistratus, a tyrant who ruled from 546 to 527 BCE, divided the estates of nobles among peasants and sponsored major building projects that created new jobs. After Pisistratus's death, **Cleisthenes** created an assembly of all male citizens over the age of twenty as well as a Council of 500 whose members were citizens. His rule promoted equality before the law and freedom of speech.

By 500 BCE, several of the poleis created a tradition of public participation, with Athens taking the lead as the most fully developed Greek democracy. Athens was a **direct democracy**, with an assembly in which all citizens could participate by proposing and debating laws. All decisions in Athens had to be approved by this assembly. Citizens participated as jurors in court trials. Judges, who were nobles, interpreted the laws, but judicial decisions could be taken to a citizen board for appeal.

But citizenship was restricted to approximately half the male population in Athens, since it was granted only to males over the age of twenty who had served in the army. Foreigners and slaves were not admitted into citizenship, and women had no opportunities for political participation.

INTERACTIONS WITH PERSIA

Democratic Athens and aristocratic Sparta were unified in the early fifth century BCE by their mutual concern over containing the threats of a common enemy: Persia. The Persians, whose empire was centered in present-day Iran, rose to be one of the most powerful civilizations in Southwest Asia from 500 BCE to 500 CE. One of the various Indo-European peoples who had migrated from central Asia, the Persians began their southward migration about 1000 BCE. At first, they were nomadic like other Indo-European peoples, but then the Persians capitalized on their trade contacts with Mesopotamia to learn agricultural techniques. Around 530 BCE, the Persians united under a strong ruler of the Achaemenid dynasty named **Cyrus**, who led the Persians to subdue their neighbors, the Medes.

Through warfare, Cyrus extended his empire from the Mediterranean coast to the borders of India. By 525 BCE, Cyrus' son and successor, Cambyses, further broadened the limits of the empire to include parts of Arabia and the Nile Valley of Egypt. The Persian Empire was extremely efficient; provincial governors called ***satraps*** administered outlying territories while inspectors known as the **King's Eyes and Ears** kept a watchful eye on the satraps and reported any irregularities to the monarch. The Persians displayed an attitude of tolerance to conquered peoples, allowing them to maintain their own laws, religious beliefs, and customs—as long as they paid their taxes, provided military support, and pledged obedience to the Persian monarch.

The Persians were also the founders of a new religion, **Zoroastrianism**. Its founder, Zoroaster, also known as **Zarathustra**, defined life as a struggle between the forces of good and evil; eventually good would prevail. A final judgment would decide the eternal destination of each person. The tenets of Zoroastrianism were outlined in their scripture, the *Avesta*, based on the teachings of Zoroaster.

Darius I (reigned 521–486 BCE), the greatest of the Achaemenid rulers, further extended the empire to include Macedonia and the coast of North Africa. From his magnificent administrative capital at Persepolis, Darius introduced standardized coinage as well as a calendar used throughout the region. The **Royal Road**, which stretched 1,600 miles from Ephesus to Sardis in Anatolia to Susa in present-day Iran, included a system of couriers who could travel the length of the road in a week's time, similar to the Incan system of roads in the fifteenth and sixteenth centuries. The Greek historian Herodotus described the efforts of the couriers along the Royal Road in his statement, "Neither snow nor rain nor heat nor gloom of night stop these couriers from the swift completion of their appointed rounds."

The Persian Wars

In 546 BCE Cyrus conquered the Greek poleis on the western shores of Asia Minor and, true to Persian tradition, allowed the Greeks to preserve their own government as long as they continued to pay tribute to Persia. In 499 BCE, however, revolts broke out in the poleis of Asia Minor, with the Athenian navy offering support. Darius crushed the revolts and subsequently decided to attempt an invasion of the Greek mainland, first to punish Athens and secondly to control the poleis on the mainland and in Asia Minor.

The Persian Wars (500–479 BCE) involved two attacks on Greece. The first, launched by Darius, culminated in the defeat of the Persians by the Athenians. When the Athenians defeated the Persians at the Battle of Marathon in 490 BCE, a runner ran the 26 miles to Athens to announce their victory, collapsing immediately after announcing the triumphant news. (Today's 26-mile **marathon** race is a tribute to his effort.)

In 480 BCE, Darius's successor, **Xerxes**, moved against Greece with a vast army and fleet. To advance toward Athens, the Persians had to march through a narrow mountain pass at **Thermopylae**. King Leonidas of Sparta, with 300 Spartans and about 6,000 Greek allies from other city-states, met an army of 200,000 Persians and held the Persians at the pass until a Greek traitor revealed an alternate route through the pass. While the Greek allies left Thermopylae to race to the defense of Athens, the 300 Spartans remained, giving their lives to delay the Persians. Although the Persians subsequently sacked Athens, they were defeated by the superior Athenian navy at Salamis in 479 BCE. Complete Greek victory was attained by a combined Greek army at the Battle of Plataea in 479 BCE.

Classical Greece, c. 400 CE

THE RISE AND FALL OF ATHENIAN POWER

Victory in the Persian Wars allowed the Greeks to preserve their political independence and individual freedom, although the Persians would continue to strive to prevent Greek unity. The most significant outcome, however, was Athens' rise to prominence as she created an empire in the Aegean. To solidify her position among the Greek city-states, Athens gathered a group of neighboring poleis into the **Delian League**. Sparta countered with a smaller alliance called the **Peloponnesian League**.

Athenian culture flowered in the years following the Persian Wars. Under the leadership of the aristocrat **Pericles** (495–429 BCE), Athens would become the center of the artistic and intellectual life of classical Greece (see "The Golden Age of Athens," below). Pericles also expanded Athenian democracy by allowing all citizens to hold public office. In order to permit poor citizens the opportunity to serve as jurors and to attend meetings of the assemblies, officeholders were given salaries. However, members of the Delian League were dependent on Athenian rule without having much voice in policymaking.

Athens' hunger for dominance of the Greek world manifested itself in her relations with the powerful poleis of Corinth and Sparta. When the Spartans came to the aid of Corinth to protest what they perceived as Athenian aggression, war broke out between Sparta and Athens and their respective allies. The resulting Peloponnesian War began in 431 BCE when Sparta marched into Athenian territory. Athens, with its superior navy, believed it could hold off the Spartans while preparing its allies to raid Sparta. During the second year of war, however, a devastating plague erupted in Athens, killing a third of the population, including Pericles. Demoralized by what some Athenians perceived as loss of favor from their gods and weakened by their significant decline in population, the Athenians argued among themselves. A failed attempt to invade Sicily further weakened Athens. Finally, in 404 BCE, the Spartans (with help from the Persians) defeated Athens at sea and surrounded the city, starving it into surrender.

THE GOLDEN AGE OF ATHENS

Under the intellectual and artistic leadership of Athens, the Greeks would achieve lasting renown in philosophy, the arts, and science.

The Three Great Greek Philosophers

Three key **philosophers** rose to prominence in Greek culture: **Socrates**, **Plato**, and **Aristotle**. Socrates (470–399 BCE) became noted for his "Socratic method," or systematic questioning, by which he continuously challenged his students to question and justify everything before accepting it as truth. In his attempt to question traditional Greek ethics, Socrates incurred the anger of some Athenians, who charged him with corrupting the morals of Athenian youth. Condemned to death by a jury of Athenian citizens, he took his own life in 399 BCE by drinking hemlock.

The message of Socrates continued in the life of his pupil, Plato (430–347 BCE). Plato's most lasting achievement was *The Republic*, in which he detailed his concept of the ideal state. Asserting that the best state was one in which philosophers ruled, Plato supported an aristocracy of intellectuals. The less intelligent classes would be confined to labor that would best fit their abilities and skills.

Aristotle (384–322 BCE) was a student of Plato. Aristotle developed rules of logic to assist him in constructing arguments to explore the universe. His comprehensive work in the fields of psychology, ethics, politics, literature, biology, physics, and astronomy earned him the respect of both the western and Islamic worlds. Among the topics Aristotle explored were slavery and the status of women. Defending the usefulness of slavery, he also supported patriarchal families that accepted a position of inferiority for women.

The Roles of Religion, Science, and Sport

In addition to philosophy, religion played an integral role in Greek life. Greek religion was polytheistic, with many gods and goddesses to whom the Greeks assigned human characteristics. Among their gods were their chief god, Zeus; his wife, Hera; Poseidon, the god of the sea; Athena, the goddess of wisdom and war; Apollo, god of the sun; and Demeter, the goddess of fertility. Those wishing to determine the will of the gods for their lives cast lots to reveal the answers to their questions or consulted diviners such as the famed **Oracle at Delphi**. In general, the Greeks did not fear death and devoted little time to anticipating the afterlife; their focus was on the concerns of this world.

The Greeks' emphasis on order and reason also led to an examination of the scientific world. Greek scientists developed theories of the motion of planets and studied the organization of the elemental principles of earth, fire, air, and water. They applied mathematics as a means of comprehending the patterns of nature. The **Pythagorean theorem** was the product of the Greek mathematician, Pythagorus (582–507 BCE).

A tribute to both the glory of the human form as well as the gods were the Olympic games, first held in 776 BCE in the polis of Olympia. The first event was a foot race in which only men could compete; women held their own games dedicated to the goddess Hera at a separate location. Eventually other events were added: jumping, javelin and discus throwing, boxing, wrestling, weightlifting, and chariot racing. A prized wreath of olive branches bestowed honor on the victor and his polis. Continued every four years for approximately 1,000 years, the games declined after the Macedonian conquest of Greece and eventually ceased altogether. After 2,300 years, the modern Olympic games were subsequently revived in 1896.

Greek Drama and Art

Theatre was popular in Greek culture; annual dramatic festivals were held for which the poor received free tickets. Greek drama involved two forms: **tragedy** and **comedy**. Tragedies were serious dramas centered around a main character who displayed exceptional attributes but also a tragic flaw that caused his downfall. This flaw was often **hubris**, or excessive pride or overconfidence. Among the most well known Greek tragedies were those of the dramatist Sophocles (*Oedipus Rex* and *Antigone)* and Euripides (*Medea*). Comedies were dramas that contained not only humorous scenes but also material that satirized leading citizens, customs, or ideas. The leading comedic dramatist was Aristophanes, author of *Lysistrata*, which portrayed the persuasive power of women.

The Greeks also excelled at other art forms. Greek painting followed the traditional ideal of combining beauty with utility. Most examples of their paintings are found as murals on public buildings or scenes on ceramic vases; paintings on Greek vases depicted mythological events or scenes from everyday life. Greek sculpture, on the other hand, displayed the Greeks' pride in the human form. The statue of Zeus at the Temple of Olympia by Phidias is considered one of the Seven Wonders of the World. As in other artistic endeavors, sculpture reflected the Greek ideals of order, balance, harmony, and moderation as typified by the **golden mean**. The golden mean involved the concept of avoiding extremes in architectural proportions as well as in the thoughts and actions of everyday life. As such, it was also reflected in Greek drama.

The **Parthenon** is considered the finest example of Greek architecture. Situated atop the **Acropolis** in Athens, the elegant proportions of the Parthenon were a tribute to the Greek ideal of the golden mean. A statue of the goddess Athena by the Athenian sculptor Phidias was the focal point in the majestic temple of the Parthenon, which was constructed in her honor.

Greek Society

The people of Greece dwelled in a **patriarchal** society where women occupied a public position very inferior to that of men. However, women could divorce their husbands and control any property they owned prior to their marriage. A woman's daily routine mostly centered around the care and management of household and family.

Greeks who were educated and who owned property regarded manual labor as beneath their position in life and, consequently, turned most of it over to slaves. Greeks and non-Greeks were often enslaved because of indebtedness. Slaves were also imported from the southern part of present-day Russia and from Egypt (which acquired its slaves from the African kingdom of Nubia). Some slaves were permitted to work for wages in craft shops or small businesses. The slaves enduring the most rigorous conditions were primarily criminals who worked the Athenian silver mines.

THE EMPIRE OF ALEXANDER

The conflict between Athens and Sparta ended Athens' position as the cultural center of ancient Greece and weakened the political and economic power of several Greek city-states. Further warfare between Athens and Sparta after Sparta's defeat of Athens in 404 BCE prompted a monarch to the north, **Philip of Macedon**, to move his efficient military against the northern Greek poleis. At the Battle of Chaeronea in 336 BCE, Philip gained mastery over Greece, returning a degree of unity to the various poleis.

His assassination shortly afterward brought his twenty-year-old son **Alexander** to the throne. In the 13 years of his reign (336–323 BCE), Alexander would create one of the largest empires up to his time and prove himself a master at linking the cultures of East and West.

A pupil of Aristotle, Alexander had been schooled in Greek science, literature, and philosophy. In an effort to continue his father's empire, he began by suppressing an insurrection in the city-state of Thebes, during which he killed large numbers of inhabitants and sold others into slavery. He then took on the weakened Persian army, defeating them in 333 BCE. By 331 BCE, Alexander had conquered Asia Minor, Syria, Egypt, and Mesopotamia. To accomplish his goal of uniting East and West, he married Persian and Bactrian princesses and urged his generals to do the same. Finally, Alexander reached his ultimate goal, India, but here at the Indus River his conquests ended. Exhausted by years of fighting, his troops refused to penetrate India. Alexander's divided army went in different directions. Alexander himself died of a fever in Babylon in 323 BCE, one month short of his thirty-third birthday.

During his brief career, Alexander built new cities, many of which were named Alexandria. The most famous was **Alexandria of Egypt**, which boasted a library, research institution, and a lighthouse that was considered one of the wonders of the ancient world. In the process of creating centers of learning, Alexander fashioned a new culture, the **Hellenistic culture**, a synthesis of the traditions of West and East (especially Persia). The Hellenistic world carried the Greek culture far beyond the borders of the poleis and gave rise to the application of the name *Hellenistic Age* to the period between the death of Alexander and the Roman conquest of Greece in 146 BCE. Although Alexander failed to conquer India, his presence at its border introduced India to western culture and boosted trade between India and the Mediterranean world.

After Alexander's death, Athens and Sparta again became independent city-states. Alexander's generals murdered the members of his family and divided his empire into three dynasties: the Ptolemaic of Egypt, which ended in 31 BCE with the suicide of Cleopatra; the Seleucid of Mesopotamia; and the Antigonid of Macedonia and Greece. Although Greek commerce and trade continued to flourish, the weakening of the Greek poleis made them vulnerable to outside attack. It was into this power vacuum that Rome entered in 146 BCE, adding the Greek city-states to its own empire.

Hellenistic Culture

Hellenistic influence permeated all aspects of life among the inhabitants of Alexander's former empire. Eastern religions found their way into the Greek world as **mystery religions** that involved faith in Eastern deities and the promise of eternal life to believers. Others looked to philosophy for an explanation to life's situations. Three philosophies were especially appealing to Hellenistic Greeks: **Cynicism**, **Stoicism**, and **Epicureanism**. Cynicism called for a return to simplicity and a rejection of materialism. Epicureanism sought pleasure (defined as the avoidance of pain) and inner peace. Stoicism, the most popular of the three philosophies, was originally attributed to a freed slave named **Zeno**. With an emphasis on the brotherhood of all humans, the Stoics taught that individuals had a responsibility to aid others and to lead virtuous lives.

Hellenistic interest in the improvement of mankind led to studies of human anatomy, particularly of the digestive and vascular systems. Galen (131–291 CE) summarized the medical knowledge of his day and performed experiments concerning the nervous and circulatory systems. Archimedes (287–212 BCE) studied mathematics and the measurement of water power and created a system of pulleys. The geographer Eratosthenes (276–194 BCE) accurately calculated the circumference of the earth. In the third century BCE, an Egyptian Greek named **Euclid** wrote the *Elements of Geometry*, considered the most significant mathematical argument ever written. The debate concerning the nature of the structure of the universe involved the findings of the astronomer Aristarchus (310–230 BCE), who taught that the earth revolved around the sun (heliocentric theory) and **Ptolemy** (second century CE), who argued that the earth was the center of the universe (geocentric theory). The culture of the Greek and Hellenistic worlds would be largely adopted by their conquerors, the Romans, and become the basis for Western civilization.

THINGS TO REMEMBER

- The Dorians ruled Greece after the fall of the Myceneans (1100 BCE).
- Independent city-states emerged, Athens and Sparta becoming most prominent.
    - Athens developed a direct democracy where all citizens participated in government.
    - Sparta established an efficient military state.
- Greek city-states joined together to fight the encroachment of Persia (500–479 BCE).
    - Important battles included Marathon and Thermopylae.
    - Victory made Athens dominant over many city-states.
- The Persian Empire extended from India to the Mediterranean and introduced the religion of Zoroastrianism to the world. It was a model of administrative organization.
- Athens and Sparta fought the devastating Peloponnesian War (431–404 BCE) in which Sparta defeated Athens.
- The Classical Age of Athens (fifth century BCE) featured achievements in philosophy (Socrates, Plato, Aristotle), drama, mathematics, and sports.
- Philip of Macedon conquered Greece in 363 BCE.
- His son Alexander (the Great) established an empire including Asia Minor, Egypt, Syria, and Mesopotamia.
    - The empire fragmented shortly after Alexander's death.
    - Its blend of Greek and Persian culture, Hellenism, spread Greek culture and learning.

REVIEW QUESTIONS

1. "Our constitution is called a democracy because power is in the hands not of a minority but of the whole people."

   The above quote of Pericles refers to

   (A) the Spartan assembly.
   (B) the reforms of Cleisthenes.
   (C) the reforms of Solon.
   (D) the government of Athens during its Golden Age.
   (E) aristocratic rule in Athens.

2. All of the following were true of the Persians EXCEPT

   (A) their language was related to that of the Aryans and Hittites.
   (B) they treated conquered peoples in a manner similar to the Assyrians.
   (C) they introduced a new religion.
   (D) they were efficient administrators.
   (E) they established an efficient communications system.

3. Classical Greek philosophy

   (A) was studied by Alexander the Great.
   (B) promoted women's rights.
   (C) was unknown beyond the western world.
   (D) resulted in the emancipation of Greek slaves.
   (E) considered scientific subjects unfit for philosophical inquiry.

4. All of the following are true of Greek geography EXCEPT

   (A) it encouraged trade.
   (B) it contributed to the rise of independent poleis.
   (C) it led to the establishment of colonies.
   (D) it fostered maritime activities.
   (E) it promoted agriculture.

5. Alexander's empire

   (A) extended throughout the Indian subcontinent.
   (B) blended eastern and western cultures.
   (C) remained stable for two centuries following his death.
   (D) ended slavery among the Greeks.
   (E) was known for its benevolence toward conquered peoples.

ANSWERS AND EXPLANATIONS

1. (D)

Pericles was the ruler of Athens during its Golden Age, when the democratic process in Athens was at its height. The other responses referring to Athens (B, C, E) pertain to eras before the rule of Pericles.

2. (B)

The Persians usually allowed their conquered peoples to maintain their cultural identity, in contrast to the Assyrians, who dispersed conquered peoples throughout their empire so that they would lose their identity. The Persians also spoke an Indo-European language (A). They introduced the religion of Zoroastrianism (C), oversaw their empire well (D), and linked most parts of their empire through the Royal Road (E).

3. (A)

Alexander studied under Aristotle. Greek philosophy advocated a patriarchal society (B), was known to the Islamic world (C), accepted slavery (D), and pursued all branches of scientific knowledge (E).

4. (E)

The mountainous terrain of Greece was a deterrent to agriculture. Because of this feature, the Greeks engaged in trade (A) and other maritime activities such as fishing (D). Independent poleis grew up in the valleys (B). The lack of arable land led the Greeks to establish colonies to support their growing population (C).

5. (B)

The empire of Alexander blended the Greek culture with that of the east, especially Persia. Alexander's army refused to march beyond the Indus River (A). Alexander supported slavery (D) and sometimes used brutal methods to accomplish his goals, as in Thebes (E). His empire broke apart shortly after his death (C).

CHAPTER 7

The Roman and Han Empires

TIMELINE

2000 BCE	Indo-Europeans move into the Italian Peninsula
800 BCE	Greeks and Etruscans move into the Italian Peninsula
509 BCE	Establishment of the Roman republic
451 BCE	Writing of the Twelve Tables
265 BCE	Romans control all of Italy except the Po Valley
264–146 BCE	Punic Wars
206 BCE	Beginning of the Han empire
150 BCE–900 CE	First era of the Silk Roads
148 BCE	Rome controls the eastern Mediterranean
100 BCE	Buddhism reaches China
60 BCE	First triumvirate
59 BCE	Julius Caesar elected proconsul
46 BCE	Julius Caesar appointed dictator for life
44 BCE	Assassination of Julius Caesar
27 BCE	Establishment of the Roman empire Octavian begins his reign
20 BCE–180 CE	Pax Romana

4 BCE	Birth of Jesus
6 CE	Overthrow of the Han by the Wang
23 CE	Restoration of the Han dynasty
73 CE	Fall of Masada
132 CE	Second Diaspora
200s CE	Civil war in Rome
220 CE	Fall of the Han empire
300 CE	Christianity reaches Anatolia
313 CE	Edict of Milan
325 CE	Council of Nicaea
330 CE	Constantine makes Constantinople the imperial capital
378 CE	Battle of Adrianople
381 CE	Christianity becomes the official religion of the Roman empire
410 CE	Sack of Rome by Alaric
451 CE	Battle of Chalons
476 CE	Overthrow of the last Roman emperor

IMPORTANT PEOPLE, PLACES, EVENTS, AND CONCEPTS

republic*
patrician*
plebeian*
consul*
Senate*
Tribal Assembly
tribune*
veto*
dictator*
Twelve Tables
legion*
Hannibal
Scipio
*latifundia**
Tiberius and Gauis Gracchus
Cleopatra
Octavian
Marc Antony
Hadrian
Marcus Aurelius
Colosseum
Zealots
Jesus
apostle*
Gospel*
New Testament
Paul of Tarsus
Gentile
Masada
Second Diaspora
Coptic Christianity
Nestorian Christianity
Arianism
Nicene Creed*
St. Augustine
Huns*
Attila
Saxons
Angles
Franks
Visigoths
Ostrogoths
Vandals
barracks emperors
Empress Lü

Marius	bishop	Han Wudi
Sulla	diocese*	Silk Roads*
Julius Caesar	Peter	shi*
triumvirate*	Nero	Manichaeism*
Pompey	Diocletian	

THE ROMAN REPUBLIC

Rome, the successor to the splendors of Greek and Persian civilization, had its beginnings about 2000 BCE when a group of Indo-Europeans moved into the Italian peninsula. But Roman legend tells quite a different tale, in which Rome was founded by Aeneas, a refugee from the Trojan War. According to the legend, two of his descendants, Romulus and Remus, nearly died in infancy when the evil Aeneas abandoned them by the flooded waters of the Tiber River. A she-wolf then discovered them and restored them to health. In 753 BCE, Romulus founded Rome and became its first king.

In reality, another group, the Etruscans, moved into the Italian peninsula around 800 BCE and remained influential in that region until about 500 BCE. The Etruscans, who probably migrated from Anatolia, were artisans and traders. They were ruled by monarchs who controlled well-disciplined and organized armies who used horses and war chariots. Many of the Roman religious beliefs and architectural forms, including the arch, were the products of Etruscan influence. The Romans also developed the Etruscan alphabet, which the Etruscans had learned from the Greeks, who ultimately had adopted the Phoenician alphabet. Sometime prior to 800 BCE, Greeks had migrated into the Italian peninsula; the early Romans also established some contacts with them.

Governing the Republic

By the eighth century BCE, the present-day city of Rome, situated along the banks of the Tiber River, consisted of a small city-state with a king. But the landed aristocrats of Rome grew tired of monarchical rule, so in 509 BCE they overthrew the Etruscan king and established a **republic**.

Republican Roman society consisted of two groups vying for power: the **patricians** and the **plebeians**. The patricians, or upper class, were the landed members of society who held most of the power in republican Rome. The patrician assembly elected the two **consuls** who held executive authority in Rome, and the 300-member **Senate** of patricians approved all major decisions.

The plebeians, on the other hand, comprised the majority of the population—farmers, artisans, merchants, and so forth. They were granted the right to vote but initially were not allowed to hold most government offices. Later the plebeians were permitted seats in the Senate and were granted their own assembly, the **Tribal Assembly**, which allowed them to elect their own representatives, or **tribunes**. The tribunes had the authority to **veto** unfair measures and make laws for the plebeians. Late in the republic, the Tribal Assembly received the right to make laws for the republic as a whole. Eventually, plebeians were allowed the opportunity to hold almost all offices; one of the consuls was selected from patrician ranks.

During times of crisis, the republic could appoint a **dictator** to attempt to restore order. Chosen by the consuls and elected by the Senate, the dictator could remain in power for six months, during which he possessed absolute power to command the army and legislate for the republic.

In 451 BCE, the **Twelve Tables** of Roman law were written. This codification of Roman law established the concept that citizens had the right to protection of the law and became the basis for later Roman law. Throughout the years of the Roman republic, the Twelve Tables were modified when needed as new laws were passed and as judges interpreted older laws to apply to new situations.

The Roman Army and Expansion of the Republic

At the center of Roman power was its army, in which all citizen landowners were required to serve. The army was organized into **legions**, or military units of 5,000 to 6,000 foot soldiers, known as infantry. Each legion was reinforced by cavalry, or soldiers mounted on horseback. Soldiers had to provide their own weapons and equipment.

By the fourth century BCE, Rome controlled central Italy. The power of the Roman army—and the wealth to be obtained through trade—promoted the expansion of the Roman republic. However, the growth of the republic suffered a major setback in 390 BCE when the Gauls sacked the city of Rome. After rebuilding the city, the Romans continued to subdue the other inhabitants of the Italian Peninsula; by 265 BCE, the Romans controlled all of Italy except the Po Valley.

The Romans divided their conquered peoples into three categories of privilege. Latins, living along the Tiber River, were granted full Roman citizenship. Conquered peoples in territories farther out from Rome were given all rights of citizenship except the vote. Other conquered peoples were granted the status of allies and were permitted to keep their local governments; however, allies were required to provide troops for the Roman army. Rome's lenient policy toward her conquered peoples promoted cooperation in the republic and later throughout the empire.

The Punic Wars

Rome's location in the Mediterranean Sea placed her in a position to carry out profitable trade relations with neighboring peoples: Over both land and sea routes, the Romans traded wine and olive oil for a variety of foods, manufactured goods, and raw materials. Rome was not without its challengers for supremacy in the Mediterranean, however. Its chief rival was Carthage, a former Phoenician colony in northern Africa.

Between 264 and 146 BCE, Rome and Carthage fought a series of wars (called the Punic Wars, after the Roman word for *Phoenician*) over control of the Mediterranean. The First Punic War, which lasted more than twenty years, broke out over Roman and Carthaginian dominance in Sicily, which was prized as a grain-producing territory. During this war, which culminated in the defeat of Carthage, Rome organized her first navy.

In the Second Punic War, the Carthaginian general **Hannibal** assembled a large army, including fifty war elephants, and marched them through the Alps into Italy. For more than a decade he inflicted great losses upon the Romans, until the Roman general **Scipio** attacked Carthage, forcing Hannibal to return to his home, where he was defeated by the Romans.

During the Third Punic War, Carthage was no longer a threat to Rome, but the Romans were bent on revenge. Their animosity toward Carthage was fueled by the Roman senator Cato, who ended all his speeches with the words, "Carthage must be destroyed." In 146 BCE, the Romans razed Carthage, salted the earth to make it unfit for agriculture, and killed its inhabitants or forced them into slavery.

Rome was now the master of the western Mediterranean. Between 215 and 148 BCE, wars in Macedonia and Anatolia gave Rome control over the eastern Mediterranean. Rome's territory now extended from Anatolia at the eastern edge of the Mediterranean to Spain in the west.

ROME IN TRANSITION

Between the end of the Punic Wars and 27 BCE, Rome made the transition from the limited democracy of the republic to the absolute rule of an empire. The transformation was prompted by problems from the expansion of Rome's territory, the most serious of which was the widening chasm between rich and poor. Conquest of land during Rome's many wars left her with many large estates called ***latifundia***. Peoples captured during these wars were often enslaved and forced to work on the latifundia. Small landowners often found themselves unable to compete with the large estates and their free labor; many of them were then forced to sell their land to the wealthy, leaving them homeless and unemployed. Many displaced former landowners fled to the cities, especially Rome, adding to an already large population of urban poor.

Into this crisis situation came two brothers, **Tiberius and Gaius Gracchus**. The Gracchi, who were tribunes, devoted their careers to relief of the poor in Rome. In 133 BCE, Tiberius attempted to limit the size of the latifundia and moved landless citizens to work on redistributed land. This offended the Senate, so they, along with their sympathizers, clubbed Tiberius and 300 of his followers to death. In 123 BCE, Gaius used public funds to purchase grain to resell to the poor at low prices. The Senate assassinated his supporters; Gaius committed suicide before he could be put to death.

Rule by Generals

A number of generals came to power and attempted to alleviate the crisis in Rome. In 107 BCE, **Marius** became consul after suppressing a rebellion in North Africa. He proceeded to substitute Rome's drafted army for a professional one; as a result, armies became loyal to their commanders rather than to the Roman government. In 105 BCE, Marius defeated Germanic invaders threatening the republic. Another general, **Sulla**, executed many of Marius's followers in 82 BCE and acted as a military dictator until 79 BCE. He placed all governmental powers in the Senate and allowed army commanders to influence Senate policy. The chaos in Rome was finally brought to a semblance of order through the efforts of a leader named **Julius Caesar**.

Julius Caesar

In 60 BCE, Julius Caesar joined a wealthy aristocrat named Crassius and a highly regarded general named **Pompey** to rule Rome for the next ten years as the first **triumvirate**. In 59 BCE, Julius Caesar was named consul. Caesar used his position to give grain to the poor and used his oratory skills to further win the favor of the masses. Making himself proconsul (provincial ruler) of Gaul, he brought all of Gaul under Roman rule. Caesar issued written reports of his campaigns that are still read today in classes in the Latin language. After the death of Crassius, Pompey became increasingly jealous of Caesar. In 49 BCE, in defiance of Pompey, Julius Caesar brought his troops back from Gaul to Rome. He then proceeded to Egypt and placed **Cleopatra** on the throne of Egypt as an ally of Rome.

In 46 BCE, Julius Caesar was appointed dictator for life by the Roman Senate. Reducing the Senate to an advisory council, he granted citizenship to many people in the provinces and distributed public land to veterans and grain to the poor. He also established a calendar of 365 days that was used in western Europe until the late 16th century. Fearing that Caesar was about to set up a monarchy, the Senate conspired against him and assassinated him on March 15, 44 BCE.

Octavian and the Beginnings of an Empire

During the thirteen years following Caesar's death, disorder and civil war reigned in Rome. The government resided in the hands of a second triumvirate comprised of **Octavian** (Caesar's nephew), **Marc Antony**, and Lepidus. After Octavian forced Lepidus into retirement, he and Marc Antony became rivals. While commanding an army in Anatolia, Marc Antony fell in love with Cleopatra and returned with her to Egypt. Antony subsequently took control of the eastern portion of the empire, while Octavian took the west. At the Battle of Actium in 31 BCE, Octavian defeated Antony and Cleopatra, who both committed suicide. By 27 BCE, Octavian firmly controlled the government of Rome. Accepting the title *Augustus*, or "exalted one," he also ruled as supreme military commander, placing all power in Rome in the hands of a single ruler.

THE PAX ROMANA

When Octavian assumed total power in 27 BCE, Rome entered upon a 207-year period of peace called the *Pax Romana*, or the Roman Peace. Except for occasional fighting with Germanic tribes living along the empire's borders, there was peace throughout the empire. Government was stabilized throughout the reaches of the empire; taxes were fair. A system of roads connected all parts of Rome as well as parts of Asia, encouraging trade and communications. A system of common coinage promoted the ease of commerce. Industry flourished; public buildings, bridges, and aqueducts were constructed. The government encouraged science, art, and literature. In the province of Palestine, Jesus was born; Roman roads would carry the news of his birth and teachings and spread the new religion of Christianity.

When Augustus died in 14 CE, the Senate chose his adopted son Tiberius as his successor. A number of capable emperors ruled during the Pax Romana, as well as some unstable rulers such as Nero and Caligula. The emperor Claudius conquered Britain and added it to the empire. The problem of succession was solved by the Five Good Emperors, each of whom adopted a respected leader as his heir. Among them were Trajan, who increased the empire to its greatest size, and **Hadrian**, who erected defensive walls in northern Britain and central Europe and encouraged frontier people to join the army. During his reign, Hadrian was forced to give up some of the Asian territories that Trajan had added. The last of the Five Good Emperors was the stoic philosopher **Marcus Aurelius**, author of *Meditations*. During his reign, the empire was already showing signs of weakening; several times Marcus Aurelius had to defend the empire from invaders from the north and east. With his death, the Pax Romana came to an end.

ROMAN CULTURE

The Roman government during the Pax Romana kept a watchful eye on its provincial governors. A provincial citizen could appeal the governor's decision on an issue directly to the emperor, giving provincial citizens the same rights as other Roman citizens. Gaul and Spain benefited from new cities constructed by the Romans; the cities boasted aqueducts, paved streets, sewer systems, public buildings, schools, and entertainment.

Roman law throughout the empire revolved around a number of concepts prevalent in western law today. Among them were the ideas that all persons are equal before the law; accused persons are guaranteed legal protection; and an accused person is innocent until proven guilty in a court of law. Women held considerable influence under Roman law and could own property. Roman law became the foundation of all European countries that had once been part of the Roman empire.

Joining the Roman army was an option for both citizens and non-citizens. Non-citizens could enlist in the Roman army for twenty-five years and then become citizens. The Praetorian Guard, a small, elite force, was stationed in Rome to protect the emperor. Legions also occupied fortified camps along the Roman frontier. Those who served along the frontier served for twenty years; some remained after the conclusion of their military commitment and formed permanent settlements along the frontier.

Lifestyles of the Wealthy and the Poor

Living conditions in Rome showed a vast disparity between wealthy and poor. Wealthy Romans owned spacious houses in town and also country estates with private baths and gardens. The lives of the wealthy included substantial leisure time for rest, exercise, banquets, and public baths. The lower classes often dwelled in three- to four-story concrete and wood tenement apartment houses or in small rooms over shops. Fire was a constant threat for tenement dwellers.

A number of amusements kept both the wealthy and poor occupied. The masses enjoyed the theater, boxing matches (performed with brass knuckles), and chariot racing in the Circus Maximus. **Colosseum** events were popular, featuring fights between wild beasts or between humans and animals. The humans who were forced to fight against the beasts were usually condemned criminals, Christians, or slaves. Fights between two or more humans, or gladiators, usually ended in death for one or both.

Education and Literature

Education among the Romans was different from that of the Greeks in that the Romans valued education only for its practical use. Roman fathers taught their sons agriculture and the duties of citizenship while mothers taught reading, writing, and arithmetic. Children also memorized the Twelve Tables. While daughters focused on learning household management, many upper-class women were well educated. Children entered school at the age of seven, with boys having the opportunity for further, advanced levels of education at ages thirteen and sixteen. All education was at the expense of the parents.

Roman literature featured histories, essays, poetry, and biographies. A historian named Levy wrote the history of Rome, while another of the greatest Roman historians, Tacitus, wrote the *Annals*, a critique of public virtue, and *Germania*, considered the best account of Germanic tribes along the Roman borders. Cicero, a noted orator who spoke on political concerns, became the father of Latin prose. Virgil, the greatest Roman poet, wrote the *Aeneid*, which extolled Rome's greatness. Horace wrote odes and satires that praised early Roman virtues, while Ovid penned love poetry and the *Metamorphoses*. The stoic philosopher Seneca wrote an essay on morals, while Plutarch produced his biographical collection, *Parallel Lives*. Universities used Latin as the language of instruction, and the Roman Catholic Church conducted Mass in Latin only. All governments in western Europe wrote their laws in Latin.

THE RISE OF CHRISTIANITY

Jesus and the Christian Bible

Another of the lasting contributions of the Romans was to serve as the vehicle to facilitate the spread of Christianity. Rome had conquered Palestine in 63 BCE, naming it the province of Judea. As a Roman province, Judea was allowed to preserve its own religious beliefs and practices as well as its own government. Within Judea, however, were **Zealots** who wanted to rid Judea of Rome's dominance. The Jewish people of Judea eagerly awaited the arrival of the Messiah promised them in their sacred writings—a Messiah some hoped would serve as their liberator from Roman rule.

Jesus was born in Judea sometime between 6 and 4 BCE. At the age of 30, he was baptized by the prophet John and began his public ministry, choosing 12 followers to serve as his disciples, or **apostles**. Throughout the three years of his ministry, Jesus spoke of a personal relationship between God and man and promised eternal life for those who repented of their sins and believed that he was the Son of God. Accounts of Jesus' life and ministry are found in the **Gospels** (Greek for "good news") of Matthew, Mark, Luke, and John, which became the first four books of the Christian **New Testament**. Although Jesus proclaimed that his kingdom was not an earthly one, Roman authorities and Jewish officials perceived him as a threat to their political authority and condemned him to death. According to the Christian Bible, Jesus was crucified outside the city of Jerusalem, rose from the dead on the third day after his crucifixion, and 40 days later ascended into heaven.

The spread of Jesus' message was now in the hands of his disciples and Christian missionaries. The greatest Christian missionary of the first century CE, **Paul of Tarsus**, was a Roman citizen from the province of Anatolia. Once a persecutor of the Christians, Paul was converted to Christianity while walking along the Damascus Road. Saint Paul, as he was later called by the Catholic Church, utilized the unity of the Roman world, particularly that of the Mediterranean basin, to spread the doctrines of Christianity. In the course of three missionary journeys, he reached distances as far apart as Anatolia and Spain before being imprisoned and later executed in Rome. Although the earliest converts to the Christian faith were Jews, Paul reached out especially to the non-Jews, or **Gentiles**.

The Second Diaspora of the Jews

After the crucifixion of Jesus, the Romans continued to pay attention to the little province of Judea and the Jews who dwelled there. In 66 CE, a group of Zealots unsuccessfully rebelled against Rome. The rebellion culminated in the Romans' destruction of the temple at Jerusalem. All that remained was the western wall of the temple, which stands today as the most noted Jewish shrine, the Wailing Wall. In 73 CE, a fortress near **Masada**—the final Jewish stronghold—fell to the Romans. After a second rebellion in 132 CE, the Jews were dispersed to faraway territories by the Romans in the **Second Diaspora**. From this time on until 1948, the Jewish people would not have their own homeland. Judaism would continue, however, in colonies of exiles, some of whose inhabitants would convert to Christianity. Christianity appealed to people of all classes; promising eternal life after death, it offered hope to the weak and downtrodden of the world.

Christianity in the Late Roman Empire

As it grew, the Christian Church became more organized. In charge of the local community parishes were priests, who were selected by **bishops**, who in turn were heads of a **diocese**, or group of local churches. According to the traditions of the Roman Catholic Church, Jesus' apostle **Peter** was the first bishop of Rome. Subsequent bishops of Rome claimed succession from Peter, claiming that Peter was the first pope, or leader of the Roman Catholic Church.

Although taught to respect and submit to the government, the early Christians refused to worship the Roman emperor as god. As a result, the Roman government (particularly the emperors **Nero** and **Diocletian**) would periodically persecute the Christians. In spite of persecution, however, the Christian Church continued to grow. Early Roman Christians frequently held their worship services in secret in the catacombs, or tunnels already in place beneath the city of Rome. The persecutions continued until 313 CE, when the emperor Constantine issued the Edict of Milan, which established Christianity as one of the religions allowed to be practiced in Rome. In 381 CE, the emperor Theodosius made Christianity the official religion of the Roman Empire.

Varieties of Early Christianity

As the Christian religion spread throughout the Mediterranean world, it sometimes took on different beliefs. **Coptic Christianity** of Ethiopia and Egypt and **Nestorian Christianity** were two such variations. The Nestorian branch, which spread eastward to China along the Silk Roads, stressed the humanity of Jesus over his divinity. Coptic Christians believed only in the divine nature of Christ. **Arianism** taught that Jesus had been a creation of God rather than a divinity who had coexisted with God from eternity. In order to resolve the disputes within Christianity, councils were convened. The first was the Council of Nicaea, which met in 325 in Asia Minor. Participants at the council issued the **Nicene Creed**, which asserted that Jesus was at the same time fully human and fully divine. Christian doctrine was further clarified by the works of **St. Augustine**, whose *Confessions* and *The City of God* further defined the teachings of the Church.

THE FALL OF ROME

While Christianity continued gaining prominence as the established religion of the Roman empire, internal and external pressures were chipping away at the empire. Several Germanic tribes, many of whom had adopted Christianity, dwelled around the borders of the Roman empire. While sometimes coexisting peacefully alongside the Romans, these tribes would periodically raid the fertile agricultural lands of the Roman frontier. Their attacks on the Roman empire escalated in the 400s when the **Huns**, a nomadic group from central Asia, came under the influence of a new leader, **Attila**. Under his leadership, the Huns moved in the direction of the Roman empire, a migration that exerted pressure on the tribes surrounding the Roman empire. As the Huns approached, the Germanic tribes, fearing for their safety, crossed the borders of the empire. The key Germanic tribes and the regions they invaded were: the **Saxons** (northern Germany), **Angles** and Saxons (England), the **Franks** (France), the **Visigoths** (Spain), the **Ostrogoths** (Italy), and the **Vandals** (North Africa).

Rome might have been able to withstand the Germanic invasions had she not already been weakened by other factors. The end of the Pax Romana in the 200s had prompted civil war. Bandits roamed the countryside, preying upon travelers along the Roman roads. Unsafe travel led to a breakdown of trade. As trade declined, there was a decline in the amount of money pouring into the empire. Wealthy Romans used gold to pay for the foreign goods they imported, causing a further drain of gold from the empire. Newly minted coins contained elements of copper or lead, which led to inflation. A series of poor harvests increased the numbers of the rural poor, who began flocking to the cities. Improper land usage had exhausted the soil; many small farmers were forced to sell their land to the owners of the larger latifundia and also flee to the cities, where they added to the strain on the coffers of Rome and other cities to provide for them. Plague also decimated the population of Rome. Emperors contributed to the weakening of the Roman empire by spending excessively on themselves and bankrupting the treasury. Political instability created a succession of 28 generals (the so-called "**barracks emperors**") in less than 100 years.

Final Attempts to Save the Empire

Two emperors attempted to remedy the problems of the empire. Diocletian, who was also the last emperor to persecute the Christians, divided the empire into East and West to provide for easier administration. To control runaway inflation, he froze wages and set prices. To prevent farmers from leaving their land and professionals and artisans from abandoning their occupations to avoid taxation, Diocletian required farmers to remain on their land and workers to remain at their job for life.

Diocletian's successor, Constantine, was made sole emperor in 324. He continued the policies of Diocletian by declaring most occupations hereditary. Recognizing the greater wealth of the eastern portion of the empire, Constantine created a new capital in 330, which he named Constantinople, on the site of the city of Byzantium on the Bosporus. Power had now shifted to the eastern sector of the empire.

The Last Days of Rome

The Germanic tribes continued to exert pressure on the borders of Rome. In 378, at the Battle of Adrianople, the Visigoths destroyed the Roman army and killed its leader, the eastern emperor Valens. Rome itself was sacked in 410 by Alaric, king of the Visigoths. A combined army of Romans and Visigoths defeated the Huns in 451 at the Battle of Chalons. The battle weakened the Roman army, rendering it incapable of combating the overthrow of the last Roman emperor, Romulus Augustus in 476 CE. Historians consider this event "the fall of the Roman empire," although in reality the empire had experienced declines for more than 200 years.

As a result of Rome's decline, central government broke down. Rome was dominated by Germanic peoples, who were accustomed to a tribal form of government. Towns and cities lay in ruins and devastated agricultural fields showed the wear of battle. Roads and bridges fell into disrepair, resulting in severe curtailment of trade and travel. Learning declined as the Romans concerned themselves with everyday survival rather than academic pursuits.

Reasons for Rome's Decline

Various historians have pointed to a combination of factors that led to the decline and fall of Rome. Among them are:

- **Slavery**, which prompted the Romans to rely on free labor to do most tasks rather than exerting themselves
- **Social decay**, especially of the wealthier classes, which resulted in their lack of motivation to ensure an effective government
- **The size of the empire**, which had become too vast for efficient government
- **The Roman army**, whose structure admitted barbarians loyal to their commanders rather than the empire
- **Economic decline and heavy taxes** compounded by failed harvests and the decrease in revenues from foreign wars during the *Pax Romana*
- **Barbarian invasions**, whose constant threat drew the attentions of the emperor away from other governmental concerns

None of these factors alone precipitated the end of Rome; rather, the combination hastened the empire's demise. Meanwhile, the eastern portion of the empire, Byzantium, would manage to survive almost one thousand years after the fall of the West. Eventually some barbarian leaders would rise to re-establish some degree of unity in fallen Rome, and the Catholic Church would continue to serve as a vehicle for the preservation of Roman ideas.

THE HAN EMPIRE

While the *Pax Romana* unified the Mediterranean basin, China's classical civilization, the Han empire, developed along similar lines. The Han empire (206 BCE to 220 CE) would prove the longest and most influential of all Chinese dynasties, prompting the Chinese of future generations to refer to themselves as "People of Han."

The Han Dynasty was preceded by the Qin Dynasty (whose internal improvements would have a bearing on the success of the Han Dynasty). The Qin arose after the collapse of the Zhou Dynasty in the third century BCE. The Qin were noted for their extensive use of bronze and iron. Their most lasting achievement, however, was the construction of public works such as canals and roadways. The Chinese had long possessed a line of walls to hold back the advances of invaders. Under the Qin, these walls were connected, resulting in the beginning stages of the Great Wall, a 1,400-mile structure that protected the Chinese from potential invaders from the west and north.

Upon coming to power, Liu Bang, the founding Han ruler, immediately instituted a strong centralized government that ensured peace and stability for the Chinese people. Particularly influential was **Empress Lü** (195–180 BCE), who seized and retained control over the throne by naming her infant sons as emperors. The achievements of the Qin were expanded by the longest ruling of the Han rulers, **Han Wudi** (141–87 BCE), who appointed provincial administrators to promote governmental efficiency.

Roads and canals encouraged trade and communication throughout the Han empire. The **Silk Roads** linked China to the Mediterranean world. Some of the Han people migrated southward into the present-day areas of Burma, Laos, and Thailand. Like Rome, the Han empire added to its borders, expanding into Korea and Vietnam and encouraging the assimilation of those areas into Chinese culture. Most Han Chinese were farmers; however, the rapid growth of the iron industry produced fine manufactured goods for trade along the Silk Roads. Knowledge of the production of silk spread to most parts of China; silk was a valued commodity in long-distance trade with the West, especially with the Roman Empire.

Funded by taxes on trade, agriculture, and the work of artisans, the Han Empire boasted an imperial university. The **shi**, or scholar class, promoted education, while the first civil service examination was instituted under the Han.

The prosperity of the Han period produced significant population growth as well as technology more advanced than that of any other classical civilization. Among the inventions and advances attributed to the Han are paper, the rudder, the compass, porcelain, the seismograph, acoustical studies, and a calendar of 365 days. It is possible that the practice of acupuncture originated with the Han.

The Decline of the Han

In spite of the achievements of the Han period, the empire also saw inequities which, as in the case of Rome, precipitated its decline and eventual fall. Land was distributed unequally between rich and poor. Women were kept in a subordinate position, although upper-class women were often educated in writing and the fine arts. The Hsiung-nu, peoples along the Han borders whom the Chinese considered barbarians, presented an ever-present threat; the Han Chinese paid them tribute to prevent them from invading Chinese territory. The economic strain of efforts to contain the Hsiung-nu and expand the empire further weakened it. Han Wudi confiscated the property of the upper class, a policy which weakened both trade and manufacturing. Peasants continued to revolt against their plight. A series of poor harvests prompted many small landowners to sell their property or even themselves into slavery.

Inept rule by the successors of Han Wudi led to the overthrow of the Han dynasty in 6 CE by the Wang. The strict control executed by the Wang, however, led to peasant rebellion resulting in the overthrow of the Wang in 23 CE and the restoration of the Han. Still plagued by poor emperors and internal weakness, the later Han were forced to contend with repeated invasions of the Hsiung-nu. Epidemic disease significantly reduced the population of the Han empire as it had in Rome. Han generals increasingly seized power as the empire declined. The collapse of the Han empire in 220 CE brought the barbarians into the Chinese borders, producing 400 years of political and economic turmoil and the division of the former empire into numerous regional kingdoms.

THE SILK ROADS

An intelligence mission undertaken by an envoy of Han Wudi led to the opening of the Silk Roads, which eventually would link western China to the easternmost reaches of the Roman empire. Embracing both land and sea routes, the Silk Roads would play a prominent role in world history at two periods, the first from 150 BCE to 900 CE. During this period, the Silk Roads were used by nearby societies who were attracted to the wealth and material goods of the classical empires. Trade routes encompassed by the Silk Roads included the regions of central Asia, North Africa, Sub-Saharan Africa, and the Indian Ocean. In the Indian Ocean, an active route linked Ceylon and India with the societies of Southeast Asia. Pastoral nomads from the steppes of central Asia proved key players in the story of the Silk Roads—sometimes by threatening to interfere with trade, and sometimes by fostering conditions that led to improved trade connections. Travelers and traders could acquire pack animals and buy protection through tribute payments to nomadic peoples.

Trade along the Silk Roads promoted the development of regional resources and manufactures offered as trade items. Among the items traded along the Silk Roads were spices, jewels, cosmetics, grain, wine, olive oil, and jewelry. The introduction of the stirrup spread both east and west, contributing to the success of the cavalry in China and the horsemanship of the European medieval knight.

Few people traveled the entire length of the Silk Roads with their merchandise; instead, they relied on middlemen to transport their goods part of the distance. Indians and Parthians (from the present-day Persian Gulf area) were particularly active as middlemen along the Silk Roads, as were the Jews, Greeks, and Armenians in the Mediterranean basin. Malay merchant mariners were noted for their long-distance voyages from the islands of southeast Asia to both India and East Africa, capitalizing on the seasonal patterns of monsoon winds to facilitate their journey.

Religion Along the Silk Roads

By the first century BCE, Buddhism had traveled the Silk Roads through the travels of merchants, reaching as far as China. Oasis towns along the Silk Roads harbored Buddhist monasteries that served as inns for early traders. Nomadic peoples along the Silk Roads would trade with oasis cities and, in the process, learn of Buddhism. By the fifth century CE, the Chinese had become sufficiently comfortable with the presence of the Buddhist monks, nuns, and traders among them to accept the Buddhist faith in a widespread fashion. Both Buddhism and Hinduism spread through Indian Ocean trade to southeast Asia, including Indonesia, the Malay peninsula, Cambodia, and Vietnam.

Christianity diffused across the land routes and sea lanes of the Silk Roads through the activity of missionaries. By the third century CE, Christianity had reached central Anatolia, and Christian communities had emerged throughout the Mediterranean basin as far as Spain and Gaul as well as North Africa. Christianity also spread to Persia and India, remaining a prominent faith in those areas even after the arrival of Islam in the 600s. By the third century CE, Christian monasteries began to form in the Roman world.

Another religion that traveled the Silk Roads was **Manichaeism**, named after its founder Mani (216–272 CE). Appealing to merchants, Manichaeism was a blend of beliefs of other major religions and considered Zoroaster (Zarathustra) as the prophet of Persia, Buddha as the prophet of India, and Jesus as the prophet of the Mediterranean basin. Manichaeism held that life was a struggle between good and evil and that good could be achieved by abandoning worldly pleasure. A life after death awaited those who achieved the good in this life in an eternity filled with goodness and light. The subject of persecution by the Sasanids of Persia and the Romans, Manichaeism was transmitted to central Asia, where it was accepted by some of the Turkish nomads.

Epidemic Disease Along the Silk Roads

Epidemic disease transmitted along the Silk Roads accounted for sharp population declines in the final days of both the Roman and Han empires, with China affected by epidemic disease slightly later than the Roman world. Persia also appears to have suffered from outbreaks of epidemic disease. India, however, apparently was spared a major outbreak of epidemic disease. In both China and Rome, Silk Road trade declined as a result of the reduction in population.

THINGS TO REMEMBER

- Rome (509 BCE–476 CE)
    - Many elements of Rome's government, religion, architecture, and military organization came from the Etruscans, a people dominant in Italy from 800 BCE–500 BCE
    - Rome's rise to power came from its military. After the Punic Wars with Carthage (between 264 and 146 BCE) Rome controlled the Mediterranean region.
    - Originally a republic, Rome became a military dictatorship and then a full-fledged empire by 27 BCE.
    - Christianity arose in the first century CE after the life of Jesus. At first, Christians were persecuted, but the faith was legalized by the Emperor Constantine in 313 CE. The stability of the empire helped the religion spread rapidly.
    - Under centuries of pressure by Germanic tribes, the empire "fell" when the last emperor was deposed in 476 CE.
- The Han dynasty (206 BCE–220 CE)
    - The Han continued the development of roads and defensive walls.
    - They expanded the empire into Korea and Vietnam.
    - The Silk Roads were opened, creating a trading network that linked China with the Mediterranean. Buddhism spread along the Silk Roads.
    - Barbarian incursions, epidemic disease, and the widening gulf between rich and poor led to the empire's collapse in 220 CE.
- Parallels between the Roman and Han empires:
    - Both enjoyed long periods of peace and prosperity.
    - Both encouraged trade through the building of roads and establishment of stability.
    - They exerted a lasting influence on the culture of the West and China, respectively.
        - Rome left a legacy of language, laws, and Christianity.
        - The Han dynasty created the Silk Roads, promoted education, and made scientific discoveries.
- Decline came to both due to similar factors.
    - Wealth led the ruling classes to focus on material possessions rather than government.
    - Both empires became too vast for effective administration.
    - Armies gained preeminence during periods of decline as generals became emperors.
    - Harassment of borderlands by "barbarians" hurt agriculture and trade.
    - Population declined due to failed harvests and epidemics spread via trade routes.

REVIEW QUESTIONS

1. During the time of the Roman republic,

   (A) the plebeians enjoyed no political representation.
   (B) only patricians enjoyed the protection of the law.
   (C) trade was regional only.
   (D) all conquered peoples were offered citizenship.
   (E) Rome became master of the Mediterranean world.

2. Which of the following is in the correct chronological sequence?

   (A) appointment of Julius Caesar as dictator; birth of Jesus; rule of the Gracchi; founding of Constantinople
   (B) rule of the Gracchi; appointment of Julius Caesar as dictator; birth of Jesus; founding of Constantinople
   (C) rule of the Gracchi; birth of Jesus; appointment of Julius Caesar as dictator; founding of Constantinople
   (D) birth of Jesus; rule of the Gracchi; founding of Constantinople; appointment of Julius Caesar as dictator
   (E) rule of the Gracchi; appointment of Julius Caesar as dictator; founding of Constantinople; birth of Jesus

3. The Silk Roads

   (A) were opened by Parthian middlemen.
   (B) featured Christian monasteries in oasis towns that served as inns for traders.
   (C) were instrumental in the spread of Buddhism to China.
   (D) created a perpetual rivalry between its travelers and neighboring pastoral nomads.
   (E) were confined to overland routes.

4. The Han empire accomplished all of the following EXCEPT

   (A) it established the first Chinese civil service examination.
   (B) it elevated the status of women.
   (C) it traded silk to Rome over the Silk Roads.
   (D) it expanded to Southeast Asia and Korea.
   (E) it produced fine porcelain.

5. Both the Han and the Roman empires experienced all of the following EXCEPT

   (A) a prolonged period of peace.
   (B) population reductions from epidemic diseases.
   (C) abundant harvests in their final years.
   (D) rule by generals during their period of decline.
   (E) threats from foreign tribes along their borders.

ANSWERS AND EXPLANATIONS

1. (E)

After winning the Punic Wars against Carthage, Rome dominated the Mediterranean. The plebeians eventually acquired their own assembly (A), and both classes were protected by the Twelves Table of the Law (B). The republic engaged in both regional and long-distance trade (C). Citizenship was not offered to those in the farthest provinces (D).

2. (B)

Choice (B) is the only response which lists the events in the proper chronological order.

3. (C)

Buddhism was spread by traders along the Silk Roads and also by Buddhist, not Christian, monks along the Silk Roads (B). The Silk Roads were opened by the Chinese (A) and featured both overland and sea routes (E). Although pastoral nomads sometimes harassed travelers along the Silk Roads, at other times they supplied them with pack animals and supplies.

4. (B)

Women were kept in a subordinate position under the Han. The other responses are all accomplishments of the Han dynasty.

5. (C)

Both the Roman and Han empires experienced poor harvests in the final days of their empires. Both enjoyed a prolonged period relatively free of military conflicts (A). Diseases spread along the Silk Roads resulted in epidemics that caused significant loss of population in both empires (B). Both experienced the rule of generals in response to weak emperors (D), and threats from tribes along their borders harassed both (E).

CHAPTER 8

Empires of South Asia

TIMELINE

321–185 BCE	Mauryan empire
320–550 CE	Gupta empire
400s CE	Hun incursions into northern India

IMPORTANT PEOPLE, PLACES, EVENTS, AND CONCEPTS

Chandragupta Maurya
Ashoka
stupa*
sati*
monsoon*

THE MAURYAN EMPIRE

When Alexander the Great and his troops departed India in 325 BCE, a local ruler from the prosperous agricultural and trading center of Magadha in the central Ganges plain rose to power. **Chandragupta Maurya** (322–298 BCE) began a program of conquest that would include northwestern India and areas of the Ganges plain and would form the first unified, centralized government in India. Relying on the advice of a treatise called the *Arthashastra*, Chandragupta and his successors amassed an empire that encompassed all of present-day India except for the southern tip.

The Mauryans supported their government by taxing agricultural crops. Standard coinage throughout their empire facilitated trade, while government control of manufactures, mines, and shipbuilding strengthened the state. A national army consisted not only of infantry and cavalry divisions, but also of chariots and war elephants.

The Rule of Ashoka

The greatest of the Mauryan rulers was **Ashoka**, the grandson of Chandragupta. One of Ashoka's greatest joys was conquest—until he witnessed the horrible results of his conquests in eastern India. Rather than continuing to devote his energy to conquest, Ashoka converted to Buddhism and embarked on a program to construct public works and to encourage vegetarianism in an effort to reduce the slaughter of animals. His policy of ending the killing of cows, combined with the already revered status of cattle from the Aryan era, contributed to the concept of sacred cows that became a part of the Indian civilization. Ashoka also attempted to live his Buddhist faith by spreading peace and building an efficient government. His efforts met with resistance from the caste of brahmins, whose power was displaced by Ashoka's central government.

The Buddhist disapproval of the caste system was advantageous for artisans and merchants, who supported the growing number of Buddhist monasteries. Buddhist law also improved the status of women by granting them more authority within their families and by allowing them to enter the monasteries as Buddhist nuns.

Ashoka publicized his tolerant Buddhist program by engraving his decisions on large rocks and sandstone pillars that he had scattered throughout his empire. Great shrines of stone, called ***stupas***, were constructed by the Buddhists to house relics of the Buddha. Ashoka also furthered the Buddhist faith by sending missionaries to Ceylon (Sri Lanka), the Himalayan regions, and the grasslands of central Asia. By means of the Silk Roads, Buddhism spread to various points of southeast and east Asia.

The End of the Mauryan Empire

After Ashoka's death in 232 BCE, weaker rulers ascended to the Mauryan throne. By 185 BCE the empire no longer existed, and political division characterized the South Asian subcontinent. Waves of invaders entered the region, until the rise of a new dynasty that would allow the brahmans to diminish the power of Buddhism and strengthen the position of Hinduism in India.

THE DECLINE OF BUDDHISM IN INDIA

The decline of Buddhist power in India was, in part, caused by the actions of the Buddhist monks themselves. The monks had become more preoccupied with philosophy than with serving the needs of the common people in India. As the monks devoted more time to the wealthy patrons who supported the monasteries, the brahmans used this opportunity to capture the attention of the ordinary people of India. The new focus of Hinduism called upon followers to become personally involved in the worship of the major gods Shiva and Vishnu. More temples arose to house statues of the gods, and even untouchables were allowed to embrace the new form of Hinduism, which eventually allowed the inclusion of the Buddha as one of the many Hindu gods. Women were also permitted to participate. The *Upanishads* acquired new prominence as Hinduism taught that the ultimate purpose of the soul was to merge with the divine essence from which it had originated. The world itself was viewed as an illusion.

After the fall of the Han empire in the third century CE, trade decreased, creating a decline in merchant support for the Buddhist monasteries. Furthermore, the arrival of a new dynasty sympathetic to Hinduism hastened the decline of Buddhism in India. The center of Buddhism would now shift to central and southeast Asia and to China, Japan, and Korea; there Buddhism would develop into the Mahayana form, which allowed rituals in worship.

THE GUPTA EMPIRE

Like the Mauryan empire, the Gupta empire was founded by a family from the kingdom of Magadha in eastern India. By the conclusion of the fourth century CE, the Gupta family had amassed an empire that included most of northern India, though not as extensive as that of the Maurya family. Although the Gupta empire was not as centralized as its predecessor, it succeeded in bringing nearly 300 peaceful and prosperous years to the people of northern India.

Women in Gupta Society

Characteristic of the Gupta rule was a further definition of Hinduism and the caste system. Restrictions upon members of the lowest castes and the untouchables became even more severe. The position of women also declined under the Guptas. Under Hindu law, women were minors subject first to their father, then to their husband, and then to their sons. Women were not allowed to own or inherit property. Marriages were usually arranged, and young girls often left home years before their marriage to live with and be molded by their future mother-in-law and future husband. Female infants were often viewed as economic liabilities and were frequently killed. Women who were widowed before they bore sons were ostracized from society; widows with sons were not permitted to remarry. The most pronounced degradation of women involved the custom of ***sati***. This practice, which was observed in some parts of India among the elite *varna*, or castes, expected a widow to throw herself on her husband's burning funeral pyre. Women who failed to honor their deceased husbands in this manner were forbidden to remarry and were excluded from society.

Gupta Achievements

While denying educational opportunities to women and members of lower castes, the Gupta empire was noted for an array of achievements, especially in mathematics and science. Gupta mathematicians accurately calculated the value of pi and the circumference of the earth. They also used decimals and developed the concept of the zero as a place holder. Another achievement was the introduction of the numbers used around the globe (the Western world would label these "Arabic" numbers because they came to the West via Arab traders and academics). Gupta physicians set up hospitals and developed treatments for numerous diseases and various surgical techniques.

The Gupta period was also renowned for its artistic and literary achievements. The poet Kalidasa, who was considered the greatest writer in the Sanskrit language, painted word pictures of Gupta life. Also noteworthy were the rock paintings and statues of the Buddha located in the caves of Ajanta; the caves also housed monasteries for Buddhist monks.

In spite of the decline in long-distance trade with China, commerce flourished between Gupta India and other areas. Archeological finds of Roman coins in southern India attest to the presence of trade between these two areas. One remaining trade route included passage through the Hindu Kush to Persia and the Mediterranean world. Mariners used the **monsoon** winds to cross the Indian Ocean to Southeast Asia and the islands of Indonesia and also sailed to Arabia. The overland route between India and China still saw some trade, despite the presence of bandits.

Decline of the Gupta Empire

Similar to the experiences of the Han and Roman empires, the Gupta empire was plagued by repeated attacks of foreigners along its border areas. The Xiong-nu, or Huns, who exerted pressure on the borders of the Han empire also raided across the Himalayas into northern India during the early fifth century CE The drain on the treasury resulting from efforts to repel Hun invaders, combined with internal struggles between Gupta rulers and their vassals, led to the eventual collapse of the Gupta empire. By 530 CE, the empire was overrun by further Xiong-nu invasions and broke up into numerous local governments.

THINGS TO REMEMBER

- The Mauryan empire
    - Chandragupta Maurya (322–298 BCE) established an empire in northwest India and the Ganges region.
        - It was the first centralized government in India.
        - His successors expanded the empire to include almost all of India.
    - Ashoka, the most famous Mauryan emperor, became a great patron of Buddhism, spreading it throughout India and beyond. The caste system was de-emphasized.
    - The Mauryan empire declined due to weak rulers and fell by 185 BCE.
- The Gupta empire
    - The Gupta family founded a state in north India (circa 400–530).
        - Hinduism experienced a revival with the help of the Gupta, and Buddhism declined in India.
        - The caste system regained prominence.
        - Women became subject to stricter controls under Hindu law. They could not own property. Widows could not remarry and some were expected to commit ritual suicide (sati).
        - Great mathematicians calculated the value of pi, created the concept of zero, and introduced the "Arabic" numerals we use today.
        - Trade, art, and Sanskrit literature flourished.
    - Invasion by the Huns caused the Gupta empire to collapse.

REVIEW QUESTIONS

1. All of the following are true of the empire of Chandragupta Maurya EXCEPT

   (A) it adopted Buddhism as a unifying force throughout the empire.
   (B) it became the first unified, centralized government in India.
   (C) it used standardized coinage to facilitate trade.
   (D) it established government control of industry.
   (E) it formed a military.

2. "But after the conquest of Kalinga, the Beloved of the Gods began to follow Righteousness, to love Righteousness, and to give instruction in Righteousness… The participation of all men in common suffering is grievous to the Beloved of the Gods."

   The sentiment above expressed in the words of Ashoka Maurya caused him to do all of the following EXCEPT

   (A) convert to Buddhism.
   (B) reduce the slaughter of cattle.
   (C) engage in conquest to enlarge his empire.
   (D) provide opportunities for women to become nuns.
   (E) send missionaries to Ceylon.

3. After Ashoka's death, Buddhism declined in India because

   (A) Buddhist monks became more interested in wealth than in the common people.
   (B) the Indian people were opposed to the rituals of Buddhism.
   (C) Buddhist monks became preoccupied with the philosophy of Buddhism.
   (D) trade increased after the fall of the Han dynasty.
   (E) Buddhism saw the world as an illusion rather than reality.

4. The Gupta empire

   (A) relaxed the restrictions of the caste system.
   (B) was noted for its achievements in science and mathematics.
   (C) engaged in regional trade only.
   (D) improved the position of women in India.
   (E) like the Mauryan empire, provided a strong, centralized government.

5. The classical empires of the Han, Romans, and Gupta experienced all of the following EXCEPT

   (A) internal weakness prior to their downfall.
   (B) the need to hold off foreign tribes along their borders.
   (C) conflicts between political and religious authorities.
   (D) financial decline.
   (E) the dissolution of their empires into numerous local governments.

ANSWERS AND EXPLANATIONS

1. (A)

Chandragupta did not favor one religion over another. He unified India for the first time (B); used standardized coinage (C); provided for government control of manufactures, mining, and shipbuilding (D); and formed a national army (E).

2. (C)

After his conversion to Buddhism (A), Ashoka devoted his attentions to wise rule rather than to expansion of his empire. He also became a vegetarian to reduce the killing of cattle (B), gave women opportunities to become Buddhist nuns (D), and sent Buddhist missionaries to Ceylon (E).

3. (A)

Buddhist monks became more interested in serving the wealthy than the common people, and also became preoccupied with philosophy rather than service (C). The Indian form of Buddhism did not involve elaborate rituals (B). Trade decreased after the fall of the Han (D). Hinduism, not Buddhism, saw the world as illusion (E).

4. (B)

Gupta scientists and mathematicians were noted for many cultural achievements, especially in mathematics and science. Under their rule the caste system was further defined (A), long-distance trade was undertaken (C), and the position of women was made considerably more subordinate (D). The Gupta empire was not as centralized as that of the Maurya (E).

5. (C)

Conflicts with religious authorities were not significant in any of the classical empires mentioned. They did experience economic weakness (D), internal political weaknesses (A), and the threat of foreign tribes along their borders (B). Sometime after their fall, their empires broke up into small local governments (E).

CHAPTER 9

The Rise of Islam

TIMELINE

570	Birth of Muhammad
622	The *hijra*
630	Muhammad's return to Mecca
632	Abu-Bakr becomes the first caliph
634	Arabia under Muslim control
661	Founding of the Umayyad dynasty
732	Battle of Tours
750	Founding of the Abbasid dynasty
1258	Fall of the Abbasids

IMPORTANT PEOPLE, PLACES, EVENTS, AND CONCEPTS

Bedouins
Muhammad
Ka'aba*
Mecca
Allah*
Medina
*hijra**
*umma**
Qur'an
Five Pillars*
hajj*
*shariah**
Abu-Bakr
people of the book*
Shia*
Sunni*
Sufi
al-Andalus
lateen sail*
caravanserais*
*sakk**

THE BEGINNINGS OF ISLAM: THE LIFE OF MUHAMMAD

The setting for the rise of Islam, a religion that would also serve as a vehicle to preserve the culture of the classical world, was the Arabian Peninsula. Originally inhabited by clans of nomadic **Bedouins**, several trade routes now crossed the sands of Arabia. Its key city of **Mecca** was a stopping point for various caravan routes. Mecca was not only a commercial center but a city of religious significance as well. Situated in Mecca was the **Ka'aba**, a house of worship that contained the Black Stone, a relic of the polytheistic beliefs of the early Arabs. The merchants of Mecca enjoyed a profitable income from the large numbers of the faithful who arrived each year to visit the holy shrine.

The founder of Islam, **Muhammad**, was born in Mecca in 570 CE At about the age of 25, he married Khadija, a wealthy widow and businesswoman. Muhammad thrived as a merchant in Mecca. Into this world of polytheism, Muhammad would introduce a radically new religious belief: monotheism, the worship of one god. Muhammad based his new belief on a revelation he claimed to have received from the Angel Gabriel. Interpreting the revelation to mean there was one god, **Allah**, and that Muhammad was his prophet, Muhammad began preaching his beliefs throughout Mecca. The Meccans, especially merchants, deeply resented Muhammad's teachings from fear of losing the position and prosperity that Mecca represented as a pilgrimage site. Animosity became so intense that some of Muhammad's followers were attacked in the streets.

The *Hijra*

As a result of the danger now faced by himself and his followers in Mecca, in 622 CE Muhammad fled 200 miles north to the town of Yathrib (later renamed **Medina**). The year of his flight, or ***hijra***, marks the first year in the Islamic calendar. In Medina, Muhammad organized his followers into the ***umma***, or community of the faithful, and set up relief services for the widowed, orphaned, and poor. He began to perceive himself as the last of the prophets of Allah, while also respecting the scriptures of both the Jews and Christians. (The three religions of Islam, Judaism, and Christianity all trace their heritage back to Abraham.) Later, after his death, Muhammad's teachings would be written down in the **Qur'an**, the holy book of the Muslims.

The Return to Mecca

In spite of the success he achieved in preaching his faith in Medina, Muhammad's ultimate goal was to return to Mecca. In 630, two years before his death, Muhammad and his followers returned to conquer Mecca and impose upon the city a government dedicated to the worship of Allah. Mosques, or Muslim houses of worship, replaced the shrines of the city's former polytheistic religion. From the minarets towering above the mosques, the faithful were now called to prayer. By 632, almost all of Arabia was under the control of Muhammad's followers.

FIVE PILLARS OF ISLAM

The teachings of Islam revolve around obligations known as the **Five Pillars of Islam**, which include:

- **Faith.** The Muslim must acknowledge that there is one god, Allah, and that Muhammad is his prophet.
- **Prayer.** The Muslim is required to pray to Allah five times a day, facing Mecca.
- **Fasting.** Muslims must fast during the daylight hours of the holy month of Ramadan.
- **Alms.** Muslims must give a portion of their material possessions for the relief of the poor and needy.
- **The Hajj.** Muslims are expected, if they have the physical stamina and financial resources, to make at least one pilgrimage to Mecca during their lifetime. This journey is intended to honor Muhammad, who himself made the hajj to Mecca in 629 and 632.

Eventually, after Muhammad's death, his followers would further define Islamic principles of living through the ***shariah***, or social and ethical law.

THE SPREAD OF ISLAM

After Muhammad's death, the Muslim community united to elect as their new head a friend of Muhammad named **Abu-Bakr**. In 632, Abu-Bakr became the first caliph, or successor to the Prophet Muhammad. By 634, all of Arabia was under Muslim control; the empire continued to expand further under the rule of Abu-Bakr's successors. Under the caliphs, the Islamic empire would expand to Syria, Palestine, Mesopotamia, North Africa, India, and Spain. Accompanying expansion of the empire was the spread of the Arabic language. The Muslims believed that only the Arabic version of the Qur'an reflected the true revelations of Muhammad; therefore, the ability to read Arabic was valued throughout the Islamic world.

The weakness of the Byzantine and Persian empires contributed to the Muslims' success in conquering them. Muslim rule was often welcomed by the inhabitants of Byzantium and Persia who had been persecuted for failing to follow the beliefs of the state religions of Christianity or Zoroastrianism. Those who converted to Islam were not required to pay a poll tax; those who chose not to convert were allowed to practice their own religion, though they were not allowed to spread their religions. Christians and Jews, respected as **"people of the book"** because they shared a belief in the same God and possessed a written scripture, could acquire exemption from military service by payment of an annual tax.

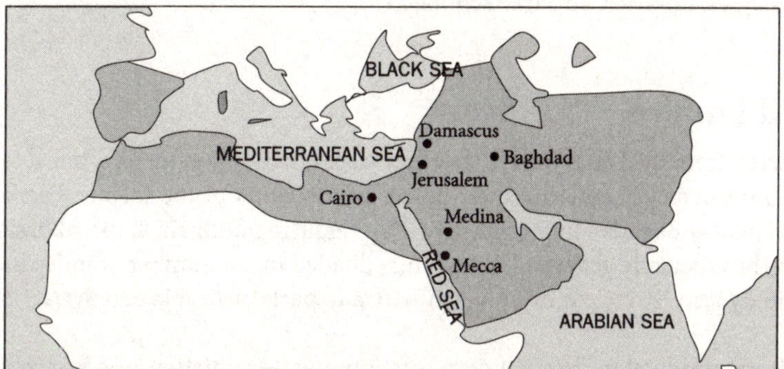

Islamic Expansions, c. 850 CE

Controversies Over Succession

Disputes soon arose over the succession to Muhammad's rule; these disputes would permanently divide the world of Islam. In 661, the elected caliphs were succeeded by a family known as the Umayyads, who set up a hereditary method of succession. To control the far reaches of the Islamic empire more easily, the Umayyads moved their capital from Mecca to Damascus in Syria. In time, the Umayyads, who ruled as conquerors, surrounded themselves more and more with wealth, a practice which alienated them from the *umma*. Their preoccupation with wealth, their taxation of non-Muslims, and the question of succession created a lasting rift in the Muslim community.

Disagreement surrounding the issue of succession led to the formation of the **Shia** sect of Islam, an alternative to the largest group of Muslims, the **Sunni**. The Shia supported Ali, a cousin and son-in-law of Muhammad, and his successors as caliphs. Ali had become the fourth caliph from 656 to 661, but had been assassinated. The Shia continued in their efforts to appoint only descendants of Ali as caliph, while the Sunni supported the authority of the Umayyad caliphs. Eventually, different rituals and laws served to further divide the Shia and the Sunni. A third Muslim group, the **Sufi**, reacted to the Umayyad preoccupation with wealth by attempting to contact Allah through chants and meditations. They served as missionaries of the Islamic faith and maintained their focus on tradition and the Qur'an. Opposition to Umayyad rule led to their fall and the rise of another dynasty, the Abbasids, in 750.

Al-Andalus

Upon coming to power, the Abbasids murdered the remaining members of the Umayyad dynasty, except for one prince who escaped to Spain, where he set up an Umayyad dynasty. In 711, the Muslim Berbers from North Africa, under the leadership of El Tariq, had invaded Spain. They would have advanced farther into western Europe had they not been halted in 732 by Charles Martel and his troops at the Battle of Tours in present-day France. The Berbers then returned to Spain, where they established an Islamic state called **al-Andalus** that produced advances in science and mathematics and at the same time aided in the preservation of the culture and learning of the Greeks and Romans. With its capital at Córdoba, al-Andalus would assure that knowledge and culture would flourish in Spain at a time when the majority of western Europe experienced cultural decline.

Islamic Spain prospered from long-distance trade during the era of Abbasid rule. Although the Islamic rulers of Spain allied themselves with the Umayyads rather than the Abbasids, this separation did not prevent them from trading with the remainder of the Islamic world. The cities of Córdoba, Toledo, and Sevilla became prosperous commercial and manufacturing centers that featured quality leather products, crystal glass, gold jewelry, and ceramics. Córdoba became an impressive cultural center complete with mosques, libraries, and free schools.

The Abbasid Empire

The Abbasids differed from the Umayyads in that they were not only conquerors, but able administrators with an efficient bureaucracy. Centering their power in the lands of the former Persian empire, they established their capital at Baghdad in present-day Iraq. Enduring until 1258, the Abbasid empire finally became too vast to be efficiently governed. It was then divided into a number of independent states; one power, the Fatimid dynasty, stretched from North Africa to parts of Arabia and Syria.

Increased agricultural production through crop rotation, the introduction of new crops such as sugar, rice, and citrus fruits, and the use of fertilizer, provided the Abbasid empire with a rich variety of foods that produced a rapid growth in population. This led to a marked growth in urban centers throughout the Islamic empire. Muslim cities housed thousands of merchants and craftsmen and were also thriving industrial centers producing cotton textiles, glassware, pottery, iron, steel, and leather. The Muslims learned about paper production from Chinese prisoners captured after the Battle of Talas in 751.

Commerce and Trade

Muslims participated in the greater economic activity of the eastern hemisphere by using the major land and sea trade routes of the time. The use of the compass, astrolabe, and **lateen sail**, all borrowed from other cultures, helped them to navigate the waters of the Indian Ocean, Red Sea, Persian Gulf, and Arabian Sea. Muslim traders sailed to the coast of East Africa to obtain slaves and animal skins. The Abbasids were also connected to the active trade routes between Scandinavia and Russia via the Dnieper and Volga Rivers; products sought were furs, honey, timber, and more slaves.

Overland trade usually employed camel caravans, made more feasible by the invention of the camel saddle in the first few centuries CE. Inns called **caravanserais** provided lodging for caravan travelers and food and water for their camels. Caravans crossed the Sahara Desert with salt, glass, copper, and steel to exchange for gold and slaves from the prosperous kingdoms of West Africa.

To facilitate commerce, both a common currency and a banking system were introduced in the Islamic world. In addition to lending and exchanging money, Islamic banks also issued letters of credit called ***sakk*** that became the forerunners of modern-day checks.

WOMEN IN THE ISLAMIC WORLD

The Arabic world into which Islam was introduced offered its women more rights than many regions in the seventh century. Women could inherit property, own their own businesses, and divorce their husbands. Later, the Qur'an provided for care for widows and orphans and outlawed female infanticide. It also proclaimed that, as believers in Islam, men and women were equal. For the most part, however, both the Qur'an and the *shariah* enforced male dominance. Islamic law recognized patriarchal inheritance; to ensure the legitimacy of their heirs, women were subjected to control by the male members of their household. Both the Qur'an and the shariah allowed Muslim men to follow the example of Muhammad and acquire up to four wives; women, however, were permitted only one husband.

In the early days of Islamic rule, women could receive an education and participate in public life. The responsibilities of Muslim women varied according to their husband's income: Wives of poor men often worked in the fields alongside their husbands, while wives of wealthy husbands managed the household and servants.

The relative early freedom for women was severely curtailed during the rule of the Abbasids, who introduced the custom of the harem and the veil. Wives of the Abbasid caliphs and the caliphs' concubines, who were often slaves, were confined to secluded quarters in the palaces. Urban women who appeared in public went accompanied by servants or chaperones and used a veil to discourage attracting the attention of men. (Islamic culture borrowed this from the societies of Mesopotamia, Persia, and the eastern Mediterranean—all areas that already practiced the veiling of women.) Eventually, however, the practice of veiling or *hijab* spread from the upper-class urban women to women of all classes in both urban and rural areas.

MUSLIM CULTURAL ACHIEVEMENTS

The Islamic world would not only enrich its occupied lands with an advanced culture; it would also influence the beginnings and progress of the European Renaissance. One of the greatest achievements of the Muslims was their foundation of great universities, especially in Córdoba, Baghdad, and Cairo. These universities taught the Greco-Roman culture, preserving it at a time when most of western Europe was generally in academic decline. Their libraries contained works passed down through the centuries, including *The Thousand and One Nights* and the *Rubaiyat of Omar Khayyam*. They spread the Arabic language, giving to the English language words such as *alcohol*, *algebra*, *almanac*, *cipher*, *coffee*, *cotton*, and *sofa*.

As expert mariners, the Muslims believed the world was round. Muslim caravans transmitted the knowledge of the India system of numbers, while Muslim mathematicians developed the study of algebra and furthered the knowledge of geometry and trigonometry. Scientists prepared chemical compounds such as alcohol and sulfuric acid and improved cloth dyeing and metal refining. Muslim physicians studied the relationship between light and vision, performed difficult surgery using anesthetics, and compiled their knowledge in medical textbooks. The Muslims designed exquisite structures including palaces, mosques, and minarets, and used intricately carved lace patterns called arabesques; the Alhambra of Granada, Spain, is a noteworthy example of Muslim architecture.

THINGS TO REMEMBER

- Islam was introduced in the seventh century by an Arab merchant, Muhammad, who claimed to have received divine revelation.
- Islam features monotheism, Five Pillars of faith, the Qur'an as its holy book, and *shariah*, codified rules for righteous living.
- The religion gained widespread popularity in Arabia, the Middle East, North Africa, and Central Asia.
- Disagreements over succession after the death of Muhammad divided the Muslim world into Shia and Sunni sects.
- The extension of the Islamic empire into Spain spread the advances of Islamic culture and helped to preserve Greek and Roman culture during the European Middle Ages.
- Islamic women, at first considered equal to men, soon were made subject to their husbands and later were required to wear the veil.
- Muslim traders in the trans-Saharan and Indian Ocean trade routes spread the Arabic language and facilitated advances in banking.
- The Islamic world produced many cultural achievements in medicine, mathematics, literature, and architecture.

REVIEW QUESTIONS

1. Which of the following is NOT a correct statement concerning the beliefs of Islam?
   (A) All Muslims must acknowledge that there is one god called Allah and that Muhammad is his prophet.
   (B) All Muslims must pray five times a day, facing Mecca.
   (C) All Muslims must fast during the daylight hours during the month of Ramadan.
   (D) All Muslims must contribute to the support of the poor and needy.
   (E) All Muslims must make at least one pilgrimage, or *hajj*, to either Mecca or Medina during their lifetime.

2. All of the following are true concerning the split between the Shia and the Sunni sects of Islam EXCEPT
   (A) it gave rise to the two most important divisions in the Islamic world today.
   (B) it arose over the issue of succession after Muhammad's death.
   (C) it resulted when the Sunni supported the Umayyad dynasty.
   (D) it resulted in separate laws for both sects of Islam.
   (E) it resulted in the appointment of the Shi'ites as missionaries of Islam.

3. Women in the Islamic world
   (A) had fewer rights in the early days of Islam.
   (B) were given equal rights by the Qur'an.
   (C) were required to wear the veil after the Islamic culture adopted the custom from the Persians.
   (D) were freed from male dominance by the *shariah.*
   (E) were introduced to the custom of the harem in the earliest days of Islam.

4. Muhammad
   (A) saw himself as divine.
   (B) scorned the scriptures of the Christians and Jews.
   (C) wrote the Qur'an after the *hijra.*
   (D) was resented because of his introduction of monotheism to Mecca.
   (E) did not return to Mecca after his flight.

5. All of the following are true of the Muslims EXCEPT
   (A) they traded across the Sahara Desert.
   (B) they caused the decline of Greco-Roman culture during their occupation of Spain.
   (C) they traded with Russia.
   (D) they developed the forerunners of present-day checks.
   (E) they traded actively in the Indian Ocean.

ANSWERS AND EXPLANATIONS

1. (E)

Muslims are required to make the *hajj* to Mecca if they are healthy and have the financial resources to make the pilgrimage. The other responses are requirements of the Five Pillars of Islam that every Muslim is expected to obey.

2. (E)

The Sufi served as the missionaries of Islam. The Islamic world today continues to experience conflicts between its two major divisions, the Shia and Sunni (A). The split arose over whether caliphs succeeding Muhammad had to be members of his family (B). The Sunni supported the caliphs of the Umayyad family (C); eventually, different laws (D) divided the two sects further.

3. (C)

After coming into contact with the Persians, the Muslims adopted the custom of requiring women to wear the veil. Islamic women had greater rights in the early days of Islam (A). Both the Qur'an and the *shariah* established a patriarchal society (B, D). The harem was introduced later, during the Abbasid dynasty (E).

4. (D)

The merchants of Mecca derived considerable income from the pilgrims who came to Mecca to honor the numerous gods of the Arabs. Muhammad saw himself as the last of the prophets of Allah (A). He respected the Jews and Christians as "people of the book" (B). The Qur'an was written after the death of Muhammad (C). Shortly before his death, he returned to Mecca to once again spread the Islamic faith in that city (E).

5. (B)

The Muslim occupation of Spain served to preserve Greco-Roman culture. They developed letters of credit, or *sakk*, that became the forerunners of modern checks (D). Muslims participated in the gold-salt trade across the Sahara (A). One of the many interactions in the Byzantine world was trade between Muslims and Russians (C). They were also one of the dominant traders in the Indian Ocean (E).

CHAPTER 10

Cross-Cultural Exchange in the Byzantine Empire

TIMELINE

200	Slavs settle the steppes
527	Beginning of Justinian's reign
533	Recovery of North Africa from the Vandals
534	Justinian Code
535	Recovery of Rome from the Ostrogoths
565	Death of Justinian
730	Iconoclastic controversy
882–1169	Kiev serves as the capital of Rus
945	End of Abbasid power in Persia
970s	Seljuks move into Abbasid empire
1054	Division of the western and eastern churches
1055	The Seljuks capture Baghdad
1071	Battle of Manzikert
1453	Fall of Byzantium to the Ottomans

IMPORTANT PEOPLE, PLACES, EVENTS, AND CONCEPTS

Justinian	iconoclastic controversy*	Magyars*
Justinian Code*	Eastern Orthodox Church	Vikings
Hagia Sophia*	patriarch*	Kiev
Belisarius	Saint Methodius	Rus
Theodora	Saint Cyril	Vladimir
Seljuk Turks	Cyrillic alphabet*	mameluke*
Ottoman Turks	steppe*	shah*
icon*	Slavs	Malik Shah

THE EASTERN ROMAN EMPIRE

For almost a thousand years after the fall of the western portion of the Roman empire, the eastern part of the empire continued as a political and cultural entity. Byzantium's unique geographical location allowed it to control the straits of the Bosporus and Dardanelles, placing it in a strategic military position. As the center of numerous trade routes, Byzantium prospered from the continuous wealth flowing through, which explains her prosperity and longevity long after Rome's fall. The emperor Constantine had seen Byzantium's value when he selected it as a new capital of the Roman empire, renaming it Constantinople in his own honor. The division of the western and eastern Roman empires became a reality in 395 CE.

The Emperor Justinian

Justinian, who came to the throne of the eastern empire in 527, was the strongest of the Byzantine emperors. Among Justinian's main goals was the recovery of territory lost by the western empire as a result of the Germanic invasions of the 400s. To execute his plan, in 533 Justinian sent a general named **Belisarius** to recover North Africa from the Vandals; in 535 CE Belisarius attacked Rome, taking it from the Ostrogoths. Justinian's military eventually recovered nearly all of Italy and portions of Spain.

Justinian maintained strict control over both church and state; his policies led to frequent threats upon his life. His wars to restore Roman territory exhausted most of the resources of the Byzantine empire, leaving few funds to devote to the defense of its eastern borders. In spite of Byzantium's economic problems, Justinian managed to mold a thriving culture in the eastern empire. Latin, the language initially used for legal matters in the empire, was gradually replaced during Justinian's reign by Greek, the language of the common people in Byzantium. Knowledge of Greek promoted the preservation of the writings of Hellenistic thinkers.

In an effort to sift through Roman laws and update archaic ones, Justinian codified a body of laws so flexible that it was used for the next 900 years: The **Justinian Code**, a compilation of Roman laws, legal treatises, and Byzantine laws passed after 534. But Justinian's achievements did not end with his codification of laws. He rebuilt the city of Constantinople, which had been demolished by riots against high taxes. Using the high dome characteristic of Byzantine architecture, Justinian constructed the magnificent church called the **Hagia Sophia**, while also enlarging the imperial palace and constructing public buildings.

Rivalry among the various factions culminated in a 532 rebellion in which rebels chose a new emperor. Suppressed by the general Belisarius, the uprising took the lives of 30,000 rebels. Justinian's efforts to contain the rebellion were supported by his wife, **Theodora**, who championed not only her husband's sovereignty but also women's rights. During Justinian's reign, Theodora campaigned for laws to protect the status of women and to grant them adequate benefits and representation in divorce cases. In spite of Theodora's efforts, Byzantine women were expected to live their lives somewhat in seclusion. While male children attended schools to study the works of their Greco-Roman heritage, female children received a similar education, but at home. However, some women were allowed to continue their education and pursue professions, becoming physicians, professors, and mathematicians.

Byzantine Power Weakens

After the death of Justinian in 565, the Byzantine empire began a slow, steady decline. An outbreak of plague dealt a crippling blow to the empire's population. When the plague finally disappeared about 700, it left a population so severely reduced that Byzantium was unable to effectively combat its enemies. Subsequent attacks by Slavs, Russians, Arabs, Persians, Turks, and Crusaders from western Europe repeatedly chipped away at portions of the once-flourishing empire. Of particular impact were the repeated attacks of the **Seljuk Turks**, who in the late eleventh century conquered most of the Asian portions of the Byzantine empire, cutting off major sources of tax income and food supplies.

Later Byzantine emperors employed a combination of diplomacy, bribes, and political marriage alliances to try to ensure the survival of the empire; the term *byzantine* came to refer to complex intrigue. By 1350, Byzantine territory was confined to a small portion of Anatolia and a strip of land in the Balkans. Finally, Byzantium weakened to the point where it could not withstand further attacks, and it fell to the **Ottoman Turks** in 1453.

THE BYZANTINE CHURCH

The centuries following Justinian's rule also saw division between the eastern and western branches of the Roman Catholic Church. Initially, the major issue between the two geographic branches of the Church was the use of **icons**, or two-dimensional religious images used by the eastern Christians in their celebrations and devotions. Prior to this time, the patriarch, or leading bishop of the eastern church, submitted to the ultimate authority of the eastern emperor in religious matters. But this imperial authority was tested in 730, when Leo III prohibited the use of icons. The emperor, who considered the icons objects of idol worship, received support from his army. **Iconoclasts**, or those opposing the use of icons, broke into churches to destroy the icons, prompting public riots. The western pope added to the controversy by supporting the use of icons and another even went so far as to excommunicate the Byzantine emperor from the Roman Catholic Church. Later, in 843, the Empress Theodora restored the use of icons in the **Eastern Orthodox Church**.

Differences concerning papal authority, clerical celibacy, and policies regarding divorce continued to plague the eastern and western branches of the Church. The division over these issues escalated until the western pope and the eastern **patriarch** excommunicated each other in 1054. This schism resulted in the permanent division between the Roman Catholic Church in the West and the Eastern Orthodox Church.

This split did not diminish the Church's zeal for winning souls. Orthodox missionaries took Christianity to the Slavs in the ninth century. Especially active in Slavic missions were **Saint Methodius** and **Saint Cyril**, who devised an alphabet to enable the Slavs to read the Bible in their own language; the resulting **Cyrillic alphabet** remains the alphabet of the Russian and other Slavic languages today. In addition to spreading literacy and Christianity to the Slavs, the missionaries of the Eastern Orthodox Church were opening doors to further cultural interaction between Byzantium and the Slavic peoples.

BYZANTINE AND RUSSIAN INTERACTIONS

By the mid-ninth century, the **Slavs** living north of the Black Sea became further acquainted with Byzantine culture through trade with Constantinople. The geographical setting for the future Russian state was the **steppe**, an almost treeless flat grassland stretching across central Asia and eastern Europe. In addition to an abundance of fertile soil, the steppe also featured several major rivers that became the vehicles for active transportation and trade. By 200 CE, the world of the steppes had already been settled by the Slavs, who spread throughout most of eastern Europe. With their iron tools, the Slavs readily cultivated the lands of the steppe. The Slavs, who had originally come from Asia, mingled with previous inhabitants of the steppes as well as new settlers, such as the Bulgarians, who adopted the Slavic language and culture.

The loose organization of the Slavic peoples into kinship-based tribes and villages made the Slavs easy prey for conquest by nomadic peoples such as the Huns, **Magyars**, and Avars. The **Viking** invasions in the 800s brought Viking traders into eastern Europe. Along one of these Viking trade routes, running from Constantinople to the Baltic Sea, was the city of **Kiev**. Viking dominance of the area was further solidified when the residents of another steppe city, Novgorod, asked the Vikings to defend their city against the incursion of steppe nomads. In time, the Slavs began to refer to the Vikings and the territory they controlled as ***Rus***, from which would come the term *Russian*.

Kievan Rus

Kiev prospered and served as the capital of Rus from 882 to 1169. Situated in the center of interactions between Vikings, Byzantines, Slavs, and Islamic Turks, Kievan Rus was in a position to observe the cultural practices of those peoples. Religious customs were of particular interest to the princes of Kiev. Rejecting Islam because of its prohibition against alcoholic beverages and Judaism because of his presumption that the Jewish God lacked political power, Prince **Vladimir** finally settled on the adoption of Eastern Orthodox Christianity for his people. Vladimir soon forced Christian baptism on many of his subjects. His control of major church appointments gave birth to a separate Russian Orthodox Church. The painting of icons emerged as a characteristic art form in Kiev, and the influence of Byzantium was apparent in the architectural style of Kievan Rus.

The Kievan state continued to prosper with an economy based on both agriculture and trade. Kiev furnished slaves for the Byzantine empire (in fact, the word *slave* is a variation of *Slav*). Kiev also traded fur, animal hides, burlap, hemp, and hops in exchange for Byzantine wine, silk, steel blades, religious art, and horses. Trade routes from western Europe brought metals, textiles, and glassware. By 1000, Kievan Rus could compete with any western European state for wealth and power.

The tide of Kievan prosperity and power began to turn in the twelfth century, when competing princes set up regional governments and differences arose concerning royal succession. While invasions from the Mongols of central Asia chipped away at Russian territory, the decline of Byzantium reduced trade and wealth in Kievan Rus. In the thirteenth century, the Mongols (or Tatars, as the Russians called them) twice invaded Russia, conquering its cities. Throughout the period of Mongol control, the Russians would continue to identify themselves with the glories of Byzantium and feel a sense of responsibility for carrying on its traditions. A unique Eurasian Slavic culture had been born on the steppes of Russia.

TURKISH INTERACTIONS WITH BYZANTIUM

By the tenth century, the Turks, who had previously raided and traded along the northeastern borders of the Islamic empires, began converting to the Islamic faith and migrating into the Abbasid empire. The Abbasids eagerly purchased Turkish children for use as slaves, soldiers, and bodyguards. Military slaves called **mamelukes** fought in the armies of the Abbasids; eventually their skill made them stronger than their Abbasid masters.

In 945, the power of the Abbasids in Persia ended when the Persians moved into Baghdad. Subsequently, beginning about 970, large numbers of Turks migrated into the Abbasid empire. Among them was a group known as the Seljuks, who had converted to the Sunni branch of Islam. The Seljuks gained control of the major trade routes between eastern Asia, the Middle East, and Europe. In 1055, the Seljuks attacked and captured Baghdad from the Persians, ridding the capital of its Shi'ite officials. In 1071, they dealt a blow to the Byzantine empire at the Battle of Manzikert. Within ten years, the Seljuks occupied all of Anatolia.

In Persia, the Seljuk rulers actively sought the support of their Persian subjects, selecting the Persian capital of Isfahan as their capital and often appointing Persians as government officials. Respect for Persian advances in learning prompted the Seljuks to adopt the Persian language as the language of culture; the Seljuks began referring to their rulers as ***shah***, the Persian word for *king*. The Seljuks' adoption of the Persian language led to the near disappearance of the Arabic language in Persia. The Seljuk ruler **Malik Shah** (1055–1092) also supported Persian architects and artists, further gaining the appreciation of the Persian people.

After the death of Malik Shah, the Seljuks were unable to develop a well-organized government and began to struggle with one another for control of the land. The Seljuks, who had been pastoral nomads, overran agricultural areas surrounding the cities. Irrigation works suffered from lack of maintenance. The canal system upon which agriculture in the Tigris-Euphrates valley depended collapsed. The successors of Malik Shah were largely uninterested in the cultural life of urban areas. Disagreements arose between Shi'ites and Sunnis, and within Sunnism itself.

The Crusades

As the Seljuk empire was beginning to disintegrate, western Europe embarked on a campaign against the Turks called the Crusades. In 1095, Pope Urban II of the western branch of the Church called for Christians to unite to drive the Seljuks out of Anatolia and Palestine and to recover the city of Jerusalem. In 1099, the First Crusade resulted in the capture of Jerusalem and the establishment of a Christian kingdom for almost a century. By the time the various crusades ended in the mid-thirteenth century, the Seljuks had regained control of the Holy Land but granted Christians the right to make pilgrimages to Palestine.

The final threat to the power of the Seljuk Turks was the invasion of the Mongols in the thirteenth century. When the Mongol empire fell in the fourteenth century, it would lead to the rise of another branch of Turks: the Ottomans. In building their own empire, the Ottomans would end that of the once-splendid Byzantium.

THINGS TO REMEMBER

- Beginning as the eastern branch of the Roman empire, the Byzantine empire endured for almost a thousand years after the fall of the western empire.
- Byzantium's location on the straits separating the Black Sea and the Mediterranean Sea made it a hub of trade routes from many parts of the world.
- The emperor Justinian preserved Roman heritage by codifying its laws. Greek became the empire's language, and the works of ancient Greek thinkers were preserved.
- While Empress Theodora and other women fought for expanded rights, Byzantine women generally were kept secluded in their homes.
- Conflicts over church authority and practices caused a division between the Roman Catholic and Eastern Orthodox Churches. This became permanent in 1054.
- The Russian Orthodox Church began when Prince Vladimir of Kiev chose Orthodox Christianity for the Russian people. Byzantine and Russian interactions led to cultural exchange.
- Kiev rose to preeminence in Russia due to its position on trade routes.
- The Seljuk Turks dealt Byzantium a critical blow in 1071, when they captured most of Asia Minor (Battle of Manzikert).
- The Ottoman Turks conquered the diminished Byzantine empire, capturing Constantinople in 1453.

REVIEW QUESTIONS

1. Byzantium

(A) owed much of its prosperity to its geographical location.
(B) received much of its strength from its steadily growing population.
(C) failed to regain territory lost by the western Roman empire.
(D) fell at the hands of the Seljuk Turks.
(E) declined abruptly in the fifteenth century.

2. Justinian is credited with all of the following EXCEPT

(A) the codification of Roman law.
(B) the restoration of Latin as the language of his people.
(C) the construction of Hagia Sophia.
(D) the rebuilding of Constantinople.
(E) the recovery of most of Italy from Germanic tribes.

3. All of the following are true of the Byzantine Church EXCEPT

(A) it witnessed clashes between papal and imperial authority.
(B) it sent missionaries to the Slavic peoples.
(C) it reunited with the western Church in 1054.
(D) it furthered cultural interaction between the Byzantines and the Slavs.
(E) it used icons as an aid to religious devotion.

4. Kievan Rus

(A) developed economic and cultural ties with Byzantium.
(B) could not compete with western Europe in wealth and power.
(C) was able to repel Mongol invasions.
(D) resisted Viking attempts to dominate their region.
(E) was ruled by princes who were uninterested in the cultures of surrounding peoples.

5. The Seljuk Turks

(A) were converts to the Shi'ite branch of Islam.
(B) improved the irrigation systems of the areas they conquered.
(C) adopted the Arabic language.
(D) contributed to the conditions leading up to the Crusades.
(E) failed to assimilate into the culture of their subjects.

ANSWERS AND EXPLANATIONS

1. (A)

The prosperity of Byzantium was largely the result of its location at the center of a number of trade routes. Epidemic disease caused a marked population decline, which weakened the empire (B). Under Justinian, it regained some of the territory lost with the fall of the western Roman empire (C). Byzantium declined gradually after the death of Justinian (E) and fell in 1453 at the hands of the Ottoman Turks (D).

2. (B)

Under Justinian, Latin was replaced by Greek as the language of the people. The Code of Justinian (A) put ancient and contemporary Roman laws in writing. During his reconstruction of Constantinople (D), Justinian built the beautiful church Hagia Sophia (C). His generals were able to recover most of Italy from the Germanic tribes that overran it after the fall of Rome (E).

3. (C)

The Byzantine Church split with the western Church in 1054. It witnessed conflicts between papal and secular authority (A), especially over the use of icons in worship (E). St. Methodius and St. Cyril were sent as missionaries to the Slavic peoples (B), which furthered cultural contacts between the two groups. The Russian Prince Vladimir adopted the Byzantine faith for the Slavs (D).

4. (A)

Kiev furnished slaves for the Byzantine empire and was further connected to Byzantium through Vladimir's acceptance of Byzantine Christianity (E). Trade and agriculture allowed Kiev to compete with western Europeans for wealth and power (B). In the thirteenth century it was dominated by the Mongols (C). Vikings dominated the area at the request of the city of Novgorod (D).

5. (D)

In the eleventh century, the Seljuk Turks occupied Jerusalem, leading to the call for a crusade. They were converts to the Sunni branch of Islam (A). They adopted the Persian language (C) and assimilated somewhat into the Persian culture, taking the name of *shah* for their leaders (E). Later groups of Seljuks destroyed the ancient irrigation systems of the peoples they conquered (B).

CHAPTER 11

East Asia and Southeast Asia

TIMELINE

500	Rise of Yamato clan of Japan
589–618	Sui empire of China
618–907	Tang dynasty of China
mid-7th century	Silla of Korea drive out the Han
794–1185	Heian dynasty
935–1392	Koryu dynasty of Korea
939	Vietnamese win their independence
960–1279	Song dynasty of China Mongol takeover of China
1009–1225	Vietnamese Lu dynasty
1185	Rise of the Minamoto clan of Japan
1200	Khmer empire reaches its height
1231–1350	Mongol attempts to conquer Korea
1392	Choson dynasty of Korea

IMPORTANT PEOPLE, PLACES, EVENTS, AND CONCEPTS

Grand Canal	foot-binding	Silla dynasty
civil service system*	Malay sailors	Koryu dynasty
Middle Kingdom	Zen Buddhism*	celadon pottery
kowtow*	Angkor Wat	Shinto*
Jurchen	Neo-Confucianism*	Heian Japan

RESTORATION OF CHINESE CENTRALIZED RULE

After the fall of the Han dynasty, China, like Rome, experienced the division of its former empire into numerous regional governments. Finally, in the late sixth century, the Sui dynasty rose, restoring a centralized government to China. After the short duration of the Sui dynasty, the Tang and then the Song dynasties brought significant agricultural and industrial growth to China.

The Sui Dynasty

The Sui emperors (589–618) united the Chinese people by constructing numerous public works, including granaries and palaces, while also repairing the many defensive walls scattered throughout China. Their most extensive undertaking was the construction of the **Grand Canal**, which linked northern and southern China. Nearly 1,240 miles long, with parallel roads on either side, the Grand Canal provided an effective and economical way to transport rice and other crops from the Yangtze River valley to the northern portions of China. Until railroads arrived in China, the Grand Canal provided the economic basis to unite the Chinese people once again. However, despite this unity, the imposition of high taxes prompted a rebellion in northern China and the subsequent assassination of the emperor Sui Yangdi in 618.

The Tang Dynasty

The Sui emperors were succeeded by the Tang dynasty (618–907), who brought power and prosperity to China. Tang Taizong (627–649), the most well-known of the Tang emperors, ruthlessly pushed his way to the throne; once he became emperor, however, Tang Taizong proved to be a benevolent ruler. During his reign, travel and trade benefited from the end of highway banditry, and the price of rice and the tax rate remained low.

The Tang united China by means of an extensive network of roads, with inns, postal stations, and stables along the route. Carriers on horseback and human runners carried messages along the highways—similar to the activities of the Persian Royal Road. Land was redistributed through a formula that took into account the fertility of a plot of land and the needs of the recipients; later this system deteriorated when some powerful families retained their land holdings and the rise of Buddhist monasteries took up even more land. The Confucian **civil service system** was resurrected under the Tang: Most governmental offices were filled with men who had passed the civil service exam, completed their education in the writings of Confucius, and mastered a curriculum of Chinese classics.

The Tang extended their imperial authority by conquering Manchuria, the northern part of Vietnam, and much of Tibet, and also by bringing the Silla kingdom of Korea under its control. The Tang perceived themselves as the **Middle Kingdom**, one in which surrounding states would have a tributary relationship to China. Representatives from these tributary states were expected to perform the

kowtow, a ritualistic bow in which subordinates knelt before the emperor and touched their forehead to the ground several times.

In the mid-eighth century, a weak emperor started the decline of the Tang empire. Eventually land reforms failed and tax receipts proved insufficient to meet imperial needs. A series of peasant rebellions forced the Tang emperors to grant increasingly more authority to local military commanders; by 907, the last Tang emperor had abdicated his rule and China underwent a period of rule by warlords.

The Song Dynasty

In the tenth century, the Song dynasty (960–1279) again restored centralized rule to China. The Song dynasty characterized itself not by military rule, but rather by an emphasis on education and the arts in addition to industrialization. In effect, the Song dynasty became a period of industrial advancement in China. Under the Song, the Confucian civil service system was expanded to include opportunities for more men to study Confucian philosophy and to take the exam.

However, the increasing number of government employees created a huge bureaucracy that eventually strained the country's finances. The bureaucracy was also incapable of handling the country's defenses, and nomadic peoples such as the Khitan began demanding tribute from the Song. In the early twelfth century, another group of nomads, the **Jurchen**, overran the northern part of China, limiting the Song dynasty to the south, with the border between the two parts situated between the Huang He (Yellow) and Yangtze Rivers. The Song dynasty would endure in the south until its takeover by the Mongols in 1279.

LIFE IN TANG AND SONG CHINA

The Tang and Song dynasties not only brought prosperity to China but also increased trade in the eastern hemisphere as a whole. A significant development was the discovery of fast-ripening rice, which was brought to China from Vietnam during the Tang dynasty. The new rice made it possible to harvest two crops per year. The use of iron plows, natural fertilizers, and irrigation increased agricultural productivity, as did the use of reservoirs, canals, and water wheels. Terraces were used along mountainsides to increase the amount of land under cultivation. The increase in agricultural productivity, along with improved food distribution through better transportation networks, contributed to a significant growth in the Chinese population. Population increases resulted in the growth of cities, with Song China distinguished as the most urbanized area in the world of its time. An abundant food supply also led to commercial agriculture, in which the various regions of China produced crops best suited to their region and exported the surplus.

Foot-binding

The innovations of the Tang and Song dynasties contributed to a new emphasis on family. Under the Song, more importance was placed on honoring one's ancestors. Unfortunately, the emphasis upon family and patriarchal authority also led to the disfiguring custom of foot-binding. **Foot-binding**, which for the most part was practiced only by wealthy families, involved tightly wrapping young girls' feet with strips of cloth. This would break some bones in the foot, preventing the girl from walking easily. The procedure was considered a measure of attractiveness, a display of high social standing, and a way to control the girl's behavior. Since foot-binding made it impossible for Chinese women to work in the fields and to walk without pain, it demonstrated that a family was so wealthy that it did not need to send its women into the fields to work. Their disability also made Chinese women with bound feet completely dependent upon their husbands or other male family figures.

Industry and Trade

The abundance of food in China under the Tang and Song furthered industrial development. Craftsmen learned the formula for making high-quality porcelain that was highly valued in the western world, where it earned the name *chinaware*. Iron production resulted in new weapons such as the flame thrower, which terrorized the inhabitants of Eastern Europe. The production of gunpowder would change the course of Eurasian history. The distribution of Buddhist texts was facilitated by the invention of moveable type centuries before the same process would be implemented in Western Europe. Technological innovations such as the magnetic compass helped long-distance trade in the Indian Ocean and the Persian Gulf, in addition to opening a direct trade route between China and the eastern coast of Africa. Trade with Vietnam introduced tea to the Chinese and also brought the knowledge of Islam and Nestorian Christianity.

Class structure was attained by the creation of a gentry (an elite upper class whose position relied on education and position in the civil service) and a middle class, expanding economic opportunities for merchants, shopkeepers, craftsmen, and minor government officials. Trade opened up contacts with other peoples such as the **Malay sailors**, who established trading communities in the southern Chinese ports of Guangzhou and Quanzhou, and other merchants from Persia, India, and central Asia, who traded in the cities of Chang'an and Luoyang. Through these contacts, Chinese trade stimulated commerce throughout the eastern hemisphere.

Buddhism in China

As commerce brought Buddhism to China, the nature of the religion changed. Spreading over the Silk Roads, Buddhism in China took on the form of Mahayana Buddhism, which dwelled on the divinity of the Buddha and surrounded itself with rituals that were unknown to Indian Buddhism. Chinese Buddhism would blend with some of the precepts of Daoism to form a faith dependent upon meditation and enlightenment called Chan Buddhism (or **Zen Buddhism** in Japan). The revival of the beliefs of Buddhism further influenced Confucianism because of its thoughts on the nature of the soul. **Neo-Confucianism**, practiced in China by the end of the Tang dynasty, reflected the influence of Buddhist tradition.

FOREIGN RELATIONS UNDER THE TANG AND SONG

The Khmer Empire

Located in present-day Cambodia, the Khmer empire was once the dominant one on the mainland of Southeast Asia and engaged in an active volume of trade with China and India. Reaching the height of their prominence around 1200, the Khmer had become prosperous through the cultivation of rice. Their most noteworthy architectural achievement was the **Angkor Wat**, a temple complex dedicated to the Hindu god Vishnu and a magnificent example of the blend of Indian and Southeast Asian cultures.

Korea

The Tang and Song dynasties undertook a number of invasions of Vietnam and Korea and also established trade connections with both countries as well as with Japan. Thus the knowledge of Chinese culture influenced these Asian neighbors, especially in the area of government and administrative styles. Korea, which had been conquered by the Han dynasty, became acquainted with Chinese centralized government in addition to Buddhism, Confucianism, and the Chinese system of writing. In the mid-seventh century, the **Silla dynasty** drove out the Han and controlled the entire Korean peninsula. Under the Silla, the Koreans developed a writing system based on Chinese characters and constructed Buddhist monasteries.

The Silla dynasty was overthrown in 935 and replaced by the **Koryu** (which gave Korea its name). Enduring until 1392, the Koryu dynasty adopted a Confucian civil service system similar to that of China. Under the Koryu, the Koreans used block printing to print the sacred texts of Buddhism and produced the first national history of Korea. Poets flourished, and artists produced Korea's prized green **celadon pottery**. Sharp class division plagued the Koryu dynasty, making it vulnerable to Mongol conquest from 1231 to about 1350. In 1392, scholars and the military overthrew the Koryu dynasty and carried out land reforms under the subsequent Choson, or Yi, dynasty.

Vietnam

Chinese relations with the Vietnamese encountered more resistance than its relations with Korea. The Viet people adopted the Chinese civil service system and bureaucracy, Confucian writings, Buddhism, and Chinese agricultural techniques. However, differences between the Chinese and Vietnamese cultures sparked animosity to Chinese rule. Women in Vietnamese society had long been accustomed to wider privileges, especially in local business and commerce, than their Chinese counterparts. After the Tang dynasty fell in the early years of the tenth century, the Vietnamese won their independence in 939. Vietnamese rulers of the Lu dynasty (1009–1225) established a capital at Hanoi and conquered peoples to the south. The Mongols attempted to conquer Hanoi three times (in 1257, 1285, and 1287) but were turned back by the Vietnamese.

Japan

Japan was also profoundly influenced by Chinese political and cultural traditions. The earliest people of the Japanese islands had migrated to Japan from northeast Asia during one of the ice ages. By about 500 CE, numerous aristocratic clans dominated Japanese society; gradually one clan, the Yamato, gained prominence as the leading class. By the sixth century, Yamato leaders began referring to themselves as the emperors of Japan. So at this early date, the Japanese had already established the tradition of an emperor who ruled only as a figurehead.

From Korean travelers and migrants to Japan, the Japanese learned of the customs and centralized government of the Chinese. During the Tang dynasty, an interest in Chinese culture prompted the Japanese to send groups to China to study its way of life. Japanese painting developed along Chinese lines, and the Japanese were introduced to Chinese writing by the Koreans. For a brief time, the Japanese also followed some aspects of the Chinese government. Full implementation of the Chinese model of potential administration was hindered by the Japanese emphasis on noble birth as a key to power.

Through the influence of Koreans, the Japanese adopted Buddhism, although their native religion, **Shinto**, retained its popularity. Eventually Shinto (which centered around the veneration of ancestors and spirits of nature) and Buddhism blended some of their rituals.

In 794, the emperor of Japan moved his court from the city of Nara to a new capital at Heian (present-day Kyoto). Japanese culture would blossom in the Heian period (794–1185). The courts of **Heian Japan** were models of elegance and etiquette. Much of what is known about Heian Japan has been handed down through an eleventh-century work of Lady Murasaki titled *The Tale of Genji*, considered the world's first novel, and Sei Shonagon's *The Pillow Book*, a tale of Heian court life.

The common people of Japan continued to live surrounded by aristocratic landowners who accumulated more and more land. In 1185, one clan, the Minamoto, emerged as the most powerful. The Minamoto proclaimed their clan leader as *shogun*, a military governor who ruled in the place of the emperor. Establishing their capital at Kamakura, south of modern Tokyo, the Minamoto clan would continue to rule Japan for most of the following 400 years.

THINGS TO REMEMBER

- The Sui dynasty (589–618) imposed a central government on China, which had been divided into regional states since the fall of the Han dynasty (third century).
- The Tang dynasty (618–907) made the Chinese state strong and prosperous.
    - They built an extensive network of roads, like the Romans and Persians.
    - They renewed the Confucian civil service, based on education and merit.
    - They conquered Manchuria, Korea, and part of Vietnam.
    - Eventually the dynasty declined due to misuse of funds, and warlords took control of China.
- The Song dynasty (960–1279) advanced industrialization and the arts, but was weak militarily.
- The Mongols conquered China in the thirteenth century.
- Both dynasties experienced prosperity and technological achievement.
    - Inventions include gunpowder, moveable type, and high-quality porcelain. Farming techniques improved.
    - Population grew and long-distance trade flourished.
    - Buddhism spread through China and the surrounding nations, and it took on new forms.
- Vietnam, Korea, and Japan adopted aspects of Chinese culture including the writing system, the form of government, and religion. They changed these models to fit their own cultures.

REVIEW QUESTIONS

1. In their system of roads, the Tang dynasty bore a similarity to

   (A) Byzantium and Kiev.
   (B) Assyria and Egypt.
   (C) Babylonia and Anatolia.
   (D) Rome and Persia.
   (E) Greece and Phoenicia.

2. All of the following are true of Buddhism in China EXCEPT

   (A) it affected land distribution.
   (B) it blended with Chinese philosophy.
   (C) it influenced Japanese Buddhism.
   (D) it adopted a simpler form of worship than in India.
   (E) it worshipped the Buddha as a deity.

3. Under the Tang and Song dynasties,

   (A) the Confucian civil service system was disbanded.
   (B) the family declined in importance.
   (C) tea was imported from Cambodia.
   (D) class divisions were abolished.
   (E) Buddhism was introduced to Vietnam.

4. All of the following were among the achievements of the Tang and Song dynasties EXCEPT

   (A) trade with the Khmer empire and Korea.
   (B) the development of gunpowder and moveable type.
   (C) the establishment of long-term dominance over Vietnam.
   (D) an abundance of food.
   (E) a subordinate status for women.

5. Japan

   (A) was governed by a powerful emperor as early as the sixth century.
   (B) adopted Buddhism to replace its native religion of Shinto.
   (C) distributed land equally.
   (D) found the Chinese style of government suitable to its needs.
   (E) was dominated by aristocratic classes.

ANSWERS AND EXPLANATIONS

1. (D)

Both Tang China and Rome boasted roads that linked all part of their empire. The Persian Royal Road, like that of the Tang, used carriers to relay messages along the length of the road. The other civilizations and societies mentioned in the other responses were not noted for their extensive road networks and, therefore, are incorrect responses.

2. (D)

Buddhism in China, or Mahayana Buddhism, adopted a more elaborate form of worship than that of Indian Buddhism. In Tang China, Buddhism affected land distribution to peasants by taking up land for Buddhist monasteries (A). Buddhism blended with both Daoism and Confucianism (B); in Japan this blend became known as Zen Buddhism (C). In Mahayana Buddhism, the Buddha was considered divine (E).

3. (E)

Under the Tang, Buddhism was introduced to Vietnam, where it became a popular religion. The Confucian civil service system was restored under the Tang (A). Under the Song, increased emphasis was placed on the family (B). Tea was imported from Vietnam, not Cambodia (C). Class divisions were apparent (D).

4. (C)

The Vietnamese won their independence shortly after the fall of the Tang dynasty. Trade connections were established with both the Khmer empire and with Korea (A). Among inventions of the Tang and Song were gunpowder and moveable type (B). An abundance of food led to commercial agriculture (D). Increased emphasis was placed upon patriarchal authority, leading to the establishment of the custom of foot-binding (E).

5. (E)

By about 500, several aristocratic clans dominated Japan, while the emperor was established as a figurehead only (A). These aristocratic clans accumulated more and more land (C). Although Buddhism was adopted by the Japanese, their native Shinto retained its popularity (B). The Japanese followed some aspects of the Chinese government, but preferred its own emphasis on nobility as a key to power (D).

CHAPTER 12

Feudal Systems in Western Europe and Japan

TIMELINE

520	Benedictine order
731	Venerable Bede's history of England
732	Battle of Tours
751–987	Carolingian dynasty
800	Charlemagne crowned emperor Beginning of Viking invasions
843	Treaty of Verdun
mid-12th century	Gempei Wars
1467–1477	Civil war in Japan

IMPORTANT PEOPLE, PLACES, EVENTS, AND CONCEPTS

Clotilda
Clovis
Rule of St. Benedict
St. Scholastica
illuminated manuscript*
major domo*
Charles Martel
Pepin the Short
Donation of Pepin
Papal States*
Charlemagne
*missi dominici**
Danes
feudalism*
vassal*
serf*
benefice*
fief*
manor*
chivalry*
Eleanor of Aquitaine
bushi*
samurai*
bushido*
seppuku*
shogun*
daimyo*

THE RISE OF REGIONAL STATES IN WESTERN EUROPE

After the chaos of the fall of the Roman empire, some areas of western Europe witnessed the rise of powerful nobles and monarchs who established unified regional governments that provided a glimpse of the future of western Europe. Historians traditionally have termed the history of western Europe between the years of 500 and 1500 as the medieval period, or the Middle Ages. More recent historians question the accuracy of the second date, believing that by around 1100 the rise of urban centers and universities signaled the end of the medieval period in western Europe.

In the decades following the fall of Rome, imperial rule was replaced by local governments in the form of small Germanic kingdoms. At the same time, the Catholic Church served as a unifying force in the territories of the former Roman empire. Eventually many of the Germanic tribes surrounding the Roman empire converted to Christianity.

Germanic rule structured itself around loyalties to families and individuals, such as the Germanic chiefs. In the former Roman province of Gaul, power was in the hands of a Germanic people called the Franks. **Clovis**, who was leader of the Franks and was perhaps influenced by his Christian wife **Clotilda**, converted to Christianity along with his army. Their adoption of Roman Christianity gained the Franks the support of the pope, thereby strengthening the power of the Frankish rulers.

Monastic Life

During the rule of the Frankish kings, the Roman Catholic Church established monasteries and convents, or religious communities where monks and nuns relinquished their private possessions in order to serve God. One of the prominent orders was the Benedictine order, founded around 520 by an Italian monk named St. Benedict. The ***Rule* of St. Benedict** required its monks to observe the rules of poverty, chastity, and obedience, and also divided the monk's day into hours of meditation and hours of manual labor. St. Benedict's sister, the nun **St. Scholastica**, adapted the *Rule* to guide the lives of women in convents.

Within the walls of the monasteries of western Europe, monks preserved education by maintaining schools and libraries. In 731, an English monk called Venerable Bede wrote a history of England; many historians consider this the best historical work of the early medieval period. Still another accomplishment of medieval monks was the copying of books and manuscripts by hand, enhancing the beauty of the manuscripts by decorating them with elaborate lettering and detailed pictures. These **illuminated manuscripts** preserved Greco-Roman culture until the invention of the printing press in the western world around 1440.

Church Authority

In addition to preserving the culture of the former Roman empire, the Church continued to solidify its authority over secular as well as spiritual matters. When Gregory the Great (Gregory I) became pope in 590, he used church finances to engage in traditionally secular roles of repairing public works, raising armies, and establishing public welfare programs. The concept of secular kingdoms under church authority would prove a source of increasing tension between popes and kings throughout the medieval period.

The Carolingian Dynasty

The Frankish kings ruled until the early eighth century, when the Carolingian family came to power in Gaul. By that time, the most powerful person in Gaul was not the king, but an official called the ***major domo***, or mayor of the palace. Officially, the mayor of the palace was in control over the royal household and its grounds, but in reality, he controlled Gaul. The most famous mayor of the palace was **Charles Martel**, who not only extended the territory of the Franks but also defeated the Muslims at the Battle of Tours in 732. This victory was significant because it halted Muslim expansion farther north into western Europe; the Muslims retreated to Spain, where they built a civilization whose cultural advances combined the knowledge of Muslim scholars with the preservation of Greco-Roman culture.

Upon his death, Charles Martel's power passed to his son, **Pepin the Short**. As a reward for fighting against the Lombards, a tribe that had invaded central Italy, the pope anointed Pepin king of the Franks. After routing the Gauls, Pepin reciprocated by presenting the territory he conquered around Rome to the pope. This **Donation of Pepin** became the basis of the **Papal States**. The Carolingian dynasty (as the family of Charles Martel became known) had now secured its hegemony over the Franks; its rule would last from 751 to 987.

The peak of Carolingian power came with the reign of Pepin's son, known as **Charlemagne**, or Charles the Great. Charlemagne set about crafting an empire larger than any that had existed since the Roman empire, including Italy as far south as Rome, all of present-day France, northeastern Spain, and Saxony in northern Germany. In 800, while visiting Rome, Charlemagne was crowned emperor by Pope Leo III. The pope's action constituted a claim that popes had the authority to crown secular rulers, a right which strengthened the relationship between church and state in western Europe.

Charlemagne set up his capital at Aachen in present-day Germany, but devoted much of his reign to travel throughout his empire to solidify his authority. Charlemagne relied on counts, or local rulers, to govern the far reaches of his empire; he kept watch over the counts by sending out imperial officials known as ***missi dominici*** to review their records. Charlemagne required monasteries to open schools to educate future priests and monks, and he also opened a palace school for his own children and the other children at his court.

Although Charlemagne was a master at governing his vast empire, his expertise was not shared by his heirs. His only surviving son, Louis the Pious (reigned 814–840), proved ineffective at keeping the empire together. After his death, Louis's three sons fought over the empire. The conflict ended in 843 when the three signed the Treaty of Verdun, which divided Charlemagne's empire into three kingdoms. The western portion was awarded to Charles the Bold, the central region to Lothair, and the east to Louis the German. The eventual loss of Carolingian power weakened the political solidarity of western Europe, creating a need for an alternative plan for providing order in western Europe.

FEUDALISM IN WESTERN EUROPE

The wave of Germanic invasions that contributed to the fall of the Roman empire in the 400s was followed in the 800s by a series of Viking invasions from Scandinavia. The Vikings (who were called **"Danes"** by the English) were a people with few class distinctions. In the 800s, climatic changes and an increased population in Scandinavia caused serious food shortages. As a result, Viking ships left Scandinavia to follow the coasts of Europe and its rivers, sailing also to Iceland, Greenland, and North America. The Viking intrusion far surpassed that of the 400s and prompted the terrified western Europeans to seek some way of providing protection to their defenseless inhabitants.

The resulting system that arose in western Europe was one based on loyalty, similar to the Japanese system of the same period. Western European **feudalism** was based on a reciprocal relationship between lord and **vassal**. Nobles, or lords, would grant protection plus a **benefice**, or privilege, to a vassal, in return for either military service or agricultural labor. The benefice could be an economic or commercial privilege, but usually it was a grant of land, or a **fief**. At any given time, one man could be the lord of a number of vassals and could also be a vassal under another noble.

The Life of the Serf

Feudalism in western Europe revolved around the **manor**, or self-sufficient estate. Some peasants living on manor lands were free men who either rented land from the lord or worked at a skilled craft. However, most peasants were **serfs** who, like the Japanese peasants, were bound to the land. But unlike the Japanese peasants, western European serfs were not bound to their lord. In western Europe, if a plot of land were sold to another noble, the serf remained with the land and transferred his or her allegiance to the new lord. Living in huts with thatched roofs and limited furnishings, the serfs owed the lord certain obligations in exchange for the lord's protection and the right to live on the manor. These obligations included services such as several days of farm labor each week on the lord's farmlands and also a payment of a portion of the crops that were raised on the serf's land.

In the early days of feudalism in western Europe, serfs had only wooden plows and crude tools to work the land. Little was known about fertilizers or crop rotation. Each serf farmed strips of land scattered throughout the manor, which further hindered productivity. In the tenth century, heavy iron plows and crop rotation were introduced to western Europe, both of which increased agricultural productivity. By the year 1000, a more plentiful supply of food produced a significant rise in population.

The Lord's Military

Some vassals served specifically in the lords' army. Those who served as knights lived under a code of conduct called **chivalry**. Chivalry required several obligations: loyalty to God and the feudal lord; protection of the helpless; defense of Christianity; gallantry toward conquered enemies; honesty; justice; and courtesy to women. Sons of nobles began training for knighthood around the age of seven, and by their early teens were often given the opportunity to accompany a knight in a local battle. Around the age of twenty-one, men who had proven themselves worthy of the honor were knighted.

In the absence of central governments in western Europe, the small, independent feudal estates engaged in frequent warfare. Battering rams and siege towers, both used earlier by the Assyrians, were frequently used, as were catapults. Noblewomen often joined in the defense of the castle; when the lord of the manor was off at war, the lady had the responsibility for organizing the remaining knights of the manor. When not engaged in actual battle, knights sometimes participated in tournaments (mock battles between two opposing armies of knights) or in jousts (mock combat between two knights).

The Role of Women

The ideal of romantic love elevated noblewomen as objects of adoration, while the concept of chivalry added to the notion that women were weak and needed the protection of men. As feudalism progressed, the status of most women continued to decline. The Church taught that women were inferior to men.

Women were limited to traditional roles in the home or to life in the convent. Noblewomen had a few more privileges than the lower classes: A noblewoman could inherit the feudal estate from her husband and make decisions for him in his absence. A noteworthy example is Queen **Eleanor of Aquitaine**, who at times ruled England for her husband, Henry II, and her two sons, Richard and John. Among the lower classes, however, there was a considerable distinction between men and women: Women were not allowed to receive land in exchange for military service and held less property than men, with fiefs being willed to sons only.

THE DECENTRALIZATION OF JAPANESE GOVERNMENT

While western Europe was organizing itself into feudal estates, Japan was experiencing a period of decentralization of its government which displayed some parallels to western Europe. Japan was indebted to the Chinese for its Confucian values, Buddhist religion, system of writing, and concept of centralized government. But although the Japanese valued the Chinese concept of centralized rule, they placed little importance upon the elaborate bureaucracy of the Chinese government, preferring instead self-discipline and military ability. As the extravagant lifestyle of the Heian court grew, the centralized rule of Japan weakened. With the loss of centrality in the government, some families began to gain control of land and labor within little kingdoms that they carved out for themselves. One of these families, the Fujiwara, built up large estates. Within these estates, the local lord lived in a fortress surrounded by wooden or earthen walls and ditches similar to the moats found around the castles of medieval Europe. The Japanese estates were self-sufficient and included granaries for storing the rice cultivated by peasants, wells, and blacksmith shops.

Society Under Japanese Feudalism

The Japanese estates were administered by a social hierarchy with a class of warrior leaders, the ***bushi***, at the top. Bushi possessed the responsibilities of enforcing laws, supervising the construction of public works, and collecting taxes. To assist them in the protection of their property, they built up their own armies of soldiers called ***samurai***. Such a system of protection proved essential in eleventh- and twelfth-century Japan, as bandits roamed the countryside. The samurai lived by a code called ***bushido***, which stressed absolute loyalty to one's lord. Bushido was followed by both men and women of the samurai class who, in addition to protecting their lord, were expected to protect the emperor. The code of bushido emphasized the preservation of family honor and willingness to face death rather than the acceptance of defeat or retreat. When faced with the prospect of defeat, bushido provided for an honorable outcome through the custom of disembowelment, called ***seppuku***.

Because they were expected to provide the lord with military services, the samurai were released from agricultural responsibilities and were allowed a portion of the produce grown by peasants. The bushi and samurai depended on peasants to supply them with food while they devoted themselves to activities preparing them for war, such as archery and riding. Japanese peasants were placed in a subordinate position similar to that of serfs in medieval Europe. Unlike serfs, who were bound only to the land they worked, Japanese peasants were bound to both the land and their lord. To alleviate their dismal lives, Japanese peasants turned to a popular form of Buddhism called "the salvation pure land sect." This sect promised future joy in heaven for those who led upright lives in this world.

By the middle of the twelfth century, feuding among key Japanese families resulted in the Gempei Wars, in which farmlands were destroyed on the island of Honshu. After these wars ended, Japan preserved her figurehead emperor and his court, but actual power now rested in the hands of the Minamoto family and their samurai, who established a military government known as the *bakufu*, a word meaning "tent." The rule of the Minamoto saw the rise of military leaders called ***shoguns***. Lands belonging to the shoguns were doled out to their samurai, who pledged their loyalty to the shogun and provided him military protection. Between 1467 and 1477, civil war reigned in Japan, resulting in hundreds of tiny kingdoms with rulers called ***daimyo***.

THINGS TO REMEMBER

- Western Europe
    - After the breakup of the Roman empire, Germanic tribes ruled various regions of Western Europe.
    - In Gaul, a series of rulers including Clovis, Charles Martel, and Charlemagne brought centralized authority to their region. Charlemagne built an empire in the eighth and ninth centuries that included France, Germany and parts of Spain.
    - Church and secular leaders kept close ties to mutually strengthen their authority.
    - The first Christian monasteries and convents arose. Monks preserved manuscripts from Greco-Roman times by copying them.
    - In the 800s, a wave of Viking invasions terrorized Western Europe. The feudal system was set up for security.
    - Under feudalism, local lords of self-sufficient manors owed allegiance and military support to other lords rather than a central government. Most peasants were serfs, tied to the land and forced to work in the lord's fields.
    - Despite the status granted to women by the ideals of chivalry and courtly love, women's position declined. Some noblewomen could govern their husband's lands in his absence.
- Japan
    - The extravagance of the Heian court weakened Japan's central government.
    - In the tenth century, after a series of civil wars the Minamoto clan took power. Their leader was called shogun, and he held political authority instead of the emperor.
    - A feudal system emerged, with warriors (samurai) pledged to support lords (daimyo). Daimyo ruled estates farmed by peasants, who were tied to the land and their lord.
    - Aspects of the warrior's code of bushido resembled the European ideal of chivalry.

REVIEW QUESTIONS

1. After the fall of the Roman empire, all of the following were true EXCEPT

   (A) the Catholic Church served as a unifying force.
   (B) urban centers began to arise around 1100.
   (C) Germanic tribes continued to resist Christianity.
   (D) unified regional states arose.
   (E) Germanic peoples owed their loyalty to families and individuals.

2. Throughout the medieval period in western Europe,

   (A) the printing press spread religious literature.
   (B) the preservation of Greco-Roman culture was realized through the culture of Islamic Spain.
   (C) popes and kings cooperated to create order.
   (D) women were forbidden to enter religious orders.
   (E) Europeans had no opportunities to acquire an education.

3. Charlemagne is credited with all of the following EXCEPT

   (A) crafting the largest empire since the time of Rome.
   (B) fostering cooperative relations between church and state.
   (C) creating the *missi dominici* to help administer his empire.
   (D) tolerance of non-Christian peoples.
   (E) educating children in palace schools.

4. Under feudalism/manorialism in western Europe,

   (A) all peasants were bound to the land.
   (B) population continued to decline.
   (C) each serf was assigned to a plot in one portion of the manor.
   (D) women were allowed to receive a fief.
   (E) the independent feudal estates engaged in frequent warfare.

5. All of the following are true of Japan during its feudal period EXCEPT

   (A) it valued military ability over bureaucratic administration.
   (B) it was carved into self-sufficient estates.
   (C) *bushido* was practiced by men of the *samurai* and *bushi* classes.
   (D) it had a decentralized government.
   (E) *samurai* were released from agricultural responsibilities in exchange for military service.

ANSWERS AND EXPLANATIONS

1. (C)

Many Germanic tribes embraced Christianity; an example is the Franks. The hope of an afterlife offered by the Church brought unity to the people of western Europe (A). Around 1100, the increase in trade gave rise to more and more urban centers (B). The Franks are an example of the rise of regional states (D). Germanic tribes continued to owe their allegiance to clans and individual military rulers rather than to a central government (E).

2. (B)

The Muslim occupation of Spain served to preserve Greco-Roman culture. The printing press was not invented in Europe until the fifteenth century (A). Popes and secular rulers continued to vie for supremacy (C). Women were allowed to enter convents (D). Europeans had some opportunities to acquire an education through instruction from their parish priest, through the palace schools sponsored by Charlemagne, and through the new universities (E).

3. (D)

Charlemagne was noted for attempting to convert non-Christian people by force. His crowning by the pope illustrated his submission to the concept that the pope had the authority to select secular rulers, a right which strengthened church-state relationships (B).

4. (E)

Frequent military conflicts were a trademark of the lack of central government of the feudal period. Some peasants were free men and women (A). The European population began to rise in the tenth century (B). Serfs often had to work plots scattered throughout the manor, which hampered their work and the manor's efficiency (C). Women were not allowed to receive grants of land (D).

5. (C)

Bushido was expected of both men and women members of the samurai class, while chivalry pertained to knights only. Because of the value the Japanese place on military ability, they only partially accepted the bureaucratic nature of Chinese government (A). During its feudal period, Japan had a decentralized government of self-sufficient estates (B, D). The samurai were to devote their attention to military service (E).

CHAPTER 13

The Mongols and Eurasian Interactions

TIMELINE

1206–1227	Conquests of Chinggis Khan
1231	Mongol conquest of Persia
1231–1350	Yuan occupation of Korea
1237	Mongol invasion of Russia
1241–1242	Mongols advance into eastern Europe
1250–1350	Mongol Peace
1258	Mongol defeat of Abbasids in Baghdad
1260–1369	Yuan dynasty in China
1335	End of Mongol rule in Persia
1346–1351	Black Death
1480	End of Mongol presence in Russia

IMPORTANT PEOPLE, PLACES, EVENTS, AND CONCEPTS

Khanate of the Golden Horde
*qanat**
Alexander Nevsky
Kublai Khan
Yuan dynasty
Marco Polo
kamikaze*
Mongol Peace*
Black Death

MONGOL SOCIETY

The people of Mongolia (located to the northwest of China in central Asia) would dramatically alter the interactions and history of Europe and Asia. The Mongols were pastoral nomads organized into families, clans, and tribes. Their unique portable tents, or *yurts*, gave them the flexibility to travel from one location to another. The Mongols were expert warriors who could ride for days, even sleeping and eating in the saddle. In the thirteenth century, they began to migrate from the steppes of central Asia toward better grazing lands to the south and southwest.

The leaders of Mongol tribal councils were always men. Women, however, were allowed the right to speak out in the tribal councils and also held considerable influence within their own family.

MONGOL CONQUESTS

From 1206 to 1227, under the leadership of the formidable Temujin (who took the name Chinggis Khan, or "Universal Ruler"), the Mongols conquered vast portions of Asia. One of the great military strategists in world history, Chinggis Khan organized his military force into units independent of family ties. After breaking up tribes and forming new military units, Chinggis Khan chose talented leaders to take charge of his men. To show his power, he constructed a palace at Karakorum in Mongolia. Adopting Chinese siege warfare technology, he employed devices such as the catapult and gunpowder technology to further his conquests of other societies. Through his knowledge of steppe diplomacy, Chinggis Khan served to link Europe and Asia. After his death in 1227, his successors continued to acquire territory from China to Poland, creating the largest land empire in history to that time. For easier administration, the empire was divided into four regional empires: China, central Asia, Persia, and Russia (the **Khanate of the Golden Horde**).

The Mongols in Persia

Sweeping into Persia in 1231, the Mongols massacred hundreds of thousands of its inhabitants, interrupted trade, and destroyed cities, some of which never recovered. In 1258, Islamic civilization was dealt a crippling blow when Mongols defeated the Abbasids in Baghdad. Throughout Southwest Asia, the invaders destroyed ancient ***qanat*** irrigation systems. Eventually the Mongols allowed the Persians to rule their local territory as long as they paid tribute and maintained law and order. Mongols retained the highest governmental positions. Gradually, the Mongols in Persia assimilated to the local culture and often adopted Islam as their religion.

The Mongols in Russia and Central Europe

The Khanate of the Golden Horde demanded tribute from the Russians. The Mongol invasion of Russia in 1237 was the only time in history that a winter invasion of Russia succeeded. Mongol rule created a long-standing mistrust between Russia and Westerners by keeping Russia isolated from the lifestyle and technology of the Western world. The lack of Mongol concern with promoting cultural interests kept Russian areas such as Moscow culturally impoverished, isolating them from the cultural and economic wealth of the European Renaissance. Inept administration maintained Russia's economic backwardness. During Mongol rule, Russian peasants became serfs of the Russian ruling class in exchange for their protection.

Moscow finally rose to prominence when Prince **Alexander Nevsky** of Novgorod cooperated with the Mongols. Acting as a tribute collector for the Mongols after 1328, Nevsky's government annexed those territories that did not pay tribute, adding to the territory and power of Moscow. Granted the title of Grand Prince, Nevsky became the first of a line of princes who became leaders of Moscow and eventually all of Russia. In 1480, Ivan III of Moscow stopped paying taxes to the Mongol leader, effectively ending the Mongol presence in Russia. The Mongols continued to rule the Crimea until the end of the eighteenth century.

Even central Europe was not exempt from Mongol advances. In 1241 and 1242, the Mongols centered on the areas of present-day Poland, Hungary, and eastern Germany, reaching the outskirts of Vienna before they were finally turned back.

The Mongols in China

The grand prize of the Mongol invaders was their occupation of China, where they set up a tribute empire beginning in 1260. Under the leadership of **Kublai Khan**, the grandson of Chinggis Khan and founder of the **Yuan dynasty**, the Mongol capital was moved to the site of present-day Beijing, solidifying the tradition of a centralized government in China. Kublai Khan also extended the length of the Grand Canal to connect the Huang He River with Beijing in order to haul food supplies, especially rice, into Beijing. He ended the Confucian system of education and reliance on civil service examinations. Although he promoted Buddhism, Kublai Khan supported the right of Daoists, Muslims, and Christians to exercise their faith.

Distrustful of the Chinese, the Mongols brought foreign merchants and administrators into China and largely remained separate from the Chinese. They outlawed marriage between Mongols and Chinese and forbade the Chinese from studying the Mongol written language. Mongol women refused to engage in the Chinese custom of foot-binding. They also retained their property rights, enjoyed more freedom to move about publicly, and had considerable control over their household.

In addition to its presence in China, the Yuan Dynasty advanced into Vietnam, briefly occupying Hanoi but failing to conquer the country. Incursions into Cambodia, Burma, and Java proved unsuccessful, largely because the Mongols did not adapt well to the hot, humid climate of those areas. Attempts to conquer Indonesia and Japan also failed. Twice, in 1274 and 1281, massive Mongol forces were turned back from a successful invasion of the Japanese islands by a mighty wind the Japanese called ***kamikaze***. The aborted invasion of 1281 was one of the largest seaborne invasions prior to World War II. The Yuan Dynasty did occupy Korea from 1231 to 1350, requiring Koreans to pay tribute to the khan. The Mongol domination of China ended in 1369 when the Chinese defeated them and established the Ming Dynasty.

THE MONGOL PEACE

The Mongol presence in Eurasia led to a period of peace and prosperity for the continent. The so-called **Mongol Peace**, which endured from the 1250s to the 1350s, ensured the safety of travelers along trade routes in Eurasia and resulted in increased trade volume between Asia and Europe, most notably along the Silk Roads. The Mongols established foreign embassies and maintained diplomatic relations with Korea, Vietnam, India, and western Europe. The Mongols also resettled people in new lands and recruited craftsmen to better the lifestyle of those they ruled.

The Black Death

Increased trade was a contributing factor to the spread of the bubonic plague, or the **Black Death**, as Europeans called the disease. The plague had been unknowingly brought into China by Mongol invaders, whose food sacks had been invaded by infected rats and fleas. Appearing initially in southwestern China in the 1330s, the bubonic plague first spread throughout China and central Asia. By the late 1340s, it had spread throughout Southwestern Asia and then into Europe and northern Africa. Mongol invaders catapulted plague-infested bodies over the city walls of the Black Sea port of Kaffa in 1346, further transmitting the epidemic. Following the path of the trade routes, the disease spread from city to town, wiping out nearly half the population in areas it infected. Merchants in the Mediterranean compounded the problem by carrying plague from port to port.

By 1351, the plague had almost run its course in Europe. Approximately one-third of the European population had died, resulting in massive shortages of labor. Workers were demanding high wages, and when some authorities froze wages, rebellions broke out. The prestige of the Church declined as Europeans questioned its inability to halt the progress of the epidemic among them. Some areas of China reported losses of up to two-thirds of their population. The ravages of the plague exacted a 100-year recovery period in Europe and China. In Egypt, the Middle East, and other areas of the Islamic empire, recovery took even longer. Population levels in Egypt failed to recover completely until the nineteenth century.

THE FALL OF THE MONGOL EMPIRE

Poor administration and economic distress brought down the Mongol empire. In Persia, the Mongols' excessive spending caused them to print relatively valueless paper money. The resulting inflation caused merchants to close their shops. When the Mongol rule in Persia ended in 1335, the Persian government returned to local rule until the Turks reinstated centralized government in the late fourteenth century.

In China, the people rebelled against the valueless paper money. The devastation brought by the bubonic plague further weakened the Mongol rule. The desire of the Chinese to reassert their cultural identity after long years of Mongol rule strengthened the ability of the Ming Dynasty to return China to the Chinese. Even though they were ousted by the Chinese in 1369, the Mongols remained a constant threat to the northwestern borders of China into the eighteenth century.

THINGS TO REMEMBER

- In the thirteenth century, the Mongols (central Asian nomads) conquered nearly all of Asia, Russia, and eastern Europe (being halted at Vienna).
- The Mongols invaded Persia in 1231 and also defeated the Islamic caliphs in Baghdad in 1258. They destroyed cities and irrigation systems.
- Mongol rule in Russia lasted from 1237–1480.
- It isolated Russia from the economic, social, and artistic innovations of the European Renaissance.

    - Moscow became prominent because its prince collected taxes for the Mongols.
- The Mongol (Yuan) dynasty ruled China from 1260–1369.
    - It moved the capital to Beijing.
    - The Mongols brought foreign administrators to China.
    - They tried and failed to conquer Japan, Vietnam, Cambodia, and Burma.
- Mongol rule brought peace and facilitated trade between Europe and Asia along the Silk Roads.
    - Increased trade spread the Black Death through Asia and Europe in the mid-fourteenth century.
- The Mongols' inept government led to inflation and the collapse of their empire.

REVIEW QUESTIONS

1. The Mongols
   (A) adopted Chinese siege warfare technology.
   (B) were skilled administrators.
   (C) were pastoral nomads from southern Asia.
   (D) gave few privileges to women.
   (E) were accustomed to centralized government.

2. The Black Death
   (A) was confined to North Africa and China.
   (B) strengthened the position of the Church.
   (C) spread along the trade routes.
   (D) was more widespread in northern Europe than in Mediterranean areas.
   (E) was initially spread by the Mongols as a deliberate warfare tactic.

3. The Mongols
   (A) succeeded in their attempt to conquer Japan.
   (B) facilitated trade along the Silk Roads.
   (C) constructed cities and irrigation systems during their conquest of Persia.
   (D) had little respect for craftsmen and their work.
   (E) established no communications with western Europe.

4. All of the following are true of the Mongols EXCEPT
   (A) they created tribute empires.
   (B) they helped to link the eastern and western hemispheres.
   (C) they kept Russia isolated from the technology of the western world.
   (D) they reached the outskirts of Vienna, Austria.
   (E) they contributed to the economic prosperity of Russia.

5. In China, the Mongols broke with Chinese tradition by
   (A) forbidding foreign merchants to enter the country.
   (B) encouraging the Confucian system of education.
   (C) continuing civil service examinations.
   (D) imposing foot-binding on their women.
   (E) allowing foreign administrators to enter China.

ANSWERS AND EXPLANATIONS

1. (A)

The Mongols used catapults and gunpowder technology, both of which were used by the Chinese. They were noted as poor administrators (B) and were not accustomed to centralized government (E). They were pastoral nomads from central Asia (C) who allowed their women to speak out in tribal councils and carry considerable influence in the family (D).

2. (C)

The Black Death was spread primarily by traders. It also spread throughout Europe (A) and was particularly virulent in areas along the seacoast where trade was most active (D). The Black Death caused Europeans to become disillusioned with the power of the Church (B). It was inadvertently carried into China by the Mongols via fleas who penetrated their food sacks (E).

3. (B)

The Mongols created safe conditions for traders to move along the Silk Roads. Twice they failed in their invasions of Japan because of the *kamikaze* wind (A). In Persia, they destroyed cities and irrigation systems (C). They established communications with western Europe (E) and recruited craftsmen to improve the lifestyle of their people (D).

4. (E)

The inept administration of the Mongols hampered economic prosperity in Russia. The Mongol empire was characterized by the collection of tribute from conquered peoples (A). In protecting trade along the Silk Roads, they helped to link the hemispheres (B). Their lack of concern with technology and cultural pursuits kept Russia isolated from western technology (C). They penetrated into western Europe as far as Vienna before being turned back (D).

5. (E)

Chinese tradition tended to prevent the entrance of foreign administrators. Their tradition was to prevent the entrance of foreign merchants (A). Kublai Khan disbanded the Confucian system of education (B) and civil service examinations (C). The Mongol women did not engage in foot-binding (D).

CHAPTER 14

African Societies and Empires

TIMELINE

2000 BCE	Beginning of the Bantu migrations
1000 BCE	Arabs cross the Red Sea into Kush
200s CE	Berbers begin using the camel
325–360 CE	Kingdom of Aksum at its height
451 CE	Split between Coptic and mainstream Christianity
600s CE	Islam spreads across northwest Africa
710 CE	Muslims destroy Adulis in Aksum
1000s CE	Almoravids conquer Morocco
1000 CE	End of the major migratory period of the Bantu Rise of Bantu kingdoms
1076 CE	Almoravids conquer Ghana and portions of southern Spain
mid-1100s	Almoravids overpower the Almohads
1200s–1500s CE	Great Zimbabwe
1235 CE	Emergence of the kingdom of Mali
1352 CE	Travels of Ibn Battuta
1403 CE	Weakening of Mali
1403–1591 CE	Kingdom of Songhai

1480s CE	Benin comes into contact with the Portuguese
1500s CE	Portuguese introduce Catholicism to the Kongo

IMPORTANT PEOPLE, PLACES, EVENTS, AND CONCEPTS

Swahili*	age grade*	Benin
kinship group*	Sundiata	Great Zimbabwe
stateless society*	Mansa Musa	Ezana
animism*	Timbuktu	stele*
griot*	Ibn Battuta	

THE BANTU MIGRATIONS

While the Mongols were facilitating trade across the Eurasian continent, the Bantu of West Africa were nearing the end of a 3,000-year-old series of migrations that would bring them into contact with a variety of African and Islamic cultures. The Bantu-speaking peoples acquired their name as a result of the common features that linked their languages. Their ancestors, the proto-Bantu, lived along the edges of the rain forest in what is now the country of Nigeria. Around 2000 BCE, the Bantu-speaking people began migrating south and east across the continent of Africa, with their major migrations occurring between 700 and 500 BCE. Although historians are unsure of the exact cause of these migrations, one assumption is that the increase in population in west Africa was a factor.

As the Bantu-speaking people spread through sub-Saharan Africa, they encountered numerous foraging, or hunting-gathering, cultures that they absorbed into their own. At first scornful of these foreigners, the Bantu eventually learned the hunter-gatherers could offer them a wealth of information that would ease their transition into central Africa, including knowledge of cattle-raising. The enterprising Bantu adapted to their new surroundings by farming lands along the edges of the rain forests.

The Bantu people also benefited from the arrival of the banana to the African mainland; the banana, which originated in Southeast Asia, was transported to the island of Madagascar off the southeastern coast of Africa by the Malay sailors, who were traders in the Indian Ocean. (Today the language of the people of Madagascar bears a strong resemblance to that of Malaysia.) The banana spread northward and westward throughout Africa, following in reverse the path followed by the migratory Bantu. The arrival of the banana provided the additional calories and nutrients that resulted in an increase in the population of the Bantu speakers.

The Bantu speakers altered the linguistic patterns of sub-Saharan Africa by spreading their language. As the Bantu migrated into eastern Africa, they encountered territories under Arabic influence. The Bantu languages, from the Niger-Congo language family, would blend with Arabic, creating a new language called **Swahili**; Swahili would become a widely spoken language among the peoples of East Africa.

Evidence exists that by 700 BCE there was iron smelting in the original homeland of the Bantu in western Africa. From there, the knowledge of iron smelting diffused throughout central and southern Africa in a pattern that corresponds to the spread of the Bantu languages throughout Africa. Thus, historians assume that the Bantu spread not only their language but also the knowledge of iron as they made their way through sub-Saharan Africa.

Bantu Settlements

By about 1000 CE, the major migratory period of the Bantu peoples had ceased. (Some migrations, however, would continue until the mid-1800s and would bring the Bantu into contact with the Khoisan of South Africa.) As the Bantu settled into a sedentary existence, they began to engage in long-distance trade in metals, pottery, canoes, and other regional crafts. Originally the Bantu were organized into villages based on family and **kinship groups**. These **stateless societies** were led by a family member who served as leader of the family or clan. Rulers and religious leaders constituted the elite of Bantu society. Private property was an unknown concept; all property was held in common. As followers of **animism**, or a religion based on a belief that spirits inhabit the features of the natural world, the Bantu especially revered the spirits of their ancestors. Tribal traditions were passed on orally through storytellers called ***griots***.

Within the villages, the most significant social group was the **age grade**, a type of cohort group in which tribal members of a common age range shared experiences common to that age group and were expected to carry out the responsibilities appropriate for their age. In addition to the age grade, gender expectations helped define society. Among the Bantu, both men and women shared the duties of planting and harvesting. Women were respected as sources of life and sometimes held positions of power in trading activities and in the military. Since the concept of private property was nonexistent among the Bantu, personal wealth was determined by the number of slaves one held.

Slaves were often captives of war, debtors, criminals, or accused witches. As the Bantu became acquainted with the Muslim societies of eastern Africa, they became connected with the Muslim slave trade in the Indian Ocean. Slaves from central and eastern Africa, frequently captured by their fellow Africans in slave raids, often found themselves transported by Muslim traders across the Indian Ocean to South Asia and the Far East. There they were purchased, usually to work as household servants.

The Formation of Kingdoms Among the Bantu

Sometime after 1000 CE, the settled Bantu people began to see the rise of kingdoms in their society. Prominent among them was the Kingdom of Kongo in central Africa. Encompassing the territory of present-day Angola and the Democratic Republic of Congo, Kongo became a centralized state among the Bantu speakers. It established a system of currency based on cowrie shells gathered from the Indian Ocean. The kingdom of Kongo would remain strong until the arrival of the Portuguese on the east coast of Africa in the mid-1500s.

EMPIRES OF WEST AFRICA

While the Bantu-speaking peoples were involved in waves of migration across the African continent, the Muslims were also making their mark in Africa. In the seventh century, Islam swept across the northwest portion of Africa, gaining converts both by conquest and by peaceful conversions. By the late seventh century, the Muslims had entered Egypt and areas along the Mediterranean coast of Africa. Among the converts to Islam were the Berbers, who would unite under the Almohad and Almoravid dynasties to bring North Africa under Muslim rule. In the eleventh century, the Almoravids conquered Morocco, founding the city of Marrakech, and took the West African empire of Ghana. They also captured portions of southern Spain, where they were known to the Spanish as the Moors. In the mid-twelfth century, the Almohads were overpowered by the Almoravids, who furthered the conquest of southern Spain. The Muslim presence in Africa would spark trade connections among African societies and kingdoms and between Africa and areas in the Indian Ocean basin.

The Kingdom of Ghana

While the Muslims were solidifying their hold in North Africa, powerful empires were rising in West Africa. Trade across the harsh Sahara was sporadic until the third century, when Berber nomads began using the camel. By the 700s, trans-Saharan trade had grown to the point that the natives of West Africa were growing increasingly wealthy from taxing trade goods that moved across their territory. The two most important items traded were gold, which could be found in abundance in the sub-Saharan region between the Niger and Senegal Rivers, and salt, a product of the Sahara. The savannas and forests of West Africa lacked salt, an element so vital to human health that it was worth nearly as much as gold.

By 800, the kingdom of Ghana in West Africa had grown into an empire. Islam was introduced into the empire by Muslim traders and merchants from North Africa. The rulers of Ghana converted to Islam, prompting a rise in literacy since those in the upper-class who followed their example had to learn Arabic in order to read the Qur'an. When the Almoravid dynasty completed its conquest of Ghana in 1076, the gold-salt trade was interrupted, causing a permanent decline in the power of Ghana. After the decline of Ghana, new gold deposits were discovered farther east and the trade routes shifted to accommodate the new discovery.

The Empire of Mali

By 1235 a new empire, Mali, had emerged. Like Ghana, Mali also became extremely wealthy from the taxation of trade goods. Mali's first great emperor, **Sundiata**, provided an efficient military and a strong government, both of which promoted the prosperity of Mali. The most famous of Sundiata's successors was the Muslim leader **Mansa Musa**, who exercised strict control over the gold–salt trade. While making the hajj to Mecca in 1324 and 1325, Mansa Musa stopped over at Cairo, where he distributed such lavish quantities of gold that he inflated the currency of Cairo for years afterward. Upon his return to Mali, he devoted his efforts to establishing the trading city of **Timbuktu** as one of the leading cities of his empire. Timbuktu would grow to offer universities and mosques that would attract religious leaders, scholars, and professionals. In 1352, a Muslim traveler named **Ibn Battuta**, who was on a tour of most of the countries of the Islamic world, visited the court of Mansa Musa. Ibn Battuta admired the splendor of Timbuktu and its lack of crime. By 1403, however, weak successors to Mansa Musa and a further shift of the gold fields farther east prompted the weakening of Mali.

The Empire of Songhai

As Mali declined, a third empire rose in West Africa in 1403: Songhai, with Gao as its capital. The people of Songhai extended their empire to embrace the new location of gold deposits. However, crippled by the lack of modern weapons, Songhai succumbed in 1591 to a Moroccan force in possession of gunpowder and cannons.

West Africa was now left in the hands of societies such as the Hansa, noted for its cloth anad leather goods, and the Yoruba, in modern-day **Benin** and Nigeria, who did fine handiwork in terra cotta, brass, bronze, and copper. The kingdom of Benin, near the delta of the Niger River, also gained fame for its craftsmanship in brass and copper. By the 1480s, the people of Benin had come into contact with the Portuguese, who, like the Muslims who would influence eastern Africa, became actively involved in the trade of leopard skins, ivory, pepper, and slaves. Thus, by 1500, both the Muslim and European worlds had already gained a firm hold in Africa.

EASTERN AND SOUTHERN AFRICAN SETTLEMENTS

As previously noted, the Bantu people had an influence on the Swahili language of East Africa. Eventually the term "Swahili" was applied to both the language blend of Arabic and Bantu and also to the people of African and Arabic descent. Residing in the coastal areas of East Africa, the originators of the Swahili society gained their livelihood through agriculture and through fishing and trade in the Indian Ocean. The trade cities that developed along the east coast of Africa (from Mozambique to the horn of Africa) reflected the contact between native African peoples and Muslims from Arabia, Persia, and India, in addition to the Chinese. By the tenth century, the Swahili people had joined many of their fellow Africans in the hunt for slaves from the interior of the continent. In addition to slaves, the Swahili obtained ivory, tortoise shells, leopard skins, and gold, all of which became profitable items in the Indian Ocean trade. From Muslim traders the Swahili acquired products such as textiles, glass, and pottery from Persia, China, and India. The prosperity of the Swahili traders could be seen in the buildings of coral that the wealthier Muslim members of their society constructed in their towns and cities. Non-Muslims dwelled in houses of mud and thatch that surrounded the more opulent coral homes of the Muslim elite.

By the fifteenth century, the larger Swahili towns boasted stone buildings. The wealthy used porcelain tableware from China. Inhabitants of the east African town of Kilwa obtained slaves, ivory, and gold from the interior of Africa to trade for cotton, perfumes, silk, and pearls from India.

Great Zimbabwe

The kingdom of Zimbabwe dominated a major portion of southeastern Africa to the coastal areas of the Indian Ocean. Discoveries of glass beads and porcelain from South Asia and the Far East are evidence of trade connections between these regions and the Arab port of Sofala, with which Zimbabwe had developed commercial ties. The city of **Great Zimbabwe** was located near a trade route that connected the gold fields of central Africa with Sofala. After Great Zimbabwe gained control of this route in the 1200s, it became the capital of Zimbabwe, thriving on the collection of taxes from the traders who used the route. The most impressive feature of Great Zimbabwe was its massive stone walls built without the use of mortar, perhaps constructed to impress outsiders. By the sixteenth century, Great Zimbabwe had fallen prey to internal strife and soil exhaustion through the overgrazing of its cattle.

Muslim Converts in East Africa

Contact with Arabs involved in the Indian Ocean trade resulted in the conversion of eastern and central African rulers and merchants to Islam. Although the elite who were involved in trans-oceanic trade readily saw the commercial value of conversion to Islam, the common people of the African villages were reluctant to convert and largely retained their tribal customs. One source of controversy between sub-Saharan Africans and the Islamic faith was the treatment of women: Some African societies tended to offer significantly greater gender equality than did traditional Islamic societies. Later, in the 1700s, when the commoners did begin to convert to Islam, they maintained some of their tribal beliefs and blended them with the precepts of Islam. Sub-Saharan women who had converted to Islam, for example, often did not wear the veil required in traditional Islamic societies.

African Christianity

The hybridization of a major world religion with local beliefs was not confined to Muslim-dominated areas of Africa. Another example was Ethiopia, where the Ethiopian version of Christianity also blended with African tribal religions. The kingdom of Aksum was located near the Red Sea in what is now Ethiopia and Eritrea. Around 1000 BCE, Arabs crossed the Red Sea into Africa, where they blended with the people of Kush, contributing their written language, Ge'ez. Aksum expanded its original territory by controlling a section of territory in the southwestern portion of the Arabian Peninsula. Aksum's geographical location placed it at the center of caravan routes to Egypt and Meroë as well as to trade routes in the Mediterranean basin and the Indian Ocean. Its trade connections to the Roman empire and areas as far away as India made its chief port city of Adulis an international trade center. The power of Aksum was further strengthened between 325 and 360 CE when its strongest ruler, **Ezana**, ascended the throne. Acquiring more territory in the Arabian Peninsula, Ezana also conquered Kush and burned the city of Meroë.

Because of the diversity of its trading partners, the culture of Aksum took on an international flavor, with Greek emerging as the major language among a wide spectrum of tongues. The merchants in Aksum brought not only exotic goods but also Christianity, which had already spread throughout the Roman empire. The conversion of Ezana to Christianity strengthened its position in Aksum. In 451 CE, the Church of Egypt and Ethiopia broke off from the mainstream Church over a controversy regarding the human and divine natures of Christ.

The prosperous Aksum minted its own coins and developed a characteristic architectural structure, a stone pillar called a ***stele***. Built of carved stones fit together without the use of mortar, the stele were among the tallest structures in the ancient world. In 710, the Muslims swept through Aksum, destroying Adulis. Cut off from other Christian territories by the advancing Muslims, Aksum was forced to move inland, where it eventually declined as an international power.

THINGS TO REMEMBER

- The migration of the Bantu-speaking people from West Africa to the south and east (2000 BCE–1000 CE) prompted many developments:
    - The Bantu-speakers spread their language. In the eastern port areas under Arabian influence, Bantu blended with Arabic to create Swahili.
    - The migrants spread the knowledge of iron-working throughout sub-Saharan Africa.
    - Bantu society consisted of kin-based villages, the concept of private property did not exist, and slaveholding was common.
    - The Kingdom of Kongo, a Bantu society, existed from after 1000 CE to the mid-1500s.
- The West African kingdoms of Ghana, Mali, and Songhai were based on profits from the trans-Saharan gold-salt trade.
- Islam spread across North Africa and into Spain via the Berbers.
- In East Africa, Muslims and later the Portuguese established trade between the interior of Africa and the Indian Ocean.
- Islam and Christianity both gained converts in East Africa.
- Slave trading was common to all African societies, whether with other African societies or with foreign merchants from Europe or Asia.

REVIEW QUESTIONS

1. All of the following are true about the banana EXCEPT

    (A) it resulted in a population increase among the Bantu.
    (B) it originated in East Africa.
    (C) it was transported by the Malay sailors.
    (D) its path was traced through linguistic connections.
    (E) it was transported through the Indian Ocean to Madagascar.

2. All of the following are true of the Bantu EXCEPT

    (A) they contributed to the origins of the Swahili language.
    (B) they knew the use of private property.
    (C) they established a stateless society.
    (D) they may have migrated to move away from areas of high population.
    (E) they allowed women to hold positions of power.

3. All of the following were true concerning the kingdoms of West Africa EXCEPT

    (A) they learned of Islam from North African traders.
    (B) they valued education so that people could read the Qur'an in Arabic.
    (C) the prospered through the trans-Saharan gold-salt trade.
    (D) they were plagued by a series of ineffective rulers.
    (E) they taxed goods transported through their territory.

4. With regard to the influence of Islam in Africa,

    (A) African women tended to have fewer privileges than Islamic women.
    (B) the lower classes were more eager to convert to Islam than the elite.
    (C) contacts with Islam were generated by the trans-Atlantic trade.
    (D) African rulers feared that conversion to Islam would undermine their authority.
    (E) converts to Islam tended to blend Islam and their tribal beliefs.

5. With regard to Christian areas in Africa, all of the following are true EXCEPT

    (A) the Ethiopian version of Christianity blended with African tribal religions.
    (B) African Christians had no commercial or cultural contacts with western Europe.
    (C) the Ge'ez language is a blend of the languages of Arabia and Kush.
    (D) Coptic Christianity differs from mainstream Christianity in its perception of the nature of Christ.
    (E) Adulis was an international trade center.

ANSWERS AND EXPLANATIONS

1. (B)

The banana originated in Southeast Asia and was transported through the Indian Ocean by the Malay sailors (C) to Madagascar (E). This fact is borne out by the similarities in the languages of Malaysia and Madagascar (D). From Madagascar the banana made its way to Africa, where it was introduced to the Bantu, whose population increased with the addition of the banana to their diet (A).

2. (B)

The Bantu did not know the use of private property, but rather communal property. They lived in a stateless society which was governed by kinship groups (C). Within this society women had opportunities to assume leadership positions (E). They blended their language with Arabic to form the Swahili language (A). Their migrations may have been caused by their original homeland in a densely populated area in the vicinity of modern Nigeria (D).

3. (D)

The West African kingdoms were known for their capable rulers, such as Mansa Musa. They prospered by taxing goods moving through their territory on the gold-salt trade route (C, E). Islam was introduced to West Africa by Islamic peoples of North Africa (A). West Africa became a center of Islamic learning (B).

4. (E)

African converts to Islam did not totally relinquish their tribal beliefs. Many African women had more privileges than Islamic women (A). The elite were more interested in conversion to Islam than the common people (B). Contacts with Islam were generated by Indian Ocean and Mediterranean trade (C). African rulers were aware that acceptance of Islam was a commercial advantage (D).

5. (B)

African Christians had contacts with Rome through trade. Christianity, like Islam, found its converts blending their new faith with their tribal beliefs (A). Coptic Christianity stresses the divine over the human nature of Christ (D).

CHAPTER 15

The Rise of Nation-States in Europe

TIMELINE

900s	Viking invasions subside
987–1328	Capetian rule
1016	Canute conquers Britain
1066	Battle of Hastings
1187	Saladin recaptures Jerusalem
1192	Truce with Saladin allows Christians to visit Jerusalem
1202–1204	Fourth Crusade, Constantinople plundered
1212	Children's Crusade
1215	Magna Carta
1265	The Great Council
1295	Model Parliament
1337–1453	Hundred Years' War

IMPORTANT PEOPLE, PLACES, EVENTS, AND CONCEPTS

Pope Urban II
Peter the Hermit
Saladin
bourgeoisie*
domestic system*
usury*
guild*
apprenticeship*
burgess*
burgher*
William the Conqueror
Magna Carta*
parliament*
Estates-General*
Third Estate
Great Schism
Joan of Arc

THE REVIVAL OF TRADE IN EUROPE

By the tenth century, the wave of Viking invasions that had caused the rise of feudalism in western Europe had subsided; the Vikings had settled down in locations such as Normandy, and many of them had accepted Christianity. The new security that accompanied the end of the Viking threat produced a revival of trade in western Europe. Between 1000 and 1300, the population of western Europe tripled and agricultural production thrived. The surplus of food made its way to the marketplaces, where it promoted a return to the usage of currency. The return of gold coins was a sure sign that prosperity was returning to the European continent.

THE CRUSADES

In 1095, **Pope Urban II** sent out a call for Christian knights to take up the mission of seizing the Holy Land from the Seljuk Turks. He was aided in his appeal by a wandering monk named **Peter the Hermit**, who assembled an army of poor knights and peasants who then left for the Holy Land without adequate weapons, supplies, or plans. This first group failed in its mission to reach the Holy Land, but it did prompt the organization of the First Crusade.

Organized by French and Norman nobles to recover the Holy Land from the Seljuks, the First Crusade was the only crusade that succeeded in capturing the Holy Land. Jerusalem was overtaken by the Christians, who carved it into feudal states and maintained control for more than 100 years. The internal division that already existed among the Seljuk Turks was a factor in the success of the First Crusade.

By 1187, the Muslim leader **Saladin** had recaptured Jerusalem. Several other Crusades were attempted, but none were successful. In the Third Crusade, led by three European monarchs (Philip Augustus of France, Frederick Barbarossa of the Holy Roman Empire, and Richard the Lion-Hearted of England), only King Richard remained to attempt to regain the Holy Land from Saladin after Barbarossa drowned en route and Philip Augustus returned home after arguing with Richard. A truce signed in 1192 maintained Muslim control over the Holy Land, and Saladin agreed to allow Christian pilgrims to visit Jerusalem. A Fourth Crusade from 1202 to 1204 resulted in the crusaders' plundering Constantinople, an event from which the city never fully recovered. Perhaps the most tragic crusade was the Children's Crusade of 1212: Of the thousands of children who set out for Jerusalem, many died from exposure or starvation; others turned back. Those that continued either drowned at sea or were sold into slavery; none reached the Holy Land.

The Role of Italian and Viking Traders

Even before the onset of the Crusades, the Italian city-states had established some contacts with rulers in the Middle East and had won commercial privileges in Constantinople, Syria, Palestine, and North Africa. By the time the Crusades were at their height, Italian fleets were large enough to move armies. Ships carrying crusaders to the Holy Land brought return cargoes of luxury goods from the East. These goods were then taken by pack train from the Italian seaports through northern Italy and into central and northern Europe; cities would rise along these trade routes.

Viking traders also served to acquaint northern Europe with the luxuries of the East. Even before 1000, the Vikings were traveling from Kiev to the Black Sea and Constantinople to acquire the treasures of the East and transport them to northern Europe.

Results of the Crusades

The results of the Crusades were many and far-reaching:

- **They created further economic growth in western Europe** as the Europeans, through knowledge of the East acquired during the Crusades, desired luxury goods and spices from the Middle and Far East, such as sugar, citrus fruits, cotton cloth, carpets, paper, glassware, and precious stones.
- Through the Crusades, **Europeans learned of new technology** such as gunpowder.
- **The Crusades increased the power of European monarchs**, as the nobles sold off their lands to kings to pay for their journeys to the Holy Land. Other nobles lost their lives in the Crusades. Merchants, who were impressed with the law and order a stable monarchy could bring, favored the rise of kings.
- **The Christian Church acquired more political power.**
- **The status of women improved** as they managed the family property while male members left on the Crusades, or participated in the Crusades themselves.
- **New ideas were exchanged** as Europeans saw in the East a prosperity with which they were not familiar, such as great cities, active trade and industry, and achievements in the arts and sciences.
- **Italian city-states flourished** from selling supplies and providing ships to transport Crusaders to the Holy Land.
- Throughout Europe, **trade increased, money increasingly replaced barter, urban populations grew, and a new social class, the middle class, or bourgeoisie, arose.** Composed largely of merchants, bankers, and professionals, the bourgeoisie would play an integral role in the future of western Europe.

These changes marked the beginning of the end of the western European Middle Ages.

LIFE IN THE HIGH MIDDLE AGES

Trade Centers, Markets, and Fairs

Another area in western Europe whose prosperity was owed to the rebirth of trade was Flanders, encompassing part of modern Belgium and northern France. The prosperity of Flanders resulted from its location as the hub of trade routes that traveled across France, down the Rhine River in modern Germany, across the English Channel, and south from the Baltic Sea. Flanders, which produced fine woolen cloth from British raw wool, eventually became the textile headquarters of Europe, and its chief cities of Bruges, Ypres, and Ghent became wealthy.

The Germanic cities of Hamburg, Lübeck, and Bremen, all commercial centers on the North and Baltic Seas, formed the Hanseatic League. Eventually adding more than seventy cities to its membership, the league set up permanent trading centers in Flanders, Russia, England, and Scandinavia. The league ensured free trade among its numbers, eliminated piracy from the northern seas, and established regulations for fair trade.

Markets and fairs also supplied avenues for the exchange of goods. Some European feudal lords set up fairs to sell imported goods and gained income by charging taxes on merchandise sold. The fairs in the Champagne region in northeastern France evolved into a central marketplace for Europe. Money changers were on hand to ease transactions. Entertainers such as musicians, clowns, and jugglers delighted fairgoers as merchants from distant places exchanged new ideas.

Manufacturing and Banking

In addition to the diversion and contacts provided through markets and fairs, the High Middle Ages also saw the rise of manufacturing, banking, and investment. Early manufacturing in western Europe was based on the **domestic system**, in which goods were produced in the homes of workers. Manufacturers would supply raw materials to home workers, who would then produce the finished product.

Money changers often turned to money lending, charging excessive interest rates of eight percent or higher. The Roman Catholic Church's prohibition of the charging of interest, or **usury**, had left most money changing to non-Christians during the early Middle Ages. During the High Middle Ages, Christians began to pursue money lending; instead of collecting interest, they charged rents and fees for services. To facilitate transporting money from one location to another along trade routes, letters of credit that somewhat resembled checking accounts were issued. As time went on, the capital earned through banking and money lending activities was often invested in enterprises such as shipbuilding, giving rise to a market economy in which entrepreneurs would combine land, labor, and capital to engage in manufacturing and business ventures.

The Growth of Towns

An increase in urbanization accompanied the rise of manufacturing, banking, and investment in western Europe, especially in Italy and Flanders. There was also an increased desire for self-government. Initially, towns were controlled by feudal lords who sometimes granted them a degree of self-rule in order to promote the towns' development. According to feudal practice, serfs who escaped the manor and lived in towns for a year and a day without capture would become free men and women.

Town merchants founded organizations called ***guilds*** to regulate trade. The guilds ensured the use of honest weights and measures and uniform prices and also acted as charitable organizations. Although guild leaders were men, most guilds allowed women members. Craft guilds had the specific task of regulating wages and setting hours and conditions of labor. They also established a system of training craftsmen known as apprenticeship. Townspeople who engaged in commerce, banking, craftsmanship, and manufacturing created a new middle class, called ***bourgeoisie*** in France, ***burgesses*** in England, and ***burghers*** in Germany.

Cities now had the opportunity to define their own laws regarding manufacturing and trade. These new autonomous cities benefited kings, who took steps to centralize the government by consolidating territories that would eventually become national kingdoms.

The Black Death

The swelling population of western Europe was dealt a devastating blow between 1346 and 1351 with the arrival of the bubonic plague, or Black Death. Introduced via disease-carrying rodents from central Asia by the Mongols, the plague first reached China, killing 25,000,000 people. The plague then proceeded to follow the trade routes to the Middle East, North Africa, and Europe, where it killed about one-third of the population. The devastation among the serf population decimated the work force and dealt a final blow to feudalism.

The Agricultural Revolution

Accompanying the economic changes of the High Middle Ages was an agricultural revolution featuring new farm tools and techniques that further increased agricultural output and population growth. Many of the new techniques had been learned from contact with eastern Europeans and Asians occupying central Europe. An improved plow allowed peasants to turn over the soil with greater ease; a more advanced harness for pulling wagons led to the replacement of oxen with horses. The two-field system of the early Middle Ages was replaced by the three-field system, in which two-thirds of the land was planted and the third section was left fallow. Rotation of crops in planted fields led to greater agricultural productivity. As productivity improved, some feudal lords developed new farmlands, giving the serfs an opportunity to leave the manor permanently.

THE RISE OF CENTRALIZED GOVERNMENT IN ENGLAND

The Viking invasions that had buffeted the European continent had extended to Great Britain. When King Alfred the Great (871–899) expelled the Vikings, he united England under one rule (naming it England after the Angles, a Germanic tribe that had invaded Britain during the 400s). In 1016, the Vikings and Anglo-Saxons were united when the Danish king Canute conquered Britain. King Edward the Confessor, a descendant of Alfred the Great, began his reign in 1042, but died in 1066 without an heir. Harold, an Anglo-Saxon, rose to claim the throne of England, but he would soon learn of another claimant to the throne. The subsequent struggle for the throne of England resulted in the invasion of the Norman people, who would add their language and culture to that of Anglo-Saxon England.

The Norman Invasion

Normandy, a region in northern France, had been settled by the Vikings during their wave of invasions beginning in the 800s. The Normans were descendants of the Vikings who had adopted the French culture and language. Their leader was William, Duke of Normandy, who was a cousin of Edward the Confessor. William was willing to battle Harold for the crown of England. On October 14, 1066, the Battle of Hastings raged between Harold and William. Harold was killed in the course of the battle, placing the throne of England in the hands of **William the Conqueror**. No foreign power has successfully invaded Britain since that time.

William began his reign by claiming all England as his personal property. He granted fiefs to Norman lords, who then owed allegiance to William personally rather than to a lesser feudal lord. William's model of feudalism set the stage for the beginnings of centralized government in Britain.

The Beginnings of Democracy in England

William the Conqueror's descendant Henry II expanded his landholdings when he married Eleanor of Aquitaine. Besides bringing to her marriage additional French lands, Eleanor had the distinction of being a wife to two kings and mother to two kings. Her first marriage to Louis VII of France ended in annulment, whereupon she married Henry Plantagenet, later Henry II of England. Two of their four sons became English kings: Richard the Lion-Hearted and John. During the reign of Henry II (1154–1189), jury trials were introduced to English courts of law. Henry also sent royal judges to various parts of England to settle disputes, punish wrongdoers, and collect taxes. As the centuries progressed, the decisions of royal judges would form the basis of English common law, which in turn would influence law in many other English-speaking countries, including the United States.

Henry II was succeeded by his son Richard and, upon Richard's death, by his son John (1199–1216). John's loss of English landholdings in France prompted his nobles to revolt against paying exorbitant taxes to finance John's wars. In June 1215, the nobles capitalized on John's weaknesses by drawing up a document of basic political rights which they then forced John to sign. The document, called the **Magna Carta**, limited the powers of the king and protected the rights of nobles. Later the English people claimed many of the rights of the Magna Carta as applicable to every English citizen, making it one of the most treasured documents in English law. Among rights guaranteed by the Magna Carta are the jury trial, protection under the law, and the right not to be taxed without representation in a legislative body.

Another critical step in the democratic process was the establishment of the first English legislative body, or **parliament**, which emerged from the Great Council. The Great Council was initially a body of key nobles and church leaders who served as advisors to the king, but in 1265 it expanded to include two knights from each shire and two burgesses, or middle-class citizens, from each town. In 1295, King Edward's need to raise taxes for a war against the French resulted in the calling of the first parliament. The first parliament, or Model Parliament, brought together two burgesses from every borough and two knights from every county. Eventually the burgesses and knights would form the House of Commons, and bishops and nobles would form the House of Lords, establishing the basic structure of today's British Parliament.

THE BEGINNINGS OF CENTRALIZED GOVERNMENT IN FRANCE

Feudal relationships in France also formed the basis for the establishment of regional monarchies. After the breakup of Charlemagne's empire, local rulers governed France under a feudal system. In 987, these feudal lords elected a minor official named Hugh Capet as their king. Capet would be the first of the Capetian kings, who would govern France from 987 to 1328. Though initially weak, the Capetian kings added to their territory by absorbing lands from nobles who died without heirs. The family of Hugh Capet ruled only a small area in the center of France around Paris, but this territory also embraced portions of major trade routes in northern France. By the early fourteenth century, the Capetians had brought centralized authority to most of France.

Several Capetian kings were especially gifted at strengthening the power of the monarchy over that of feudal lords. Philip Augustus, or Philip II (1180–1223), expanded French territory by taking Normandy from King John of England and seizing other lands as well. He also installed a system by which bailiffs, or royal officials, would travel throughout France, presiding over royal courts and collecting taxes. Philip's grandson Louis the Pious, or Louis IX, who reigned from 1226 to 1270, created an appeals court that had the authority to overturn decisions of local courts. When Louis experienced a conflict with the pope over payment of taxes to the monarchy, he created a new government group of common people called the **Third Estate** to participate in the French legislative body, or **Estates- General**. The Third Estate united with the already existent First Estate, (the clergy) and the Second Estate (the nobility).

SECULAR V. PAPAL AUTHORITY

As both England and France took significant steps to develop democratic traditions among their people, the power of the monarchy was challenged by the Church. The subject of the controversy was the Church's assertion that monarchs were subject to the authority of the popes. Philip IV of France responded to this edict by holding Pope Boniface VIII prisoner in 1303; the pope was eventually released, and he died shortly thereafter.

Under Philip's persuasion, the College of Cardinals chose a French archbishop as pope. The new pope, Clement V, chose to reside in Avignon, France, rather than in Rome. The popes would remain headquartered in Avignon until 1378, when Pope Gregory XI died while on a trip to Rome. The College of Cardinals then angered the French by selecting an Italian reformer, Urban VI, as pope. French cardinals responded by choosing the French-speaking Pope Clement VII—meaning that the Roman Catholic Church now had two popes. This controversy, known as the **Great Schism**, culminated with each pope excommunicating the other. Ultimately the issue was resolved by the Council of Constance, which in 1417 chose a new pope, Martin V. Division within the Church, accompanied by the loss of confidence in the Church resulting from the Black Death, would create a disillusionment that would set the stage for the religious upheaval known as the Protestant Reformation.

THE HUNDRED YEARS' WAR

The final blow to feudalism was dealt by the Hundred Years' War. When the last member of the Capetian dynasty died without an heir, King Edward III of England (grandson of Philip IV) claimed the throne. This claim set up a war for the French throne that lasted from 1337 to 1453. Although English longbowmen demonstrated their superiority by defeating the French in the battles of Crécy, Poitiers, and Agincourt, the French monarchs were the ultimate victors.

The heroine of the Hundred Years' War was a French teenager named **Joan of Arc**. In 1429, convinced that heavenly voices were directing her to rescue France from the English, Joan of Arc led the French army to move against an English fort blocking the way to Orléans. Leading the French army in a charge against the English fort, Joan of Arc succeeded in breaking the siege of Orléans. After the battle, she convinced the son of the previous French king, Charles VI, to accompany her to Reims; there he was crowned king, restoring the French throne to a French monarch. Captured the following year by the English, Joan of Arc was condemned as a heretic and burned at the stake in 1431.

The Hundred Years' War contributed to the development of the nation-state in Europe by elevating the power of the French king and promoting a spirit of nationalism in both England and France. The demise of feudalism, accompanied by the growth of towns and the rise of universities, would lead to an ever-increasing appreciation for learning and the development of self-rule in western Europe.

THINGS TO REMEMBER

- In Western Europe between 1000 and 1300, new agricultural tools and techniques led to population increases and food surpluses.
- The end of the Viking raids created the stability required for trade in Europe, while people returning from the Crusades brought knowledge of new products from the Middle and Far East.
- Growth in trade and population led to the rise of towns, craftsmanship, banking, and investment. A middle class of townspeople emerged from the peasant population.
- Merchants supported the strengthening of the power of monarchs because it halted feudal wars.
- The Crusades and the Hundred Years' War increased the power of the kings and weakened the nobles.
- In 1215, English nobles forced King John to sign the Magna Carta. This document guaranteed basic rights to the nobles, including protection under the law, jury trials, and representation in a legislative body.
- In France, the Capetian royal family asserted its power. Common people gained a voice in government with the creation of the Third Estate, a representative group in the French legislature (Estates-General).
- The Black Death struck Europe between 1346 and 1361. It killed one-third of the people, causing labor shortages that crippled the manors. It weakened the power of the Church.

REVIEW QUESTIONS

1. As a result of the Crusades,

   (A) the power of the Church weakened.
   (B) the power of European monarchs weakened.
   (C) the middle class arose.
   (D) the status of women declined.
   (E) Italian city-states suffered economically.

2. All of the following were features of city life in the High Middle Ages in western Europe EXCEPT

   (A) fairs and central marketplaces.
   (B) the beginnings of a market economy.
   (C) police protection.
   (D) trade.
   (E) manufacturing.

3. All of the following were true of towns in medieval Europe EXCEPT

   (A) they were characterized by a desire for self-government.
   (B) they featured guilds comprised of male members only.
   (C) they allowed some escaped serfs to remain free.
   (D) they featured training for craftsmen.
   (E) they contributed to the power of monarchs.

4. The centralization of government in England

   (A) was one result of the Norman invasion.
   (B) was delayed because of the lack of a written constitution.
   (C) was hindered by the signing of the Magna Carta.
   (D) saw a parliament emerge as early as the twelfth century.
   (E) was accomplished by the English monarchy alone.

5. The controversy over secular v. papal authority

   (A) was a response to the failure of England and France to develop strong democratic institutions.
   (B) was resolved by the tragedy of the Black Death.
   (C) went unresolved by the Roman Catholic Church.
   (D) was resolved by the Great Schism.
   (E) set the scene for the Protestant Reformation.

ANSWERS AND EXPLANATIONS

1. (C)

The middle class, many of whom were merchants, rose to prominence as a result of the increased trade after the Crusades. The Crusades and its religious fervor strengthened the power of the Church (A). Monarchs became stronger as many nobles died in the Crusades or had to sell off their landholdings to them to offset the cost of their journey (B). The status of women rose as they participated in the Crusades or maintained family property while male family members were away (D). Italian city-states prospered as they sold supplies and to crusaders and transported them across the Mediterranean (E).

2. (C)

Police protection would not be a part of city life until the Industrial Revolution. Medieval European cities did often sponsor fairs; the larger fairs gradually became central marketplaces (A). The increased trade in the cities (D) marked the beginnings of a market economy (B). Manufacturing also added to the economic activity of medieval cities (E).

3. (B)

Although guilds were led by male members, they often allowed female members. The independence of cities from the feudal manors increased the desire of urban dwellers for self-government (A). According to medieval European tradition, a serf who could flee to a city and remain there for a year and a day would be free from servitude (C). Through the guilds, the cities featured apprenticeship training (D). Urban artisans and traders tended to favor the rise of monarchs, whose power promoted law and order that would provide a safer environment for carrying out trade (E).

4. (A)

Williams's model of feudalism, in which lords owed their allegiance personally to the monarch, provided the beginnings of centralized government in England. Although the rights of Englishmen were not in written form, a body of common law evolving from court decisions unified them (B). The nobility, and later all the English, were unified by the prvileges granted them in the Magna Carta (C). The Great Council, the forerunner of the British parliament, was formed in the thirteenth century (D). The centralization of the English government was accomplished not only by the monarchy but also in the Magna Carta, which was initiated by English nobles, and in the beginnings of a parliament (E).

5. (E)

The issue of papal authority was among the controversies that precipitated the Protestant Reformation. Both England and France were establishing democratic traditions at the time of the battle over secular v. papal authority (A). The Black Death (B) was one of the causes of the decline in confidence in the Church and papal authority. The controversy over papal authority was left unresolved by the Great Schism (D), which resulted in the naming of two popes, one French and the other Italian, in 1378. In 1417, the Council of Constance, called by the Roman Catholic Church, appointed a new pope, resolving the Great Schism (C).

CHAPTER 16

Peoples of the Americas and Oceania

TIMELINE

250–900	Height of the Mayan civilization
900s	Rise of the Chimu
950–1200	Toltec empire
1000s	Expansion of Polynesian societies
1200	Arrival of the Aztecs in the Valley of Mexico Kingdom of Chucuito
1325	Founding of Tenochtitlán
1519	Spanish conquest of the Aztecs
1525	Civil war in the Inca empire

IMPORTANT PEOPLE, PLACES, EVENTS, AND CONCEPTS

Tikal
Chichén Itzá
truncated pyramid*
Popol Vuh
glyph*
Quetzalcoatl
Lake Texcoco
Tenochtitlán
*chinampa**
Triple Alliance
Quechua
Lake Titicaca
Pachacuti
Cuzco
*quipu**
parallel descent*
Hiram Bingham
Machu Picchu

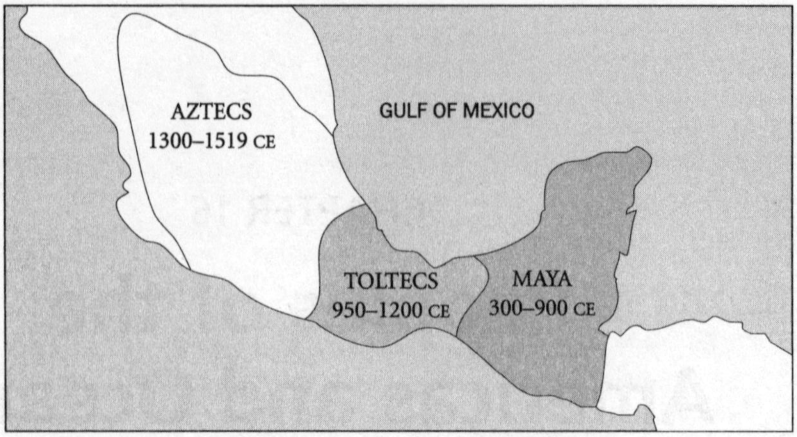

Peoples of Mesoamerica, 300–1519 CE

THE MAYA

The story of the people of Mesoamerica and South America is a continuum of cultural borrowing from one civilization or society to another. The Maya adopted many of the customs of their contemporaries, the Olmec. From 250 to 900, the Mayan civilization (located in the Yucatán Peninsula and modern Belize and Guatemala) was at its height. Their magnificent cities, such as their capital at **Tikal** and their ceremonial center at **Chichén Itzá**, featured massive **truncated pyramids** and temples dedicated to their gods. Agriculture formed the basis of Mayan life, with maize, beans, and squash as the main crops. The various independent city-states were linked by trade, especially in jade, salt, flint, honey, feathers, and shells; sometimes cacao beans were used as currency.

Among the many achievements of the Maya was the development of both a lunar and a solar calendar; the solar calendar contained eighteen months of twenty days each, with a final period of five days that was dedicated to religious observation. The Maya were able to perform complex mathematical and astronomical calculations because of their understanding of the concept of the zero as a placeholder. They developed the most advanced writing system in the Americas, using **glyphs**, or symbols representing either words or syllables.

Religion and Society

The Mayan version of the story of creation can be found in the ***Popol Vuh***, one of their books. Like many of the societies of Mesoamerica, the Maya believed in the legend of **Quetzalcoatl**, a god who would one day return to rule his people in peace. The Maya, who were polytheistic, sometimes practiced human sacrifice to appease their gods. The Maya also played a type of ball game that was believed to satisfy the gods so that natural order would be maintained.

Mayan families were patriarchal, although the wealthier and more prominent families traced their lineage through parallel descent. Women of the elite classes retained some rights and were considered important to the society. The majority of women, however, performed the traditional roles of homemaker and childbearer.

By the 800s, many of the Mayan cities were suddenly abandoned; this may have been the result of warfare, or perhaps soil depletion from improper land usage. Whatever the reason, by the 900s the once-glorious civilization of the Maya had been reduced to a number of independent city-states.

THE TOLTECS

After the collapse of Teotihuacán in the eighth century, the Valley of Mexico experienced several decades without the influence of a dominant culture. Nomadic peoples saw the opportunity to migrate into central Mexico; the most significant among them arrived around 900. The Toltecs, from the southwest, rose to power and established a capital at Tula in the mid-tenth century. Like others before them, the Toltecs adopted many of the cultural practices and beliefs of the sedentary Mesoamerican peoples, constructing temples and truncated pyramids and perpetuating the legend of Quetzalcoatl. A warlike people, the Toltecs based their empire on conquest and, in spite of their belief in the peaceful Quetzalcoatl, sacrificed humans to appease their war god.

Toltec influence spread beyond central Mexico, reaching the former Mayan city of Chichén Itzá. Some historians believe that the Toltecs may have traded obsidian from northern Mexico for turquoise from the Anasazi in present southwestern United States. Around 1200, the Toltec empire collapsed, but not before it transmitted the legend of Quetzalcoatl to another more powerful group—the Aztecs.

THE ARRIVAL OF THE AZTECS

The Aztecs, or Mexica, were nomads from northern Mexico who arrived in the Valley of Mexico around 1200. For the next century they migrated from one location to another in central Mexico, often encouraged to move on because of their warlike disposition and their inability to live peacefully with the other peoples of central Mexico. In their wanderings, the Aztecs became acquainted with the customs of other Mesoamericans, adopting a brutal ball game played in a court in addition to a solar calendar of 365 days similar to that of the Maya.

Finally, the Aztecs settled in a location given to them by one of their legends: According to the legend, they were supposed to build their capital city at the location where they saw an eagle perched on a cactus, holding a snake in its mouth. The Aztecs found the prophesied sign on an island in the center of **Lake Texcoco** in central Mexico. In 1325, they established their capital city at this site, naming it **Tenochtitlán**. The splendid city shone with pyramids, temples, and canals; three causeways connected the island city with the mainland.

To augment the amount of agricultural land, the Aztecs created plots of land called ***chinampas***. These floating plots were constructed of intertwining reeds and vines upon which the Aztecs deposited fertile soil dredged from the bottom of the lake. Like other Mesoamerican societies, the staple crop of the Aztecs was maize, although beans and squash were also widely cultivated.

A Tribute Empire

As the Aztecs solidified their wealth and power in the Valley of Mexico, they demanded tribute from neighboring peoples. By the middle of the fifteenth century, they had attained sufficient power to create the **Triple Alliance** with the neighboring city-states of Tlacopan and Texcoco. The alliance controlled most of Mesoamerica, except for a few areas such as the desert regions of northern and western Mexico. The collection of tribute in the form of exotic items such as jade, emeralds, animal skins, and parrot feathers, in addition to cacao and vanilla beans from the tropical lowlands, supplied items that the Aztecs then bartered in their active long-distance trade network. Although trade and commerce were controlled by the government, the Aztecs did not have a complex bureaucracy, nor did they maintain a standing army; instead, military forces were assembled when the need arose.

Society and Religion

Much of what is known about Aztec society is derived from books and other written material that survived the Spanish conquest. Aztec society was hierarchical, with the military elite receiving the highest honors. Other than trading in the marketplaces, women played almost no role in public life. However, within their families, women received high regard as mothers of future warriors; even the women of the wealthiest classes were respected for their childbearing and childrearing responsibilities. Aztec society also included large numbers of slaves who were often fellow Aztecs sold by their families to pay their debts or accused of criminal behavior.

Aztec religion, like that of other Mesoamerican peoples, was based on the worship of gods who had made sacrifices to establish the world and its order. To appease their gods and ensure prosperity, the Aztecs practiced human sacrifice regularly (and to a greater extent than their Mesoamerican predecessors). Among the victims sacrificed to the war god Huitzilopochtli were criminals from the Aztec society and prisoners of war from neighboring societies.

The violent habits of the Aztecs contributed to the weakening of their empire under their ruler Montezuma II, who began his reign in 1502. Several provinces under Aztec dominion rose up in protest after a century of the Aztecs' demanding tribute and sacrificing victims. Thus, internal problems had already debilitated the Aztec empire by the time the Spaniards came to conquer in 1519.

THE INCAS

While the Aztecs were dominating central Mexico, the Incas, or **Quechua**, were establishing a vast, powerful, and well-organized empire in the highlands of the Andes Mountains in South America. The Incas are credited with establishing the largest empire in the Americas.

The Inca empire was built upon the cultural traditions of their predecessors, the Chavín and Moche, as well as the later societies of the Chucuito and Chimu. Around 1200, the kingdom of Chucuito occupied the Andes highlands around **Lake Titicaca**. In these highlands the people of Chucuito cultivated potatoes as their staple crop and herded llamas and alpacas. They traded with societies in the lowlands to get maize and coca, whose leaves acted as a mild stimulant. The lowland peoples, the Chimu, used irrigation to cultivate sweet potatoes in addition to maize. Their society, which rose around the tenth century, featured large brick buildings. Into the domain of the Chucuito and Chimu came the Quechua people around the middle of the thirteenth century. The Quechua would later be named the *Incas* by the Spanish, after the term applied to rulers.

The Expansion of the Inca Empire

Settling in the highland region around Lake Titicaca, the Incas grew into an empire under the leadership of their ruler **Pachacuti**, who reigned from 1438 to 1471. After conquering the highland areas to the north and south of Lake Titicaca through a series of military campaigns, Pachacuti gained control over the coastal Chimu by interrupting their irrigation system. By 1500, the Incas ruled an extensive empire 2,500 miles long—from present-day Ecuador to Chile and Argentina along the western coast of South America. With a population of perhaps twelve million people of various ethnic and cultural backgrounds, the Inca empire, or *Tihuantinsuya*, distinguished itself as the largest political unit ever established in South America.

The Incas allowed conquered peoples to largely retain their own culture and local leaders if they pledged their allegiance to the Inca state. At the same time, the Incas would take a few hostages from among the elite classes of conquered peoples, forcing them to reside in the Inca capital at **Cuzco**. Reliable Quechua people were sometimes recruited as colonists to settle in conquered areas in order to assure the loyalty of subject peoples. Only when subjects became rebellious were they forced to resettle in a portion of the empire far away from their homeland.

Inca Empire, 1525

The Incas as Administrators

The Incas distinguished themselves as able administrators of their vast empire. In spite of lacking a written language, they managed to maintain efficient government records by means of a device known as a ***quipu***. The quipu was a thick cord from which were suspended a number of cords, each containing knots of various sizes, shapes, and colors; the colors represented the categories of information recorded in the quipu, such as population counts, economic and financial matters, and religious concerns.

The other factor that maintained the superb organization of the Inca empire was a highly efficient system of roads that stretched the length of the empire. Two routes carried messengers and military forces throughout the Inca world: one route went through the mountain areas, and the second went through the lowlands. A system of runners carried messages throughout the Inca empire. Like the Persians, the Incas set up a system of way stations along their roads to provide lodging and supplies.

Inca Society

Unlike the Aztecs, the Incas did not administer a tribute-based empire. Instead, they required communities to participate in public building projects, in mining, or in working the land. These shifts of required labor were called *mita*. Within Inca communities, small groups of people known as *ayllu* worked together on projects in order to keep the community self-sufficient. While most men were herders, women occupied themselves by weaving cloth, caring for the household, and working in the fields. In addition, Inca women were required to weave fine cloth for government and religious use. Although labor was divided along gender lines, the roles of both males and females were equally respected. Inheritance progressed through **parallel descent**, with daughters inheriting from their mother and sons from their father.

The cooperation required of members of the Inca society helped to ensure plentiful food supplies in times of scarcity. Irrigation systems from earlier societies in the area were expanded to meet the needs of the empires in times of drought. The Incas also devised a method of freeze-drying potatoes and storing them against the possibility of poor harvests.

Long-distance trade also fell under the control of the imperial government. The lack of a market economy discouraged the rise of skilled artisans, which was a noticeable difference between the Incas and the peoples of Mesoamerica.

Although most members of the Inca community were peasants, Inca society included rulers, aristocrats, and priests. The Inca, or chief ruler, was deemed a god descended from the sun; his main wife (who was usually his sister) represented the moon. Even after death, Inca rulers were esteemed as an integral part of the government; rulers would often make their major decisions in the presence of their predecessors' mummies in order to benefit from their wisdom. Aristocrats wore more elaborate clothing than commoners, with some wearing large ear spools that distended their earlobes, prompting the Spanish to call them "big ears." Priests were assisted in their ritual duties by "virgins of the sun" who devoted a lifetime to religious service.

In addition to the sun god, or Inti, many Incas also worshipped the creator god, or Viracocha. While humans were occasionally sacrificed, the vast majority of sacrifices were animals such as llamas or guinea pigs. The Incas had a concept of sin as a violation of the social order and believed in an afterlife in which humans would be rewarded or punished according to their earthly deeds. The city of Cuzco served as the ceremonial, as well as the administrative, capital of the Inca empire. Another possible religious center was **Machu Picchu**, whose ruins were discovered high in the Andes by **Hiram Bingham** in 1912. Typical of Incan cities, Machu Picchu featured a central plaza, irrigation system, public buildings, and a temple to the sun.

Decline of the Incas

About 1525, after the death of their ruler Huayna Capac, civil war broke out in the Inca empire between Huayna's two sons, Atahualpa and Huascar. Atahualpa won, but he had to rule over an empire weakened by the conflict. The once mighty Inca empire was now easy prey for foreign conquerors.

SOCIETIES OF OCEANIA

While the peoples of Mesoamerica and South America were developing their distinctive, largely isolated cultures, the societies of Oceania were also taking on their own unique flavor. The peoples of Australia maintained their traditional foraging culture, which they did not relinquish until the arrival of European migrants during the nineteenth and twentieth centuries. Although long-distance trade among the peoples of Oceania may not have been common, trade goods often passed over short distances from one island to another. Migrations of Australian aborigines also promoted contact with and knowledge of the various cultures of the region. Australian aborigines in the northern part of the continent carried on some trade with societies of New Guinea and the islanders of Southeast Asia, in addition to trading with nearby islands.

The polytheistic Polynesians particularly revered gods of agriculture and war; their place of worship in early Polynesian societies was a terraced pyramid. Population numbers in Polynesia grew significantly in the years after 1000 CE, perhaps as the result of planned expansion by the Polynesians. Trade networks grew in areas where islands were closely grouped together, giving the various Polynesian peoples opportunity for cultural and economic interactions. Cultural groups were further united by intermarriage among some of the Pacific islanders.

Other islands (notably the Hawaiian Islands, New Zealand, and Easter Island) were so remotely situated that trade and social contacts were basically limited to their own inhabitants until the arrival of European sailors in the Pacific. In New Zealand and the eastern Pacific, the islanders domesticated pigs and dogs and also grew yams, taro, breadfruit, bananas, and coconuts. The Hawaiians supplemented their diet with fish from man-made fishponds that prevented larger fish from escaping into the ocean waters.

Population growth was especially rapid in Hawaii, Samoa, Tonga, and Tahiti. As the number of islanders increased, stratified societies arose with class distinctions among the elite and commoners. High chiefs organized military forces, carried out public works projects, and controlled land distribution. Isolated from other societies, the Pacific Islanders managed to maintain prosperous societies without the assistance of technology and metallurgy known to other societies.

THINGS TO REMEMBER

- Pre-Columbian Mesoamerican peoples
    - Common characteristics include maize as a staple crop, ball playing, the use of the terraced truncated pyramid, human sacrifice, and belief in the god Quetzelcoatl.
    - The Maya (250–900)
        - Lived in Mexico's Yucatán peninsula, Belize, and Guatemala.
        - Created a solar calendar.
        - Invented a hieroglyph-based writing system, the most advanced in the Americas.
        - Used the concept of zero to perform complex calculations.
    - The Toltecs (circa 900)
        - Settled in southwest Mexico.
        - Were a warlike, formerly nomadic people.
        - May have traded with the Anasazi people (in the southwest of what currently is the United States).

- The Aztecs (1200–1521)
    - Established an alliance of central Mexican peoples and created an empire.
    - Engaged in long-distance trade.
    - Were particularly devoted to human sacrifice.
- The Incas (circa 1250–1533)
    - Created the largest empire in the Americas.
    - Did not have a written language, but used the *quipu* system for record keeping.
    - Built roads throughout the empire and were efficient administrators.
- Peoples of Oceania
    - Were isolated from other societies and developed their own traditions.
    - Practiced local trade between islands.
    - Did not have much technology or any knowledge of metallurgy.
    - Prospered and built highly organized societies.

REVIEW QUESTIONS

1. When the Aztecs, or Mexica, arrived in the valley of central Mexico,

    (A) they established their own more advanced traditions.
    (B) they adopted many of the existing Mesoamerican traditions.
    (C) they were noted for their adaptability to other regional peoples.
    (D) they developed independently from other Mesoamerican cultures.
    (E) they insisted that other societies adopt their traditions.

2. The Incas did NOT fit the traditional definition of a civilization because they did not have

    (A) advanced cities.
    (B) specialized workers.
    (C) advanced technology.
    (D) a system of writing.
    (E) complex institutions.

3. The Toltecs

    (A) were a peaceful people.
    (B) did not practice human sacrifice.
    (C) were the only major cultural group that denied the legend of Quetzalcoatl.
    (D) based their empire on efficient administration.
    (E) may have been involved in long-distance trade of obsidian for jade.

4. All of the following are true of the Mayas EXCEPT

    (A) they based their livelihood on the cultivation of maize.
    (B) they transmitted the legend of Quetzalcoatl.
    (C) their wealthier families traced their lineage through parallel descent.
    (D) they were monotheistic.
    (E) they constructed truncated pyramids.

5. Regarding the societies of Oceania,

    (A) the Australians based their society on the cultivation of various grains.
    (B) Australians remained isolated from other peoples.
    (C) the Polynesians maintained their prosperous society without the knowledge of metallurgy.
    (D) New Zealanders carried on an active long-distance trade.
    (E) Polynesian societies developed few class distinctions.

ANSWERS AND EXPLANATIONS

1. (B)

The Aztecs adopted many Mesoamerican traditions such as the cultivation of maize, the construction of truncated pyramids, picture writing, a solar calendar, and the legend of Quetzalcoatl. Since they borrowed so heavily from other civilizations, they were not noted for the development of more advanced traditions of their own (A). During their migratory period before settling in the valley of Mexico and after their civilization developed, they were noted for their aggressive nature toward other peoples (C). Because of their cultural connections with other Mesoamerican peoples, their culture did not develop independently (D); at the same time, they were not intent upon imposing their society upon others (E).

2. (D)

The Incas did not have a system of writing, but rather used a system of knotted cords called the *quipu* for recordkeeping. That they possessed specialized workers and advanced technology is evident in the architecture of their cities, that of Machu Picchu serving as an example (A, B, C). An example of Incan institutions is their highly efficient imperial government (E).

3. (E)

There is archeological evidence that the Toltecs traded obsidian for the jade of the Anasazi of what is today the southwestern portion of the United States. The Toltecs were a warlike people (A) who practiced human sacrifice (B). They based their empire on conquest (D), in spite of their belief in the peaceful Quetzalcoatl (C).

4. (D)

The religion of the Mayas was polytheistic. Choices (A), (B), and (E) were true of the Mayas and other Mesoamerican peoples. Their wealthier families practiced parallel descent; women traced their lineage through their mother and men through their father (C).

5. (C)

The Polynesians achieved an advanced society without the use of metals, which were extremely limited in their geographic location. The Australians were foragers, not farmers (A), who maintained contact with other peoples through migration (B). New Zealanders were unable to carry on long-distance trade because of their isolated location (D). Polynesians had a stratified society with definite class distinctions between commoners and the elite (E).

CHAPTER 17

Renaissance and Reformation

TIMELINE

1300–1600	Renaissance
1400s–1500s	Northern Renaissance
1440	Invention of the Gutenberg printing press
1517	Beginning of the Protestant Reformation
1529	English Reformation
1534	Completion of Luther's translation of the Bible Society of Jesus founded
1544	Charles V sends armies against Protestant princes
1545	Council of Trent
1555	Peace of Augsburg
1598	Edict of Nantes

IMPORTANT PEOPLE, PLACES, EVENTS, AND CONCEPTS

humanism*
Medici
Renaissance*
fresco*
Johannes Gutenberg
indulgence*
Martin Luther
Protestant Reformation*
justification by faith*
Peace of Augsburg
Ulrich Zwingli
John Calvin
predestination*
John Knox
Anabaptists*
Huguenots*
Edict of Nantes*
Catholic Reformation*
Society of Jesus*
Ignatius of Loyola
Inquisition*
Council of Trent*
Index of Forbidden Books
Henry VIII

THE EUROPEAN RENAISSANCE

The fascination with new ideas and products that had been spawned by the Crusades sparked a rebirth of learning and awareness in Europe known as the **Renaissance**. This period, which lasted from approximately 1300 to 1600 (and to 1700 in Northern Europe), emphasized human reason and celebrated humanity. No longer would men and women rely solely on the teachings of the Church as they had done during the European Middle Ages. The Renaissance marked a transitional period between the medieval and modern ages in Western Europe.

The ideal Renaissance man was one who was educated in many different subjects, including the arts. The Renaissance woman, on the other hand, was expected to be an object of beauty and was not encouraged to pursue learning. Although Renaissance women were more educated than women in medieval times, the average woman of the Renaissance enjoyed no more privileges, and perhaps even less, than her medieval counterpart.

Among the chief characteristics of the Renaissance was a belief in ***humanism***, which:

- emphasized reason.
- admired Greco-Roman civilization as a model.
- concerned itself with everyday human problems.

The Renaissance is also known for its unparalleled achievements in literature and the arts, characterized by realism.

Italy: Birthplace of the Renaissance

The Renaissance began in the city-states of northern Italy for several reasons. Many Italians had become wealthy from Mediterranean trade and from selling supplies to Crusaders. The culture of Italy was already based on Greek and Roman traditions. Italy had become familiar with the Byzantine and Muslim worlds through the Crusades. The culture of Islam had already shown its magnificence in the Muslim occupation of Spain, and with the weakening of the Byzantine empire and its demise in 1453, the Islamic peoples of the eastern portion of the former Roman empire added their vast wealth of knowledge to further spark the Renaissance in Italy.

Key Italian cities during the Renaissance were Florence, Rome, Venice, Milan, and Naples. Among the noteworthy families of Florence were the **Medici**, who were initially bankers, then leaders of their city-state, and finally patrons of the arts. Other major figures of the Renaissance were:

Writers

Francesco Petrarch (1304–1374) of Florence. A poet, he admired the ethical example of the Romans and wrote that leading a full life on earth was more important than devotion to religious pursuits.

Niccolo Machiavelli (1469–1527), also of Florence. Macchiavelli wrote *The Prince*, in which he justified the right of the ruler to use any means to govern his state.

Dante (1265–1321), an early writer in the Italian vernacular, wrote *The Divine Comedy*, which describes a soul's journey to salvation.

Artists

Renaissance painting was characterized by realism and perspective.

Leonardo da Vinci (1452–1519). An ideal model of the well-rounded "Renaissance man," da Vinci was an artist, architect, musician, mathematician, and scientist. His observations of animals led him to draw a flying machine and a parachute, and studies of human anatomy gave him the expertise to draw the human body. His most famous paintings are the *Mona Lisa* and *The Last Supper*.

Michelangelo (1475–1564), who considered sculpting his greatest joy, is noted for his statues of David and Moses. His most remembered achievement, however, is his **fresco** painting of the ceiling of the Sistine Chapel in the Vatican. Michelangelo also designed the dome of St. Peter's Basilica in Rome.

Raphael (1483–1520) was known for his painted frescoes (painting on wet plaster) in papal chambers and for his madonnas.

Titian (1477–1576). With the king of France and the Holy Roman Emperor as his patrons, Titian was known for his use of rich colors. His most famous work was *The Assumption of the Virgin*.

Donatello (1386–1466) of Florence studied statues of Greeks and Romans. His statue of Saint George is a model of realism.

The Northern Renaissance

By the fifteenth century, scholars from northern Europe had journeyed to Italy to study with its artists. Italian merchants leaving Italy also carried with them the ideas of the Renaissance. As a result, by the fifteenth and sixteenth centuries the Renaissance had spread to Germany, the Netherlands, France, England, and Flanders; Flanders especially would distinguish itself for its artists. Renaissance ideas traveled even more rapidly after the invention of the printing press around 1440 by **Johannes Gutenberg,** a German.

The figures of the northern Renaissance would combine the realism and humanism of the Italian Renaissance with the religious devotion of Northern Europe. The result would be the setting for the next significant movement of the age, the **Protestant Reformation.**

The Northern Renaissance produced its own fine writers and artists:

Writers

Desiderius Erasmus (1466–1536) of the Netherlands, considered the greatest humanist of northern Europe. Learning of the ideas of the Italian humanists through literature printed on the new printing press, Erasmus wrote the book *In Praise of Folly* in which he criticized the lack of spirituality of the Roman Catholic Church and urged a return to the basic message of Jesus.

Thomas More (1500s) of England. His book *Utopia* described an imaginary ideal society.

William Shakespeare (1564–1616) of England is considered the greatest poet and playwright of the English language.

François Rabelais (early 16th century) of France pointed out the problems of his day while expressing his own appreciation for life.

Artists

A trademark of Northern Renaissance art was portrait painting, which reflected the Renaissance emphasis on individual persons.

Rembrandt (1606–1669) of the Netherlands became the greatest painter of northern Europe. His portraits are characterized by their contrasts between light and shadows.

Albrecht Dürer (1471–1528) of Germany became famous for his copper engravings and woodcuts.

Jan Van Eyck (1400s) of Flanders painted in oils on canvas.

Pieter Bruegel (mid-1500s) of Flanders used his paintings of the countryside and peasants to criticize the intolerance of society.

THE PROTESTANT REFORMATION

The Northern Renaissance, with its religious fervor, provided fertile ground for a revolution in religious thought, while the invention of the printing press supplied the means by which new ideas would sweep through Europe. The spark that ignited the reform movement in Germany was the sale of **indulgences** to offset the cost of rebuilding St. Peter's Basilica in Rome. (Indulgences were papers whose purchase would guarantee the buyer the forgiveness of sins.) Among the opponents of the sale of indulgences was a priest and former monk named **Martin Luther**. While studying the Bible in the monastery, Luther had come to believe that man is saved through faith in Jesus. On October 31, 1517, Luther nailed his *95 Theses*, or topics for debate, on the door of the church in Wittenberg, Germany, to encourage debate on the issue of the sale of indulgences. Later he began to openly teach his doctrine of

"justification by faith" and was subsequently excommunicated by Pope Leo X. When Luther refused to recant his teachings at the Diet of Worms, Holy Roman Emperor Charles V banished him from the empire. Sheltered in a castle by Frederick the Wise, Elector of Saxony, Luther completed his translation of the New Testament of the Bible into the German language in 1522. By 1534, he had completed the translation of the entire Bible from Hebrew and Greek.

Charles V continued to try to halt the spread of Lutheranism and in 1544 sent armies against the Protestant princes in Germany. The **Peace of Augsburg** in 1555 allowed each German ruler to choose the religion for his state; the princes in northern Germany selected Lutheranism, and those in southern Germany chose Roman Catholicism.

The English Reformation

In England, Reformation arose not because of religious fervor, but because of political and personal concerns. King **Henry VIII** petitioned the pope for an annulment from his marriage to Catherine of Aragon, who had failed to give him a son, so that he could marry another young lady, Anne Boleyn. When the pope refused, Henry persuaded Parliament in 1529 to place him as head of the new Church of England, or Anglican Church. He also added to royal land by seizing the vast amounts of property formerly owned by the Roman Catholic Church in England.

Other Protestant Reformers

Other reform movements and new religious denominations emerged from the Reformation. **Ulrich Zwingli** began the Swiss Reformation. Upon his death, the continuation of his work fell to **John Calvin**, a theologian who also believed in justification by faith. Calvin taught a doctrine known as **predestination**. According to this belief, God, before the beginning of the world, had chosen some people for heaven and others for hell. In the 1530s and 1540s, Calvin established a theocracy in Geneva, Switzerland, featuring an orderly but strictly regulated society.

John Knox of Scotland founded the Presbyterian Church. The **Anabaptists**, who stressed adult baptism and the separation of church and state, split into a number of denominations including Mennonites, Amish, Quakers, and Baptists. French Protestants, or **Huguenots**, had been subjected to persecution, including a massacre by French Catholics in 1572. In 1598, they were granted religious freedom by the **Edict of Nantes.**

The Catholic Reformation

In response to the reform movement, the Roman Catholic Church also entered into a period of renewal. The principal arm of the **Catholic Reformation**, or Counter-Reformation, was the **Society of Jesus**, or the Jesuits, founded in 1534 by **Ignatius of Loyola**. The function of the Jesuits was threefold:

1) To promote education (Jesuit colleges were founded throughout Europe).
2) To establish missions.
3) To stop the spread of Protestantism.

Although the Jesuits did not believe in executing heretics, another branch of the Counter-Reformation did. The **Inquisition**, a Church court, was established to try accused heretics and punish the convicted. The Inquisition in Spain was an especially powerful arm of the Roman Catholic Church.

In 1545, the **Council of Trent** was convened to examine the teachings and practices of the Roman Catholic Church. At this council, the Church reaffirmed its teachings that:

- The Church's interpretation of the Bible was the final authority.
- Both faith in Christ and good works were necessary for salvation.
- Both the Bible and Church tradition were of equal authority.
- Indulgences were expressions of faith; however, a ban was placed on their sale.

The council also created an **Index of Forbidden Books** which Roman Catholic laymen were forbidden from reading. The Index would be in effect until 1966, when it was abolished by the Second Vatican Council.

Effects of the Reformation

The subsequent effects of the Reformation were numerous. Nations were strengthened, and a new interest in education arose. From the 1530s through the mid-1600s, Europe would see a series of religious wars arising from the Protestant and Catholic Reformations. Religion continued to divide Europe as new religions were established and the power of the pope declined.

THINGS TO REMEMBER

- The Renaissance was characterized by humanism, which:
  - emphasized reason.
  - looked to Greco-Roman civilization as a model.
  - concerned itself with everyday problems.
  - featured great achievements in art and literature, characterized by realism.
- The Northern Renaissance featured:
  - a concern for spiritual matters.
  - the invention of the printing press.
  - great achievements in art and literature, often emphasizing the individual.
- The Protestant Reformation:
  - taught justification (salvation) by faith alone.
  - led to the rise of new denominations.
  - strengthened the position of nation-states.
  - promoted an interest in education.
  - helped in the development of vernacular languages.
  - sparked reform in the Catholic Church

REVIEW QUESTIONS

1. The European Renaissance

   (A) encouraged independent thought for both men and women.
   (B) centered around current, rather than ancient, traditions.
   (C) relied solely on Western traditions.
   (D) concentrated on the present world rather than on the afterlife.
   (E) greatly increased privileges for women in general.

2. All of the following were typical of the Northern Renaissance EXCEPT

   (A) religious devotion.
   (B) independent development.
   (C) the invention of the printing press.
   (D) portrait painting.
   (E) an influence on the Protestant Reformation.

3. Humanist philosophers taught that

   (A) people could lead moral lives while still concentrating on life in this world.
   (B) monasticism was the purest lifestyle.
   (C) the pagan Greco-Roman culture should be ignored.
   (D) a life of faith was superior to the pursuit of the new ideas of the Renaissance.
   (E) human reason could lead men and women astray.

4. Renaissance painting was NOT characterized by

   (A) an emphasis on individual persons.
   (B) perspective.
   (C) the use of themes from nature.
   (D) realism.
   (E) frescoes.

5. All of the following are true of the Protestant Reformation EXCEPT

   (A) it caused the Roman Catholic Church to reaffirm its traditional beliefs.
   (B) it was based on the belief in salvation through Christ alone.
   (C) it promoted education.
   (D) it strengthened the power of monarchs.
   (E) it produced radical changes in religious devotion in England.

ANSWERS AND EXPLANATIONS

1. (D)

The Renaissance concentrated on issues in the current world rather than relying on the life of faith characteristic of the medieval period in Europe. Renaissance-era men were admired if they devoted themselves to the pursuit of many branches of knowledge; women were not expected to show interest in the learning of the period (A). Renaissance women possibly enjoyed fewer privileges than women of the medieval period (E). The Renaissance centered around the culture of the ancient Greeks and Romans (B). Learning of the period revolved around not only Western traditions, but also the Islamic world (C).

2. (B)

The Northern Renaissance sprang from the ideas of the Italian Renaissance. The religious emphasis of the Northern Renaissance (A) influenced the thinking of the Protestant Reformation (E). Ideas of the Northern Renaissance were spread by the new European invention of the printing press (C). The emphasis on humanity was evident in the prevalence of portrait painting (D).

3. (A)

Humanist philosophers attempted to rationalize earthly life with the moral teachings of the Church. The purest lifestyle was one of service to humankind in this world, not a retreat into monastic life (B). Greco-Roman traditions (C) and reason (E) were emphasized. Faith was not so important as the Renaissance emphasis on reason (D).

4. (C)

The use of themes from nature was characteristic of the later romantic period, not of Renaissance art. Renaissance art was characterized by portrait painting (A) and realistic representations (D). Frescoes, or painting on wet plaster, were common (E). The use of perspective, or three dimensions, was also a Renaissance technique (B).

5. (E)

The English Reformation was caused, not by doctrinal issues, but by the conflict between King Henry VIII and the pope over the issue of Henry's proposed divorce. The Council of Trent, part of the Catholic Counter-Reformation, was a reaffirmation of the traditional teachings of the Roman Catholic Church (A). Education was promoted as the Protestant reformers wanted the general public to be able to read the Bible (C). As the power of the papacy declined because of the Protestant Reformation, the power of monarchs rose (D).

CHAPTER 18

Expansion of the Islamic World

TIMELINE

1000	Turkish armies move into India
1300	Mongols conquer the Seljuk Turks
1326	Ottomans conquer Bursa
1361	Ottomans conquer Adrianople
1398	Tamerlane destroys Delhi
1402	Battle of Ankara
1453	Ottoman conquest of Constantinople
1514	Battle of Chaldiran
1521	Ottomans conquer Belgrade
1526	Babur conquers Delhi
1529	Ottoman seige of Vienna
1534	Ottomans conquer Baghdad

IMPORTANT PEOPLE, PLACES, EVENTS, AND CONCEPTS

*ghazi**
Osman Bey
emir*
Balkans*
Tamerlane
Mehmet II
Bosporus Strait*
Selim the Grim
Suleiman I
janissary*
*devshirme**
millet*
Dar al-Islam*
Ismail
Abbas the Great
Rajput
Delhi Sultanate
Babur
Hindi
Urdu*
Aurangzeb
Sikhs*
Shah Jahan
Taj Mahal
Mumtaz Mahal
Goa

THE RISE OF THE OTTOMANS

By 1300, the Mongols had ended the power of the Seljuk Turks, who in turn had repeatedly chipped away at the territory of the Byzantine empire. As the physical size of Byzantium began to shrink, its power steadily eroded as well.

Anatolia was settled by nomadic Turkish tribes who were not unified under a central authority. Many of these Anatolian Turks sought to become warriors for Islam, or ***ghazi***. In their zeal to conquer the territories of infidels, or non-Muslims, they targeted their raids on those who lived along the borders of the Byzantine empire. One of the most noteworthy of the *ghazi* was **Osman Bey**, who ruled the Ottoman dynasty from 1259 to about 1326. ("Ottoman" is derived from "Osman.") Osman's dynasty would rule in unbroken succession from 1289 until 1923. He and his successors formed alliances with other ***emir***, or Muslim rulers, and engaged in one conquest after another. In 1326, they conquered the Anatolian city of Bursa, which became their capital. In 1361, the Ottomans added a second capital, Adrianople, which gained them a secure foothold in the **Balkans**.

The Ottomans owed their military success to their use of gunpowder and cannon. After they had conquered a group of people, they appointed local officials approved by their ruler, the sultan, to govern them. Most Muslims were required to serve in the Turkish army. Non-Muslims could be exempt from military service upon payment of a tax.

Tamerlane

While the Ottomans were quickly rising to power, a rebellious warrior from Samarkand in central Asia came onto the scene in the early fifteenth century. Called Timur-i-Lang, or Timur the Lame, the Europeans dubbed him **"Tamerlane."** Claiming descent from Chinggis Khan, Tamerlane set about conquering Russia and Persia. He burned the city of Baghdad to the ground, and in 1378 moved through northern India, leaving a path of death and destruction. While in India, he massacred the population of Delhi, making a pyramid of their skulls. At the Battle of Ankara in 1402, Tamerlane crushed the Ottomans, effectively halting the expansion of the Ottoman Empire. He then took the sultan back to Samarkand in an iron cage; there the sultan died in captivity.

The Conquest of Constantinople

After a civil war among the sons of the Ottoman sultan, Mehmet I took the Ottoman throne. His son, Murad II, restored the power of the Ottoman army. **Mehmet II**, son of Murad II, captured Constantinople in 1453, giving the Ottomans control of the **Bosporus Strait**. Marching to Hagia Sophia, Mehmet declared the church a mosque. He then opened the city of Constantinople to new citizens of various religions and backgrounds. People from these varied backgrounds helped rebuild the city of Constantinople, which was renamed Istanbul.

The Expansion of the Ottoman Empire

Another infamous sultan was **Selim the Grim**, who came to power by murdering family members, including his own father and sons. In 1514, at the Battle of Chaldiran, Selim defeated the Persians, afterwards sweeping into Syria, Palestine, and North Africa and adding these areas to his empire. He continued by capturing the holy cities of Mecca and Medina. Upon taking Cairo, the Islamic world's intellectual center, Egypt became part of the Ottoman empire.

The Ottoman empire reached its greatest height under the rule of **Suleiman I**, who reigned from 1520 to 1566. Called Suleiman the Lawgiver by his subjects, he was known to the Europeans as Suleiman the Magnificent. He expanded the Ottoman empire by conquering Baghdad in 1534 and the city of Belgrade in 1521, and advancing into Hungarian and Austrian territory. In 1529 he briefly laid siege to Vienna; his failure to conquer Vienna ended Ottoman hopes of expansion into Europe. The Ottomans also became a major naval power, capturing Tripoli and other areas along the North African coastline; through these conquests, they gained influence in the interior of Africa.

Ottoman Administration

The Ottomans would rule their empire for 600 years, during which they would build up an extensive bureaucracy, using slave labor to further their control. Included among the sultan's slaves were **janissaries**, or slaves taken from the people of conquered Christian territories. Under a policy called ***devshirme***, the Ottoman sultan's army removed boys from their families, gave them an education, taught them the principles of Islam, and then trained them for military service. The brightest and most capable janissaries could rise to prestigious posts in the government. Non-Muslim girls were also taken from their families, but to become slaves in wealthy homes.

The Ottomans granted religious freedom to their subjects. Jews and Christians, as "people of the book," were allowed to pursue their own religious beliefs and practices. Their status as **millets**, or nations, allowed them a representative who served as a voice before the sultan and his bureaucrats. This arrangement promoted fairly peaceful relations between the sultan and his subjects, but did little to promote unity among the variety of ethnic and religious groups in the Ottoman empire—a problem that would continue into the modern era.

THE SAFAVID EMPIRE

Discord within **Dar al-Islam** emerged with the creation of the Safavid empire. Named after their first ruler, Safi al-Din (1252–1334), the Safavids were originally members of the Sufi sect in northwestern Persia. Claiming they were descended from Muhammad, the Safavids adopted the Shia branch of Islam. The Safavids were subsequently persecuted by the Ottomans, who followed the Sunni form of the Islamic faith.

Believing that a powerful military was their best defense against the Ottomans, the Safavids set about strengthening their army. Their foremost military leader, a 14-year-old named **Ismail**, would seize most of present-day Iran and adopt the Persian title *shah*. The Ottoman Turks, fearing that the Safavids might alienate some of their own followers, ordered the execution of Shia Muslims within the Ottoman empire, while Ismail wiped out the Sunni in Baghdad. Facing off against each other at the Battle of Chaldiran in 1514, the Ottomans and their artillery weakened the Safavids, but did not defeat them completely. The conflict between Ottomans and Safavids would continue for another 200 years.

The Rule of Shah Abbas

In spite of the animosity between Ottomans and Safavids, Shah **Abbas the Great** (reigned 1588–1629) created a culture that blended the Persian tradition with that of the Ottomans and Arabs. Among the accomplishments of Shah Abbas were moving the Safavid capital to the more centrally-located Isfahan, and incorporating into his army royal slaves similar to the Ottoman janissaries. He also formed trade and political relationships with European countries, using these alliances to contain both the Ottomans and the Portuguese in Southwest Asia. In a further effort to promote cultural blending, Shah Abbas called in Chinese artisans to contribute their expertise to the design of architectural structures in Isfahan. Organized largely along the lines of the Ottoman empire, the Safavids expanded their territory to include the Caucasus area and much of Mesopotamia.

THE MUGHAL EMPIRE

After Shah Abbas assassinated or incapacitated his most promising sons, the Safavid empire was left in the hands of weak rulers who fell to the armies of Afghanistan in 1722. To the east, however, another Islamic empire had risen, this time in northern India. After the fall of the Gupta empire, India had been invaded by both Arabs and Muslims from central Asia, who had divided the subcontinent into a number of tiny kingdoms under the control of rulers called **Rajputs**, or Rajahs.

The Muslim invasion of India was especially devastating to Hindus. Around the year 1000, Turkish armies moved into India, destroying cities and Hindu temples. The weakened subcontinent was brought into some degree of organization when Delhi became the capital of a loosely unified Turkish empire called the **Delhi Sultanate**. The Hindus, however, continued to be oppressed, creating the source of future conflict between Muslims and Hindus in India.

The Rule of Babur

After Tamerlane's annihilation of Delhi in 1398, Indian unification was not realized until 1523 with the reign of **Babur**, a Turk from central Asia. Claiming that he was descended from both Chingghis Khan and Tamerlane, Babur eventually created an army that would conquer India in 1526 and provide the basis for the Mughal, or "Mongol" empire.

The Golden Age Under Akbar

The golden age of Mughal power would be realized under the rule of Babur's grandson Akbar (reigned 1556–1605). By outfitting his army with heavy artillery, Akbar was able to consolidate his rule of Gujarat and Bengal. Akbar, a Muslim, tolerated a variety of religions within his realm and permitted both Hindus and Muslims to rise to prominent governmental positions. In a further effort to unite his people, Akbar imposed a system of graduated taxes that were affordable even to poorer subjects.

Akbar's policy of blending the cultures of India extended to language usage. Persian served as the language of Akbar's government and of high society. Commoners spoke **Hindi**, a local language which is still widely spoken in India today. A new language called **Urdu** emerged from the cultural blend of soldiers in the Mughal armies; a blend of Persian literary forms and Arabic characters, Urdu is the official language of Pakistan today.

Division Under Aurangzeb

The extent of the Mughal empire reached its height under **Aurangzeb** (reigned 1659–1707), who widened his rule to include the entire subcontinent except for a small area at its southern tip. Aurangzeb also sowed the seeds of future discord in his empire by abandoning the tolerant policies of Akbar. By taxing Hindus and destroying their temples and rebuilding them as mosques, he garnered the hatred of the Hindus for generations to come.

Another group angered by the policies of Aurangzeb were the **Sikhs**. Once a nonviolent people whose philosophy blended Hinduism and Islam, the Sikhs responded to the policies of Aurangzeb by forming a militant union and devoted themselves to building a state in the Punjab, an area in northwest India.

SOCIETY UNDER ISLAMIC IMPERIAL RULE

Muslim rule in the Ottoman, Safavid, and Mughal empires strongly reflected their heritage in the steppes of central Asia, especially in the importance attached to the warrior class and the autocratic rule of imperial leaders. Battles and assassinations among family members over succession issues were also typical of steppe empires.

Women Under Islamic Imperial Rule

General Muslim belief that women had no place in government or public life gave way to the reality that some Muslim women were finding a place for themselves in the male-dominated world of politics. Within imperial Islam, a ruler's mother or favorite wife was often shown special privileges and power. Muslim rulers frequently consulted with their wives in matters of state. One woman even raised an army to put down a rebellion against her family's rule. Perhaps the best example of spousal devotion was that of **Shah Jahan**, who in 1631 began the construction of the magnificent **Taj Mahal** as a tomb to memorialize his beloved wife and political adviser, **Mumtaz Mahal**, who had died in childbirth.

Agriculture and Trade

Agriculture was the backbone of the Islamic economy. After the voyages of Columbus to the New World, products such as coffee, tobacco, and sugar grown in the Americas eventually found their way back across the Atlantic to Muslim marketplaces. The lands the Muslims conquered had long been actively involved in long-distance trade. The Ottoman and Safavid rulers continued to trade extensively, especially with European countries, offering them silk, carpets, and fine ceramics. In return, the English brought the knowledge of gunpowder technology to the Safavids. The Mughals preferred to permit European merchants to establish trading stations within their territories and left most long-distance trade in the hands of private Indian merchants. The Portuguese trading post of **Goa** was allowed to set up a Christian mission to India.

Trade between the Islamic empires and the West would have proven even more profitable had the Islamic empires taken more initiative in establishing their own trading posts. Instead, imperial rulers were content to maintain more of a unilateral relationship in which foreigners had to establish trading posts within Islamic territory. Also, by the end of the seventeenth century, the once advanced technology of the Islamic empires had leveled off while that of the Europeans had progressed dramatically. The resulting technological gap between Islam and the West served to hasten the decline of the Islamic empires. Even the introduction of printing to the Islamic empires by Jewish exiles from Spain in the late fifteenth century was not enthusiastically received. The Muslims' conservative attitudes toward technological innovation markedly weakened the Islamic empires.

The Beginnings of Decline

By the eighteenth century, the economy of the Islamic empires began to decline, due in part to its lack of full participation in long-distance trade. The costs of maintaining advanced military organizations and complex bureaucracies began to take their toll, as did the drain on the economy of numerous and protracted wars. Outdated technology made it increasingly more difficult to maintain a strong military presence in Islamic-occupied territories. The beginning of the end had come for the once formidable Islamic empires.

THINGS TO REMEMBER

- Between 1300 and 1700, three great Islamic empires emerged.
    - The Ottoman Turks
        - Osman Bey (1259–1326) and his successors conquered an empire that included Constantinople (now Istanbul), Palestine, Egypt, Syria, Iraq, North Africa, Greece, and parts of Eastern Europe.
        - The Ottoman empire was marked by bureaucracy, tolerance of religious diversity, and the use of slaves as warriors.
    - The Safavids
        - These rulers of Persia conquered most of present-day Iran.
        - They were Shia Muslims, which brought them into conflict with the Sunni Ottomans.

        - Shah Abbas the Great established trade relations with European nations and blended Persian, Arab, and Central Asian culture.
    - The Mughals
        - In 1526, a Turk named Babur defeated the Seljuk Turk rulers of North India and united the subcontinent.
        - His successors were the Mughals. The most famous is Akbar (1556–1605), who encouraged religious tolerance and a Hindu-Muslim cultural blend.
        - Aurangzeb (1659–1707) instituted policies of religious intolerance that led Hindus and Sikhs to revolt. This hastened the decline of the Mughal empire.
- Reasons for the decline of these empires included:
    - Failure to take full advantage of opportunities for global trade.
    - Rejection of new technology.
    - Many protracted wars.
    - Contested successions.

REVIEW QUESTIONS

1. Under the Ottomans,

    (A) Muslims were exempt from military service.
    (B) non-Muslims were forced to serve in the military.
    (C) the power of gunpowder empires was made evident.
    (D) Turkish tribes were not subjected to a central authority.
    (E) conquered peoples were separated from other members of their ethnic group.

2. All of the following areas were included in the Ottoman empire EXCEPT

    (A) North Africa.
    (B) southern France.
    (C) Anatolia.
    (D) Hungary and Austria.
    (E) the Balkans.

3. Under Ottoman administration,

    (A) religious freedom was denied Jews and Christians.
    (B) labor was carried out by free men called janissaries.
    (C) millets promoted ethnic unity in the empire.
    (D) non-Muslim girls were educated in the principles of Islam.
    (E) millets tended to promote peaceful relationships between the sultan and his subjects.

4. All of the following were true of the Muslim rule of India EXCEPT
   (A) it contributed to the animosity between Muslims and Hindus in India.
   (B) it followed upon the rule of the Gupta empire.
   (C) it was united under the strong centralized government of the Delhi Sultanate.
   (D) it greatly lessened the tax burden under Akbar.
   (E) it resulted in the appearance of a new language.

5. The weakening of the Ottoman empire was caused by all of the following EXCEPT
   (A) the discrepancy between Western European and Ottoman technology.
   (B) limited agricultural resources to support their growing population.
   (C) the costs of maintaining the military.
   (D) conservative, traditional attitudes among its leadership.
   (E) their failure to establish trading posts.

ANSWERS AND EXPLANATIONS

1. (C)

The key to Ottoman conquests was their possession of gunpowder. Muslims were required to serve in the military (A), while non-Muslims were exempt from military service if they paid a tax (B). Under the Ottomans the Turks were centrally organized (D), while conquered peoples were settled in areas with members of their own ethnic group (E).

2. (B)

Southern France was not included in the Ottoman empire, while all the other choices were Ottoman areas.

3. (E)

Millets created a direct, and usually harmonious, relationship between ethnic groups and the sultan. Jews and Christians, as "people of the book," were allowed religious freedom (A). The janissaries were slaves taken from conquered Christian peoples (B), while non-Muslim girls were not educated, but used as household servants (D). Millets tended to promote ethnic discord because they depended upon a relationship with the sultan rather than with other ethnic groups (C).

4. (C)

The Delhi Sultanate was loosely-unified. Destruction of Hindu shrines increased animosity between Muslims and Hindus (A). Akbar lessened the tax burden (D). Muslim rule resulted in the appearance of the Urdu language (E).

5. (B)

The Ottoman empire had abundant agriculture resources. The advances in European technology were occurring at a faster rate than those of the Ottomans, placing them farther and farther behind (A). Conservative attitudes among its leadership led to the reluctance to engage widely in trade (D, E).

CHAPTER 19

An Age of Exploration and Exchange

TIMELINE

1368–1644	Ming dynasty
1405–1423	Expeditions of Zheng He
15th century	Arrival of the Portuguese to the African coast
1453	End of Hundred Years' War
1492	Reconquest Expulsion of the Jews from Spain First voyage of Columbus
1493	Horses are reintroduced to the Americas
1494	Treaty of Tordesillas
1498	Da Gama rounds the Cape of Good Hope
1500	The globe is linked by long-distance trade
1514	Portuguese gain control over Macao
1519–1522	Magellan's circumnavigation of the world
1521	Conquest of the Aztecs by Hernán Cortés
1533	Conquest of the Incas by Francisco Pizarro
1542	Portuguese reach Japan and set up a missionary post Portuguese trading posts founded in Mozambique Portuguese trading posts founded in Goa

1565–1815	Voyages of the Manila galleons
1571	Battle of Lepanto
1588	England's defeat of the Spanish Armada
1644–1911	Qing dynasty
1652	Dutch establish Cape Colony
18th century	Height of the trans-Atlantic slave trade
1756–1763	Seven Years' War
1767	Great Britain and France establish trade with Tahiti
1770	Captain James Cook charts the southeast coast of Australia
1788	Great Britain settles Australia as a penal colony
1795	Great Britain seizes Cape Colony from the Dutch
1807	Great Britain abolishes the slave trade
1888	Abolition of slavery in Brazil End of slavery in the Americas

IMPORTANT PEOPLE, PLACES, EVENTS, AND CONCEPTS

Emperor Yongle
Zheng He
Reconquest*
Ferdinand and Isabel
caravel*
lateen sail*
astrolabe*
Treaty of Tordesillas*
Forbidden City*
Neo-Confucianism*
Malinche
*encomienda**
Bartolomé de las Casas
*repartamiento**
Captain James Cook
Columbian Exchange*
polygamy*
harem*
Boers*
Great Trek
triangular trade*
Middle Passage*
William Wilberforce
John Wesley

GLOBAL AWARENESS IS HEIGHTENED

In the fifteenth century, the ties between East and West that had grown more pronounced during the Crusades, the Mongol Peace, and the many centuries of Silk Road trade started becoming even more evident. Improved navigational methods and more sophisticated technology facilitated long-distance trade and exploration. The combination of knowledge and ideas of both East and West that had erupted in the Renaissance created an awareness of life beyond one's immediate borders that would permanently broaden European perceptions of global citizenship. Even civilizations such as the Chinese and Japanese, who attempted long periods of isolation from global connections, would gradually give way to limited participation in the global economy.

CHINESE EXPLORATION OF THE INDIAN OCEAN

After ridding China of the Mongol presence, the Ming dynasty embarked on a period of intensified interest in the trade and exploration of the eastern hemisphere. In an effort to explore other lands and display the splendors of the Ming dynasty, the **Emperor Yongle** dispatched his advisor **Zheng He** on seven overseas expeditions between 1405 and 1423. His fleet of sixty-two ships and 28,000 sailors, soldiers, and merchants was much larger than the European expeditionary forces that would enter the Indian Ocean during the following century. The distances covered in the voyages were comparable to those of the Portuguese in their voyages around the coast of Africa. Zheng He explored southern Asian kingdoms, parts of Persia and Arabia, and the eastern coast of Africa. A direct trade route was established between East Africa and China.

In spite of interest and expertise that allowed China to explore the Indian Ocean and reach such distant shores, the Ming Chinese suddenly abandoned the voyages because of pressures from many of the scholar-bureaucrats in China who felt that funds spent on the expeditions could be better spent back home. Their greatest concern was the Mongols who were again posing a threat along China's northwestern borders. The Great Wall had fallen into disrepair and funds were needed to shore up its defenses. Because of these national defense issues, the Chinese pulled out of the Indian Ocean scene in the early 1430s.

EUROPEAN EXPLORATION OF THE INDIAN AND ATLANTIC OCEANS

The end of the Hundred Years' War in 1453 had prompted the rise of nation-states in Europe, among them Portugal and Spain. Both nations increased taxes and the power of their military, preparing to augment their status among the nations of the world. A few attempts at exploration had already been undertaken; in the late fourteenth century, ships from Barcelona in Spain had sailed along the western coast of Africa as far south as Sierra Leone. The new European kingdoms proved efficient at managing their resources and displayed a competitive spirit with one another. By the fifteenth century, the rapidly improving technology of the European nations, along with the desire to spread the Christian faith and a spirit of economic competition, facilitated the European entry into the world of exploration.

The Portuguese Initiative

By the fifteenth century the Portuguese were already experienced fishermen in the Atlantic waters. Under the direction of Prince Henry, a navigation enthusiast, the Portuguese colonized the islands of the Madeiras and Azores and collaborated with the Italians to set up sugar plantations on the Cape Verde Islands off the coast of West Africa. They also sailed down the coast of West Africa, interacting with African kingdoms engaged in the slave trade. The Portuguese helped increase the volume of the already-existing slave trade in Africa, sending slaves to Europe and to the sugar plantations on the islands of the Atlantic.

The principal motive behind Portuguese exploration was to find a route to the East that would break the monopoly of the Italian middlemen. Before the Crusades, the Italians had traded in the Mediterranean, connecting with Islamic trade routes in the Middle East and the famed Silk Roads. The Portuguese accomplished their goal in 1498 when Vasco da Gama rounded the southern tip of Africa and reached India by using the power of the monsoon winds in the Indian Ocean. The roots of Portuguese economic interest in Asia began with that nation's arrival in the Indian Ocean.

Spain Enters the Scene

The year 1492 was pivotal in Spanish history. It was the year of the *Reconquista,* or **Reconquest**, of Spain from the Muslims, who had occupied Spain since 711. Under the consolidation of power brought about by the marriage of **Ferdinand** of Aragón and **Isabel** of Castilla, the last Muslim stronghold of Granada fell to the Christians in 1492, unifying Spain. As a reaction to the Reconquest, the "Catholic Kings" (as Ferdinand and Isabel were called) expelled not only the Muslims from Spain but also the Jews. The end result was to rid Spain of some of her most educated people, creating an academic void which would take its toll upon the future development of the nation.

Accompanying the power created by the unification of Spain was the capacity to collect taxes to finance national ventures, including exploration. After weighing the relative merits of Columbus's proposal to sail west to find an alternative route to the riches of the East, the Catholic Kings agreed to outfit the expedition. Columbus's four voyages across the Atlantic would not only rediscover new territories but also set the stage for the great exchange of plant and animal life across the Atlantic.

TRADE: A GLOBAL PROCESS

By 1500, distant areas of the globe were involved in either long-distance trade networks or in active local trade routes. The Indian Ocean linked China with East Africa, and the Silk Roads connected China with the Mediterranean world. Along these routes traveled trade goods and agricultural crops, technology, diplomatic messages, religions, and epidemic disease. In the New World, trade routes emerged from Mexico to the Great Lakes. The inhabitants of Pacific islands traded locally from island to island. The balance of power had now shifted to the new European nations, as they utilized their entrepreneurship and their newly acquired advanced technological knowledge to dominate other regions of the world. With the voyages of the European mariners, the world entered into a permanent trade relationship; a global era had truly begun.

EUROPEAN DOMINANCE OF THE OCEANS BEGINS

Technology borrowed from Mediterranean and Chinese peoples made feasible European navigation of the oceans. One example was the **caravel**, a small ship with a sternpost rudder (invented by the Chinese) that facilitated steering of the vessel. Control of the ships was also accomplished through the use of the **lateen sail** (of Mediterranean origin). The **astrolabe** (perfected by the Muslims) allowed mariners to determine latitude.

Portugal and Spain

The **Treaty of Tordesillas** in 1494 had granted the bulk of the Americas to Spain. Turning their attentions to the Indian Ocean basin and the Far East, by 1514 the Portuguese had sailed as far as Indonesia and China, establishing control over Macao, an island port. In 1542 they reached Japan, where they set up a successful missionary post and also founded trading posts on the African coast in Mozambique and at Goa in India.

The circumnavigation of the globe by Magellan's crew allowed Spain to claim a number of Pacific islands, among them the Philippines. Spain became a dominant maritime force after her conquest of the Aztec and Incan empires in the Americas. The immense wealth of gold and silver she now controlled from the Americas proved an initial boost to the Spanish economy. Later, however, the tremendous influx of silver and gold from the mines of New Spain produced an inflationary crisis in Spain and the continent of Europe as a whole.

Between 1565 and 1815, the Manila galleons, or Spanish ships, sailed the Pacific between the Philippines and Mexico, picking up cargoes of silver from the Spanish colonies in Mexico and trading them for luxury goods from the East. Since the Chinese currency was based on silver, the Chinese readily traded their gold for Mexican silver. Europeans sent so much silver to China in return for luxury goods that the bulk of silver in the age of exploration ended up in China.

The Spanish continued asserting their dominance in maritime activity by defeating the Ottoman navy at the Battle of Lepanto in 1571, effectively ending Muslim competition in the world's oceans. Spain's navy, however, met defeat off the coast of England in 1588, when her armada, or naval force, was defeated by the English.

England, France, and the Netherlands

England, France, and the Netherlands also had a stake in the exploration of new lands. France claimed present-day Canada and the Ohio and Mississippi valleys. England claimed much of the northeastern coastal section of what is now the United States, while the Netherlands controlled a small portion of the northeastern coast as well. For a short time the Dutch claimed a small portion of Brazil, while their settlement on the southern tip of Africa would become Cape Colony.

World Response to European Influence

As time went on, international trade proved beneficial, not only to the world at large but also to the economies of individual regions. Where direct control over a particular area was not won, often the Europeans would gain some other type of agreement with native inhabitants. European merchants set up trade agreements with Ottoman Istanbul. In Russia, European shipping agents were allowed in Moscow and St. Petersburg. While Japan had entered a period of isolation from most Westerners, the Dutch gained access to the port of Nagasaki. The Spanish and Portuguese traded in Japan until they were expelled by the Tokugawa in the mid-seventeenth century.

Colonial Rivalries

Commercial rivalries among the European nations led to the Seven Years' War (1756–1763), which also played itself out in North America as the French and Indian War. This global conflict pitted Britain and Prussia against France, Austria, and Russia. Britain and France battled for dominance in the Indian Ocean, while the British battled against the Spanish and the French in the Caribbean and in North America. The long-term result of the Seven Years' War was the beginning of a 150-year period of British dominance.

CHINA'S RESPONSE TO FOREIGN INFLUENCE: THE MING AND QING DYNASTIES

The Ming Return to Chinese Tradition

China's reaction to foreign influence was to re-establish her traditional culture and identity. After a period of exploration in the Indian Ocean basin, the Ming dynasty (1368–1644) withdrew into itself to form a highly centralized state that reflected the Chinese tradition of strong government. The capital was moved to Beijing, which was more centrally located and, therefore, easier to defend against possible Mongol threats. The Confucian civil service examinations, which had fallen into disuse during Mongol rule, were reinstated. Dishonest or incompetent government officials were publicly beaten, while those who spoke out against the government were also punished. As time went on, the Ming rulers withdrew into the **Forbidden City**, a lavish community forbidden to commoners, where the Ming could lead a self-indulgent lifestyle. Disgusted with the apparent lack of interest on the part of their rulers and disheartened by a major famine in China, the peasants revolted and supported the invasion of another people, the Manchu.

The Qing

The scholar-bureaucrats and Chinese generals were particularly supportive of the Manchu takeover of China. The Manchu were pastoral nomads from Manchuria who had already won control of Manchuria and Korea. In China, they would rule from 1644 to 1911 as the Qing dynasty, which would be the last dynasty in Chinese history. During their rule they would expand their control to Taiwan, central Asia, Vietnam, Nepal, and Burma. In order to maintain a distinction between the Chinese and Manchu, the Qing prohibited intermarriage between the two ethnic groups and forbade the Chinese from either traveling to Manchuria or from learning the Manchurian language. The Qing interest in improving the lives of their subjects led to their sponsorship of irrigation and flood control projects.

Life for Women

Under the Qing, the idea of the patriarchal family continued, with the traditional veneration of ancestors part of family life. Upon her marriage, a woman became part of her husband's family. Women could not divorce their husbands. Foot-binding continued and was broadened to include some of the less wealthy families who hoped to marry their daughters into wealthier families. Since daughters were often considered a social and financial liability, female infanticide was common. Although most girls were not educated, the daughters of the elite classes were often taught to read and write.

Economic Conditions

Under the Ming and Qing, China continued to base its economy on agriculture; farmers were a highly respected class in society. Maize, sweet potatoes, and peanuts—all American crops—were introduced and became popular with the Chinese. Although relatively isolated from other nations, the Ming exported silk, porcelain (the highly-valued Ming vases), and tea. During periods when Chinese isolation curtailed exports, the Dutch responded by producing Delft porcelain, whose blue- and white-colored patterns closely resembled that of the Ming porcelain. From Europe the Chinese imported exotic animal skins, spices, and woolen goods. In spite of some continued long-distance trade, merchants were considered at the bottom rung of Chinese society, while scholar-bureaucrats and the landed gentry occupied the most privileged positions. While China had been highly advanced in her technological achievements earlier in her history, the abundance of workers discouraged the Ming and Qing dynasties from devoting much effort to technological advancement—a decision that eventually placed China behind Europe in scientific and industrial achievement.

Religion and Philosophy

Neo-Confucianism was particularly popular with Ming rulers. As a blend of Confucianism and Buddhism, neo-Confucianism emphasized traditional Chinese values of self-discipline, family loyalty, and obedience to authority. Christianity, whose practice had largely disappeared after the collapse of the Yuan, or Mongol, dynasty, was reintroduced to China in the sixteenth century by Jesuit missionaries. The Jesuits attempted to spark the interest of the Chinese by displaying the wonders of European technology; nevertheless, Christianity did not gain a strong following among the Chinese. The efforts of the Jesuits did promote knowledge between East and West, however. European rulers became intrigued with the Chinese civil service system and began instituting it in some of the European countries while the rational thought of Confucianism fascinated European Enlightenment thinkers. Again, the age proved to be one of exchange between East and West.

CULTURAL EXCHANGE IN THE NEW WORLD: EUROPEAN CONQUESTS

The Aztec and Inca Empires

The ultimate goal of European exploration was conquest. In the New World, Spain executed the takeover of both Mexico and South America. In 1519, the Spanish, led by Hernán Cortés, were dazzled by the appearance of Tenochtitlán, the capital city of the Aztecs. The Mesoamerican legend of Quetzalcoatl allowed the Spanish easier entry into the Aztec empire as its ruler, Moctezuma II, considered the arrival of Cortés and his men as a possible manifestation of the return of the god of peace. The conquest of the Aztec empire in 1521 was further facilitated by the interpretations of a native woman named **Malinche** and with the cooperation of native peoples who had been subjugated by the Aztecs. The most significant factor in bringing down the Aztec empire was the introduction of smallpox by a carrier among the men who sailed with Cortés; lacking immunity to the disease, the Aztecs died by the thousands. The Spanish culminated their conquest of Tenochtitlán by burning it to the ground and rebuilding it as modern Mexico City; unfortunately, many Aztec artifacts were destroyed.

In 1533, the Inca empire, weakened by internal conflicts, was also conquered by the Spanish under Francisco Pizarro. As in the case of the Aztec empire, the Spanish were more interested in the acquisition of gold and silver than in the preservation of native artifacts. The Inca capital city of Cuzco was burned to the ground, with the modern city of Lima built in its place.

The Organization of the Spanish Colonies

The Spanish who came to settle the American colonies set up a patriarchal system, although women were given a voice within their families. The government of Spain awarded some of the colonists ***encomiendas***, or grants of land that gave owners the right to exploit the Native Americans on the land as laborers. A Spanish monk living in the Americas, **Bartolomé de las Casas** (1484–1566), championed the cause of the Native Americans, suggesting instead the use of Africans as a source of labor. His reports to the Spanish crown reached receptive ears, leading to the eventual replacement of the *encomienda* system with the ***repartamiento***, which allowed for improved treatment of the Native Americans, including payment for their labor. While Native Americans continued to die at alarming rates from diseases such as smallpox, measles, and tuberculosis, African slaves had the advantage of being able to withstand both tropical diseases and the diseases of the Europeans.

Other European Colonies

In the seventeenth century, England, France, and the Netherlands colonized some of the islands in the West Indies and imported slaves to work on plantations there. The holdings of the three colonial powers in present-day Canada and the Atlantic coast were minor compared to those in the West Indies and the Indian Ocean. In North America, there was less intermarriage and cultural blending with the Native Americans in these countries' colonies than in the Spanish colonies. While the French respected the Native Americans and made an effort to learn their ways, the British tended to be less concerned with learning Native American customs. The British North American colonies were distinct in that they established their own assemblies, paving the way for democratic rule along the Atlantic.

Like the Native Americans, the native peoples of the Pacific also died in large numbers when exposed to European diseases. Europeans had begun exploring the Pacific in the sixteenth century and had permanently settled the Mariana Islands and Guam before the end of the eighteenth century. By 1767, the English and French had established trade with Tahiti. Throughout the eighteenth century, European whalers were a familiar sight in the Pacific. In 1770, **Captain James Cook** charted the southeast coast of Australia and reported it suitable for settlement. The British would establish Australia as a penal colony, with the first settlers arriving in 1788. By the nineteenth century, the European presence in the Pacific had been widely established.

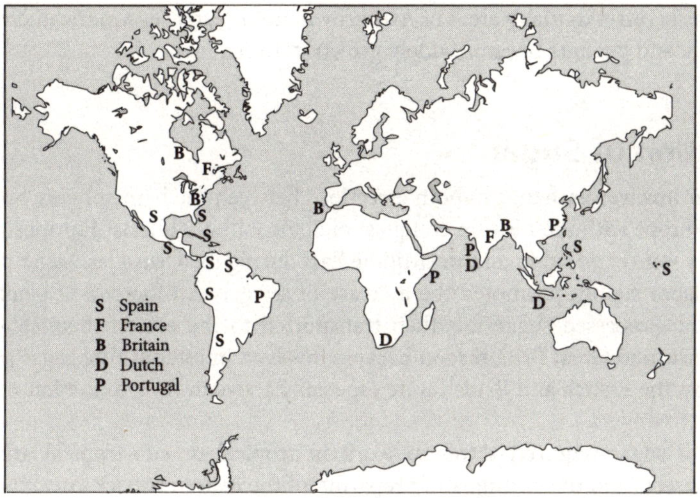

European Global Expansion, 1760

THE COLUMBIAN EXCHANGE

When the European explorers and conquerors landed in the Americas, they found a world that was truly unique. Largely isolated from the rest of the globe since the last Ice Age, the Americas featured plant and animal life distinct from other regions of the world. The Native Americans were good farmers, but they had no domesticated animals larger than the llama. The isolation of the Americas meant that the Native Americans were not exposed to the major diseases of humankind, resulting in weakened defenses against common diseases. The arrival of Europeans on American soil set up a great exchange between the eastern and western hemispheres in plant and animal life, diseases, and African slaves.

From the Eastern Hemisphere to the Western

On his second voyage to the Americas, Columbus brought with him cuttings and seeds for a variety of crops, including wheat, melons, onions, grapes and other fruits, and sugar cane. The first horses to be re-introduced to the Americas by the Spanish also arrived with Columbus in 1493. The arrival of the horse would be especially important to the culture of the Plains Indians, who could then both hunt the buffalo and resist the white man more easily. Dogs had been domesticated on both sides of the Atlantic, but those introduced from Europe were larger than those of the Americas.

From the Western Hemisphere to the Eastern

A large variety of plants also made their way from the western to the eastern hemisphere. The white potato, which originated in the Andes highlands, was transported to Europe, where it was cultivated widely in Ireland, Germany, and Russia. When the Scotch Irish emigrated to North America in the 1700s, they took the white potato with them. The sweet potato, which, like the white potato, also produces a high yield, grows well even in poor and dry soil; it became widely cultivated in Indonesia, China, and Japan. Manioc, or cassava, from which tapioca is made, is a hardy root crop that grows in various climates; it became a staple in the African diet. The introduction of American food crops into Africa produced such an increase in population that the population decline caused by the African slave trade was easily offset in many areas of Africa by natural increase. American crops such as chiles, pumpkins, squash, and peanuts became widely grown in India.

The Production of Sugar

The story of sugar involves exchange in both directions between the hemispheres. Sugar cane was first introduced into Europe with the Muslim conquest of Spain, although most Europeans did not learn of the crop until they were exposed to it in the Middle East during the Crusades. Sugar production, which required a large labor supply, promoted the increase of slavery and the rise of plantations, especially in the New World. Processed sugar was then transported to the eastern hemisphere. Portugal, the Netherlands, France, and Great Britain soon became involved in establishing sugar plantations. By the eighteenth century, the French and British were especially active in the production of sugar.

The processing of sugar required slaves to work in tropical or sub-tropical areas abounding in disease-bearing insects and the cutting and preparing of the cane was back-breaking labor. Although highly profitable for the plantation owners, life on the sugar plantations was one of the most difficult situations in which a slave could be placed.

THE TRANS-ATLANTIC SLAVE TRADE

A final feature of the **Columbian Exchange** was the transport of slaves across the Atlantic from Africa to the New World. Slavery was certainly not a novel concept to Africans in the sixteenth century; on the contrary, a number of slave routes had been in operation, some for hundreds of years. The arrival of the Portuguese to the African coasts in the fifteenth century broadened the slave trade and altered the nature and focus of many of the African kingdoms. By the eighteenth and nineteenth centuries, several African kingdoms (most notably Asante, Benin, and Dahomey) based a large portion of their respective economies on the slave trade.

In Africa, wealth was based not on private property, but on the acquisition of slaves. Africans usually did not enslave the people of their own kingdom or society, but rather captured prisoners of war or engaged in slave raids on other African peoples in order to supply themselves with forced labor. Reforms in Islamic western Africa resulted in increased literacy and the establishment of new trade centers that also specialized in slaves. The African kingdoms of the Sahara used slaves for gold mining and salt production as well as workers in the caravans that crossed the Sahara.

Within African societies, women were frequently enslaved. A large number of women in proportion to males in Africa led to **polygamy** and the creation of **harems**. Often African women were sold as slaves for the households and harems of Arabia and the Middle East or to labor on European-owned plantations on the islands of the Indian Ocean.

Europeans Enter the African Slave Trade

The European nations found that they could easily enter the slave trade by tapping into the existing slave routes in Africa. African rulers turned slaves over to the Europeans in exchange for commodities such as iron, cloth, tobacco, and especially, guns; guns could, in turn, be used in slave raids upon other African societies. The gun-for-slaves trade relationship with the Europeans promoted distrust among the various societies of Africa and made the Africans dependent upon European aid and technology. Traditional African societies were disrupted as the kingdoms of western and central Africa refocused their trade toward the coast to accommodate the European entry into the slave trade. Areas such as Senegambia created large plantations which required the labor of even more slaves.

The existence of the slave trade also entered into the history of South Africa. Cape Colony, established in 1652 by the Dutch, depended in part on slave labor. In 1795, Great Britain seized the colony. After the British abolished slavery, the Dutch, or **Boers**, traveled farther north in order to free themselves of British control; this is known as the **Great Trek**.

The Trans-Atlantic Journey

The eighteenth century was the major era of the trans-Atlantic slave trade. Between 1450 and 1850, about 12 million slaves were shipped across the Atlantic with an overall mortality rate of 10 percent to 20 percent. Mortality was not confined to the trans-Atlantic journey; perhaps as many as one-third of the slaves died en route from central Africa to the coast to await loading on the slave ships or as a result of the ongoing slave raids within Africa.

The majority of the African slaves were sent to the Caribbean islands and South America, primarily Brazil. Although slaves worked in mines and sometimes as household slaves, most of them were enslaved for work on the sugar plantations. The scarcity of female slaves and the high mortality rate of slaves on the sugar plantations guaranteed a constant need for further slave shipments to Brazil and the Caribbean. Other slaves were sold to Europe, where they generally worked as household servants. Only about five percent of slaves were carried to what is now the United States, and most of them arrived in North America after first spending some time in the Caribbean islands.

The Triangular Trade

The trans-Atlantic slave trade was one leg of the **triangular trade** routes across the Atlantic. The voyage across the Atlantic took from four to six weeks, depending upon the final destination of the slaves. Slave cargoes could go as high as 700 slaves, although 400 to 500 was a more typical cargo size. The typical triangular trade pattern involved:

- European products taken to the coast of Africa, where they were traded for slaves
- Slaves carried from Africa to the Americas (the **Middle Passage**)
- Goods such as sugar, rum, and tobacco carried to Europe

The End of the Slave Trade

The humanitarian thinking of the Enlightenment prompted some Europeans to campaign for the termination of the slave trade. Particularly active in the movement were the British humanitarians **William Wilberforce** and **John Wesley**. In 1807, Britain responded by ending the slave trade in her empire and by taking it upon herself to capture the illegal slave ships of other nations. The practice of slavery would continue in the Americas until 1888, when it was abolished in Brazil.

THINGS TO REMEMBER

- Ming China explored the Indian Ocean and established trade with East Africa. But the continued Mongol threat caused China to focus instead on defense.
- Technological innovations and the desire for profit led the European nations to establish colonies and trading posts in the Americas, India, Africa, and the Far East.
    - The Reconquest of Spain from the Muslims in 1492 allowed the Christian rulers to invest resources in the voyage of Columbus, who wanted to reach the East by sailing west.
    - European powers fought one another for control of the world's oceans and international trade. After the Seven Years' War (1756–1763), Britain became dominant.
- Contact with European nations caused the Chinese to reassert their national identity and the Japanese to retreat into isolation. This placed them at a technological disadvantage.
- The Columbian Exchange was the exchange of plant life, animal life, and disease between the eastern and western hemispheres, after Europe's "discovery" of the Americas.
- The American colonies, particularly the sugar plantations of the Caribbean and Brazil, required a great number of African slaves. African cultural traits such as religious beliefs and music were transferred to the Americas.
- The slave trade disrupted African societies, and the exchange of European technology for slaves made Africans dependent on Europeans.

REVIEW QUESTIONS

1. European dominance of the oceans in the sixteenth century

   (A) caused the Japanese to resist efforts to Christianize Japan.
   (B) depleted China's silver supply.
   (C) caused China to more actively pursue its Indian Ocean trade.
   (D) gave the Boers the opportunity to establish a colony in southern Africa.
   (E) was made possible by inventors from China and the Muslim world.

2. In Ming and Qing China,

   (A) the practice of foot-binding declined.
   (B) merchants occupied the most prestigious position in society.
   (C) technological advancement was a goal.
   (D) Christianity gained a strong following.
   (E) Neo-Confucianism was valued because of its emphasis on loyalty to the government.

3. All of the following are true of the Columbian Exchange EXCEPT

   (A) peanuts were introduced from the Americas to China.
   (B) sweet potatoes were cultivated in Japan and Indonesia.
   (C) the white potato became a staple of Germany.
   (D) India resisted the introduction of American food crops.
   (E) the introduction of new food crops into Africa produced a population increase that somewhat offset the population decline from the slave trade.

4. The African slave trade

   (A) promoted unity among the various African kingdoms.
   (B) was an outrage to the Islamic rulers of West Africa.
   (C) was restricted to sub-Saharan Africa.
   (D) began in the fifteenth century with the arrival of the Portuguese.
   (E) was one aspect of the Columbian Exchange.

5. Trans-Atlantic trade between 1450 and 1850

   (A) was part of a larger triangular trade.
   (B) carried the majority of slaves to the cotton plantations of North America.
   (C) transported tobacco and sugar to the western hemisphere.
   (D) saw an overall mortality rate of 40 percent for African slaves.
   (E) transported some slaves to Europe to work in the mines.

ANSWERS AND EXPLANATIONS

1. (E)

Improvements and inventions such as the lateen sail, astrolabe, and sternpost rudder from the Chinese and Muslim worlds eased exploration for Europeans. In the sixteenth century, Japan permitted Christian missionaries from Portugal to enter their country (A). China's silver supply was replenished by the voyages of the Manila galleons that sailed from Manila to Mexico, then carried Mexican silver to China (B). China under the Ming dynasty continued to have limited trade contacts (C). The Boers would not establish control in southern Africa until the seventeenth century (D).

2. (E)

Neo-Confucianism and its emphasis on fidelity created loyal citizens. The practice of foot-binding continued (A). Scholars occupied the most prestigious position in society (B). Technological advancement was not emphasized nearly so much as in previous dynasties (C), and Christianity did not gain much popularity among the Ming and Qing because of their return to traditional Chinese values (D).

3. (D)

Many American crops, such as chiles and pumpkins, were transferred to India. The cultivation of manioc in Africa was a particular boon to population growth in Africa (E).

4. (E)

The trade in human beings from the eastern to the western hemisphere was part of the Columbian Exchange. The slave trade promoted discord among the African kingdoms (A) and was carried out throughout most parts of Africa (C). It was promoted as a profitable business practice of West African rulers (B) and had been a part of African life for centuries before the arrival of the Portuguese (E).

5. (A)

The African slave trade, or the Middle Passage, was part of one section of the triangular trade. Only about 5 percent of the slaves were carried to British North America (B). Tobacco and sugar were transported to the eastern hemisphere (C). Mortality rate was about 10 percent to 20 percent (D). Slaves taken to Europe usually worked as domestic servants (E).

CHAPTER 20

Rise of Absolute Monarchs and the Enlightenment

TIMELINE

1571	Battle of Lepanto
1579	Northern provinces of the Netherlands win independence
1588	England's defeat of the Spanish Armada
1605	First modern European novel, *Don Quixote de la Mancha*
1613–1917	Rule of the Romanov dynasty of Russia
1618–1648	Thirty Years' War
1648	Treaty of Westphalia
1687	Isaac Newton's principles of motion
1701–1713	War of the Spanish Succession
1740–1748	War of the Austrian Succession
1776	Publication of *The Wealth of Nations*

IMPORTANT PEOPLE, PLACES, EVENTS, AND CONCEPTS

nation-state*
Inquisition*
constitutional monarchy*
absolute monarch*
divine right of kings*
Hohenzollerns
Junkers*
War of the Austrian Succession
czar*
Time of Troubles*
Johannes Kepler
Vesalius
Galileo
John Harvey
Francis Bacon

Bourbons
War of the Spanish Succession
William of Orange
El Greco
Diego Velázquez
Miguel de Cervantes
Thirty Years' War
Treaty of Westphalia
Hapsburgs
balance of power*
mercantilism*
capitalism*
laissez faire*
joint-stock companies*
Scientific Revolution*
Copernicus
geocentric theory*
Rene Descartes
Isaac Newton
Deism*
Enlightenment*
John Locke
Denis Diderot
feminist*
Mary Wollstonecraft

THE GROWTH OF NATION-STATES IN EUROPE

At a time when India, China, and the Ottoman lands had already developed strong centralized states, Europe remained a region of independent states. The Holy Roman Empire appeared the most likely area in Europe to develop a centralized state, but it had its limitations. Comprised of only Germany and northern Italy, it did not have authority over a significant portion of the European population. Also, the people of the Holy Roman Empire came from cultures that were too different from each other to promote real national unity. Furthermore, other states, such as France and the Ottoman Empire, were actively engaged in preventing the Holy Roman Empire from becoming too powerful.

The most powerful European states in the fifteenth and sixteenth centuries were England, France, and Spain. To consolidate their power they developed new sources of income from taxes and the acquisition of colonies, enlarged their administrative bureaucracies, and maintained standing armies. They also acquired power over the Church, confiscated Church lands, and used Church disciplinary instruments such as the **Inquisition** in Spain and Italy. While England and the Netherlands developed **constitutional monarchies**, absolute monarchies grew in France, Spain, Austria, Prussia, and Russia.

ABSOLUTE MONARCHS

Absolute monarchs had several characteristics in common:

1) They were the ultimate authority in the state.
2) They claimed to rule by **divine right,** the belief that
   - rulers received power from God.
   - rulers were responsible only to God.
3) They had power to
   - levy taxes.
   - enact laws.
   - administer justice.
   - manage bureaucracy.
   - execute foreign policy.

Philip II of Spain (1527–1598)

Philip II (great-grandson of Ferdinand and Isabel of Spain) inherited Spain, the Spanish Netherlands, and the Spanish colonies in the New World. To this empire he added Portugal and Portugal's possessions around the globe. Victorious against the Ottoman empire in the Battle of Lepanto in 1571, Philip later suffered a devastating defeat of his naval forces at the hands of the English in 1588.

As silver bullion flooded the European market from Spain's colonies, the price of silver dropped, causing severe inflation. Spain's wars placed further financial strain on the nation. In 1579, after a lengthy revolt against the heavy taxes imposed on them by the Spanish, the largely Protestant northern provinces of the Netherlands, led by **William of Orange**, declared their independence.

Spain's tremendous wealth during the sixteenth and seventeenth centuries produced a Golden Age of art and literature. The artist **El Greco** demonstrated his religious devotion by painting saints and martyrs, while **Diego Velázquez** painted portraits of court life and the royal family. Lope de Vega became the father of Spanish drama. *Don Quixote de la Mancha*, published in 1605 by **Miguel de Cervantes**, is considered by some the first modern European novel.

Louis XIV of France (1638–1715)

The classic example of an absolute monarch was Louis XIV of France, of the **Bourbon** family of rulers. His famous remark, "*L'état c'est moi,*" or "I am the state," defined his perception of the right to levy excessive taxes, spend public funds on his lavish estate at Versailles, and engage in costly wars to extend the power of France. (However, in the **War of the Spanish Succession**, Great Britain was the real victor instead of France, taking not only Gibraltar from Spain but also the territories of Nova Scotia, Newfoundland, and the Hudson Bay from France.) During his reign, Louis XIV made France a cultural model, but in the process incurred extensive debts and abused his power, preparing the way for future revolution in France.

Monarchs of Central Europe

From 1618 to 1648, central Europe was devastated by the **Thirty Years' War**, a conflict between Catholic and Lutheran princes in Germany prompted by a mutual fear of the spread of Calvinism. The war, which caused great population loss and devastated agriculture and trade in Germany, prevented German unification. It also weakened Spain and Austria but strengthened France. The Thirty Years' War ended the religious wars in Europe, weakened the Holy Roman Empire, and began the modern state system; the **Treaty of Westphalia**, which ended the war, was the first official use of negotiation to resolve a conflict.

Both the economies and political structures of central Europe were weaker than in western Europe. By the seventeenth century, western Europe was a highly commercialized region based on capitalism, while central Europe was still organized along feudal lines. Strong feudal lords prevented the development of strong monarchies.

The **Hapsburgs** of Austria took several steps to increase their power, among them reconquering the territory of Bohemia, ending Protestantism during the Thirty Years' War, and establishing a stronger centralized government by creating an army. The Empress Maria Theresa of Austria (1717–1780) used her authority to decrease the power of the nobles.

A contemporary of Maria Theresa, Frederick the Great of Prussia (1712–1786) followed in the footsteps of the other members of his powerful family, the **Hohenzollerns**. The Hohenzollerns instituted a military state in Prussia by creating a standing army with the landowning classes, the **Junkers**, as officers. They also weakened the power of the territorial assemblies. Frederick the Great opposed Maria Theresa in the **War of the Austrian Succession** and won Silesia for Prussia.

Absolute Monarchs in Russia

Ivan IV, or Ivan the Terrible (1533–1584), the first Russian ruler to call himself ***czar***, established an autocracy by setting up a secret police and executing those who opposed him. The **Time of Troubles**, which followed the rule of Ivan's son, saw more needless executions. In 1613, the Russians chose a new czar, Mikhail Romanov, whose family would rule Russia from 1613 until 1917. The Romanovs established serfdom more strictly and increased absolute rule. Another well-known Romanov, Peter the Great (1672–1725), increased the number of serfs, making them virtual slaves. To gain a foothold on the sea, he engaged in a war with Sweden. Peter the Great also attempted to westernize Russia and established a new capital at St.Petersburg. Under his rule, noblewomen took a greater part in community life, and trade and manufacturing flourished.

As centralized governments emerged in Europe, there also arose a concern that one nation might gain preeminence over another. A key concept in European diplomacy from the eighteenth to the early twentieth centuries was the **balance of power**, or the assurance that no one nation would acquire the power to dominate another. To assure this balance, the European nations competed over the acquisition of the latest technology and of colonies.

NEW ECONOMIC POLICIES

New economic policies strengthened the rule of absolute monarchs. The concept of **mercantilism** asserted that nations needed to amass as much wealth as possible. One of the ways to gather wealth was to acquire colonies, an idea that prompted European nations to become engaged in a race for colonies worldwide.

The wealth of European nations was also increased by the rise of **capitalism**. Capitalism is an economic system that allows:

- private ownership
- private decisions regarding production
- profits
- laws of supply and demand

Reliance upon the laws of supply and demand was part of the economic philosophy of Adam Smith of Scotland. In 1776, Smith published *The Wealth of Nations*, in which he proposed the doctrine of ***laissez faire***, or of government non-interference in national economies. Smith was also an advocate of economic independence for women.

With the Commercial Revolution came the use of banks, insurance companies, and stock exchanges. Exploration and colonization were facilitated and financed by **joint-stock companies,** the forerunners of modern corporations. Strong governments also served as protectors of economic rights.

THE SCIENTIFIC REVOLUTION

While absolute monarchs were establishing strong centralized governments across Europe, a **scientific revolution** strengthened the power of Europe among the other regions of the world. During the sixteenth century, scientific research had been built on the traditions of the High Middle Ages. **Copernicus** disproved the popular **geocentric theory** of Ptolemy, who had believed that the earth was the center of the universe. **Johannes Kepler** used the work of Copernicus and his own observations to prove that the orbits of the planets around the sun were ellipses rather than circles. The study of anatomy by **Vesalius** furthered the medical sciences.

In the seventeenth century, new technology and further research continued to advance the study of science. New instruments such as the microscope and improved telescopes promoted studies in biology and astronomy. **Galileo** substantiated the Copernican theory while engaging in his own research concerning the laws of gravitation and planetary motion. Chemical research brought forth new information about the nature of gases. **John Harvey**, an English physician, studied and explained the circulatory system. **Francis Bacon** encouraged experimental research, while **Rene Descartes** determined that the universe was governed by natural laws and also developed analytical geometry. In 1687, **Isaac Newton** set forth the basic principles of all motion, defined the forces of gravity, and established the basic scientific method.

The Philosophy of the Scientific Revolution

Some educated persons held to a belief called **Deism**, which argued that although there may be a god, the role of the deity was simply to set natural laws, or the orderly working of the universe, in motion. Deists were unconcerned with Christian views of human sinfulness; the new intellectuals were more preoccupied with the possibility of human progress. The thought behind the scientific revolution would combine with that of a new movement called the **Enlightenment**.

THE ENLIGHTENMENT

The Enlightenment of the seventeenth and eighteenth centuries was centered in France but progressed throughout the Western world. The basic ideas of the Enlightenment stated that human beings were basically good and could be improved further through education, and that reason, not faith, was the key to truth. Enlightenment thinkers continued to support the scientific advances of the time period. Chemists gained new understanding of major elements while biologists developed a new classification system for the species of plant and animal life.

Enlightenment thinkers were especially concerned with applying the principles of science to society. Criminologists came to believe that cruel punishments failed to deter crime. Political theorists such as the Englishman **John Locke** wrote about the nature of society and government. **Denis Diderot** edited the *Encyclopedia*, a compilation of scientific and social scientific knowledge.

Feminists such as **Mary Wollstonecraft** of England campaigned for political rights and freedoms for women. Reading clubs and coffeehouses allowed artisans and businessmen to discuss the latest ideas to improve human society. Family life changed as physical discipline was replaced by discipline that respected the goodness of children. Wealthy families provided their children with children's books and educational toys. Arranged marriages became less popular, and romantic love within marriage was considered the ideal.

THINGS TO REMEMBER

- The rise of nation-states in Europe in the seventeenth and eighteenth centuries was accompanied by new methods of finance, large bureaucracies, standing armies, and the protection of trade.
    - Absolute monarchies existed in France, Spain, Austria, Prussia, and Russia, where sovereigns claimed to rule by divine right.
    - Constitutional (limited) monarchies existed in Britain and the Netherlands.
- England, France, and Spain were the strongest powers.
- Capitalism developed as nations engaged in colonization and commercial endeavors.
    - Capitalism comprises private ownership, private decisions regarding production, profits, and laws of supply and demand.
- The Scientific Revolution and the Enlightenment led people to examine their world and traditional beliefs. These movements emphasized human potential and political and social rights. Reason was considered the key to truth.

REVIEW QUESTIONS

1. All of the following are true concerning the growth of nation-states in Europe in the seventeenth and eighteenth centuries EXCEPT

    (A) the Holy Roman Empire was a potential nation-state because of its ethnic homogeneity.
    (B) the strongest states in Europe in the eighteenth century were France, England, and Spain.
    (C) England, France, and Spain sought new colonies.
    (D) nation-states acquired power over the Church.
    (E) England and the Netherlands developed constitutional monarchies.

2. All of the following were true concerning absolute monarchs EXCEPT

    (A) ultimate state authority resided in them.
    (B) they claimed to rule by divine right.
    (C) they lacked a bureaucracy to assist them.
    (D) they could make laws.
    (E) they had the power to tax.

3. In central Europe in the seventeenth and eighteenth centuries,
   (A) the Thirty Years' War strengthened German unification.
   (B) the region was highly commercialized and based on capitalism.
   (C) strong monarchies prevailed.
   (D) the Thirty Years' War began the modern state system.
   (E) the Thirty Years' War weakened France.

4. Capitalism is characterized by all of the following EXCEPT
   (A) the elimination of financial risks.
   (B) private ownership.
   (C) the ability to make profits.
   (D) the laws of supply and demand.
   (E) the ability to make private decisions regarding production.

5. The Enlightenment
   (A) was unrelated to the Scientific Revolution.
   (B) believed in the basic goodness of human nature.
   (C) was incompatible with feminism.
   (D) was a global movement.
   (E) supported the use of harsh punishments to deter crime.

ANSWERS AND EXPLANATIONS

1. (A)

Comprised of small German states and northern Italy, the Holy Roman Empire lacked the ethnic homogeneity to become a nation-state. England, France, and Spain sought colonies in the western hemisphere (C). Nation-states confiscated Church lands and used Church disciplinary instruments (D). England and the Netherlands developed monarchies whose authority was curbed by a constitution (E).

2. (C)

Absolute monarchs tended to have a number of lesser officials to assist them in their rule. The other four choices are characteristics that define the nature of the absolute monarch.

3. (D)

By ending religious wars in Europe, the Thirty Years' War allowed for the unification of small regional states, paving the way for the rise of the modern state system. The devastation caused by the war hindered German unification (A). Central Europe was still organized along feudal lines (B). Strong feudal lords prevented the development of strong monarchies (C). France was strengthened by the war (E).

4. (A)

Capitalism allows for the possibility for making a profit (C) and for assuming a loss. It is based on private, rather than state, ownership (B). The laws of supply and demand (D) allow for the consumer to make private decisions regarding production (E).

5. (B)

The Enlightenment held that humans are basically good and can be further improved by education. Confined to Europe (D), it was preceded by the discoveries of the Scientific Revolution (A). During the Enlightenment period, feminists worked to secure rights for women (C), and other reformers came to believe that punishment did not deter crime (E).

CHAPTER 21

Revolution and Nationalist Movements

TIMELINE

1603	End of the Elizabethan Age
1611	King James Version of the Bible
1628	English Petition of Right
1642–1649	English Civil War
1649–1658	The Commonwealth of Oliver Cromwell
1659	The Restoration
1679	The Habeas Corpus Act
1688	The Glorious Revolution
1689	English Bill of Rights
1772	First Partition of Poland
1776	Declaration of Independence
1789	First meeting of the Estates-General in 175 years Beginning of the French Revolution Storming of the Bastille Great Fear Bread riot in Paris Declaration of the Rights of Man
1791	Declaration of the Rights of Woman

1792	French National Convention establishes a republic
1793	Execution of Louis XVI Second Partition of Poland
1793–1794	The Reign of Terror
1795	Third Partition of Poland
1799	The Directory chooses Napoleon to command the French army Napoleon becomes dictator of France
1803	Louisiana sold to the United States
1804	Haiti declares its independence Napoleon crowns himself emperor of France
1805	Battle of Trafalgar
1806	Napoleon's Continental System
1808–1813	The Peninsular War
1812	Napoleon's invasion of Russia
1813	Battle of Leipzig
1814	Napoleon is banished to Elba
1815	The Hundred Days
1816	Argentina wins independence Battle of Waterloo Congress of Vienna
1821	Venezuela wins independence Mexico wins independence from Spain
1822	Brazil declares independence with Dom Pedro as ruler
1823	Central America wins independence from Spain and Mexico
1824	Battle of Ayacucho
1827	Greece wins independence
1830	Liberal revolutions in Europe
1848	Failed liberal revolutions in Europe Treaty of Guadalupe Hidalgo
1862	Otto von Bismarck becomes prime minister of Prussia
1862–1867	French occupation of Mexico

1870	Unification of Italy Franco-Prussian War
1871	Unification of Germany
1910–1919	The Mexican Revolution
1911–1912	Revolution in China End of Chinese dynastic rule

IMPORTANT PEOPLE, PLACES, EVENTS, AND CONCEPTS

constitutional monarchy*
Elizabeth I
James I
King James Version
Charles I
Petition of Right
Oliver Cromwell
Charles II
Whigs
Tories
James II
William and Mary
Glorious Revolution
English Bill of Rights
Thomas Hobbes
social contract*
John Locke
Voltaire
Montesquieu
separation of powers*
checks and balances*
Jean Jacques Rousseau
direct democracy*
enlightened despot*
Frederick the Great
Catherine the Great
Joseph II
Declaration of Independence
National Assembly
Tennis Court Oath
Bastille
Great Fear
Declaration of the Rights of Man
Olympe de Gouges
Declaration of the Rights of Woman
Legislative Assembly
radical*
moderate*
conservative*
National Convention
Jacobins
Jean Paul Marat
Georges Danton
First Coalition
Maximilien Robespierre
Directory
Napoleon Bonaparte
Napoleonic Code
Horatio Nelson
Duke of Wellington
reactionary*
Klemens von Metternich
Concert of Europe
balance of power*
legitimacy*
German Confederation
Simón Bolívar
José de San Martín
Gran Colombia
Bernardo O'Higgins
Miguel Hidalgo
José María Morelos
Agustín de Iturbide
liberal*
Louis Napoleon
Count Cavour
Red Shirts
Giuseppe Garibaldi
Vatican City
Wilhelm I
Otto von Bismarck
*realpolitik**
kaiser*
romanticism*
Lord Byron
Ludwig von Beethoven
realism*
impressionism*
Santa Anna
Benito Juárez
Archduke Maximilian
Porfirio Díaz
Francisco Madero
Emiliano Zapata

Thomas Jefferson	Kingdom of Sardinia-Piedmont	Pancho Villa
creole*	nationalism*	Victoriano Huerta
Old Regime	Toussaint L'Ouverture	Venustiano Carranza
estate*	*peninsular**	PRI
bourgeoisie*	*mestizo**	Sun Yixian
Estates-General*	mulatto	

THE ENGLISH REVOLUTION

While many European nations continued to be ruled by absolute monarchs, England established a **constitutional monarchy**, or a government in which the monarch's power is limited by law. Like their European contemporaries, the English monarchs believed that they ruled by divine right. Consequently, they experienced frequent conflicts with Parliament, England's legislative body. **Elizabeth I**, daughter of Henry VIII, had managed Parliament with skill, though she had found it increasingly difficult to prevent the Puritans in Parliament from challenging her decisions. When Elizabeth I died childless in 1603, she was succeeded by her cousin James Stuart of Scotland, who became **James I** of England. During his reign, in 1611, the **King James Version** of the Bible (still used today) was published. Unlike Elizabeth, James I spent his reign battling with Parliament, especially over money.

In 1625, **Charles I** became king. Charles asked Parliament in 1628 to grant him funds, but Parliament did not consent until Charles signed the **Petition of Right**. This document placed several conditions upon the monarch's rule, preventing him from:

- imprisoning his subjects without due cause
- housing the military in private homes
- imposing martial law in times of peace
- imposing taxes without the consent of Parliament

The English Civil War

Charles promptly refused to agree to the Petition of Right and further angered the Puritans in England and the Presbyterians in Scotland by refusing to allow them to worship as they chose. Conflict between Charles and non-Anglicans and Parliament erupted in the English Civil War from 1642 to 1649. In 1649, the victorious Puritans and their leader, **Oliver Cromwell**, executed Charles I for treason. Cromwell initially established a republican form of government called the Commonwealth, but eventually governed as a military dictator until his death in 1658.

The Restoration and the Glorious Revolution

In 1659, the English asked the older son of Charles I to rule; his reign would be called the Restoration. In 1679, the Habeas Corpus Act ensured that prisoners would not be held without reason. After the death of the childless **Charles II**, a debate concerning succession divided the English into two groups—**Whigs** and **Tories**—that would be the predecessors of England's political parties.

When Charles II died in 1685, he was succeeded by his brother, **James II**, a Catholic. In 1688, Protestants in Parliament invited Protestants William of Orange and his wife Mary, daughter of James II, to rule England. The resulting bloodless revolt was called the **Glorious Revolution**. During the reign of **William and Mary**, Parliament wrote a **Bill of Rights**, which William and Mary agreed to in 1689. The document stated that monarchs could NOT:

- suspend a law of Parliament
- levy taxes without the consent of Parliament
- hinder freedom of speech in Parliament
- prevent a citizen from petitioning the monarch regarding grievances

POLITICAL THOUGHT OF THE ENLIGHTENMENT

While the English were forming their constitutional monarchy, the humanitarian thought of the Enlightenment caused some philosophers to consider the nature of government. In his work *Leviathan* (1651), **Thomas Hobbes** of England wrote that people were naturally cruel, greedy, and selfish. He proposed the idea of government as a **social contract** in which people gave up the state of nature to a ruler in order to obtain law and order. Hobbes concluded that the best government was an absolute monarchy.

The ideas of English philosopher **John Locke** particularly inspired the leaders of the American Revolution. In *Two Treatises on Government* (1690), Locke wrote that all men are born with the natural rights of life, liberty, and property. He stated that governments exist to protect these rights, and that governments who fail to protect these rights may be overthrown.

The French philosopher **Voltaire** (1694–1778) admired the English style of government and campaigned for freedom of religion and speech. Another French philosopher, **Montesquieu**, wrote *On the Spirit of Laws* (1748), in which he advocated a government that provided for **separation of powers** and a system of **checks and balances**. Both these concepts were written into the United States Constitution.

The ideas of French philosopher **Jean Jacques Rousseau** captivated leaders of the French Revolution. In his work *The Social Contract* (1762), Rousseau supported the idea of **direct democracy**. He proposed the idea of a social contract as a contract between free persons in order to form a society and government, and he also believed in the equality of all people and abolition of titles.

Enlightened Despots

As a response to Enlightenment thinking, some of Europe's absolute monarchs embraced reforms in their respective countries. These **enlightened despots**, as they were called, maintained that the monarch must rule with the welfare of his subjects and the state foremost in his or her policies. Among the enlightened despots were Frederick II (the Great) of Prussia, **Catherine the Great** of Russia, and Holy Roman Emperor **Joseph II** of Austria. **Frederick the Great** granted some degree of religious freedom and broadened freedom of speech, but stopped short of ending serfdom in Prussia. Catherine the Great continued the policies of Peter the Great to further modernize Russia, but to appease Russian nobles, she gave them increased power over the serfs. In collaboration with the monarchs of Prussia and Austria, Catherine participated in the First Partition of Poland in 1772, in which the three countries each seized a slice of Polish territory. Followed by the Second Partition in 1793 and the Third Partition in 1795, these divisions served to wipe Poland off the map until its reappearance after World War I as an independent nation. Joseph II introduced freedom of religion and of the press in Austria. He also abolished serfdom, but this was reversed after his death.

THE AMERICAN REVOLUTION

The philosophy of the Enlightenment fed the fire of revolution in the British North American colonies. The **Declaration of Independence**, written by **Thomas Jefferson**, borrowed heavily from John Locke, stating that the colonies were justified in breaking away from Great Britain after its monarch failed to uphold the social contract. One alteration made by Jefferson was to change Locke's description of natural rights to read "life, liberty, and the pursuit of happiness." Like many revolutions that would follow its pattern, the American Revolution was initiated by the middle class. The middle class often found themselves with the financial support and the educational background that fostered their position as leaders.

THE FRENCH REVOLUTION

In France, key citizens who had been discouraged by the excesses of absolute monarchs were noting the progress of the American Revolution. The *ancien régime*, or the **Old Regime**, continued the division of social classes into three **estates**. The First Estate, comprised of the clergy, made up about 1 percent of the population but controlled 10 percent of the land. The Second Estate, made up of the landed nobility, consisted of about 2 percent of the population who owned about 20 percent of the land. While the Second Estate paid only minimal taxes, the First Estate was not taxed at all. The remainder of the French—merchants, laborers, and peasants—belonged to the Third Estate. The most populous Third Estate group was the peasants, who were heavily taxed. The leaders of the Third Estate were artisans and merchants of the middle class, or **bourgeoisie**; many of these middle-class leaders had been educated in Enlightenment thought.

The Revolution Begins

When Louis XVI's extravagant spending nearly bankrupted the French treasury, in May 1789 the Second Estate forced him to call a meeting of the **Estates-General**, or French assembly, which had not convened for 175 years. The traditional voting procedure in the Estates-General was for each estate to have one vote—allowing the First and Second Estates to outvote the Third. In 1789, members of the bourgeoisie proposed changing the rules to allow one vote per delegate, giving the Third Estate the same number of votes as the other two estates combined. Their request was denied, so the Third Estate formed the **National Assembly** to legislate for France. Subsequently locked out of their meeting place, Third Estate delegates met in a tennis court, where they took a pledge ("the **Tennis Court Oath**") to write a new constitution for France.

The symbolic act of revolution among the French was the storming of the **Bastille**, a Paris prison, on July 14, 1789. A time of panic and riots ("the **Great Fear**") ensued, with French peasants burning some of the feudal manor houses. In October 1789, the women of Paris, in a riot over the high price of bread, demanded that Louis XVI and his wife, Marie Antoinette, leave Versailles for Paris.

Declarations of Rights

The key document accepted by the National Assembly was the **Declaration of the Rights of Man** (1789). Reflecting the ideals of the Enlightenment and the Declaration of Independence, it stated that men were born equal and that men enjoy the natural rights of "liberty, property, security, and resistance to oppression."

A noticeable omission in the French Declaration was any reference to the rights of women. To rectify this, in 1791 a feminist French journalist, **Olympe de Gouges,** wrote the **Declaration of the Rights of Woman,** which was not accepted by the National Assembly. (Later in the course of the revolution she would be executed by the guillotine.) French women were allowed to fight for the revolution, but could not share in its rewards.

The Fall of the French Monarchy

The government forged by the National Assembly was a constitutional monarchy. In 1791, the National Assembly, having completed its constitution, created the **Legislative Assembly**. The Legislative Assembly divided itself into three factions, each of which sat in a separate section of the assembly hall. The seating position of these groups in the Legislative Assembly—**radicals** (left), **moderates** (center), and **conservatives** (right)—gave rise to the terms *right*, *left*, and *center* we still use today to refer to positions on political issues.

The course of the French Revolution was complicated by war with Prussia and Austria in 1792. Prussia's statement of support for the royal family angered Parisians. In August 1792, the Parisians imprisoned Louis XVI, Marie Antoinette, and their children after the family tried to escape from France. The Legislative Assembly dissolved itself, setting up a **National Convention** that abolished the limited monarchy and established a republic in September 1792; male citizens were given the right to vote. By this time, control of France was in the hands of a radical political club known as the **Jacobins.** Among the Jacobin leaders were **Jean Paul Marat** and **Georges Danton.** In January 1793, the National Convention, under Jacobin influence, executed Louis XVI by the guillotine. To continue the war against the **First Coalition** (which now included Great Britain, the Netherlands, and Spain in addition to Prussia and Austria), the National Convention drafted an army that included women.

The Reign of Terror

The aftermath of the execution of Louis XVI was a period known as the Reign of Terror. Its leader, **Maximilien Robespierre,** headed the Committee of Public Safety, which guillotined alleged enemies of the republic; among its victims was Marie Antoinette. The Reign of Terror saw the execution of both Marat and Danton. When Robespierre was guillotined in 1794, the Reign of Terror came to an end.

A new government now ruled France: the legislature and the **Directory,** or executive branch composed of five men. To command the French army, the Directory chose a young army officer named **Napoleon Bonaparte.**

THE EMPIRE OF NAPOLEON

In November 1799, the Directory put Napoleon in charge of the French army; the following day, in a *coup d'état*, Napoleon seized power as the dictator of France. In 1802, Napoleon's government signed peace treaties with the members of the Second Coalition against France—Great Britain, Austria, and Russia. With the immediate threat of war resolved, Napoleon went to work making changes in the French government and society. He set up a national bank and equalized taxation while also setting up a public school system. The most well-known of Napoleon's achievements was his system of laws known as the **Napoleonic Code**. The code affirmed the equality of all adult men before the law, but at the same time restored the idea of a patriarchal family and disallowed women the same property rights as men. It also restricted the freedoms of speech and of the press. Slavery, which had been abolished in France's Caribbean colonies during the Revolution, was now reinstated.

After failing to put down a rebellion in Saint Dominigue, and needing funds to carry out war against the Third Coalition of European nations, Napoleon sold his territory in Louisiana to the United States in 1803. In 1804, Napoleon crowned himself emperor of France and went about acquiring more territory. By 1805, his only remaining opponent was Great Britain. Napoleon's loss to English Admiral **Horatio Nelson** at the Battle of Trafalgar in 1805 guaranteed the supreme status of the British navy.

The Fall of Napoleon

By 1812 Napoleon's empire controlled most of Europe, excluding Great Britain, Portugal, Sweden, and the Ottoman empire. In his attempt to extend his empire, Napoleon made three errors that sealed his fate:

- the Continental System, or blockade against Great Britain (1806)
- the Peninsular War against Spain (1808–1813)
- the invasion of Russia during the winter of 1812

Napoleon's power began to wane with his defeat at the hands of the Fourth Coalition at the Battle of Leipzig in 1813. In 1814, imminent defeat forced Napoleon to give up his throne; his opponents banished him to the island of Elba in the Mediterranean. Escaping from Elba in March 1815, he returned to France and reestablished his power during a period known as The Hundred Days. Finally, the forces of Great Britain and Prussia defeated Napoleon at the Battle of Waterloo in Belgium in June 1815. Afterwards, Napoleon was banished to the island of St. Helena in the South Atlantic.

THE CONGRESS OF VIENNA

The defeat of Napoleon created a desire for stability in Europe once again. In 1815, a number of key European powers assembled in Vienna, Austria, to create a plan that would promote stable relations among the European nation-states. The general mood of the delegates was **reactionary**, advocating a return to the status quo. Participating in the Congress of Vienna were heads of state or foreign ministers from Austria, Prussia, Russia, Great Britain, and France. As chairman of the sessions, Austrian Prince **Klemens von Metternich** sought to maintain peace among the European nations by creating a **balance of power** among rival countries. A balance of power would assure that no one nation could be a threat to the others. To guard against future revolutions, Metternich set up a series of alliances called the **Concert of Europe**, which required nations to come to the aid of one another if war erupted.

Goals and Action of the Congress

The participants in the Congress of Vienna shared the following goals:

- The establishment of lasting peace and stability in Europe
- The prevention of future French aggression
- Restoration of the balance of power
- **Legitimacy**, or the restoration of royal families to their thrones

To realize their goals, the delegates:

- Formed the Kingdom of the Netherlands
- Created the **German Confederation**
- Recognized the independence of Switzerland
- Added Genoa to the Kingdom of Sardinia
- Required France to return territories conquered by Napoleon, but left France a major power
- Affirmed the principle of legitimacy

Results of the Congress of Vienna

The long-term results of the Congress were felt, not only in Europe, but also in the western hemisphere.

- Conservatives regained control of governments.
- Colonial Latin American governments declared their independence.
- An age of peace was created in Europe.
- The power of France was diminished and the power of Great Britain and Prussia was increased.
- The growth of **nationalism** was encouraged.

THE HAITIAN REVOLUTION

The principles of the American and French revolutions sparked ideas of revolution and national independence in Latin America. The first Latin American territory to assert its independence was the French colony of Saint Dominigue on the western third of the Caribbean island of Hispaniola. Most of the population of Saint Dominigue was composed of African slaves who were kept under strict subjection by the territory's minority group, the white slaveholders. When in August 1791 an African priest called for revolution, 100,000 slaves revolted. An ex-slave, **Toussaint L'Ouverture**, emerged as a capable leader. In 1802, after the arrival of French troops in Saint-Domingue, L'Ouverture was lured onto a ship to sign an agreement for independence. Taken to France against his will, L'Ouverture died in a French prison in 1803. One of his generals, Dessalines, continued the struggle for freedom. The new country of Haiti declared its independence on January 1, 1804, making it the first colony in which African slaves gained their freedom from Europeans.

SOUTH AMERICAN INDEPENDENCE

Social Classes in Spanish America

The social structure of Spanish America was rigidly stratified. The most elite position was held by the ***peninsulares***, who were those who had been born in Spain. Beneath them were the ***creoles***, or people of European descent born in the colonies. The third level in the social structure was that of the ***mestizos***, or those of mixed European and Indian heritage. Africans and ***mulattos*** (those of mixed European and African ancestry) comprised the fourth class. At the bottom of the social structure were the Indians. The peninsulares and creoles controlled power and wealth, but the creoles soon gained prominence as leaders of the revolutions that would sweep across Latin America. Generally very well educated, often in European universities, they were familiar with Enlightenment thought.

When in 1808 Napoleon replaced the Spanish king with his brother Joseph, the creoles of Latin America no longer felt a loyalty to the monarch on the Spanish throne. By 1810 rebellion had erupted in Latin America; even the restoration of King Ferdinand VII to the throne of Spain did not curb revolutionary fervor.

Spain's Colonies Gain Independence

The leaders of South American independence were the highly capable generals **Simón Bolívar**, a creole from Venezuela, and **José de San Martín** of Argentina. Bolívar dreamed of creating a strong nation which he called **Gran Colombia**. By 1821, he had led Venezuela to independence and then proceeded to Ecuador, where he met with San Martín. After achieving Argentine independence in 1816, San Martín crossed the Andes into Chile, where he was joined by **Bernardo O'Higgins**. The two armies freed Chile in 1818. In 1822, Bolívar was left in command of revolutionary forces. At the Battle of Ayacucho in December 1824, Bolívar led the remaining Spanish colonies to independence.

Bolívar had long anticipated greater prosperity for the Latin American countries after independence had been attained. His hopes, however, fell short of reality as the aftermath of independence brought destruction of both cities and fields and economic devastation because of the disruption of trade. Both his Gran Colombia and the United Provinces of Central America had divided into smaller national states within a few years.

Independence for Brazil

The colony of Brazil followed a different, peaceful pattern in winning its independence. When Napoleon invaded Spain and Portugal in 1807, the Portuguese royal family escaped to Brazil. Upon the arrival of Prince John (later King John VI), the city of Rio de Janeiro became the capital of both Brazil and Portugal. After Napoleon was defeated, the creoles demanded independence from Portugal. In 1822, the Portuguese monarch returned to Portugal, leaving his son Dom Pedro to rule Brazil. Under Dom Pedro, Brazil became an independent monarchy and the only country in Latin America to be ruled by a king after independence.

INDEPENDENCE FOR MEXICO

Mexico Wins Independence From Spain

The Mexican revolt for independence against Spain was unique among the revolts of the western hemisphere because it was initiated by mestizos rather than by the creole class. The cry for independence in Mexico went out on September 16, 1810, when Father **Miguel Hidalgo**, a priest from the village of Dolores, assembled his parishioners to encourage rebellion against Spain. A subsequent march of mestizos and Indians toward Mexico City alarmed the Spanish and creoles, who then defeated Hidalgo in 1811. Another priest, Father **José María Morelos**, took over the revolution until he was defeated in 1815 by the creole **Agustín de Iturbide**. When revolution in Spain resulted in a **liberal** government, the alarmed creoles of Mexico decided to back Iturbide. In 1821 Mexico achieved its independence from Spain. In 1823, Central America won its freedom from both Spain and Mexico.

The Mexican Revolution

After Mexico's successful revolution against Spain in 1821, Antonio López de **Santa Anna** dominated Mexico's political scene by serving as the country's president four times. During his administration, Santa Anna was unsuccessful in preventing the independence of Texas and also lost a border dispute with the United States in the Mexican War. In 1848, the Treaty of Guadalupe Hidalgo ended the Mexican War and granted to the United States the territories of California and the Southwest portion of the United States.

Benito Juárez

In the mid-nineteenth century, an Indian named **Benito Juárez** came to power in Mexico. Although he was deposed by Santa Anna in 1853, Juárez had carried out a reform program that redistributed land, increased educational opportunities, and maintained the separation of church and state. Returning to power in 1861, Juárez's presidency was again cut short by a French takeover of Mexico in 1862; Napoleon III of France appointed Austrian **archduke Maximilian** to rule Mexico as a puppet emperor. When France withdrew in 1867, Juárez resumed his presidency, encouraging foreign trade and the construction of railroads.

Porfirio Díaz

In 1876, **Porfirio Díaz** rose to power in Mexico. An authoritarian ruler of Indian descent, Díaz built banks and railroads and encouraged foreign investment. Mexico was not without its troubles, however. Land was distributed unevenly; industrial workers had low wages and poor working conditions. New political parties formed in the hopes of alleviating these conditions; among these new parties was one led by **Francisco Madero** of Mexico's elite class.

The Beginnings and End of Revolution

Educated in the United States and France, Madero believed in democracy. Exiled to the United States by Díaz, Madero called for revolution. Among the leaders of the revolution were the farmer **Emiliano Zapata** and the cowboy Francisco **"Pancho" Villa**. The revolutionary years were marked by frequent assassinations and changes in leadership, from Madero to **Victoriano Huerta** to **Venustiano Carranza**. After the murder of Zapata in 1919 at the hands of Carranza, the Mexican Revolution came to an end.

The revised Mexican constitution that emerged from the revolution promoted land reforms, workers' rights, and education. In addition, some legal rights, such as the power to initiate lawsuits, were granted to women. In 1929 a new political party, the Institutional Revolutionary Party (**PRI**) came to power. Forbidding opposition, PRI would be the dominant party of twentieth-century Mexico and would be responsible for bringing long-term stability to Mexico.

NATIONALIST STRUGGLES IN EUROPE

While colonies in Latin America were declaring their independence, a strong sense of nationalism swept throughout Europe in the nineteenth century, fueling further revolutions.

Greece

Greece was part of the Ottoman empire in the nineteenth century. Bolstered by the memories of her own glorious past, Greece declared independence in 1821. Out of respect for ancient Greek traditions, other European nations supported the Greeks. The English poet Lord Byron joined the Greek cause and in 1824 died of a fever in Greece. In 1827, Greece won her independence.

1830 Revolutions

In the 1830s, the revolutionary movement would place liberals and nationalists against conservatives.

- **Conservatives** wanted to maintain Europe's traditional monarchies.
- **Liberals** advocated limited governmental interference and representation of landowners in the government.
- **Radicals** wanted broader voting rights and often supported democracy and social reforms to alleviate the plight of the lower classes.

The Belgians achieved their independence in 1830, but revolution failed in Italy and Poland. A French revolution of 1830 brought a more limited monarchy.

Revolutions of 1848

The year 1848 witnessed another revolutionary wave. The Hungarians, under the leadership of Louis Kossuth, called for representative government within the Austrian empire. The Czechs called for the independence of Bohemia. Mob actions in Vienna caused Metternich to resign. Liberal revolts then occurred in the German states. Revolts in some of the states of northern Italy, supported by Giuseppe Mazzini's Young Italy, failed.

In France, revolts ended the rule of Louis-Philippe, who had come to the throne during the 1830 revolution. When radicals turned to violence in the streets of Paris, the French reacted by writing a constitution calling for a parliament and an elected president. They met their goal with the election of **Louis Napoleon**, a nephew of Napoleon Bonaparte, in 1848. Calling himself Emperor Napoleon III, he improved the French economy by constructing public works and railroads and promoting the growth of industry.

The Unification of Italy

The movement for Italian unity began in 1832 with the organization of a group called Young Italy by an Italian named Giuseppe Mazzini. Believing strongly in the importance of nation-states to ensure democracy in Europe, Mazzini's hopes faded when the revolutions of 1848 failed in Italy. Mazzini and his supporters were then driven from Italy by the previous rulers of the Italian states.

The Congress of Vienna had left the Italian peninsula a region of independent territories, with Austria ruling a number of northern provinces and the Bourbons of Spain in control of the Kingdom of the Two Sicilies. The **Kingdom of Sardinia-Piedmont** eventually became the leader in Italian unification. Its prime minister, **Count Cavour**, gained control of northern Italy by starting a war with Austria. Cavour then cooperated with the **Red Shirts** of **Giuseppe Garibaldi** to capture Sicily. An election granted Cavour the power to unite the northern and southern provinces. In 1866, the Austrian province of Venetia was added to Italy, and in 1870, the Papal States came under Italian control. One exception was **Vatican City**, a section of Rome that would continue to be governed by the pope. Although unified, Italy continued as an unstable state; its most pressing problem was the economic disparity between the industrial north and the agricultural south.

The Unification of Germany

After the Congress of Vienna, a loose union of 39 German states constituted the German Confederation. The confederation was dominated by its two largest states, Prussia and Austria-Hungary. With its industrial might, powerful army, and ethnic cohesion, Prussia became the leader in German unification. The Prussian King **Wilhelm I's** choice for prime minister in 1862 was the Junker **Otto von Bismarck**. Believing in ***realpolitik***, or "reality politics," Bismarck would lead Prussia to unify Germany. Ruling without the consent of the Prussian parliament, Bismarck stated that his goals would be accomplished "by blood and iron." Bismarck's policy was to win territory by stirring up conflicts with weaker states that controlled territory he desired. By 1867, the northern states of Germany had formed a North German Confederation dominated by Germany. By publishing a falsified version of a diplomatic telegram, Bismarck made it appear as if Wilhelm I had insulted the French; the incident resulted in the Franco-Prussian War in 1870, a conflict won by the Prussian army. Southern Germany, which had previously resisted German unification, now accepted the leadership of Prussia, finalizing German unification. In 1871, Wilhelm I of Prussia was crowned ***kaiser***, the German word for "emperor." The German empire, or Second Reich, had begun.

REVOLUTION IN CHINA

The reform movement also came to China in the early twentieth century. Young Chinese men educated in European schools dreamed of building a nation-state in the Western tradition. Among these men was **Sun Yixian**, who also wanted to implement social programs to assist the peasants and working classes. In 1911, uprisings of secret societies and student demonstrations protested the reliance of the Manchu dynasty on railway loans from the West. Unable to contain the rebellion, the Manchus relinquished their power in 1912, ending dynastic rule in China. Perceiving Confucian teachings as outdated and irrelevant, the new order in China abandoned the civil service exam. The traditional civilization was being abandoned and the Qing dynasty was no more. China faced an uncertain future and more days of upheaval in the decades ahead.

REVOLUTION IN ART AND LITERATURE

The political revolutions of the nineteenth century were mirrored in the art and literature of the day. During the first half of the century the major movement was **romanticism**, which reflected an admiration for nature and also an emphasis on individual thoughts and feelings. **Lord Byron**, who fought for Greek independence, was a leading romanticist. In politics, romanticism valued the common person and promoted democracy. In music, composers such as **Ludwig van Beethoven** produced works emphasizing emotion and expression.

After the mid-nineteenth century, the ills of industrialization became the focus of the arts. A new movement called **realism** produced paintings and novels that described the unsanitary, overcrowded conditions in which industrial laborers lived and worked. In the 1860s, a group of Parisian painters reacted to realism by creating the school of **impressionism**. Impressionists portrayed their subjects as they appeared to the artist at a given moment in time, as if the painter had captured only a fleeting glimpse of the subject.

THINGS TO REMEMBER

- From the seventeenth to the early twentieth centuries, citizens of Europe, the Americas, and China were engaged in various forms of revolution that demonstrated their zeal in advocating the principles of self-rule. The results of the revolutions were:
    - The **English** bloodless **Glorious Revolution** (1688) limited the power of the monarchy.
    - The **American Revolution** created a republic based on Enlightenment principles (1775–1783).
    - The **French Revolution** ended an absolutist monarchy, limited the power of the elite, and, like the American Revolution, spread Enlightenment ideas and influenced revolutions in the western hemisphere (1789–1799).
    - The **Haitian Revolution** resulted in Haiti's becoming the first colony in which African slaves gained their freedom from Europeans (1791–1804).
    - The **South American revolutions** led to independence from Spain, but failed to bring prosperity to South America (1810–1824).
    - The **Mexican revolt against Spain** was unique in that it was initiated by mestizos (1810–1821).
    - The **Mexican Revolution** produced a constitution that brought some legal rights to women and also furthered land reform, worker rights, and education (1910–1919).
    - **Greece** won its independence from the Ottoman empire in 1827.
    - The **1830 Revolutions** brought independence to Belgium and brought a more limited monarchy to France.
    - The **Revolutions of 1848** largely failed to bring more liberal governments to Europe.
    - **Revolution in China** in 1911 ended dynastic rule in China and promoted social programs.

REVIEW QUESTIONS

1. The English Revolution guaranteed all of the following rights EXCEPT

   (A) the right to legal counsel.
   (B) no taxation without the consent of Parliament.
   (C) the right of petition.
   (D) no imprisonment without due cause.
   (E) no housing the military in private homes.

2. Which of the following is paired correctly with an element of his philosophy?

   (A) Hobbes—abolition of titles
   (B) Locke—life, liberty, and property as natural rights
   (C) Rousseau—freedom of religion and speech
   (D) Montesquieu—absolute monarchy as the best government
   (E) Voltaire—separation of powers

3. The French Revolution

   (A) was a significant step forward for women's rights in France.
   (B) saw its ideals suppressed during the rule of Napoleon.
   (C) ended in the establishment of a republic for France.
   (D) was initiated by the peasant classes.
   (E) displayed the typical pattern of revolutions by undergoing a period of extremism during its course.

4. All of the following proved true of the Age of Revolution EXCEPT that

   (A) Chinese dynastic rule ended.
   (B) South American revolutions brought peace and prosperity to that continent.
   (C) the French Revolution influenced revolutions in Latin America.
   (D) the Mexican Revolution furthered land reforms.
   (E) Haitian slaves won their freedom.

5. The Congress of Vienna

   (A) resulted in peace and stability in Europe throughout the nineteenth century.
   (B) restored the balance of power until the outbreak of World War I.
   (C) discouraged the growth of nationalism.
   (D) discouraged Latin American independence movements.
   (E) assisted in the unification of both Italy and Germany.

ANSWERS AND EXPLANATIONS

1. (A)

The right to legal counsel was not guaranteed by the English Revolution. Choices (B), (D), and (E) were guaranteed by the Petition of Right. Choices (B) and (C) were also guaranteed by the Bill of Rights.

2. (B)

Locke is paired correctly with the natural rights of life, liberty, and property. Hobbes should be paired with "absolute monarchy as the best government." Rousseau corresponds with "abolition of titles," while Montesquieu belongs with "separation of powers." Voltaire should be paired with "freedom of religion and speech."

3. (E)

Most revolutions undergo a period of extremism. The Declaration of the Rights of Woman was not accepted by the National Assembly (A). The ideals of the French Revolution were spread through the rule of Napoleon (B). It ended in the establishment of rule by the Directory of five men (C). The revolution was initiated by the bourgeoisie, or middle class, of the Third Estate (D).

4. (B)

South American revolutions failed to bring prosperity. Chinese dynastic rule ended after the revolution of 1911–1912 (A). The French Revolution especially influenced the Haitian Revolution (C). The Mexican Revolution redistributed lands formerly held by the wealthy to the peasants (D). The Haitian Revolution culminated in an independent Haiti and an end to slavery (E).

5. (E)

By creating the German Confederation and adding Genoa to the Kingdom of Sardinia, the Congress promoted the unification of these two states. It failed to restore peace in Europe (A) throughout the entire nineteenth century (i.e., the Franco-Prussian War). The balance of power would erode before World War I with the race for colonies (B). It encouraged the growth of nationalism (C) and independence (D).

CHAPTER 22

Industrialization and the Growth of Democracy

TIMELINE

1700s	Enclosure movement
1750s	Beginning of English industrial revolution
1770s	Invention of the steam engine
1830s	German industrialization
1832	English Reform Bill
1837	Invention of the telegraph
1838	Chartist movement
1840s	Irish Potato Famine
1848	Declaration of Sentiments
1850s	France industrializes Self-rule for Australia and New Zealand
1861–1865	U.S. Civil War
1867	Formation of the Dominion of Canada
1868	Meiji Restoration Beginning of Japanese industrialization
1875	The Third French Republic begins
1876	Invention of the telephone

1888	*The Communist Manifesto*
1895	Invention of the radio
1903	Wright Brothers' flight
1904	Trans-Siberian railroad

IMPORTANT PEOPLE, PLACES, EVENTS, AND CONCEPTS

enclosure movement*
factors of production*
capital*
entrepreneurship*
James Watt
Eli Whitney
Robert Fulton
macadam road*
turnpike
Samuel F.B. Morse
Alexander Graham Bell
Muhammad Ali
commercial agriculture*
capitalism*
suffrage*
Thomas Malthus
David Ricardo
utopian socialist*
John Stuart Mill
utilitarian*
Robert Owen
socialism*
communism*
Karl Marx
Friedrich Engels
bourgeoisie*
proletariat*
collective bargaining*
abolition*
rotten borough*
Chartist movement
Declaration of Sentiments
Lucretia Mott
Elizabeth Cady Stanton
Emmeline Pankhurst
Thomas Edison
Guglielmo Marconi
Henry Ford
Wilbur and Orville Wright
Louis Pasteur
pasteurization*
germ theory of disease
Joseph Lister
Dmitri Mendeleev
Marie and Pierre Curie
Albert Einstein
Charles Darwin
theory of evolution*
natural selection*
Sigmund Freud
psychoanalysis
Social Darwinism*

EASTERN MODELS OF INDUSTRIALIZATION

In Europe and the Americas, the political revolutions of the eighteenth and nineteenth centuries brought new forms of government. A second revolution would now sweep these regions—an industrial revolution that would alter manufacturing methods, raise standards of living, and change the structure of family life. The western world was not unique in its transition to industrialization: During the Song dynasty, the Chinese had experienced the beginnings of industrial organization in its iron industry, and India's widespread textile industry, although not based on mechanization, inspired the industrial revolution in Great Britain.

THE AGRICULTURAL REVOLUTION

Before industrialization started in England, there were dramatic changes in the way agriculture was practiced. In the early 1700s, the "**enclosure movement**" saw wealthy landowners purchase land from small farmers. Enclosing their land with fences or hedges, the holders of larger plots of land then had opportunities to experiment with new farming methods. It also enclosed common areas used by the public to graze their animals. The enclosure movement required small farmers to either take up tenant farming or move to cities and become part of the urban labor force.

Among agricultural improvements were crop rotation, scientific breeding of animals, and more sophisticated farm implements. The increase in food supply boosted population growth and the desire for new products. Population growth also resulted in a migration of large numbers of former landholders from the southeastern portion of England to the northwest, where conditions were especially suitable for the growth of factories.

BEGINNINGS OF THE INDUSTRIAL REVOLUTION IN ENGLAND

By the mid-eighteenth century, England was an ideal location to begin industrialization because it enjoyed an abundance of the **factors of production**:

- Land (including water power, coal, and iron ore)
- Labor (former small landowners)
- **Capital** (availability of bank loans to purchase machinery and buildings)
- **Entrepreneurship** (the ability of persons to organize the factors of production and assume risks)

Industrialization in England was also enhanced by its participation in world trade and by a government willing to legislate measures to promote banking and industrialization.

The English industrial revolution began in the cotton textile industry, where new machines for spinning and weaving increased production. By the late eighteenth century, machinery became large enough to require its placement in factories. The earliest factories required water power and so were constructed along rivers and streams. In the 1770s, the invention of the steam engine by **James Watt** led to its application to power factory machinery. Much of England's cotton in the late eighteenth century came from the plantations of the American South, where **Eli Whitney**'s patent on the cotton gin provided the mechanization to speed up the cleaning of raw cotton. (Other sources of raw cotton were Egypt and India; the English had long valued the importation of colored cotton fabric, or calico, from India.)

Improvements in Transportation

Accompanying the industrial revolution were improvements in transportation. In 1807, **Robert Fulton** of the United States inaugurated the first commercial steamboat service in the world. The construction of canals, **macadam roads**, and **turnpikes** in both England and the United States facilitated the distribution of manufactured goods. Distribution was further improved with the invention of the railway locomotive in the early nineteenth century. Railroads also created new jobs and made travel easier. The movement of goods and information was assisted by the inventions of the telegraph in 1837 by **Samuel Morse** and the telephone in 1876 by **Alexander Graham Bell**.

EXPANSION OF THE INDUSTRIAL REVOLUTION

The United States

The industrial revolution quickly spread to the textile industry of the United States, which enjoyed the same factors of production as England. Railroads played a major role in industrialization in the United States, especially after the conclusion of the Civil War in 1865. Industrialization led to the rise of large corporations owned by stockholders who shared in the profits but assumed very limited risks.

Continental Europe

Railroads were also a key factor in the expansion of the industrial revolution throughout Europe. With Belgium taking the lead, other nations followed, frequently bringing the factory system to small regions rather than to entire nations. Germany began to industrialize in the 1830s, and by the end of the nineteenth century, became a strong industrial and military power. The industrial revolution came to France in the 1850s after the government began building railroads.

Not all of Europe was able to set up factories. Obstacles such as mountainous terrain that prevented adequate construction and insufficient waterways kept empires like Austria-Hungary and countries such as Spain from early industrialization.

Egypt

Industrialization came to Egypt as a result of the efforts of the Ottoman ruler **Muhammad Ali** (1769–1849). In addition to improving communications in Egypt, he also set up factories to produce cotton cloth, refined sugar, and glass. Turning to **commercial agriculture** in order to realize huge profits, he forced village farmers to leave their own plots and work instead on commercial plantations, growing cash crops for sale to European markets.

Russia

The Russian czars encouraged industrialization by promoting the building of railroads. Especially significant was the trans-Siberian railroad, completed in 1904, which linked Moscow and the port of Vladivostok on the Pacific. Russian railroads linked western Europe with East Asia. Russian industrialization also reached the armaments industry, which received government support.

Japan

The Japanese Meiji government also encouraged industrialization, hiring foreign industrial experts to instruct the Japanese. Railroads, business and technological schools, and banks received government support. When businesses were stable enough to function on their own, the Japanese government sold them to private owners. By 1900, Japan was the most highly industrialized land in Asia.

DOMESTIC EFFECTS OF THE INDUSTRIAL REVOLUTION

The industrial revolution had a profound effect on both societal and family life. Among changes brought about by the implementation of the factory system were:

- Rapid urbanization, or growth of cities
- An emerging middle class of merchants and factory owners
- Unsanitary and unsafe working conditions in the early factories
- Child labor
- Low wages and long hours
- Inadequate housing in tenements with no running water or indoor plumbing, frequent fires, lack of police protection, and epidemic disease
- A rising standard of living, cheaper goods, improved working conditions, and better housing

THE GLOBAL IMPACT OF THE INDUSTRIAL REVOLUTION

As a result of industrialization in the eighteenth and nineteenth centuries:

- The gap between industrialized and non-industrialized nations widened
- A race for colonies ensued, as European nations and Japan sought sources of raw materials and new markets
- Europe gained greater economic power
- The middle class was strengthened and became politically active
- Political participation produced an interest in reform
- World trade increased
- Various societies of the world became more closely connected

REFORM MOVEMENTS

Government and Industry

As the industrial revolution spread throughout Europe and other world regions, various theories arose concerning the role of government in the regulation of industry. The *laissez-faire* theory of Adam Smith argued that government should not interfere with the natural laws of supply and demand. Others who supported laissez-faire were the economists **Thomas Malthus** and **David Ricardo**. Both believed in **capitalism**, an economic system which allows private ownership in order to produce profits. Malthus stated that the food supply could not compete with rapid population increases and, unless the excess population was decreased by war or disease, most people would live in poverty. Ricardo, another predictor of economic gloom, wrote in 1817 that the abundance of laborers produced by high population growth would force wages to remain low.

A number of other philosophers encouraged the direct involvement of government in business and industry. **John Stuart Mill** was a **utilitarian** (or person who believed that government policies were useful only when they promoted the common good) who supported women's **suffrage**, prison reform, and improved education. A few factory owners, such as **utopian socialist Robert Owen**, believed that humans would demonstrate their natural goodness if they resided in cooperative environments. To illustrate his philosophy, Owen built a model factory at New Lanark in Scotland. His attempt to establish a model community at New Harmony, Indiana, in the United States during the 1820s failed because of disagreements among community members.

Another economic system that materialized in the nineteenth century was **socialism**. In a socialist system, the factors of production belong to the public and are operated for the common welfare. A radical form of socialism was **communism**, first proposed by the Germans **Karl Marx** and **Friedrich Engels**. In their booklet *The Communist Manifesto*, Marx and Engels taught that human society was in an ongoing conflict between the middle class of employers, called ***bourgeoisie***, and the workers, or ***proletariat***. According to Marx, the proletariat would eventually revolt against their adverse working conditions; they would seize factories and control production. Workers would then control the government in a "dictatorship of the proletariat." Eventually a classless society would develop and the government or state would cease to exist. In this last phase, or "pure communism," private property would no longer exist and the factors of production would be shared by all the people.

Social Reform

A number of additional reforms emerged from the efforts to change industrial society. One was the union movement, which initiated **collective bargaining**, or negotiations between employees and employers for higher salaries and improved working conditions. Women factory workers were receiving much smaller salaries than men; to alleviate these concerns, they started forming trade unions. Child labor laws were passed in the mid-1800s to increase the ages and decrease the working hours of children in factories. Free public education became common in western Europe, the United States, and Japan, and prison reform favored rehabilitation. The wave of reform sentiment sparked the **abolition** movement to end the slave trade and slavery itself.

Women who had campaigned for the abolition of slavery then began a public movement to guarantee themselves suffrage, or the right to vote. In 1848, women suffragists held a convention in Seneca Falls, New York, where they issued the **Declaration of Sentiments**, a statement of rights based on the Declaration of Independence. In addition to **Lucretia Mott** and **Elizabeth Cady Stanton** of the United States, women such as **Emmeline Pankhurst** of Britain demonstrated for suffrage. However, not until after World War I did women in the United States and Great Britain gain the right to vote in national elections.

THE GROWTH OF DEMOCRACY

Industrialization and the growth of urban areas resulted not only in economic and social reform, but in political change as well. In England, the new middle class carried out protests to achieve the right of suffrage. Parliament responded by easing property restrictions for suffrage in the Reform Bill of 1832. It also redrew districts to eliminate "**rotten boroughs**," or districts without residents, and to properly reflect the population of the growing industrial cities. In 1838, the **Chartist movement** presented to Parliament a document requesting universal manhood suffrage, annual elections for Parliament, the use of the secret ballot, an end to property requirements to become a member of Parliament, and salaries for members of Parliament. Although Parliament initially was unresponsive to these demands, by 1900 Parliament had granted all of them.

Another change in the British government in this period was to shift power to Parliament, especially to the elected members of the lower house, the House of Commons. The British monarch would be reduced to the status of a figurehead rather than a powerful head of state.

Further Demands for Self-Government

The industrial age witnessed many other instances of struggles for political rights. The French Third Republic, begun in 1875, would rule for more than sixty years. The Irish desire for home rule was intensified after the great potato famine of the 1840s, in which the British refused to alleviate the plight of debt-ridden Irish farmers; the Irish would not be granted home rule until the dawn of World War II. In 1867, the Dominion of Canada was formed, allowing Canada self-government but including it in the British empire. Self-rule was won in the 1850s for Australia, originally settled as a British penal colony, and New Zealand. The United States saw a struggle for states' rights in the 1860s and the abolition of slavery as a result of the Civil War.

ADVANCES IN SCIENCE AND TECHNOLOGY

The demands of the industrial revolution encouraged further experimentation and advances in science and technology. By the end of the nineteenth century, the internal combustion engine and the electric generator revolutionized industry. The American inventor **Thomas Edison** invented the phonograph, the light bulb, and motion pictures, while in 1895 the Italian inventor **Guglielmo Marconi** produced the first radio. **Henry Ford** of the United States manufactured inexpensive automobiles through the use of the assembly line. In 1903, two American brothers named **Wilbur and Orville Wright** flew the first gasoline-powered airplane.

In science, **Louis Pasteur** developed the process of **pasteurization** to kill bacteria in milk and other liquids. His experiments also led him to explain the **germ theory of disease**. Knowledge of Pasteur's work led **Joseph Lister** of Great Britain to cleanse his surgical wards with an antibacterial solution, drastically reducing the number of post-surgical deaths among his patients. A Russian chemist named **Dmitri Mendeleev** developed the Periodic Table of the elements. **Marie and Pierre Curie** discovered radioactivity, and **Albert Einstein** and others studied the nature of the atom. **Charles Darwin**, an English biologist, proposed the controversial **theory of evolution**, which advocated change through the process of **natural selection**.

In the social sciences, the new study of psychology investigated human behavior. The Austrian physician **Sigmund Freud** developed **psychoanalysis**, an intensive therapy to assist patients in dealing with psychological problems. Some social scientists applied the theories of Charles Darwin to create the notion that some races were superior to others; **social Darwinism** would be used by some nations to justify their quest for an empire.

THINGS TO REMEMBER

- The industrial revolution ushered in an era of rapid technological advances.
    - Critical inventions include the steam engine, electric lighting, the telegraph, the telephone, and the radio.
- Social changes brought on by industrialization led to increased participation in government.
- Poor working conditions in factories prompted political action to improve factory life and address other social problems.
- Workers organized themselves into unions for the purpose of collective bargaining with employers.
- As industrialization spread around the globe, standards of living increased.
- Trade and communications connected the nations of the world.
- Self-rule came to more areas of the world (including Canada, Australia, and New Zealand).
- Slavery was abolished around the world by 1888.
- The women's suffrage movement began.
- The new economic theory of communism became a major force in the economies and societies of the modern world.

REVIEW QUESTIONS

1. All of the following are true of the Industrial Revolution in England EXCEPT

    (A) it was affected by the enclosure movement.

    (B) it quickly spread to the European continent.

    (C) it was hampered by lack of governmental interest.

    (D) the factors of production were present in England.

    (E) it was enhanced by England's role in world trade.

2. A major factor common in world industrialization was the development of

    (A) commercial agriculture.

    (B) technological schools.

    (C) corporations.

    (D) railroads.

    (E) utopian socialism.

3. On a global scale, the Industrial Revolution
   (A) increased world trade.
   (B) decreased the desire of industrialized nations for colonies.
   (C) saw the nonwestern world increase in power at the expense of Europe.
   (D) caused the middle class to lose political power.
   (E) narrowed the gap between industrialized and non-industrialized countries.

4. All of the following reforms arose from industrialization EXCEPT
   (A) the women's movement.
   (B) collective bargaining.
   (C) abolition of slavery.
   (D) public education.
   (E) capitalism.

5. Demands for self-government in the industrial age produced all of the following EXCEPT
   (A) a decrease in the power of the British monarch.
   (B) home rule for the Irish.
   (C) independence for Australia.
   (D) self-government for Canada.
   (E) a republican government in France.

ANSWERS AND EXPLANATIONS

1. (C)

The English government legislated measures to promote banking and industrialization. The labor force for the factories largely came from farmers forced off their land by the enclosure movement (A). It quickly spread to Germany, France, Belgium, and other countries of continental Europe (B). The four factors of production were present in England (D), and England participated in world trade (E).

2. (D)

The railroad was a key factor in the industrialization of the United States, France, Russia, and Japan. Commercial agriculture was typical of Egyptian industrialization (A), while technological schools (B) were common in Japan, and corporations to the United States (C). Utopian or ideal societies (E) were not significant to any of the societies mentioned.

3. (A)

World trade grew with the increased volume of manufactured goods. It heightened the race for colonies (B). The nonwestern world lost out to the technological advances of the western world (C), while the gap between wealthy and poor countries increased (E). As a result of the reform movement stemming from the Industrial Revolution, the power of the middle class rose (D).

4. (E)

Capitalism existed before the Industrial Revolution. The other reforms materialized as a result of the Industrial Revolution.

5. (B)

The Irish would not be granted home rule until the period prior to World War II. France (E) saw a republican government in 1875. The British monarch acquired the status of a figurehead (A). Australia became self-governing in the 1850s (C), and the Dominion of Canada was founded in 1867 (D).

CHAPTER 23

Imperialism and Global Transformation

TIMELINE

1549	Christian missionaries arrive in Japan
1603	Beginning of the Tokugawa Shogunate
1637	Elimination of Christianity from Japan
1757–1947	The Raj
1823	The Monroe Doctrine
1834	The Great Trek
1839	Outbreak of the Opium War
1842	Treaty of Nanjing
1844	United States and other countries given extraterritorial rights in China
1850–1864	Taiping Rebellion
1853	Crimean War Commodore Perry sails into Tokyo Harbor
1854	Treaty of Kanagawa
1857	The Sepoy Rebellion
1860	European nations granted extraterritorial rights in Japan
1867	Diamonds discovered in South Africa End of the Tokugawa Shogunate

1868–1912	Meiji Restoration
1869	Opening of the Suez Canal
1882	King Leopold II gains control over the Congo British occupation of Egypt Invention of the refrigerated railroad car
1884–1885	Berlin Conference
1885	Formation of the Indian National Congress
1886	Gold discovered in South Africa
1887	Fall of the Zulu nation
1894–1895	Sino-Japanese War
1896	Ethiopian resistance to Italian imperialism
1898	Spanish-American War Annexation of Hawaii
1899	The Boer War Open Door Policy
1900	Boxer Rebellion
1901	Cuba wins independence from Spain
1902	Foundation of the Union of South Africa United States puts down the Filipino bid for independence
1904	Roosevelt Corollary
1905	Russo-Japanese War
1906	Formation of the Muslim League
1908	Belgium gains control over the Belgian Congo Discovery of gold in Persia
1910	Japan annexes Korea
1914	Opening of the Panama Canal

IMPORTANT PEOPLE, PLACES, EVENTS, AND CONCEPTS

David Livingstone
Henry Stanley
King Leopold II
imperialism*
quinine*
Berlin Conference
colony*
protectorate*
sphere of influence*
economic imperialism*
Shaka
Boers*
Great Trek
Boer War
sepoys*
Sikh
Ram Mohun Roy
sati*
Emilio Aguinaldo
Queen Liliuokalani
Crimean War
Suez Canal
concession*
Opium War
Treaty of Nanjing
extraterritorial rights*
Hong Xiuquan
Taiping Rebellion
Empress Cixi
Open Door Policy
Boxer Rebellion
Tokugawa Shogunate
daimyo*
Matthew Perry
Treaty of Kanagawa
Mutsuhito
Meiji Restoration
Sino-Japanese War
Russo-Japanese War
Treaty of Portsmouth
*caudillo**
Monroe Doctrine
Spanish-American War
Panama Canal
Roosevelt Corollary

THE RACE FOR EMPIRE BEGINS

The industrialized nations of Europe needed raw materials for their factories. They also needed markets in which to sell their manufactured goods. The answer to both of these problems: **imperialism**.

Factors Favoring Imperialism

The takeover of a territory or country by a more powerful nation in order to dominate it politically, socially, and economically is called imperialism. A number of circumstances and technological advances helped to promote European imperialism in Africa in the nineteenth century:

- Europeans enjoyed superior technology, especially more sophisticated weapons.
- The invention of the steam engine allowed Europeans to navigate African rivers into the interior of the continent.
- Cables and railroads provided means of communication between the colony and the nation that controlled it.
- The discovery of **quinine** allowed Europeans to enter the interior of Africa without fear of contracting malaria.
- The trans-Atlantic slave trade had created rivalries among African societies and dependence upon European technology.
- Africa's various ethnic and language groups promoted disunity.

Types of Colonial Dominance

Europeans used four different patterns to exercise their dominance over Africa and other colonial possessions:

- **Colonies** were areas in which the controlling power had a direct influence over the government.
- **Protectorates** were regions that were allowed to keep their own governments, but were controlled by an outside power.
- **Spheres of influence** were areas which granted investment or trading privileges to another country.
- **Economic imperialism** was the control of a region by private businesses rather than by an outside government.

EUROPE DIVIDES AFRICA

The Congo

Interest in the Congo in central Africa was created in the late 1860s, when a clergyman from Scotland, **David Livingstone**, journeyed to Africa to search for the source of the Nile. After Livingstone did not communicate with anyone for a number of years, the person sent to find him, American newspaperman **Henry Stanley**, not only found Livingtone but also later returned to Africa to sign treaties with some of the chiefs in the valley of the Congo River. These treaties gave King **Leopold II** of Belgium personal control over the Congo region.

Leopold II devastated the economy and society of the Congo by establishing large rubber plantations and forcing the natives to work on them. Not only were working conditions on the plantations extremely harsh and wages extremely low, but work on the commercial plantation prevented the Congolese from tilling their own private farm plots. By 1908, the efforts of humanitarians worldwide forced the Belgian government to take control of the Congo (now renamed the Belgian Congo). With Belgium's acquisition of the Congo, the race for empire in Africa intensified.

The Berlin Conference

In the 1880s, the French, who already had interests along the Congo River, began to expand their holdings. Although Africans did not display much interest in purchasing European manufactured goods, the industrialized European countries continued their quest for African colonies to appropriate their mineral wealth and other raw materials. The Belgian Congo contained rich deposits of copper and tin. Diamonds were discovered in South Africa in 1867 and gold in 1886. The controlling nations established cash-crop plantations to produce rubber, cocoa, and palm oil, which was used for lubricating the machinery of European factories.

Fearing the competition for colonies in Africa might result in conflict among the European nations themselves, the imperialist powers agreed to meet at the **Berlin Conference** in 1884–1885 to peacefully divide Africa. Noticeably absent from the Berlin Conference were representatives from any African tribes. The divisions imposed on Africa by the conference were executed with little regard to partitioning the continent along ethnic or cultural lines. By 1914, all of Africa had been divided among the European powers except for Liberia and Ethiopia. The Africans made several attempts to resist the colonial powers; only one, the 1896 Ethiopian resistance against Italian intrusion, succeeded.

Rivalries in South Africa

The vast territories of southern Africa were peopled by numerous ethnic groups that had for years been engaged in local rivalries. The most prominent of these ethnic groups were the Zulus, who rose to power in the early nineteenth century under their chief, **Shaka**. But Shaka's successors did not possess his military skill, and by 1887 the Zulus fell to the superior technology of the British.

The Dutch had first established the Cape Colony at the southern tip of Africa in 1652 as a supply station for their ships sailing in the Indian Ocean. The Dutch, or **Boers**, were farmers who pushed the Africans from their land in southern Africa and relied on the labor of African slaves. When the British took over control of the Cape Colony in the nineteenth century, the Boers found themselves in conflict with them over land usage and British anti-slavery policies. In 1834, the Boers moved northward in the **Great Trek** and, in the process, clashed with the Africans who inhabited the land.

The Boer War

War broke out between the Boers and the British in 1899 when the Boers blamed the British for trying to undermine their policies against political rights for newcomers to South Africa. The two groups also competed over land and over the gold and diamonds discovered in South Africa in the late 1800s. After brutality on both sides, the British won the conflict. In 1902, the British joined the Boer republics into the Union of South Africa; the union was self-governing, but controlled by the British.

Results of Colonial Rule in Africa

The impact of European imperialism in Africa was far-reaching:

- Hospitals were constructed and sanitation improved.
- Schools improved literacy rates. Classes were taught in European languages, transmitting knowledge of European culture and history rather than native cultures.
- Railroads, public works, and telephones and telegraphs improved transportation and communication and, in many cases, remained in place even after the independence and the departure of the Europeans. However, these improvements in infrastructure were initially designed primarily for the use of the imperialist powers.
- Africans lost control over their traditional lands.
- The transition from individual farm plots and subsistence agriculture to cash-crop plantations not only forced Africans to work in European-owned businesses but also reduced food crops for individual families.
- New political units formed by the European imperialist powers interfered with traditional African village life and imposed political divisions that disregarded African linguistic, ethnic, and cultural groups. The artificial boundaries drawn by the Europeans remain a problem in Africa today.

BRITISH CONTROL OF INDIA

The British had established trading posts in India in the 1600s during the active trade among both Europeans and Muslims in the Indian Ocean. The East India Company became even more influential in India after the weakening of the Mughal empire in the mid-1700s. By the beginning of the nineteenth century, the British government had begun its control over India, setting up policies that restricted the independent operation of the Indian economy. The British nearly destroyed the Indian industry in handmade textiles when they imported cheaper manufactured fabrics and clothing from Great Britain.

Among the raw materials in India that were attractive to the British were tea, coffee, jute, indigo, opium, and cotton. Indian cotton was especially desirable during the 1860s, when the blockade of the Confederate states during the American Civil War disrupted the importation of cotton to Britain. Indian-grown opium would cause serious societal problems for the Chinese when the British started selling the opium to the Chinese in exchange for tea.

Effects of British Imperialism in India

In addition to hospitals, schools, and improved sanitation, the British constructed a railroad in India that would not only transport raw materials but also served as passenger transportation linking the various parts of India. But British imperialism nearly eliminated the Indian textile industry, and the conversion to cash-crop plantations destroyed local agriculture and caused a famine. Some Indians resented the presence of Christian missionaries, and the racist attitude of many of the British officials promoted increasing animosity among the Indian people.

The Sepoy Rebellion

Indian resentment of the British escalated in 1857, when the Indian soldiers, or **sepoys**, were presented with new rifles. The cartridges of the rifles could not be used until the soldiers bit off the cartridge seal. Problems arose when a rumor spread that convinced the sepoys that the cartridges were sealed with pork and beef fat. This information angered the Hindus, to whom the cow is sacred, and the Muslims, whose faith forbids the eating of pork. The resulting uprising, called the Sepoy Rebellion (or the Sepoy Mutiny), spread throughout northern India.

Indian unification against the British was hindered by the inability of the Muslims and Hindus to cooperate with each other. The **Sikhs**, a religious group, remained loyal to the British and became an integral part of the British army in India. After the Sepoy Rebellion, the British government established the Raj (1757–1947), or direct control over part of India. Resentment and racial tension between the British and Indians increased after the rebellion.

Indian Nationalism

By the early 1800s, educated Indians were already calling for independence from British rule. Under the leadership of **Ram Mohun Roy**, a campaign began to end the caste system and the practice of **sati**, in which favored wives threw themselves on the burning funeral pyres of their husbands. The British responded by outlawing sati. The new spirit of nationalism eventually led to the beginnings of two nationalist groups: the Indian National Congress (1885) and the Muslim League (1906). During the early twentieth century, both groups began promoting independence from Great Britain.

IMPERIALISM IN SOUTHEAST ASIA AND THE PACIFIC ISLANDS

The thrust of imperialism did not confine itself to Africa and India, but extended to the territories of Southeast Asia. The centuries-old European interest in Indian Ocean trade now expanded to include Pacific islands, because of their strategic location as potential supply stations. Great Britain would establish a trading post at Singapore, the French would continue a prolonged period of influence in Indochina, Germany would claim the Marshalls, Solomons, and New Guinea, and the United States would gain the Philippines and the Hawaiian Islands.

Dutch and British Colonies

The Dutch had established their hold in Indonesia in the 1600s. Interested in the oil, tin, and rubber that Indonesia could provide, by the early 1800s the Dutch dominated all of Indonesia, which they renamed the Dutch East Indies. Large numbers of Dutch settlers migrated to Indonesia to set up plantations and trading posts. The British acquired the busy port of Singapore off the coast of the Malay Peninsula, and also Malaysia and Burma (present-day Myanmar); these areas were rich in tin, rubber, and teak. Chinese workers were encouraged to migrate to the area, eventually forming a Chinese majority. Today, ethnic conflicts remain between the Chinese majority and the native Malay people.

French Indochina

Since the nineteenth century, the French had been active in Southeast Asia, which became known as French Indochina. Rubber became a key crop. Rice, originally grown by subsistence farmers, now became a major export crop whose production decreased the amount of rice available to the Vietnamese people. The French agricultural and export polices started causing resentment among the Vietnamese.

Siam

As a result of imperialism, most of Southeast Asia saw a wave of migrations from Asia and Europe, creating an ethnic and cultural mixture that has produced misunderstandings that continue today. One exception: Siam (modern-day Thailand), which did not fall to imperialist control. Disputes over Siam between France and Great Britain resulted in Siam's status as a "buffer zone" between the colonies of Burma and French Indochina. As a result of its continued autonomy, Siam was able to provide its people with a lifestyle that included the railroads, schools, and communications systems that the imperialist nations provided.

U.S. Acquisition of the Philippines and Hawaii

As a result of the Spanish-American War, the United States acquired Puerto Rico, Guam, and the Philippines. Filipinos under the leadership of **Emilio Aguinaldo** immediately declared their independence from the United States, causing the United States to fight the Filipinos. After defeating the Filipinos in 1902, the United States promised to prepare the Filipinos for self-rule. Despite the health and educational improvements of the United States, American business interests persisted in setting up large sugar plantations that prevented sufficient cultivation of basic food crops.

American businesses had also set up sugar plantations in the Hawaiian islands, achieving significant political power in the process. When new tariff laws reduced the profits on the importation of sugar to the United States, American planters began pushing for the annexation of Hawaii to the United States. This proposal was strengthened in 1893 when Queen **Liliuokalani** of Hawaii attempted to increase the political power of the Hawaiians at the expense of the American sugar planters. In 1898, five years after the overthrow of the Hawaiian queen, Hawaii was annexed to the United States.

IMPERIALISM IN THE OTTOMAN EMPIRE

In the nineteenth century, the weakening Islamic powers also became objects of European imperialism.

The Crimean War

The Russians, wanting access through the Black Sea to the Mediterranean Sea, were particularly interested in Ottoman lands. When efforts to negotiate with the Ottomans did not provide the desired results, Russia went to war. The **Crimean War** (1853) pitted Russia against the Ottomans, who were joined by the French and British. The defeat of Russia did not hide the weakness of the Ottoman empire; the Russians subsequently gained opportunities for alliances with Slavic peoples in the Balkan area of the Ottoman empire. Meanwhile, the Ottoman empire continued to lose lands in the Balkans and in North Africa. By the beginning of World War I, the Ottoman empire was only a small fraction of its original size.

The Suez Canal

The deterioration of the Ottoman empire prompted Egypt to modernize during the reign of Muhammad Ali in the hope that modernization would provide the strength to resist European imperialism. Muhammad Ali's son and successor, Isma'il, continued his father's policies by constructing the **Suez Canal**, which connected the Red Sea with the Mediterranean. Partially financed by the French, the canal opened in 1869. The British were especially dependent upon the Suez Canal to shorten distances to its Asian and African possessions. When Egypt could not repay debts to its European lenders, the British occupied Egypt in 1882 to manage the finances of the canal.

Imperialism in Persia

Russia and Great Britain also had commercial interests in Persia. Russia, wanting access to the Indian Ocean through the Persian Gulf, acquired land from Persia in the early nineteenth century. Great Britain gained the territory of Afghanistan from Persia, with the goal of using Afghanistan as a buffer zone between Russia and the British colony of India. When riots broke out in Persia over the issue of exporting tobacco to Great Britain, the Russians and the British took over Persia in 1907 and divided the country into spheres of influence. Great Britain's interest in Persia increased after the discovery of gold in 1908.

CHINA RESPONDS TO WESTERN INFLUENCE

While the nations of western Europe were interacting with other societies and establishing colonies, China maintained its isolation from foreigners. Foreign trade was restricted to only one port: Guangzhou in southern China. By the late 1700s, the British had realized that the Chinese would purchase opium from foreign merchants. The result of the opium trade was massive opium addiction among the Chinese—a problem that prompted a Chinese government official to write a letter to Queen Victoria, trying to halt the importation of opium into China. Britain's refusal to comply with the request caused the outbreak of the **Opium War** in 1839. The **Treaty of Nanjing** in 1842 granted the victorious British the port of Hong Kong. A second treaty in 1844 gave the United States, France, Germany, and Russia **extraterritorial rights**, or special exemptions from Chinese law, in four additional Chinese ports.

The Taiping Rebellion

Rapidly increasing population, continued opium addiction, and corrupt government caused a young man from southern China named **Hong Xiuquan** to begin a revolt around 1850. Influenced by Christian missionaries, he wanted to save China and the world. Envisioning the establishment of a kingdom of peace, Hong captured large areas in the southeastern portion of China. By 1864 the Qing regained control of China, but the **Taiping Rebellion** had left vast acres of farmland devastated and perhaps twenty million or more Chinese dead.

Some Chinese leaders responded to the destruction of the Taiping Rebellion by calling for the modernization of its educational system and military. Other leaders insisted on maintaining Chinese traditions and values. The Dowager **Empress Cixi** (1861–1908), while committed to Chinese values, encouraged the country to begin to manufacture gunboats and weapons in factories. Many of these factories, however, would be operated by foreigners.

The Open Door Policy and the Boxer Rebellion

Increasingly, other nations began to gain financial interests in China. Great Britain, France, Germany, Russia, and Japan set up spheres of influence in China. This arrangement allowed each nation to control trade and financial matters within its respective sphere of influence. Fearing further foreign influence in China, the United States announced the **Open Door Policy** in 1899. The policy, designed ultimately to protect United States trading rights in China, gained the approval of several European countries by suggesting that China's ports be open to traders of all nations.

Foreign privileges angered many of the peasants and workers in China. After forming a secret society that became known as the Boxers, they carried out a siege against Beijing in 1900. A force of soldiers from Europe, Japan, and the United States descended upon the Boxers, easily defeating them. After the **Boxer Rebellion**, China continued to experience political disorder.

JAPAN BEGINS MODERNIZATION

The Tokugawa Shogunate

By 1603, Japan had been unified under the **Tokugawa Shogunate**. With its capital at Edo (which would later become Tokyo), the Tokugawa family would continue to rule Japan until 1868. During the eighteenth century, Japan became increasingly urbanized. Urbanization gave some Japanese women opportunities for employment outside the home.

European influence had entered Japan in 1543, when a group of Portuguese sailors was shipwrecked off the coast of southern Japan. Soon afterward, Portuguese merchants arrived with a number of trade items, including firearms. Firearms were valuable in defeating the enemies of the shogunate and in unifying the Japanese islands. The large landowners, or **daimyo**, were forced to fortify their castles to withstand the power of cannon. The protective walls of the castles attracted artisans and merchants to settle the land surrounding the castles; eventually some of these settlements became centers of bureaucracy.

Japanese Isolation

In 1549, Christian missionaries arrived in Japan. Seeing them as a source of European technology, the Japanese welcomed them, and Christianity spread rapidly throughout Japan. After 1637, fear of religious uprisings resulted in persecution of the Christians and the elimination of Christianity from Japan. Reaction against missionaries and merchants motivated the Japanese to close its doors to foreign influence. Only one port, Nagasaki, was kept open for Dutch and Chinese merchants.

In 1853, Commodore **Matthew Perry** of the United States sailed into Edo Harbor (modern Tokyo) to attempt to break Japanese isolation. The following year, the **Treaty of Kanagawa** allowed the United States to use two Japanese ports to receive supplies and to open an embassy in Japan. By 1860, several European nations had also received extraterritorial rights in Japan.

The Meiji Restoration

Angered that their shogun had succumbed to foreign demands, the Japanese turned against the Tokugawa shogun, who stepped down in November 1867. The emperor **Mutsuhito** set up a new government in the spring of 1868, calling it Meiji. The Meiji period, which would last from 1868 to 1912, saw feudal lords relinquish their lands to the emperor. In order to compete with other nations, Mutsuhito would embark upon a modernization program for Japan. Japanese modernization involved the creation of a strong, centralized government and a powerful military and the introduction of universal public education.

At the heart of Japanese modernization was rapid industrialization. During the late nineteenth century, the Japanese constructed railroads and increased coal production. Large state-supported factories sprang up throughout the country. By the early twentieth century, the Japanese economy could compete with any other modern nation, and the Japanese began to turn their thoughts toward imperialism.

Japanese Imperialism

When China invaded Korea in 1894, Japan responded by sending troops to Korea to fight the Chinese. In the **Sino-Japanese War**, Japan drove the Chinese from Korea and began the takeover of Manchuria. A peace treaty signed in 1895 gave Taiwan and the Pescadores Islands to Japan.

The emerging power of Japan was further reinforced by its victory in the **Russo-Japanese War** in 1905. In the course of the conflict, which originated over territory in Manchuria, Japan inflicted devastating losses upon the Russian fleet. In the **Treaty of Portsmouth**, Japan received Russian's lease on the Liaodong Peninsula, including Port Arthur, and control of the southern portion of the Chinese Eastern Railway. Russia was required to withdraw from Manchuria and agreed to stay out of Korea.

After the Russo-Japanese War, Japan devoted its attention to Korea, annexing the country in 1910. Although the Japanese brought industry and modern communications systems to Korea, they also instituted land policies that favored Japanese settlers in Korea. Control over the Korean press and the curriculum of Korean schools further encouraged an emerging nationalist movement in Korea. Japan's occupation of Korea demonstrated to the world that the aim of modernized Japan was imperialism.

IMPERIALISM IN LATIN AMERICA

The aftermath of independence in Latin America did not include the prosperity that its liberators had envisioned. Land ownership continued to be inequitable, and improper land usage was common. Political power often resided in the hands of revolutionary leaders who ruled as ***caudillos***, or dictators. Lacking a tradition of political participation, most Latin Americans were accustomed to political power for the elite classes only.

Foreign Economic Influence

Upon achieving independence, the independent nations of Latin America began active trade with Great Britain and the United States. The invention of the refrigerated railroad car in 1882 facilitated the export of perishable products such as fruits, vegetables, and beef. On the other hand, the growth of industry in Latin America remained very limited. After independence, Latin America imported American and European manufactures and paid little attention to developing its own industry, preventing itself from competing with other modern nations. Also, instead of investing in the improvement of their own infrastructure, the new republics preferred to borrow money at high interest rates from foreign nations in order to fund their export industries. When the Latin American nations could not repay their debts, foreign powers would exert force against the debtor nation, or sometimes occupy it, to collect payment.

The Monroe Doctrine

After Latin American independence had been achieved, the United States feared that the weak new republics would be incapable of warding off imperialist interests of European countries. Consequently, in 1823, U.S. President James Monroe issued the **Monroe Doctrine**, which stated that the Americas were not open to colonization by any European power. Great Britain reinforced the impact of the Monroe Doctrine by pledging to support it.

The power of the Monroe Doctrine was demonstrated in 1898 when the United States joined the Cubans in their struggle for independence from Spain. As a result of the six-week-long **Spanish-American War**, Cuba won its independence in 1901. The Spanish also relinquished the last of their colonies—Puerto Rico, Guam, and the Philippines—to the United States.

The Panama Canal

As the United States and other nations became increasingly involved in global trade, they began investigating the possibility of digging a canal across Central America. Traveling through a canal would be much quicker and cheaper than having to travel around the tip of South America in order reach the opposite coast by sea. In the 1880s, the French had already been financially unsuccessful in their plans to cut a canal across Panama.

President Theodore Roosevelt favored the construction of a canal across Panama, which was a part of Colombia. When Colombia wanted too high a price for the purchase of territory in Panama, the

United States backed a revolution in Panama. When the Panamanians won their independence, they granted the United States a ten-mile-wide zone for the construction of a canal. Completed in 1914, the **Panama Canal** attracted ships from around the globe.

In 1979, U.S. President Jimmy Carter negotiated a treaty with Panama that would eventually return ownership of the canal to Panama. Carter responded to criticism of the treaty by saying that resentment of the Panamanians toward U.S. colonialism had left the United States with no other option than the return of the canal. Over the next twenty years, the United States would gradually relinquish its ownership of the Canal Zone until it reverted to Panama in 1999.

Increased U.S. Economic Interest in Latin America

The United States continued its presence in Cuba and its investments in the new Latin American republics. To protect its interests and to strengthen the Monroe Doctrine, in 1904 President Roosevelt issued the **Roosevelt Corollary**, which made the United States a "police power" in the Americas. In the years to come, the United States would frequently use the Roosevelt Corollary to justify their intervention and occupation in the nations of Latin America. The Latin American republics, however, would resent the intrusion of the colossal power to the north.

THINGS TO REMEMBER

- Multiple factors fueled the imperialism of the nineteenth and early twentieth century.
    - Industrialized nations wanted new markets and raw materials.
    - Colonizers believed in their racial superiority.
- Major imperialist powers included Great Britain, France, Belgium, the Netherlands, Germany, the United States, and Japan.
- While native peoples benefited from European technology, often they were forced to work on cash-crop plantations or in mines instead of growing food for their families.
- Colonial economies remained undeveloped due to an excess of cheap, imported manufactured goods from the controlling nation.
- Types of colonial dominance included the establishment of colonies, protectorates, spheres of interest, and economic imperialism.
- Europeans first competed for territory in Africa. Imperialism also was extended to India, the Pacific Islands, Southeast Asia, and lands of the weakened Ottoman empire.
- China unsuccessfully fought to resist foreign intrusion, opium imports, and being carved up by Europeans into spheres of influence.
- Japan responded to foreign imperialism by modernizing and becoming an imperialist power itself.
- American and British business interests dominated Latin America. The Monroe Doctrine and Roosevelt Corollary established the United States as the dominant power in this region.

REVIEW QUESTIONS

1. As European imperialists began to divide Africa,
   (A) the Berlin Conference resolved the issues of European rivalry.
   (B) Africans welcomed the opportunity for employment on cash-crop plantations.
   (C) all of Africa was divided among European powers.
   (D) Africa became a profitable marketplace for European manufactures.
   (E) Africans made no attempts to resist the Europeans.

2. Which of the following areas is paired correctly with the type of control by its imperialist power?
   (A) French Indochina—colony
   (B) Hawaii—economic imperialism
   (C) Belgian Congo—protectorate
   (D) China—economic imperialism
   (E) Latin America—sphere of influence

3. In both Africa and India, European imperialism resulted in all of the following EXCEPT
   (A) the reduction in food crops for individual families.
   (B) railroads built primarily for European use.
   (C) schools with lessons taught in European languages.
   (D) improvements in native industries.
   (E) hospitals and improved sanitation.

4. Western influence on China resulted in all of the following EXCEPT
   (A) extraterritorial rights for some European nations.
   (B) opium addiction among the Chinese.
   (C) Chinese acquisition of the port of Hong Kong.
   (D) the Taiping Rebellion.
   (E) the Boxer Rebellion.

5. Japanese modernization
   (A) was governed by private individuals.
   (B) produced an interest in the resources of Manchuria.
   (C) was a gradual process because of lack of government support.
   (D) diverted the country's attention from developing a military.
   (E) was eased because of Japan's abundant natural resources.

ANSWERS AND EXPLANATIONS

1. (A)

The Berlin Conference divided Africa to accommodate European rivals. Africans were forced to work on the cash-crop plantations under harsh conditions (B). Liberia and Ethiopia were not assigned to European powers at the conference (C). Africans were largely uninterested in trade products from the western world (D). Africans made some attempts to resist the Europeans, such as the Ethiopian resistance to the Italians in 1896 (E).

2. (B)

Hawaii was an example of economic imperialism, or the control of a country by the businesses of another, in this case the U.S. fruit companies. French Indochina is an example of a protectorate; the Belgian Congo of a colony; China of spheres of influence; and Latin America of economic imperialism.

3. (D)

Native industries were often harmed or nearly destroyed by competition from the industries of the imperialist nation. Individual food crops were reduced as a result of the natives' being forced to work on cash-crop plantations (A). Railroads were constructed primarily to carry raw materials and manufactures as well as passengers for the benefit of the Europeans (B). Schools set up by imperialist powers were usually taught in the European languages (C), while improved sanitation and medical care were provided (E).

4. (C)

The Treaty of Nanjing (1842) ceded the port of Hong Kong to the British. Some western nations gained the right of extraterritoriality, or the right to be tried in their own courts rather than those of the Chinese (A). As a result of Great Britain's trading Indian opium for Chinese tea, opium addiction was spreading among the Chinese (B). The Taiping Rebellion was in part a reaction against opium addiction (D), while anger at foreign privileges caused the Boxer Rebellion (E).

5. (B)

Japan's lack of natural resources (E) prompted an interest in the coal and iron deposits of Manchuria. Japanese modernization accelerated because of the support of the government (A, C). Japan's military traditions continued during the period of modernization (D).

CHAPTER 24

World War I

TIMELINE

1879	Dual Alliance
1882	Triple Alliance
1887	Alliance between Germany and Russia
1907	Triple Entente
1908	Austria annexes Bosnia
1914	Assassination of Archduke Franz Ferdinand and Duchess Sophie Austria declares war on Serbia Germany declares war on Russia Great Britain declares war on Germany
1915	Sinking of the *Lusitania*
1917	Germany announces unrestricted submarine warfare Zimmerman telegram The United States declares war on Germany Czar Nicholas abdicates the Russian throne The Communist Party takes control of Russia
1918	Influenza epidemic The Treaty of Brest-Litovsk Armistice ending World War I
1919	Treaty of Versailles

IMPORTANT PEOPLE, PLACES, EVENTS, AND CONCEPTS

nationalism*	Gavrilo Princep	propaganda*
imperialism*	two-front war	armistice*
militarism*	Schlieffen Plan	Paris Peace Conference
mobilization*	Central Powers	Woodrow Wilson
Dual Alliance	Allied Powers	Fourteen Points*
Triple Alliance*	trench warfare*	Treaty of Versailles*
Kaiser Wilhelm II	Gallipoli	reparation*
Triple Entente*	Mohandas Gandhi	League of Nations*
Archduke Franz Ferdinand	U-boat	mandate*
Duchess Sophie	Zimmerman telegram	

TENSIONS MOUNT IN EUROPE

Competition over colonies and economic interests in Asia, Africa, and Latin America led to uneasy relations among the European countries in the early years of the twentieth century. Three forces were combining to create the scenario for future conflict:

- **Nationalism.** A deep sense of pride in one's nation, while in many respects a positive force, also caused an intense rivalry among several European nations. As the twentieth century unfolded, the delicate balance of power that had been the goal of Europe since the end of the Napoleonic Wars was slowly eroding to witness the rise of the major powers of Germany, Austria-Hungary, Great Britain, France, Italy, and Russia.
- **Imperialism.** Competition among the industrialized European nations for colonies to supply raw materials created disputes over territorial control. As these disputes heightened, so did mistrust among the nations of Europe.
- **Militarism.** As international rivalries increased, European nations attached greater importance to a strong military and to the maintenance of a standing army prepared for war at any time. Great Britain already boasted the most powerful navy in the world, although Germany's navy seemed poised to become the largest. By 1914, all other major powers in Europe had created formidable armies that were constantly on alert for **mobilization**, or movement to an area in conflict.

ENTANGLING ALLIANCES

Compounding the forces of nationalism, imperialism, and militarism were networks of secret defense alliances among the European powers. German Chancellor Otto von Bismarck saw France as the greatest threat to Europe. In an effort to cut off France from the support of other powers, he forged the **Dual Alliance** with Austria-Hungary in 1879. When Italy joined the powers in 1882, the **Triple Alliance** was born. In 1887, Germany also entered into an alliance with Russia. While accomplishing their purpose of isolating France, the alliances made by Germany were initiated without regard for already existing rivalries, especially between Austro-Hungarian and Russian interests in the Balkans.

The European alliances became even more involved when **Kaiser Wilhelm II** of Germany, in an effort to augment his own influence, fired Bismarck as Chancellor. In 1890, the new kaiser ended Germany's alliance with Russia, prompting Russia to form an alliance with France in 1891. Wilhelm also began building up a navy to rival that of Great Britain, causing Britain to strengthen its own naval forces. By 1907, Great Britain had entered into an *entente*, or alliance, with France and Russia. Although the resulting **Triple Entente** did not obligate Great Britain to fight on the side of France and Russia, it implied that the British would not fight against its two allies. By 1907, the nations of Europe were aligned so that the slightest incident between rival powers could mean war.

RIVALRIES ERUPT IN THE BALKANS

In the early twentieth century, the once mighty Ottoman empire was rapidly declining, resulting in the rise of several fiercely nationalistic new countries in the Balkans. The Balkans were the "powder keg" of Europe: Ethnically diverse, each new Balkan nation had its own agenda. Serbia, with a primarily Slavic population, enjoyed the support of Russia in its efforts to unite all Slavic peoples in the Balkans. Austria-Hungary, which embraced very few Slavic peoples, opposed Serbia's goals. Furthermore, Russia and Austria-Hungary both wanted to become the dominant power in the Balkans. In 1908, Austria-Hungary annexed the largely Slavic nation of Bosnia. An angry Serbia waited for the opportunity to take Bosnia from Austria-Hungary.

The Powder Keg Explodes

An incident in Bosnia set off the spark that ignited war in Europe. On June 28, 1914, the heir to the Austrian throne, **Archduke Franz Ferdinand**, and his wife, **Sophie**, paid an official visit to Sarajevo, the capital of Bosnia. While riding through the streets of Sarajevo, they were assassinated by **Gavrilo Princep**, a young member of an organization devoted to the restoration of Bosnian self-rule. Austria, backed by Germany, issued an ultimatum to Serbia to end all resistance to Austria. Although Serbia agreed to most provisions of the ultimatum and offered to submit the others to international decision, Austria declared war against Serbia on July 28, 1914. In response, Russia mobilized its army toward the Austrian and German borders.

WAR BEGINS

The chain reaction that was produced as the members of the alliances honored their pledges drew most of Europe into war. Germany responded to Russia's mobilization by declaring war on Russia on August 1, 1914, and on France on August 3. Knowing that Germany might have to fight a **two-front war** against France and Russia, the kaiser put into action the **Schlieffen Plan**, which called for war against France before turning against Russia. When neutral Belgium refused to allow Germany to pass through its borders to reach France, Germany invaded Belgium. Great Britain, which had ties to Belgium, declared war on Germany on August 4, 1914.

The Opposing Sides

The warring powers were divided into two camps. On one side were the **Central Powers** of Germany and Austria-Hungary, who would be joined later in the war by the Ottoman empire and Bulgaria. The **Allied Powers**, or Allies, included Great Britain, France, and Russia, who were later joined by Japan and Italy. Italy had left the Triple Alliance in opposition to Germany's invasion of neutral Belgium.

THE GREAT WAR

France's early victory over Germany at the Battle of the Marne ensured that Germany would have to fight on two fronts. The conflict on the Western Front, or the northern region of France, settled down into **trench warfare**. Trench warfare involved two opposing armies digging parallel trenches from which they each would face the enemy. Barbed wire dotted an area known as "no man's land" between the two lines of trenches. Trench warfare produced minimal gain of territory at a tremendous loss of life.

On the Eastern Front, along the border between Russia and Germany, the war involved greater troop mobility. Both Germany and Austria-Hungary gained an early advantage over Russia. The weakened Russia, which was not as heavily industrialized as the western European nations, found it increasingly difficult to carry on a war and at the same time provide essential supplies for its armies. Although Russia suffered devastating human losses, its huge population ensured a steady supply of replacement soldiers.

Gallipoli

As the first year of the war drew to a close, the opposing sides tried to acquire greater power by extending the war to areas outside Europe. The **Gallipoli** campaign was a failed attempt by the Allies to establish a supply line to Russia by controlling the Dardanelles. Most of the casualties in the Gallipoli campaign were suffered by the armies of Australians, New Zealanders, and Canadians. The heavy sacrifices made by these three countries resulted in weakened ties with the British empire, creating in them a heightened interest in independence.

After Gallipoli, the Ottoman armies began retreating. The British enlisted the services of recruits from Australia, New Zealand, India, and Egypt to crush the Ottomans. An Arab revolt against the Turks furthered the advances of the British and their recruits.

The War in the Colonies

The Japanese, English, and French captured some of Germany's colonies and posts in the Pacific, in China, and in Africa. In the French and British colonies, subjects joined in the war effort to support the nations that controlled them. Indians, under the leadership of **Mohandas Gandhi**, particularly hoped that supporting the British would help them in any future movements geared toward Indian independence. Joining the Allied armies were troops from Senegal, South Africa, Algeria, Egypt, and Indochina who served as soldiers and support personnel.

The United States Enters the Conflict

Since the early weeks of the war, the Germans had engaged in submarine warfare in the Atlantic. Submarine, or **U-boat**, activity had diminished somewhat after the 1915 sinking of the *Lusitania*, a British passenger liner. The Germans claimed that the ship was carrying ammunition, which proved true upon further investigation. But the loss of 128 U.S. citizens among the 1,198 dead on board the *Lusitania* outraged Americans. Eventually the American outcry caused Germany to announce that it would cease attacking passenger and neutral ships.

In 1917, in retaliation for a British naval blockade of Germany, the Germans announced that they would sink with no warning any ship that ventured into the waters surrounding Great Britain. Their policy of unrestricted submarine warfare soon resulted in the sinking of three U.S. ships.

Within a few weeks, another incident would move the United States closer to entering the world war. British intelligence intercepted a telegram from the German foreign secretary, Arthur Zimmerman, to the German ambassador to Mexico. The **Zimmerman telegram** stated that, if Mexico would enter the war on the side of Germany, the Germans would assist Mexico in reacquiring the land that it had lost to the United States.

This last incident was more than the Americans could bear. Americans were already sympathetic to the British because of common cultural ties, and Allied **propaganda** increased American sympathy for their side. Also, the United States had traded more actively with France and Great Britain than with Germany. So on April 2, 1917, the United States declared war on Germany. The entry of the United States would soon alter the balance of power in favor of the Allies.

Russia Withdraws from the War

In Russia, protests caused in part by wartime shortages of food and supplies had seriously weakened the power of the czar, Nicholas II. In March 1917, Czar Nicholas abdicated the Russian throne, and a provisional government took over. Although the new government intended to continue fighting with the Allies, tremendous loss of life drained the morale of the Russian army. In November 1917, the Communist Party, under the leadership of Vladimir Ilyich Lenin, took control of Russia. In March 1918, Lenin's Russia signed the Treaty of Brest-Litovsk, which ended the war between Germany and Russia. By the terms of the treaty, Russia was forced to cede to Germany the territories that include present-day Poland, Finland, Estonia, Latvia, Lithuania, and Ukraine.

The War's Final Days

Russia's withdrawal from the war allowed Germany to concentrate its forces on the Western Front. Launching a massive offensive against France in March 1918, the Germans appeared on the verge of victory until they were met by the newly arrived American troops. In the Second Battle of the Marne in July 1918, the Allies turned the tide and began their advance toward Germany. Shortly afterward, the Bulgarians and the Ottoman Turks surrendered to the Allies. Austria-Hungary suffered a revolution that broke up its empire, and the Germans protested against their government. In November 1918, Kaiser Wilhelm II was forced to abdicate, and the Germans formed a republic. Representatives of the opposing sides signed an **armistice** on November 11, 1918, ending the world's first global war.

THE NATURE OF THE WAR

The Great War, as it was called at that time, saw a number of firsts. It was the first time that blimps and airplanes were used in combat. Weapons such as poison gas, machine guns, armored tanks, and larger artillery were also implemented for the first time.

World War I was fought as a total war, with the nations involved devoting all their energies and resources at the battle front and on the homefront. The wartime governments of the European combatants commanded the amount and types of goods produced by factories. Governments imposed wage and price controls and rationed goods that were necessary to the war effort. Government censorship was common among the European nations at war. Widespread propaganda was used by governments to generate further fear and distrust of the enemy.

Opportunities for Women

With the shortage of men on the homefront, women were given new opportunities to assume their jobs in businesses, factories, and offices. Many women worked in dangerous munitions factories, some dying from the blast of explosions. In most instances, women received lower wages than men who performed the same duties. Although the return of the men after the war meant the loss of jobs for many women, their wartime experience produced a change in attitudes concerning the role of women in society.

BUILDING THE PEACE

Although the war had concluded, the terms of peace remained undetermined. In January 1918, the Allies held a conference at the Palace of Versailles near Paris to outline the a plan for peace. Among the key delegates at the **Paris Peace Conference** were Georges Clemenceau of France, David Lloyd George of Great Britain, Vittorio Orlando of Italy, and **Woodrow Wilson** of the United States.

The Fourteen Points

During the last days of the war, President Wilson had outlined a plan for peace which he called the **Fourteen Points.** Among the major provisions were plans for altering national borders and creating new nations along the principle of self-determination. This point involved the goal of allowing various ethnic groups to decide for themselves the government under which they wanted to live. The fourteenth and most critical point called for an association of nations that could negotiate a peaceful resolution to future international conflicts.

The Treaty of Versailles

Great Britain and France approached the peace conference with a much different attitude than that of Wilson. Both countries wanted to assure the drastic disarmament of Germany. France, whose land lay devastated from the war, wanted Germany punished for her role in the war. The eventual treaty provisions reached a middle ground between the two sentiments. On June 28, 1919, the **Treaty of Versailles** was signed.

The treaty provided for the following:

- The German territory of Alsace-Lorraine was ceded to France.
- Germany lost its colonies in Africa and the Pacific.
- The size of the German army was limited.
- Germany could not have submarines or an air force and could not manufacture or import weapons.
- A "war guilt" clause placed sole responsibility for the war on Germany.
- Germany was forced to pay **reparations** of $33 billion over a period of 30 years.
- A **League of Nations** of Allied and neutral nations was created. Russia and Germany were excluded from membership.

Additional Peace Treaties

The victorious Allies negotiated four other peace treaties with the Ottoman empire, Bulgaria, Austria, and Hungary. From the Austro-Hungarian empire were created the independent nations of Austria, Hungary, Czechoslovakia, Yugoslavia, and Poland. The Ottoman empire was reduced to the territory of present-day Turkey. Ottoman lands in Southwest Asia were organized as **mandates**, with Syria and Jordan controlled by France, and Palestine, Transjordan, and Iraq controlled by Great Britain. Russia, abandoned by the Allies for withdrawing early from the war, lost territory to both Poland and Romania. The former Russian territories of Estonia, Latvia, Lithuania, and Finland became independent.

Europe, 1919

THE IMPACT OF THE GREAT WAR

Most of the original members of the new League of Nations were non-European nations, demonstrating the global nature of the Great War. The Treaty of Versailles was unsuccessful in forging a lasting peace. The United States, fearing involvement in another global conflict, refused to join the League of Nations, thereby weakening the association from its very inception. Several years after the war, the United States signed a separate peace treaty with the former Central Powers. In spite of its lack of participation in the League of Nations, the United States would emerge from the war as an economically strong world power. Germany was angered at its humiliation by the war guilt clause and the exorbitant reparations it could hardly afford to repay. Subject peoples of the European colonies were outraged by their failure to win independence. Italy and Japan felt the treaty should have awarded them additional territory. The unfinished issues of the Treaty of Versailles would provide the groundwork for a second world conflict.

The Cost of the War

The war eliminated an entire generation of Europeans through the deaths of both soldiers and civilians. About 9 million soldiers died and another 21 million were injured. Genocide reduced the European population further, due to the massacre of thousands of Christian Armenians by the Ottoman Turks from 1915 to 1919. At the end of the nineteenth century the Armenians had attempted to achieve independence from the Ottomans. When World War I erupted, the Armenians supported the Allies. In retaliation, the Ottomans deported almost two million Armenians, many of whom died of starvation or at the hands of Ottoman soldiers.

Economic devastation plagued Europe after the war. The finances of the European nations were depleted and farmland and towns were destroyed. In 1918, a powerful strain of influenza, called the Spanish flu, swept through Europe, Asia, and the United States, killing around 20 million soldiers and civilians.

THINGS TO REMEMBER

- World War I (1914–1918) was the first global war, with fighting extended to colonial possessions of the European powers.
- The major combatants were:
    - Central Powers: Austria-Hungary, Germany, Ottoman empire, Bulgaria
    - Allies: Great Britain, France, Russia, Italy, Japan, the United States
- New technologies and weapons made this conflict more devastating than any to date.
- A generation of European men lost their lives.
- Women gained opportunities outside the home by filling factory jobs vacated by soldiers.
- The Treaty of Versailles established many new nations, most of which had borders drawn without consideration of ethnicity or language.
- Subject peoples in Asia and Africa had hoped for independence after the war, due to their service in their controlling nation's army. Their hopes were not realized.

- The Russian Revolution of 1917 came about partially due to war shortages of goods and loss of life. The communist leadership of Russia made an early peace with Germany in 1918.
- In Germany, the Treaty of Versailles was resented for its harsh provisions. Germany had to pay expensive reparations, it lost territory, and the size of its military was sharply restricted.

REVIEW QUESTIONS

1. The immediate cause of World War I was

   (A) nationalism.
   (B) secret alliances.
   (C) militarism.
   (D) the outcome of ethnic conflict in the Balkans.
   (E) independence.

2. Which of the following characteristics of World War I illustrates the concept of total war?

   (A) The implementation of laissez-faire economics
   (B) The guarantee of freedom of the press for wartime correspondents
   (C) Rationing
   (D) Bans on wage and price controls
   (E) Fewer employment opportunities for women

3. Which country became an early member of the League of Nations?

   (A) Russia
   (B) Germany
   (C) France
   (D) The United States
   (E) Israel

4. In the treaties ending World War I,

   (A) European imperialism came to an end.
   (B) Russia was granted part of Poland as a token of her participation in the war.
   (C) Japan's hopes for empire were crushed.
   (D) numerous nations and peoples other than Germany were left angered.
   (E) boundaries of new nations created after the breakup of the Austro-Hungarian empire were drawn along ethnic lines.

5. Which of the following was a result of World War I?
   - (A) Genocide carried out by the peoples of a declining empire
   - (B) A homeland in Palestine for the Jews
   - (C) Economic prosperity in France and Great Britain
   - (D) The increased power of Russia
   - (E) Ethnic harmony in Yugoslavia

ANSWERS AND EXPLANATIONS

1. (D)

Ethnic conflict in the Balkans led to the assassination of Austrian archduke Ferdinand, the immediate cause of World War I. Nationalism, secret alliances, militarism, and imperialism were underlying causes of the war.

2. (C)

Total war is the complete dedication to warfare of not only armies, but also the government and civilians on the homefront. In a total war, governments control a command economy (A), often curtail freedom of the press (B), and impose wage and price controls (D). In a total war, women receive additional opportunities for employment as a result of their need to fill in at jobs vacated by men (E).

3. (C)

France was an early member. Russia, and Germany were initially not allowed to join the League, the United States declined to join, and Israel was not a nation when the League was founded in 1918.

4. (D)

Russia was not granted a part of Poland and, in fact, lost territory as a penalty for her early withdrawal from the war (B). European imperialism would continue after the war in locations such as Africa, Asia, and the Pacific islands (A). Subject nations were angered at their failure to achieve independence; Italy and Japan desired additional territory (D). Austria-Hungary was broken into several nations without respect for the location of ethnic groups (E).

5. (A)

Armenians supportive of the Allied cause were deported or massacred by the Ottomans after the war started. Israel was not created until after World War II in 1948 (B). The war produced economic devastation in France and Great Britain (C) as well as in Russia (D). Yugoslavia, formed from the breakup of the Austro-Hungarian empire, was comprised of different ethnic groups, a situation that promoted discord (E).

CHAPTER 25

Totalitarianism and Nationalism

TIMELINE

1861	Alexander II frees the serfs in Russia
1902	Saud unifies the Arabs
1904	Trans-Siberian Railway constructed
1905	Russo-Japanese War Bloody Sunday
1906	First meeting of the Russian Duma
1911–1912	Overthrow of the Qing dynasty
1917	China declares war on Germany March Revolution Bolshevik Revolution
1918	Treaty of Brest-Litovsk Assassination of Czar Nicholas and family
1918–1920	Russian civil war
1919	Amritsar Massacre Greeks invade Turkey
1921	Lenin's New Economic Policy Organization of the Chinese Communist Party
1922	Creation of the Union of Soviet Socialist Republics Last Turkish sultan deposed

1923	Kemal becomes president of Turkey
1925	Jiang Jieshi assumes leadership of the Guomindang Reza Shah Pahlavi assumes power in Persia
1928	First Five-Year Plan Stalin initiates collective farming Jiang becomes president of the Nationalist Republic of China
1930	Civil war begins in China Indian protest against the Salt Acts
1931	Japanese invasion of Manchuria
1933	Stalin's Second Five-Year Plan
1934	The Long March in China
1934–1939	Stalin's Great Purge
1935	Government of India Act
1937	Japanese invasion of China

IMPORTANT PEOPLE, PLACES, EVENTS, AND CONCEPTS

Alexander II
Alexander III
pogrom*
Nicholas II
Mensheviks*
Bolsheviks*
V.I. Lenin
Bloody Sunday
Duma*
Czarina Alexandra
Rasputin
March Revolution
Alexander Kerensky
soviet*
Bolshevik Revolution
dissidents*
White Army
Red Army
Leon Trotsky
New Economic Policy (NEP)*
Communist Party
totalitarian state*
Great Purge
command economy*
Five-Year Plans*
collective farming*
kulak
Revolutionary Alliance
Sun Yixian
Guomindang*
Nationalist Party
Yuan Shiakai
May Fourth Movement
Mao Zedong
Jiang Jieshi
Long March
Amritsar Massacre
Mohandas K. Gandhi
Indian National Congress
civil disobedience*
Salt March
Government of India Act
Muslim League
Mustafa Kemal
Reza Shah Pahlavi
Abd al-Aziz Ibn Saud

THE RUSSIAN REVOLUTIONS

The revolution in Russia, which contributed to Russia's early withdrawal from World War I, was precipitated by conditions that had existed for decades. The harsh rule of the Romanov czars during the nineteenth century had resulted in unequal land distribution among the Russian people, in addition to shortages of bread and fuel among the peasant classes.

Nineteenth-Century Russia

Nineteenth-century Russia, which was not as heavily industrialized as the nations of western Europe, had a largely agrarian economy. Feudalism hindered Russia's economic development, binding serfs to the nobles who owned the land they worked. Russia's loss in the Crimean War resulted from the lack of industrial efficiency and adequate transportation, both of which neglected to provide the Russian army with necessary supplies.

After the Crimean War, the new czar, **Alexander II**, decided Russia needed to take steps in order to keep pace with the modernization of other nations. Alexander II began his reforms by freeing the serfs in 1861. Peasant communities replaced serfdom. But peasants had to pay the Russian government for their land, while nobles received government payment for their land.

The Policies of Alexander III

In 1881, Alexander II was assassinated. **Alexander III**, his successor, increased the czar's control over Russia while promoting industrial development. The nationalist sentiment that was present in western Europe was motivating the Russians to try to make their nation a modern, powerful state. Alexander III, however, continued along the path of autocracy by encouraging the activities of the secret police and imposing strict censorship of written materials. Political **dissidents** were exiled to remote Siberia.

In order to establish a national culture for Russia, Alexander III took strict measures to oppress ethnic minorities within the empire. Making Russian the official language, he forbade the use of minority languages in Russian schools. Jews were forced to live within areas segregated from other Russians and were subject to frequent ***pogroms***, or organized violence against them.

Nicholas II Continues Autocratic Rule

When **Nicholas II** came to the Russian throne in 1894, he vowed that he would continue in the autocratic tradition of his father, Alexander III. Realizing, however, that Russia needed to modernize to compete with other nations, Nicholas began to industrialize Russia. This involved primarily state-sponsored heavy industries such as railroads, armament factories, and iron foundries. During his reign, the Trans-Siberian Railway was constructed.

Industrialization in Russia brought additional problems, such as poor working conditions, low wages, and child labor. Revolutionary movements continued to grow within the empire; some of these were fueled by the doctrines of Karl Marx. In 1903, the Marxist groups divided over strategies: The **Mensheviks** wanted to further industrialization before gaining support from the proletariat for revolution, while the **Bolsheviks** wanted radical change executed by a small group of extremely committed revolutionaries. The leader of the Bolsheviks was the exiled leader **Vladimir Ilyich Lenin**, who maintained contact with the Bolsheviks until he could return to Russia from Europe.

Prelude to Revolution

A number of events in the early twentieth century proved the incompetence of the czars. The defeat of the Russian empire by the seemingly insignificant islands of Japan in the Russo-Japanese War in 1905 was a major blow to Russian prestige. Another troubling event was **Bloody Sunday** in January 1905, in which workers and their families marched on the czar's Winter Palace in St. Petersburg. The petition they planned to present to the czar included requests for improved factory working conditions and an elected national legislature. Although Nicholas was not present at the palace, his generals and police officials were. They ordered soldiers to fire on the protesters, killing between 500 and 1,000 people.

After a series of more violent protests across Russia, Czar Nicholas conceded to popular demands and allowed the creation of the first Russian parliament, the **Duma**. Meeting for the first time in May 1906, the Duma was led by moderates who wanted to pattern the Russian government after the constitutional monarchy of Great Britain. The first Duma was to meet for only ten weeks before it was dissolved by Nicholas. Although the Duma would reconvene from time to time, it never wielded enough power to reform the Russian government.

Problems in the Russian Royal Family

As Russia suffered one defeat after another in World War I, Czar Nicholas moved his headquarters to the front, leaving his wife, **Czarina Alexandra**, to run the government in his absence. While her husband was away at war, Alexandra became increasingly preoccupied with the health of their son and heir to the Russian throne, Alexis. The boy had hemophilia, but his symptoms were seemingly relieved by a mysterious self-proclaimed holy man named **Rasputin**. Alexandra fell under the spell of Rasputin, eventually allowing him to make key decisions regarding governmental policy. Rasputin, who opposed reform and granted governmental positions to his friends, was feared by the Russian nobility. In 1916, a group of nobles assassinated him.

While Alexandra was distracted by her son's condition, the Russian people were finding it increasingly difficult to procure adequate food and fuel. Prices on available supplies were highly inflated. Protests increased, and the czar and czarina were faced with ruling a people who had lost faith in their government and were ready for change.

The March Revolution

In March 1917, riots sprang up throughout Russia to protest the scarcity of bread and fuel. A general protest against the czar (the **March Revolution**) forced Czar Nicholas to abdicate the throne for himself and his son, Alexis. In July 1918, Bolshevik revolutionaries executed the czar and his family. In the place of czarist rule, a provisional government was set up with **Alexander Kerensky** as the head.

Kerensky was determined to continue Russian participation in World War I. Protests continued against poor factory conditions, shortages of supplies, and inequitable land distribution. Some of the revolutionaries organized themselves into ***soviets***, or local councils of peasants, laborers, and soldiers.

Meanwhile, the Germans arranged for Lenin to return to Russia, where they hoped his socialist leanings would promote further internal dissension that would lead Russia to withdraw from the war.

The Bolshevik Revolution

Arriving in Petrograd (formerly St. Petersburg) in April 1917, Lenin and the radical Bolsheviks gained control of the soviets in the principal Russian cities. In November 1917, Bolshevik-controlled armed factory workers (the Red Guards) marched on the Winter Palace in Petrograd and arrested the leaders of Russia's provisional government.

Lenin immediately placed control of factories in the hands of workers and ordered the redistribution of farmland among peasants. In March 1918, Russia and Germany signed the Treaty of Brest-Litovsk, which withdrew Russia from World War I. The treaty, which caused Russia to cede a large amount of land to the Central Powers, was a source of humiliation and anger among many Russians, who objected to Bolshevik policies.

Civil War: White v. Red

Before the Bolsheviks could carry out their plans for changing the Russian government and society, they had to deal with a civil war that would rage in Russia from 1918 to 1920. Opponents of the Bolsheviks had formed the **White Army**, which received aid from the United States and other Western nations. The **Red Army** was led by Bolshevik leader **Leon Trotsky**. Most Russian peasants supported the Reds for fear that the Whites might return the czarist rule. About ten million people would die during the civil war and perhaps another five million during the famine that followed. The Red Army won the civil war, leaving the future of Russia and its numerous problems in the hands of the Bolsheviks.

Lenin Builds a New State

The Russian civil war had destroyed industry and trade. Lenin was now left with the responsibility of restoring the Russian economy. In March 1921, Lenin announced his **New Economic Policy (NEP)**. Breaking with Lenin's vision of a state-controlled command economy, the NEP allowed a degree of capitalism and also sought foreign investment. Peasants were permitted to sell their surplus crops, and individuals could sell goods for profit. While the government controlled major industries, banks, and communications, private owners operated small factories, businesses, and farms. The central government undertook electrification projects, and technical schools trained technicians and electricians. By 1928, the economy had recovered.

Lenin's restructuring of the Russian government in 1922 involved organizing the country into self-governing republics under the central government, named the Union of Soviet Socialist Republics (USSR). In 1924, the Bolsheviks, now calling themselves Communists, created a constitution; actual power, however, resided in the **Communist Party**.

Stalin Forms a Totalitarian State

When Lenin died in 1924, Leon Trotsky and Joseph Stalin vied for leadership of the Communist Party. In 1928, Stalin assumed total control of the Communist Party, and in 1929, he forced Trotsky into exile. Stalin immediately went about establishing a **totalitarian state** in the Soviet Union. Totalitarian states are characterized by the rule of only one party whose beliefs support the welfare of the state above all else. The state controls all aspects of public and private life, and force is often used to crush any opposition.

Stalin's totalitarian government used the secret police as informants against imagined traitors. In the **Great Purge** (1934–1939), Stalin executed anyone who opposed him. His government sponsored youth groups to indoctrinate young people in the glories of the state. The government controlled newspapers, radios, and motion pictures. Christians and Jews were persecuted, and churches and synagogues were destroyed.

Stalin's Economic Policies

Stalin's economic program was aimed at transforming the Soviet Union from an agricultural to an industrial economy. A **command economy** was imposed on the Soviet people; economic decisions were in the hands of the government, not the consumer. In 1928, Stalin imposed the first **Five-Year Plan** to increase production of commodities such as coal, oil, steel, and electricity. Because of the emphasis on heavy industry, consumers experienced shortages of clothing and household goods. Although the first Five-Year Plan was less successful than Stalin had hoped, it did improve the Soviet economy. A second Five-Year Plan also increased industrial output.

In 1928, Stalin launched his agricultural program, which involved government seizure of millions of private farms. The farms were then combined into large collective farms owned by the government; profits were to be shared by all the farmers. **Collective farming** was enforced most harshly against the Ukrainian ***kulaks***, or wealthier peasants who had become prosperous during the days of the NEP. Recriminations against the kulaks led to a great famine in which many of them lost their lives.

Society Under Stalin

During Stalin's regime, women worked alongside men in factories and public works projects. Equal educational opportunities allowed many women to prepare for careers in the sciences, especially medicine. In addition to the responsibility of working for the state, Soviet women were also expected to carry out their traditional responsibilities of homemaking and childcare.

Under Stalin's economic plans, state-sponsored education provided new opportunities for university and technical training. All levels of schooling were under government control, and children were indoctrinated in the glories of Communism. Teachers who opposed Communist ideology faced job loss or imprisonment.

NATIONALISM IN CHINA

At the start of the twentieth century, the Chinese witnessed the stirrings of nationalist sentiment. After hundreds of years of foreign domination of both their government and economy, the Chinese were ready to reassert their national identity. To some Chinese, this meant modernization, while to others it involved clinging to tradition.

The Overthrow of the Qing Dynasty

In 1912, the Qing dynasty, which had ruled China since 1664, was overthrown by the **Revolutionary Alliance** under the leadership of **Sun Yixian**, a physician who had lived in the United States. Sun would also become the first leader of the **Guomindang**, or the **Nationalist Party**, and the first leader of the new republic of China. After six weeks, Sun turned over his power to **Yuan Shiakai**, who ruled as a military dictator. After his death, civil war broke out in China. Warlords ruled the land, reviving the opium trade and often neglecting irrigation projects. The outbreak of World War I caused additional misery as millions of peasants died during a wartime famine.

China's Response to World War I

In 1917, China declared war on Germany in the hopes that the Allies would win the war and then return German-controlled areas of China to the Chinese. The Treaty of Versailles, however, granted Japan the privileges and territories in China that had belonged to Germany. The Chinese reacted to the news of the treaty with demonstrations that became known as the **May Fourth Movement**. The Guomindang supported the goals of the movement, but it was too weak to impose central rule on China. Many educated Chinese abandoned Sun Yixian's support of democracy and instead adopted Lenin's type of communism. Among these young people was a teacher named **Mao Zedong**.

Communism in China

In 1921, a group of Marxists, including Mao Zedong, met in Shanghai and organized the Chinese Communist Party. When the Western democracies failed to support the Guomindang, Sun allied his movement with that of the Communist Party and accepted Lenin's offer to send military advisers to China.

When Sun Yixian died in 1925, the Guomindang came under the leadership of **Jiang Jieshi**. Jiang's supporters, primarily businesspeople and merchants, feared the creation of a socialist economy in China. In April 1927, Nationalist troops carried out executions in major Chinese cities that nearly eliminated the Chinese Communist Party. In 1928, Jiang became president of the Nationalist Republic of China, which was recognized by Great Britain and the United States.

As time went on, Jiang's government proved ineffective in addressing the plight of Chinese peasants and became progressively less democratic. Many peasants began supporting the Communist Party, which divided the land it controlled among the peasants. Mao and other Communists also supported extended rights for women, including the right to divorce their husbands, and spoke out against the practice of foot-binding.

Civil War in China

In 1930, civil war broke out between the Nationalists and the Communists. Mao Zedong recruited peasants and trained them in guerrilla warfare. In 1933, Jiang's army surrounded the Communist army; in 1934, the Communists began their 6,000-mile-long retreat, called the **Long March**. Only a fraction of those who began the trek reached safety in northwestern China.

In 1931, while civil war raged in China, Japan invaded Manchuria, an industrialized province in northeastern China with ample deposits of coal and iron which were needed by Japanese industries. With the Japanese invasion, World War II had begun in Asia. The Manchurian invasion was followed in 1937 by Japan's invasion of China along the Yangtze River. The Japanese invasion eventually served to temporarily halt the civil war between the armies of Jiang and Mao.

THE DRIVE FOR NATIONALISM IN INDIA

The people of India also longed for changes in their government. Muslims and Hindus, while often divided along religious lines, shared similar expectations for independence from British rule. The push for Indian independence had begun in earnest during World War I, as Indian troops fought on the side of the British. India had hoped that, in return for its assistance to the war effort, the British would carry out previously made promises to begin preparing the Indian people for independence.

When Indian armies returned home after World War II, they found no sign of the promised independence. On the contrary, in order to contain radicals who were carrying out acts of violence, in 1919 Great Britain passed an act which allowed them to jail protestors for up to two years without trial by jury. A peaceful demonstration of Hindus and Muslims at Amritsar, capital of the Punjab region, turned violent when the alarmed British commander ordered his troops to fire on demonstrators. After the so-called **Amritsar Massacre**, which killed about 400 of their people, millions of Indians now called for independence.

Gandhi's Philosophy of Nonviolence

Emerging as leader of the independence movement was **Mohandas K. Gandhi**, called the Mahatma, or "Great Soul." Gandhi was to transform the **Indian National Congress** from an organization appealing to a basically elitist group into a mass organization that carried out the ideals of Indian nationalism. Gandhi's philosophy was derived from the major world religions, especially Islam, Hinduism, and Christianity. Key to his strategy was **civil disobedience**, or passive resistance—public refusal to obey a law perceived as unjust. Gandhi wanted Indians to refuse to buy British manufactures, attend British schools, vote, or pay taxes to the British government. He particularly targeted the British textile industry, urging Indians to weave their own cloth. Gandhi's efforts saw a sharp decrease in the purchase of British cloth.

The Salt March

In 1930, Gandhi organized his followers in a march of two hundred forty miles to protest the Salt Acts. This legislation required Indians to buy salt only from the British government and imposed taxes on salt. Reaching the sea, the protestors made their own salt from evaporated seawater. Further protests gained worldwide support for India's independence movement while leading to the arrests of thousands of Indians, including Gandhi.

India Moves Toward Independence

Gandhi's efforts saw results in 1935, when the British Parliament passed the **Government of India Act**, granting local self-rule and some democratic elections. The act also reinforced antagonism between Muslims and Hindus. Indian Muslims were afraid that the Hindu majority would control an independent India. The head of the **Muslim League** proposed a separate state for Muslims, which he named Pakistan.

NATIONALIST MOVES IN SOUTHWEST ASIA

Turkey

The breakup of the Ottoman empire after World War I and Muslim interest in Southwest Asia stirred nationalist feelings in that region. After the war, the only Ottoman territory that remained was Anatolia and a strip of land surrounding Istanbul. The empire was further weakened in 1919 when the Greeks invaded Turkey. In 1922, under the leadership of reformer **Mustafa Kemal**, the Turks deposed the last Ottoman sultan.

In 1923, Kemal became the president of the Republic of Turkey. He separated Islamic law from secular law by abolishing Islamic courts. Kemal's legal system was based on Western law, and provided for women's suffrage and the right of women to hold public office. Government programs encouraged the development of industry.

Persia

After World War I, British attempts at control produced a Persian revolt, which resulted in **Reza Shah Pahlavi's** rise to power in 1925. Changing the name of his country in 1935 from Persia to Iran, the new shah created public schools, promoted industry, built up the country's transportation network, and assured greater rights for women. At the same time, the shah reserved total governmental power for himself.

Saudi Arabia

Modernization also came to Arabia, but it was a limited change in compliance with Islamic tradition. An effort to unify Arabs had begun in 1902 under the direction of **Abd al-Aziz Ibn Saud**, who introduced some modern technology and, in 1932, renamed his country Saudi Arabia. A major change to the Saudi economy came in the 1920s and 1930s with the discovery of vast petroleum deposits not only in Saudi Arabia but also in Iraq, Iran, and Kuwait. Saudi Arabia would become a country of wealthy oil exporters, but it would also have to deal with Western nations' attempts to control the oil-rich area.

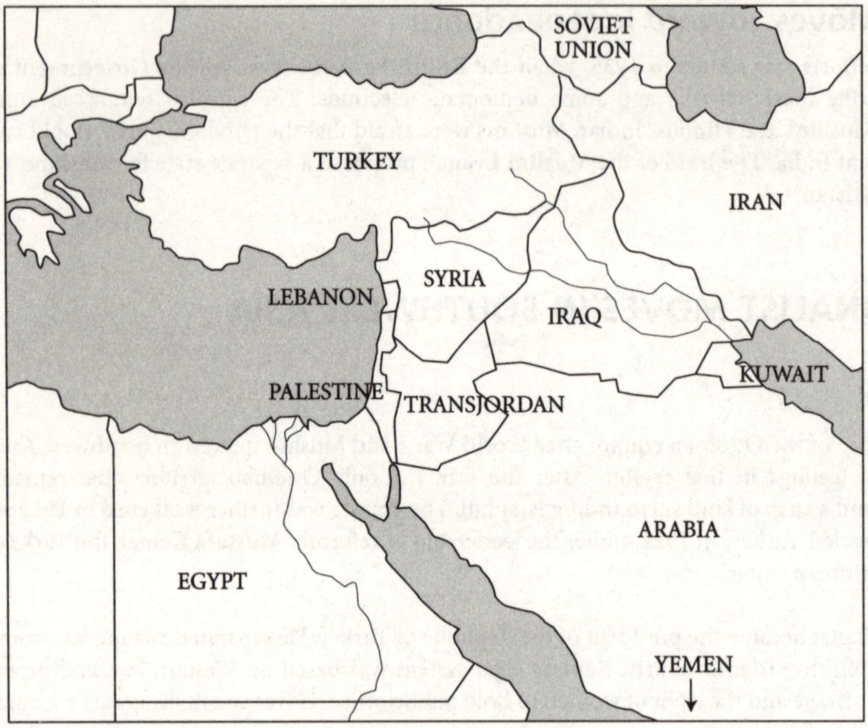

Southwest Asia After World War I

THINGS TO REMEMBER

- After World War I, nationalist movements throughout Asia gained momentum.
- In Russia, revolution came due to the people's frustration with the czar's absolutism and problems related to the war effort.
    - The czar abdicated in March 1917, and in November Lenin's Communist Party seized control, withdrawing from the war in 1918.
    - After winning a two-year-long civil war, the new communist government eventually established a totalitarian state under Joseph Stalin. The state controlled all land and means of production.
- The collapse of China's foreign Qing dynasty led to the formation of rival parties: the Nationalists (led by Jiang Jieshi) and the Communists (led by Mao Zedong).
    - China's loss of territory to Japan in the Treaty of Versailles was seen as a betrayal, since it fought on the side of the Allies.
- In India, Mohandas Gandhi's nonviolent protests led to greater self-rule.

- The Middle East also saw the rise of nationalism with the emergence of the nations of Turkey, Iran (formerly Persia), and Saudi Arabia.
    - The discovery of vast oil fields in the Persian Gulf region brought lasting conflict between local inhabitants and Western interests.

REVIEW QUESTIONS

1. Both the Weimar Republic and Kerensky's provisional government in Russia after the March Revolution
   (A) reflected the optimism prevalent after World War I.
   (B) provided sound economic footing for their respective countries.
   (C) were followed by the rise of totalitariansim.
   (D) received economic assistance from international committees.
   (E) posed a threat to their respective states because of the strength of their pro-democratic stance.

2. Which of the following is in the correct chronological order?
   (A) March Revolution, Bolshevik Revolution, Bloody Sunday, Russian withdrawal from World War I, Russian civil war
   (B) Russian civil war, March Revolution, Bolshevik Revolution, Bloody Sunday, Russian withdrawal from World War I
   (C) Bolshevik Revolution, Russian withdrawal from World War I, Bloody Sunday, March Revolution, Russian civil war
   (D) Bloody Sunday, March Revolution, Bolshevik Revolution, Russian withdrawal from World War I, Russian civil war
   (E) March Revolution, Russian civil war, Russian withdrawal from World War I, Bolshevik Revolution, Bloody Sunday

3. Stalin's economic policies
   (A) were designed to provide equal economic opportunities for all persons.
   (B) placed control of the economy upon all consumers.
   (C) concentrated on the manufacture of consumer goods.
   (D) increased the Soviet Union's industrial output.
   (E) culminated in disappointing results for his Five-Year Plans.

4. Nationalist movements in Southwest Asia
   (A) delayed industrialization in the region.
   (B) resulted in the final overthrow of the Ottoman empire.
   (C) were realized in opposition to Islamic law.
   (D) repelled Western influence.
   (E) culminated in fewer rights for women throughout the region.

5. All of the following are true of the independence movement in India EXCEPT that
   (A) it failed to permanently resolve issues between Hindus and Muslims.
   (B) it was an outgrowth of Indian participation in World War I.
   (C) it created a common desire among Muslims and Hindus to achieve independence.
   (D) it involved placing the leadership of the Indian National Congress into the hands of the elite.
   (E) it was intensified by the Amritsar Massacre.

ANSWERS AND EXPLANATIONS

1. (C)

The Weimar Republic was followed by the rise of Hitler, while the Kerensky government was followed by the rise of Lenin. The weakness of both governments prevented them from becoming a powerful advocate of democracy (E).

2. (D)

The correct order is Bloody Sunday (January 1905), March Revolution (March 1917), Bolshevik Revolution (November 1917), Russian withdrawal from World War I (March 1918), Russian civil war (1918–1921).

3. (D)

Although the First Five-Year Plan had disappointing results, the Second Five-Year Plan increased industrial output.

4. (B)

Nationalist moves finally overthrew the Ottoman empire, which had been reduced in size after World War I. The new nation of Turkey, Persia, and, to some extent, Saudi Arabia, became industrialized after the end of the Ottoman empire (A). Saudi Arabia modernized while keeping in compliance with Islamic law, while Kemal of Turkey separated Islamic and secular law (C). Kemal's legal system was based on Western law (D). Turkey allowed women to vote and hold office (E).

5. (D)

Under Gandhi, the Indian independence movement placed the Indian National Congress in the hands of commoners. After World War I, Indians thought their combat and support efforts would bring them independence (B). Both Hindus and Muslims desired independence, though each wanted to dominate an independent India (C). The Amritsar Massacre convinced the Indians to fight for independence (E).

CHAPTER 26

Depression and Dictatorship

TIMELINE

1919	Foundation of the Weimar Republic
1922	Mussolini forms a government
1923	Hitler writes *Mein Kampf*
1928	Kellogg-Briand Pact
1929	Crash of the New York Stock Exchange
1931	Japan invades Manchuria
1933	Hitler named Chancellor of Germany Japan withdraws from the League of Nations
1935	Italy invades Ethiopia
1936	Hitler occupies the Rhineland Formation of the Axis Powers
1936–1939	Spanish Civil War
1937	Japan invades China Hitler annexes Austria
1938	Munich Conference Kristallnacht
1939	Franco becomes dictator of Spain Hitler annexes Czechoslovakia Mussolini seizes Albania Nonaggression pact between Germany and Russia

IMPORTANT PEOPLE, PLACES, EVENTS, AND CONCEPTS

Albert Einstein	Walter Gropius	*Mein Kampf*
theory of relativity*	jazz*	lebensraum*
psychoanalysis*	Igor Stravinsky	*Der Führer*
Sigmund Freud	Margaret Sanger	SS
existentialism*	Emma Goldman	Gestapo
Jean Paul Sartre	Charles Lindbergh	Hitler Youth
Karl Jaspers	Amelia Earhart	League of German Girls
Friedrich Nietzsche	coalition*	Kristallnacht
Franz Kafka	Weimar Republic	Emperor Hirohito
James Joyce	Dawes Plan	Haile Selassie
stream of consciousness*	Kellogg-Briand Pact*	Rome-Berlin Axis
Erich Maria Remarque	Black Thursday	Axis Powers
Ernest Hemingway	Popular Front	Francisco Franco
expressionism*	New Deal*	Nationalists
cubism*	fascism*	Republicans
Pablo Picasso	Benito Mussolini	Anschluss
Dadaism*	Black Shirts	Sudetenland
surrealism*	*Il Duce*	Munich Conference
functionalism*	Adolph Hitler	Neville Chamberlain
Frank Lloyd Wright	Nazis	appeasement*
Bauhaus school	Storm Troopers	Winston Churchill

THE WORLD OF THE EARLY TWENTIETH CENTURY

The rivalry among nations that had culminated in World War I had largely shattered the illusion that peace and prosperity would mark the modern era. Even before and during the war, in science, literature, and the arts, old ideas were called into question and new patterns emerged. The popular culture of the day saw a sense of rebellion in a world whose future seemed uncertain.

New Concepts in Science

The most renowned scientist of the period between the wars was the German-born physicist, **Albert Einstein**. Einstein's most notable achievement was the **theory of relativity**, which stated that the measurement of motion varies relative to a specific observer. He further observed that a small amount of mass can be converted into a vast amount of energy. The theories of Einstein were controversial in that they broke with the findings of Isaac Newton to maintain that events occur not only in the dimensions of space but also in that of time.

Another scientific achievement which broke with tradition was the science of **psychoanalysis**, created by an Austrian physician named **Sigmund Freud**. Freud proposed the idea that most human behavior is irrational and focused on psychological, rather than physiological, causes of mental disorders. Believing in the importance of unconscious behavior, Freud taught that the analysis of dreams was vital to understanding the human mind.

Literature Breaks with Tradition

Literature saw the emergence of a philosophy called **existentialism**. Among its proponents were **Jean Paul Sartre** of France and **Karl Jaspers** of Germany. Existentialists believed that life in itself has no meaning, but that each person decides what life means personally. The philosophy was built upon the works of the German philosopher **Friedrich Nietzsche**, who advocated the notion that through courage and effort some humans could become superhumans. Criticizing the Western ideals of democracy and progress, Nietzsche's ideas found support among Italians and Germans in the years between the world wars. This philosophy also appealed to other European intellectuals who had abandoned democratic ideals, favoring instead the rule of elitist groups.

Novelists mirrored the anxiety of the era, choosing themes that reflected the inability of humans to control their fate, such as in **Franz Kafka**'s *The Trial* (1925) and *The Castle* (1926). **James Joyce**, influenced by psychoanalysis, used a literary technique called stream of consciousness in his novel *Ulysses* (1922). Novels such as **Erich Maria Remarque**'s *All Quiet on the Western Front* (1929) and **Ernest Hemingway**'s *A Farewell to Arms* (1929) reacted to the events of World War I by portraying the meaningless suffering of war.

New Forms in Art and Music

In the arts, a number of new schools arose during and after the war, many reflecting the influence of African and Asian styles. **Expressionism** featured the use of bold colors and distortion of forms. **Cubism**, represented in the works of **Pablo Picasso**, changed the normal shapes of objects or persons into geometric forms. A movement called **Dadaism** (1916–1924) produced works that were whimsical and meaningless, representing the concept that the events of World War I had rendered established traditions meaningless. The subsequent movement of **Surrealism** featured paintings demonstrating a dreamlike quality.

Non-traditional patterns were implemented in architecture. The school known as **functionalism** was initiated by **Frank Lloyd Wright** of the United States and was continued by the **Bauhaus school** of **Walter Gropius** of Germany. The practical nature of the movement featured buildings constructed so that their design reflected their function.

Musical forms were characterized by irregular rhythms. A new style called **jazz** was developed by white musicians from New Orleans and African American musicians. The frenetic moves of dances such as the Charleston showed the abandonment of tradition that was characteristic of the period. Russian-born composer **Igor Stravinsky**'s *The Rite of Spring* (1913) created a stir at its first performance; breaking with musical tradition, it involved different instruments played in different keys at the same time.

A More Open Society

New developments in the arts and literature merely reflected Western society in the period after World War I. The defiance of tradition particularly found a home among youth, resulting in the first teenage rebellions of the modern era. Furthermore, women, who had taken on new responsibilities and roles outside the home during the war, achieved political gains and social change. After the war, women's suffrage was enacted in several countries, including the United States, Great Britain, Sweden, Germany, and Austria. The number of women entering professions increased. Women's fashions favored shorter, less restrictive clothing, as well as shorter hairstyles. New freedoms for women were promoted as **Margaret Sanger** and **Emma Goldman** campaigned for the use of artificial contraception.

Advances in Transportation and Communication

New technology transformed society. Prices of automobiles dropped, making them affordable for the middle class. In the United States, the automobile changed teenage life and promoted the growth of suburbs and the practice of commuting from home to work in the cities. The airplane, which had been used in combat for the first time in World War I, was now used for carrying airmail, and major passenger airlines arose. In 1919, two British pilots flying from Newfoundland to Ireland made the first successful flight across the Atlantic. **Charles Lindbergh** flew from New York to Paris in the first trans-Atlantic solo flight. In 1932, **Amelia Earhart** became the first woman to fly solo across the Atlantic.

Radio and motion pictures led to the creation of a mass culture. The radio had proven indispensable to communication during World War I. Peacetime interest in wireless communication led to the founding of the first commercial radio station—KDKA in Pittsburgh, Pennsylvania—which broadcast for the first time in 1920. The radio quickly became the mainstay of family entertainment in the United States in the 1920s and 1930s. In many countries outside the United States, communications came under the control of the government. In Europe, the use of the radio spread slowly as governments reserved the air for cultural and government programs and taxed the owners of radios to finance this service.

Motion pictures had begun in France in 1895 and by the 1920s had become a major industry in Europe and the United States. At first, movies played on a silent screen, but sound was added in the late 1930s. Like the radio, the movies would become a favorite form of family entertainment in the United States and Europe.

POLITICAL AND ECONOMIC CHALLENGES

Throughout the 1920s, the European nations had undertaken the task of recovering their prewar economies. Torn by battle, most European nations were nearly bankrupt, and Europe was no longer in a position to dominate world affairs. On the other hand, Japan and the United States, neither of which had been a World War I battleground, prospered significantly after the war and expanded their volume of trade.

Postwar Governments in Europe

During and immediately following the war, the Europeans saw the fall of the last autocratic dynasties. Inexperience with democratic government often resulted in rule by a number of political parties, none of which was powerful enough to effectively run a government. Decisions were often realized by the formation of **coalitions**, or temporary alliances of a number of small parties. In times of crisis, the weakness of coalition governments became apparent. Some Europeans, therefore, began to look toward the stability of totalitarianism.

The Weimar Republic

In 1919, Germany set up a democratic government called the **Weimar Republic**. This was the German government that had signed the Treaty of Versailles, and it displayed serious weaknesses from its inception. The end of dynastic rule in Germany had produced a number of political parties, and the Germans were unaccustomed to democratic rule. Many Germans viewed the Weimar Republic as a symbol of the humiliation Germany had suffered in the postwar settlement.

Germany's political problems were compounded by economic concerns. Burdened by huge reparations debts, the Germans responded, not by raising taxes, but by printing more money. The German currency, or mark, became nearly worthless, producing severe postwar inflation. Economic woes caused many Germans to distrust their new democratic government. At this point, an international committee stepped in to rescue Germany's economy. The **Dawes Plan** rescheduled Germany's reparation payments to make them more manageable, and also provided for a $200 million loan from U.S. banks to stabilize the German economy. Implemented in 1924, the Dawes Plan was effective in curbing inflation in Germany, and by 1929 German factories were producing at their prewar level.

Postwar Peace Attempts

As Germany stabilized economically, it made efforts to ensure its economic and political stability by preventing future wars. In 1925, the German foreign minister, Gustav Stresemann, and the French foreign minister, Aristide Briand, signed a treaty agreeing that Germany and France would never again go to war against each other. Germany also agreed to respect the current borders of Belgium and France. As a result of her efforts toward peace, Germany was admitted to the League of Nations.

The treaty between France and Germany inspired another agreement: the **Kellogg-Briand Pact** (1928), negotiated between Briand of France and U.S. Secretary of State Frank Kellogg. The pact, whose purpose was to effectively outlaw war, was signed by almost every country on the globe. The treaty, however, had no means of enforcement. Nevertheless, it was a sign of genuine movement toward peace and prosperity—that is, until the economy of the world began to crumble.

THE GREAT DEPRESSION

In spite of the apparent prosperity returning to Europe in the late 1920s, the global economy was fragile. The future prosperity of Europe involved a complex entanglement of reparations owed by Germany and Austria to France and England, as well as the need for U.S. funds to flow to debtor countries so that these payments could be met. To complicate matters, the French and British governments depended upon the reparations payments from Austria and Germany to pay off their war debts from loans received from the United States. In 1928, lenders from the United States began withdrawing capital from Europe, increasing the strain on the financial network.

Effects on the Global Economy

Economic problems in the late 1920s were not confined to Europe or the United States. Advances in manufacturing decreased the need for some raw materials, causing prices to drop. The situation was devastating to some colonial economies. The popularity of oil decreased the need for coal, and the cotton textile industry was hurt by the production of synthetic fabrics. Increased agricultural production worldwide caused a decline in prices. Farm families could no longer purchase as many manufactured goods, which, in turn, lowered industrial production and resulted in worker cutbacks.

The U.S. Economy Crashes

The marked prosperity of the United States after the war prompted some Americans to buy stock "on the margin," in which they initially put up only a small percentage of the purchase price. By October 1929, hints of a coming global economic slowdown caused some investors to withdraw from the market. On October 24, 1929 (known as **Black Thursday**), a wave of sales on the New York Stock Exchange caused stock prices to crash. The economy continued to fall throughout the early 1930s.

Global Response to the Depression

Since so much of the world depended on U.S. capital and imports, the Great Depression in the United States had a profound effect around the globe. Particularly weakened were banks in central Europe.

Countries heavily dependent upon foreign trade, such as Great Britain, were the most seriously affected by the Depression. Great Britain's largest party, the Labour Party, fell in 1931 and was replaced by the Conservatives. The British government encouraged industrial growth by lowering interest rates and passing high protective tariffs to protect its manufactures from foreign competition. Great Britain also imposed higher taxes on its citizens and took measures to stabilize the currency.

France, more agricultural and less dependent on foreign trade than Great Britain, felt the effects more profoundly in the political arena. Several coalitions rose and fell. In 1936, Socialists, Communists, and moderates formed a coalition called the **Popular Front**. Its aim was to initiate reforms to assist French workers, including pay increases and a 40-hour work week. In spite of these measures, unemployment remained high, and inflation counteracted wage increases.

The Scandinavian countries continued the traditions of their Socialist governments, taking community action to alleviate the effects of the Depression. Retirement incomes were protected by the governments of these countries, and welfare programs and subsidies were underwritten by increased taxes.

Japan, which relied on exports to pay for the food and fuel it imported, suffered greatly during the Great Depression. The silk export industry collapsed. Fishermen and farmers especially struggled. The Japanese government began to increase its military, hoping to acquire an empire with resources to meet its needs.

In Latin America, the Depression produced political policies which involved government planning and input. While these measures did not cure the Depression, they pointed to a new era of greater economic independence.

In the United States, President Franklin Delano Roosevelt began a reform program called the **New Deal**. Businesses and farms received government assistance, and public works projects provided jobs. Welfare and relief programs were instituted. The banking system was reformed. Like Great Britain, France, and the Scandinavian countries, the United States maintained its democratic government. Other nations, however, would turn to fascist dictatorships to handle the problems caused by the Great Depression.

THE RISE OF FASCISM IN EUROPE

Fascism stressed loyalty to the state; it was an extreme form of nationalism that appealed to the Europeans who had been humiliated by the peace treaties of World War I and financially destroyed by the Great Depression. Fascists owed their devotion to an authoritarian ruler and favored the use of symbols such as a particular uniform and prescribed salutes. Mass rallies stirred the hearts of the people as fascist leaders alluded to the nation's cultural heritage and traditions.

Fascism and Communism Compared

Both fascism and communism permitted only one-party rule; both revolved around the control of a single dictator. Communism and fascism upheld loyalty to the state as their highest goal. Unlike communists, whose goal was a classless society, fascists believed in maintaining social classes. Communists sought worldwide revolution, while fascists concerned themselves with promoting nationalist objectives in one country only.

Fascism in Italy

Italians were angry over their failure to acquire large amounts of territory after World War I. Postwar Italy was troubled by inflation and unemployment. **Benito Mussolini**, who had founded Italy's Fascist Party in 1919, vowed to strengthen Italy's economy and armed forces. In October 1922, thousands of Fascists, or **Black Shirts**, marched on Rome to demand that King Victor Emmanuel step down and allow Mussolini to form a government. The king complied, making Mussolini ***Il Duce***, or the leader, of Italy. His one-party state used censorship and secret police to assure loyalty to the state. Strikes were forbidden as Mussolini strived to gain the support of manufacturers and major landowners.

Hitler Assumes Control of Germany

After World War I, Austrian-born **Adolph Hitler** had settled in Munich, Germany. There he joined a political group called the Nationalist Socialist German Workers' Party, or the **Nazis**, whose goals were to prevent communism and reverse the terms of the Treaty of Versailles. Hitler became a member of the military arm of the Nazi Party called the **Storm Troopers**, or Brownshirts. Arrested after an attempt to seize power in Munich in 1923, Hitler was jailed. While in jail he wrote a book called ***Mein Kampf*** (My Struggle), which outlined his goals for Germany. In the book, Hitler proclaimed that Germans were in fact a master race, whom he called "Aryans." He pledged to regain lands taken from Germany at Versailles and acquire more ***lebensraum***, or living space, by conquering Russia and eastern Europe.

In 1933, in the midst of the Great Depression, the Nazis asked German President Paul von Hindenburg to name Hitler chancellor. With Hitler in office, the Nazis quickly solidified their control. Hitler, called ***Der Führer***, turned Germany into a totalitarian state with a special, black-uniformed group called the **SS** and a secret police called the **Gestapo**. In 1934, the SS murdered hundreds of Germans opposed to Hitler. Hitler revived the economy by promoting industrialization and constructing public works. He also strengthened his control over Germany by imposing strict censorship. Children were forced to join the **Hitler Youth** for boys or the **League of German Girls**, where they were indoctrinated in the propaganda of the state.

Hitler and the Jews

Hitler particularly targeted the Jewish minority, blaming them for all of Germany's current problems. In 1933, the Nazis began passing laws to deprive Jews of their rights. A wave of anti-Semitic violence culminated in **Kristallnacht** (November 9, 1938), in which Nazis attacked Jews in their homes and in the streets and destroyed Jewish-owned businesses. After Kristallnacht, Jews were banned from entering public buildings and were not permitted to own or work in retail businesses.

Dictatorships Spread to Other Countries

Other European countries fell to dictators, among them Hungary, Poland, Romania, Bulgaria, Albania, and Yugoslavia. By 1935, the only democracy in eastern Europe was Czechoslovakia. Many Europeans felt that dictatorship was necessary to maintain stability. But in countries with fascist dictatorships, aggression, not stability, would be the goal.

AGGRESSION LEADS TO WAR

Japanese Militarism

The Great Depression, which had resulted in the rise of dictatorships in several European countries, led to the rise of military rule in Japan. During its medieval period, Japan had developed along military lines, so militarism was not unknown in the Japanese tradition. In the 1920s, however, Japan's democratic government had demonstrated the desire for peace by signing the Kellogg-Briand Pact. But when the initial postwar prosperity waned and the Great Depression hit, the Japanese blamed their democratic government, facilitating a takeover of the country by the military. The **Emperor Hirohito** became the symbol of power in Japan.

Japan now decided that the solution to its problems was territorial expansion. An empire would provide Japan with raw materials and new markets for its exports and also alleviate its growing population. Japan was immediately attracted to Manchuria, whose iron and coal deposits were needed in Japanese factories. Japan invaded Manchuria in 1931, signaling the start of the Asian arena phase of World War II. The League of Nations condemned the Japanese aggression but was powerless to enforce its decision. In 1933, Japan withdrew from the League.

In 1937, Japan invaded northern and central China. When the Chinese capital of Nanjing fell, the Japanese killed thousands of soldiers and civilians in the city. Jiang Jieshi fled westward, while Chinese guerillas under the command of Mao Zedong stayed on to fight the Japanese in the conquered region.

Mussolini Invades Ethiopia

When the League of Nations failed to halt Japanese aggression, the Italians saw a chance to begin their own quest for a colonial empire in Africa. Ethiopia, one of the few remaining independent nations in Africa, had resisted Italian aggression in the 1890s. Now Mussolini would retaliate by invading Ethiopia in October 1935. The easy Italian victory caused Ethiopian Emperor **Haile Selassie** to appeal to the League of Nations. The League condemned the attack, but, as before, its members did nothing to reduce aggression.

Hitler Resists the Treaty of Versailles

The League of Nations demonstrated its weakness once again when Hitler decided to defy the provisions of the Treaty of Versailles and began to rearm Germany in March 1935. The following year, he moved German troops into the industrialized Rhineland, again in open defiance of the treaty. The Rhineland served as a buffer zone between Germany and France. Neither the League nor surrounding European nations stepped in to halt Hitler's advances. Hitler was now in a position of strength to further his goals of conquest on the European continent.

Other nations were noticing the potential power of Germany. In October 1936, Mussolini decided to ally himself with Hitler, and the **Rome-Berlin Axis** was born. When Japan forged an alliance with Germany the following month, the **Axis Powers** of Germany, Italy, and Japan were now unified and prepared for any future aggression.

The Spanish Civil War

A prelude to the coming world conflict played out in Spain when leaders of the Spanish army, following the models of Germany and Italy, revolted against the republican government in favor of a fascist government under the leadership of General **Francisco Franco**. In the ensuing Spanish Civil War (1936–1939), Hitler and Mussolini sent military assistance to Franco's troops, the **Nationalists**. The **Republicans**, who supported Spain's elected republican government, received limited aid from only the Soviet Union and a volunteer International Brigade. Great Britain and France, still feeling the effects of the Great Depression, remained neutral, while the United States maintained its isolationism. In 1939, the republican government collapsed and Franco became the fascist dictator of Spain.

Hitler Continues His Policy of Expansion

By November 1937, Hitler, unopposed by the Western powers or the League of Nations, was again on the move to seize more territory. In opposition to the Treaty of Versailles, Hitler proceeded to achieve **Anschluss**, or the unification of Austria and Germany. Knowing that some Austrians supported the unification movement, Hitler moved into Austria and annexed it. Again, France and Great Britain remained neutral, failing in their agreement to preserve the independence of Austria.

Hitler's next goal was the seizure of a portion of western Czechoslovakia known as the **Sudetenland**, home to about three million German-speaking people. In September 1938, Hitler demanded that the Sudetenland be annexed to Germany. The Czech government refused to comply with the demand and asked its ally France for assistance.

The Munich Conference

In response to Hitler's move on the Sudetenland, Mussolini requested a conference of Germany, France, Great Britain, and Italy to meet in Munich in September, 1938. Czech representatives were not invited to the meeting. British Prime Minister **Neville Chamberlain** followed a policy of **appeasement**, believing that giving in to Hitler would permanently satisfy his lust for more territory. On September 30, 1938, Great Britain and France announced that Hitler could take the Sudetenland in exchange for his pledge to respect the new borders of Czechoslovakia. Chamberlain referred to the Munich agreement as "peace in our time." A member of the British Parliament named **Winston Churchill** warned of the somber consequences that the appeasement policy of Munich would produce in the years to come.

Within six months of the **Munich Conference**, Hitler annexed Czechoslovakia; soon after, Mussolini seized Albania. Hitler then demanded that Poland return the former German seaport of Danzig. When Poland refused to comply, Great Britain and France promised to guarantee Polish independence and requested the support of the Soviet Union in stopping Hitler's advances. Stalin had resented not being invited to the Munich Conference, so while he was engaged in talks with France and Great Britain, he was also involved in a dialogue with Hitler. The leaders of the opposing political forms of fascism and communism now came to an agreement. On August 23, 1939, Russia and Germany signed a nonaggression pact, in which they agreed never to attack one another. The nations of the globe now awaited the outbreak of war.

THINGS TO REMEMBER

- The Great Depression began in 1929 and lasted through the 1930s.
  - Great Britain, France, the United States, and the Scandinavian countries preserved their democratic governments. Government intervention, such as Roosevelt's New Deal, helped shore up the economies.
  - Japan, Italy, Germany, and some other European countries turned to ultra-nationalist authoritarian governments.
    - Fascist governments were totalitarian and promoted an ideology of nationalism.
    - Mussolini became leader of the Italian government in 1922.
    - Hitler took power in Germany in 1933. That nation was particularly harmed by the Depression because of crippling war debt imposed by the Treaty of Versailles.
    - Under Emperor Hirohito, Japan increased its military, seeing conquest as a means to obtaining the resources to support its population. To this end, Japan invaded Manchuria in 1931 and China in 1937.
  - Latin American dictatorships took a more active role in economic planning.
  - As Hitler defied the Treaty of Versailles and began to rearm and seize territory, the nations of the world remained neutral.

REVIEW QUESTIONS

1. In Europe during the Great Depression,
   (A) democracies were strengthened throughout the continent.
   (B) coalition governments arose.
   (C) countries heavily dependent on foreign trade weathered the crisis more easily than those who were not.
   (D) Scandinavian countries abandoned their concept of the welfare state.
   (E) Great Britain continued the same government.

2. During the postwar economic decline,
   (A) economic decline went unnoticed in the colonies of Africa.
   (B) decreased agricultural production brought a drop in prices.
   (C) the need for oil decreased.
   (D) jobs in industry depended on the economic plight of farmers.
   (E) raw materials commanded a higher price than during World War I.

3. All of the following events indicated to the postwar world the political power of fascism EXCEPT
   (A) the Spanish Civil War.
   (B) the Kellogg-Briand Pact.
   (C) Japan's withdrawal from the League of Nations.
   (D) the Anschluss.
   (E) the Munich Conference.

4. The power of fascism was supported by all of the following EXCEPT
   (A) the allusion of fascist leaders to past national glories.
   (B) the existentialist philosophy of Nietzsche.
   (C) the general stability of European governments after World War I.
   (D) the provisions of the Treaty of Versailles.
   (E) the weakness of the League of Nations to control fascist aggression.

5. Japanese aggression in Manchuria and China
   (A) echoed Japan's reception of the Kellogg-Briand Pact.
   (B) was incompatible with the ideals of Japan's feudal period.
   (C) resulted from the successes of its postwar democratic government.
   (D) sparked worldwide efforts to stem Japanese actions.
   (E) was prompted by Japan's rapid industrialization.

ANSWERS AND EXPLANATIONS

1. (B)

Coalitions arose because of the inexperience of democratic governments (A). Countries dependent upon foreign trade were more vulnerable because of the ripple effect of the depression (C). Scandinavian countries continued their established welfare programs (D). Great Britain's Labour Party was replaced in 1931 by the Conservatives (E).

2. (D)

Industry suffered when farm families no longer had the income to purchase as many manufactured goods as before. In the colonies, the price of raw materials dropped (A, E). Increased agricultural production brought a drop in prices (B), and the need for oil increased as that of coal decreased (C).

3. (B)

The Kellogg-Briand Pact of 1928 appeared to indicate a worldwide trend toward the elimination of war. The Spanish Civil War was a prelude to World War II in pitting fascism against the republican government of Spain (A). Japan's withdrawal from the League followed its invasion of Manchuria in 1931 (C). The Anschluss was Hitler's unification of Austria and Germany (D). The Munich Conference illustrated how European leaders bowed to the power of fascism by appeasing Hitler (E).

4. (C)

The weak governments of postwar Europe tended to be unstable. Fascist leaders owed part of their charisma to their ability to refer to the past power of their respective peoples (A). The philosophy of Nietzsche pointed to the possibility of a race of supermen such as the Aryans (B). The Treaty of Versailles was a tool used by European fascists to point to the ill treatment of their country and to stir up public support for fascism (D). The weakness of the League led to further fascist aggression from Japan, Italy, and Germany (E).

5. (E)

Japan invaded these territories because of its need for their resources to support Japanese industry. Japan had signed the Kellogg-Briand Pact (A). Both Japan's feudal period and its activity at the beginning of World War II relied on militarism (B). The Japanese blamed their economic depression on their democratic government (C). The League of Nations and its members did nothing more than confirm Japanese aggression (D).

CHAPTER 27

World War II

TIMELINE

1931	Japanese invasion of Manchuria
1935	Nuremberg Laws
1937	Japanese invasion of China
1939	Hitler's invasion of Poland France and England declare war on Germany
1940	Fall of France
1940–1941	Battle of Britain Hitler's invasion of the Soviet Union Atlantic Charter Japanese seize French Indochina Bombing of Pearl Harbor
1942	Battle of the Coral Sea Battle of Midway Battle of Guadalcanal Battle of El Alamein
1943	British and American forces defeat the Afrika Korps
1944	The Allies enter Rome D-Day Liberation of France Battle of Leyte Gulf Battle of the Bulge

1945	Marines take Iwo Jima Fall of Germany/Victory in Europe Battle of Okinawa Bombings of Hiroshima and Nagasaki Victory in the Pacific Japanese War Crime Trials
1945–1946	Nuremberg Trials

IMPORTANT PEOPLE, PLACES, EVENTS, AND CONCEPTS

Third Reich*
blitzkrieg*
Axis Powers
Allied Powers
sitzkrieg
Maginot Line
Siegfried Line
Dunkirk
Vichy government
Henri Pétain
Charles de Gaulle
Free French
Winston Churchill
Operation Sea Lion*
Luftwaffe*
RAF
Erwin Rommel
Afrika Korps
Tobruk
Operation Barbarossa*
scorched-earth policy*
Lend-Lease Act*
U-boats*
Atlantic Charter*
Manchukuo
Rape of Nanjing
Isoroku Yamamoto
James Doolittle
Chester Nimitz
Douglas MacArthur
island-hopping*
Greater East Asia Co-Prosperity Sphere*
Holocaust*
Nuremberg Laws
ghetto*
Final Solution*
Dwight Eisenhower
Nisei
Operation Overlord*
D-Day
George Patton
kamikaze*
Harry Truman
Manhattan Project*
Robert Oppenheimer
Nuremberg Trials*
Emperor Hirohito

THE STAGE IS SET IN EUROPE

The Japanese invasions of Manchuria in 1931 and China in 1937 were the opening events in the Asian phase of World War II. While the initial battles of the second world conflict were being played out in East Asia, Hitler's **Third Reich** was seizing territory in Europe. The European nations consistently either ignored or appeased Hitler's aggressive advances. Now Hitler had added to his accomplishments the signing of a nonaggression pact with Stalin. In August, 1939, the world was unaware that beneath the surface of the pact was a secret agreement that both the Soviet Union and Germany would share in the division of Poland. Another hidden term was that the Soviet Union could annex Latvia, Lithuania, Estonia, and Finland. As Hitler plotted the seizure of still more territory, Poland would provide the stage for the opening battle of World War II in Europe.

Axis Conquests in Europe, 1942

THE WAR IN EUROPE BEGINS

Blitzkrieg

With the threat of Soviet attack removed by the signing of the nonaggression pact, Hitler made a surprise air attack against Poland on September 1, 1939. Hitler's attack was termed a ***blitzkrieg***, or "lightning war." At the same time, German armies and tanks crossed the Polish border. The bombing was particularly heavy over Warsaw, which fell quickly. France and Great Britain responded by declaring war on Germany on September 3. After devastating Poland, Hitler annexed the western portion of the country, which had a largely German population.

In mid-September, Stalin occupied the eastern half of Poland, then began seizing Latvia, Lithuania, and Estonia. The rigors of the Finnish winter took its toll upon the Soviet army, and the Finns put up a fierce struggle against the invaders. By March 1940, however, they had succumbed to the larger Soviet army.

By the early 1940s, two major alliances were once again facing each other. Japan, Germany, and Italy and their conquered territories constituted the **Axis Powers**. The **Allied Powers** included Great Britain and its empire as well as its Commonwealth allies (Canada, Australia, and New Zealand); France and its empire; China; the Soviet Union; and the United States and its Latin American allies.

Sitzkrieg

The next six months of the war involved such little combat activity that the Germans nicknamed it ***sitzkrieg***, while others called it "the phony war." French and British troops settled in along the **Maginot Line**, a fortified line along the French-German border. The Germans occupied a comparable line of fortifications called the **Siegfried Line**. The phony war ended on April 9, 1940, when Hitler invaded Norway and Denmark. Within hours, Denmark fell, and by June Norway was also overtaken by the Germans.

HITLER MOVES AGAINST FRANCE AND GREAT BRITAIN

Dunkirk

After his conquest of Denmark and Norway, Hitler invaded the Netherlands, Belgium, and Luxembourg. When the Germans reached the northern coast of France, Belgium surrendered. Outnumbered and under heavy fire from the air, the Allies escaped to **Dunkirk** on the English Channel. There, while trapped against the sea, one of the most heroic and miraculous rescues of the war occurred.

The Fall of France

On June 10, 1940, Mussolini declared war on France and Great Britain. He then joined forces with Hitler and attacked France from the south. On June 24, France fell. The Germans assumed control of northern France. In the south, a Nazi-controlled government, the **Vichy government**, was set up with French Prime Minister **Henri Pétain** as its puppet leader. A French general, **Charles de Gaulle**, set up a government-in-exile in London. Committed to reconquering France, De Gaulle's **Free French** armies would battle Germany until the liberation of France in 1944.

The Battle of Britain

Great Britain now stood against the Nazis without the aid of its ally, France. Britain, however, enjoyed the advantage of having as prime minister the tenacious **Winston Churchill**, who refused to surrender to the Germans. Hitler's plan against Great Britain, **Operation Sea Lion**, began with the bombing of Britain by the German air force, or **Luftwaffe**, between September 1940 and May 1941. The air war, called "The Blitz" by the British, showered bombs in major metropolitan areas, including London. Still the British continued fighting, in spite of more than 40,000 civilian casualties.

The British Royal Air Force (**RAF**), assisted by a new invention called radar, tracked incoming German aircraft and quickly reached them in the air. RAF resistance caused Hitler to suspend the bombing of Britain in May 1941. The Battle of Britain had proved to the Allies that Hitler's forces could be repelled.

WAR IN THE EAST AND IN AFRICA

While the attacks against Great Britain were in process, Mussolini turned his attentions to Africa. In September 1940, Mussolini commanded his North African army to move toward the Suez Canal, the path to the oil fields of Southwest Asia. The British retaliated, routing the Italians and taking more than 100,000 prisoners. To support the Italians, in February 1941, Hitler sent General **Erwin Rommel** ("The Desert Fox") to Libya to command a tank corps called the **Afrika Korps**. After Rommel defeated the British in Libya, they retreated to **Tobruk**. At first resisting the Germans, the British were eventually overpowered by Rommel's forces.

Hitler's Invasion of the Soviet Union

To prepare for the eventual invasion of the Soviet Union, in 1940 Hitler expanded into the Balkans. In 1941, Bulgaria, Romania, and Hungary joined the Axis Powers. When Greece and Yugoslavia resisted, Hitler successfully invaded both in 1941. He could now proceed with his plans against the Soviet Union.

On June 22, 1941, **Operation Barbarossa**, or Hitler's invasion of the USSR, began. The Soviet army, the largest in the world, was unprepared for the invasion. Using the **scorched-earth policy**, a tactic that the Russians had used against Napoleon, the Soviets burned everything in the path of the invading Germans. Stalin had already relocated centers of Soviet industry to areas away from the war front. By the time of the German invasion, the Soviet industrial strength was greater than that of Germany. It was this industrial capacity that was key to Allied victories in Europe and Asia. The Soviet people again showed their stamina and courage when, surrounded by Hitler's forces and starving, the people of Leningrad held out against the Germans, refusing to surrender their city. Proceeding to Moscow in December 1941, the Germans were turned back by Siberian troops under the command of Georgi Zhukov. The harshness of the Russian winter cost the lives of 500,000 Germans in their successful effort to hold Moscow.

The forced entry of the Soviet Union into World War II proved significant to the defeat of the Nazis. With both the United States and the Soviet Union involved, the war was fought in two theaters: one Asian-Pacific, and the other Eurasian.

THE HOLOCAUST

As part of his efforts to capture the allegiance of the German people, Hitler had alluded to the "traditions" of the German people. One of these traditions was distrust of and animosity toward the Jews. Hitler blamed the Jews for the defeat of Germany in World War I and Germany's economic problems after the war. In 1933, the Nazis passed laws prohibiting Jews from holding public office. The **Nuremberg Laws** in 1935 prohibited Jews from becoming German citizens and owning property. Jews were also forced to wear a bright yellow Star of David on their clothing for identification.

After the violence of Kristallnacht, some of the German Jews had emigrated to other countries. At first the Nazis allowed Jewish emigration; other European nations, Latin America, and the United States, however, were reluctant to receive them and placed limits on the number of Jewish immigrants entering their respective countries.

The Final Solution

By 1941, Hitler had decided on the **Final Solution**, or the elimination of the Jews. To protect the purity of the Aryan race, Hitler also targeted other groups he perceived inferior, such as Poles, Russians, homosexuals, gypsies, and the sick or disabled. Some of the Jews in Poland were gathered into segregated communities called **ghettos**. The Nazis closed off the ghettos with walls and barbed wire. Some Jews formed resistance organizations, such as the one in the Warsaw ghetto, while others coped by taking measures to preserve their traditions within the ghettos. Other Jews were rounded up and executed or sent to concentration camps located primarily in Germany and Poland.

In 1942, the Nazis built extermination camps equipped with gas chambers. The people who were killed in the gas chambers were then cremated in large ovens located in the camps. Of the ten million Jews who lived in Europe before World War II, six million died in the Holocaust.

U.S. RESPONSE TO THE WAR

As the war raged in Europe, the Americans attempted to maintain their isolation. Between 1935 and 1937, the U.S. Congress had passed a series of acts that made it illegal for Americans to sell weapons or lend money to warring nations. By 1941, however, President Roosevelt had convinced Congress to pass the **Lend-Lease Act**, which authorized the president to lend or lease arms and other supplies to any nation considered vital to the United States. When the United States Navy began escorting British ships carrying U.S. arms, Hitler ordered his **U-boats** to sink any cargo ships. In September 1941, a German submarine fired upon a U.S. destroyer in the Atlantic. When Roosevelt ordered U.S. ships to respond, he was, in effect, engaging the United States in an undeclared war on Germany.

On August 9, 1941, Franklin Roosevelt and Winston Churchill had met secretly on a battleship off the coast of Newfoundland. The product of the meeting was the **Atlantic Charter**, which advocated free trade among nations and the right of people to select their own government.

THE JAPANESE STRIKE AGAINST THE UNITED STATES

In the 1940s, the Japanese continued their quest for empire to provide land for their growing population and raw materials for their factories. They had already taken over Manchuria, establishing a puppet state called **Manchukuo**. By invading China after the Manchurian conquest, the Japanese continued their "Asia for Asians" policy. During the invasion of China, the Japanese used warfare methods that inflicted untold suffering and mass death. In an incident known as the **Rape of Nanjing**, the Japanese raped thousands of women and murdered hundreds of thousands of civilians and unarmed soldiers. They then turned their attention to Southeast Asia, seizing French Indochina in July 1941 in order to create a defense perimeter against possible future Allied assaults. Roosevelt, afraid that Japan's advances might endanger Guam and the Philippines, suspended oil shipments to Japan.

Pearl Harbor and Its Aftermath

On December 7, 1941, the strategy of Japan's Admiral **Isoroku Yamamoto** erupted in a Japanese attack on the U.S. Pacific fleet anchored at Pearl Harbor in Hawaii. In less than two hours, the Japanese sank or severely damaged most of the U.S. Pacific fleet and killed about 2,400 American sailors. On December 8, 1941, the United States declared war on Japan.

After the attack on Pearl Harbor, the Japanese seized Guam and Wake Island in the western Pacific before attacking the Philippines. They then defeated American and Filipino soldiers on the Bataan Peninsula and the island of Corregidor. Still the Japanese continued, taking Hong Kong, Malaya, Singapore, and the Dutch East Indies. Their conquest of Burma and the Burma Road closed off China's supply line.

ALLIED RETALIATION AGAINST THE JAPANESE

In 1942, the United States retaliated by sending Lieutenant Colonel **James Doolittle** to bomb Tokyo and other key Japanese cities. Although the Doolittle raid did little damage, it was important psychologically because it demonstrated that the Japanese could be attacked.

By May 1942, the Allies were beginning to reverse the advances of the Japanese empire. When a U.S. fleet supported by the Australians intercepted a Japanese strike force, the Battle of the Coral Sea ensued. This battle halted Japanese expansion and also had the distinction of being the first battle in which both sides fought from aircraft carriers.

The Battle of Midway

In June 1942, the Japanese assembled the world's largest naval force and approached Midway Island, a U.S. possession west of Hawaii. Admiral **Chester Nimitz**, commander of the U.S. Pacific Fleet, surprised the larger Japanese force by attacking with carrier-based planes. The Battle of Midway turned the tide in the Pacific in favor of the Allies.

General **Douglas MacArthur**, commander of the Allied land forces in the Pacific, proposed the strategy of **island-hopping**, or seizing key strategic islands around Japanese strongholds. In a six-month-long struggle known as the Battle of Guadalcanal, U.S. and Australian forces took the Japanese-held island of Guadalcanal in the Solomon Islands.

Victory for the Allies

In late 1942, the Allies began reversing the progress of the war by winning the Battle of El Alamein in Egypt. In May 1943, under General **Dwight Eisenhower**, the Allies defeated the Afrika Korps. At Stalingrad, the Russian winter took the lives of over 200,000 German soldiers.

In July 1943, the Allies captured Sicily. Mussolini temporarily fell from power, only to have his government restored by the Germans. The Allies entered Rome on June 4, 1944. In April, 1945, as the Germans were retreating from Italy, Mussolini was discovered hiding in a truck. On April 29, 1945, he was shot and his body hanged in the town square at Milan.

LIFE DURING THE WAR

The Japanese American Internment

Some Japanese Americans living in Hawaii and many along the West Coast of the United States became victims of prejudice after the Pearl Harbor bombing. In February 1942, President Roosevelt set up a policy that would round up Japanese Americans into internment camps and confiscate their property. Most of the interned were ***Nisei***, or Japanese Americans who had been born in the United States. The camps were located away from the coast, some within the boundaries of Native American reservations.

Women in the War

Hundreds of thousands of women in Great Britain and the United States worked in war industries or joined the military. After the war, however, they were expected to return to their traditional homemaking roles. Women in the United States and Great Britain were forbidden to take up arms, but Soviet and Chinese women participated in combat. Soviet women and girls also worked in industries and mines and on railroads. They dug ditches and served as air raid wardens. In Great Britain, women served as pilots in noncombatant roles, as workers in the fields, and as drivers of armed service transport vehicles and ambulances. Although German women were encouraged to take up wartime employment, the number of women taking jobs increased only slightly during the war. In Japan, the traditional government was somewhat reluctant to employ women except in areas such as farming and the textile industry. As an alternative, the Japanese brought in laborers from Korea and China to work in their wartime industries.

VICTORY IN EUROPE

One of the final Allied pushes toward victory was **Operation Overlord**, the invasion of Normandy in northwestern France. Under the command of General Dwight Eisenhower, the operation was launched on June 6, 1944—**D-Day**. Massive casualties did not prevent the Allies from holding the beachheads. By July 1944, the Allies had penetrated the German defenses, and General **George Patton**'s Third Army marched on to liberate France, Belgium, Luxembourg, and much of the Netherlands. The Germans made a last valiant attempt when they penetrated Allied lines at the Battle of the Bulge in December 1944. The Allies, however, rallied and pushed back the Germans.

After the siege of Stalingrad, Soviet armies began gradually moving westward, in the process pushing the Nazi armies back into Germany. Their offensive would take them through the countries of eastern Europe, and in 1945 into Germany. By late April 1945, Soviet and American troops met at the Elbe River in Germany.

Berlin fell to the Allied forces. Hitler and his wife, Eva Braun, committed suicide. On May 7, 1945, Germany surrendered; the signing of the surrender on May 8 would be celebrated as V-E (Victory in Europe) Day. War in the European theater had ended.

VICTORY IN THE PACIFIC

The war in the Pacific had yet to be won. In October 1944, the Allies under General MacArthur landed on the island of Leyte in the Philippines. At the Battle of Leyte Gulf, the Japanese navy was decisively defeated. In March, 1945, after suffering heavy losses, U.S. Marines took Iwo Jima. The bloodiest land battles of the war, the battles for Okinawa, ended in June, 1945, with an American victory. During this battle, Japanese ***kamikaze***, or suicide pilots, dove their planes into American ships.

Hiroshima and Nagasaki

In spite of the victory in Europe, the Japanese continued their effort to maintain the "**Greater East Asia Co-Prosperity Sphere**," or an Asia free from Western influence and dominated by Japan. After the battles for Okinawa, the next step in the war was to be the invasion of Japan, an undertaking that would cause heavy Allied loss of life. Another alternative that President **Truman**, the successor of Franklin Roosevelt, had to consider was to bring down the empire of Japan by using the atomic bomb. The A-bomb had been developed by the **Manhattan Project** under the direction of scientist **Robert Oppenheimer**. The first atomic bomb had been detonated at Los Alamos, New Mexico, in July 1945. President Truman warned the Japanese that refusal to surrender would bring dire consequences. When the Japanese did not respond, the United States dropped an atomic bomb on Hiroshima on August 6, 1945, and on Nagasaki on August 9. No atomic weapons have been deployed in battle against another country since that time. On September 2, 1945, the Japanese surrendered to General Douglas MacArthur. World War II had finally ended.

THE AFTERMATH OF WAR

World War II left 60 million dead. Europe was in ruins, with thousands of displaced people from several nations trying to reach their former homes. Many of the great European cities, including Berlin, Warsaw, and London, were in ruins. The war had disrupted agriculture. Thousands of civilians died as famine and disease spread through the devastated cities of Europe.

In response to the horrors of the Holocaust, the Allies put the Nazis on trial. At the **Nuremberg Trials** in Germany in 1946, 22 Nazi leaders were charged with war crimes; 12 were sentenced to death.

Postwar Japan

The war also left Japanese cities destroyed, and Nagasaki and Hiroshima were completely annihilated. Japan no longer possessed a colonial empire. After the signing of the surrender document, Japan was demilitarized, and its war criminals were put on trial. In 1946, under U.S. supervision, a new constitution transformed Japan into a government modeled on that of the United States. **Emperor Hirohito** was forced to declare that he was not divine and took on the role of a figurehead in the Japanese government. The new Japanese government granted men and women over the age of 20 the right to vote. A provision of the constitution insured that Japan could no longer make war, and would be able to fight in its own defense only if attacked.

During its occupation of Japan beginning in 1945, the United States initiated Japan's economic revival. Japan became dependent upon direct U.S. economic aid and investments. The abandonment of wartime reparations also boosted the Japanese economy. Japanese products entered the U.S. market.

In the spring of 1952, the American occupation of Japan ended, and the United States and Japan became allies. The two nations would sign a mutual defense treaty in 1952. Meantime, another wartime ally, the Soviet Union, would soon prove to have an agenda different from the Western democracies.

THINGS TO REMEMBER

- Causes of World War II
    - Germany resented the harsh conditions imposed on it by the Treaty of Versailles.
    - The global depression of the 1930s led to the rise of fascist governments in Germany and Italy.
- The war began when:
    - Japan invaded China in 1937.
    - Germany and the Soviet Union signed a nonaggression pact in August 1939, agreeing to divide Poland between them.
    - Germany invaded and took Poland in September 1939. France and Great Britain declared war.
- By 1942, the Axis Powers included Japan, Germany, Italy, and conquered territories.
- The Allied Powers were Great Britain and its Commonwealth, France, China, the Soviet Union (after Hitler's betrayal), and the United States.
- The colonial possessions of these countries also became involved in the war.
- The course of the war
    - France fell in 1940. Great Britain suffered heavy bombardment but did not surrender.
    - Two pivotal events occurred in 1941: Hitler turned against the Soviet Union, and Japan attacked the United States at Pearl Harbor.
    - After the invasion of Normandy (June 6, 1944), the Allies took back France and the rest of Europe.
    - Several naval battles, including the Battle of Midway, and long bloody campaigns to take Pacific islands led the United States to Japan's doorstep.
    - The United States dropped atomic bombs on the cities of Hiroshima and Nagasaki, leading Japan to surrender.
- Effects of the war
    - Women filled jobs vacated by men who were at war. After the war they returned to the home.
    - Japanese Americans were imprisoned in internment camps.
    - Six million Jews were exterminated in the Holocaust.
    - Japan lost its empire and became an ally of the West.
    - European global hegemony declined.
    - The Soviet Union acquired dominance in Eastern Europe.

REVIEW QUESTIONS

1. When the *London Times* wrote that the Germans were merely "going into their own back garden," it was advocating a policy of

   (A) détente.
   (B) nonaggression.
   (C) demilitarization.
   (D) appeasement.
   (E) brinkmanship.

2. The key to Allied victories in both Asia and Europe during World War II was

   (A) their superior navies.
   (B) their more capable leaders.
   (C) their industrial capacity.
   (D) their more advanced radar equipment.
   (E) their superior intelligence.

3. During World War II, the Japanese

   (A) gave favored treatment as part of their "Asia for Asians" policy.
   (B) seized French Indochina to exploit its raw materials.
   (C) closed off British supply lines at the Burma Road.
   (D) were subjected to an oil embargo.
   (E) successfully combated allied island-hopping strategies.

4. During World War II,

   (A) women served only as noncombatants.
   (B) women played an especially diverse role on the Japanese homefront.
   (C) women in the Soviet Union went into battle.
   (D) women in Europe tended to continue in their positions in industry after the war.
   (E) women in German war industries more than doubled.

5. All of the following were results of World War II EXCEPT

   (A) displaced persons.
   (B) famine and disease in European cities.
   (C) a constitutional monarchy for Japan.
   (D) the end of Japan's colonial empire.
   (E) the extension of Soviet hegemony.

ANSWERS AND EXPLANATIONS

1. (D)

The quote describes the Munich Conference, in which European leaders appeased, or gave in to, Hitler as he occupied more and more territory in an effort to unite all the German-occupied areas of Europe. Détente (A) was the relaxing of tensions between the superpowers during the Cold War. Nonaggression (B) is a policy of refraining from entering into a conflict. Demilitarization (C) is the reduction in the size or strength of a military force. Brinkmanship (E) was the state of constant readiness to go to war.

2. (C)

Allied factories were generally much more productive than those of the Axis powers. It was the capability of the Allies to replenish their supplies throughout the conflict that, more than any of the other answer choices given, won them the victory.

3. (D)

The United States placed an oil embargo on Japan, after Japan's seizure of French Indochina in July 1941. Japan's occupation of other Asian countries was brutal (A). Japan's main interest in taking Indochina was to form a defensive perimeter around the Japanese islands (B). Japan closed off Chinese supply lines at the Burma Road (C), and was unsuccessful at combatting the Allies' island-hopping strategy in the Pacific (E).

4. (C)

The Soviet Union and China were the only two countries that allowed women combatants during World War II (A). Japanese and German women maintained more traditional women's roles at home during the war (B, E), and most European women relinquished their wartime jobs after peace returned (D).

5. (C)

Japan adopted a representative government modeled on that of the United States. Thousands of displaced persons were found in Europe after the war (A), while famine and disease were commonplace in the ruins of European cities (B). Japan was forced to relinquish her colonial empire (D), and Soviet hegemony was extended to Eastern Europe (E).

CHAPTER 28

The Postwar World

TIMELINE

1941	Ho Chi Minh founds the Vietminh
1945	Yalta Conference United Nations founded Potsdam Conference
1946–1949	Chinese civil war
1948	Marshall Plan France, Britain, and the United States end occupation of West Germany Berlin Airlift
1949	NATO founded Warsaw Pact founded Nationalists flee to Taiwan People's Republic of China founded
1950	Sino-Soviet friendship pact Agrarian Land Reform Law in China
1950–1953	Korean Conflict
1952	United States ends occupation of Japan
1953	Mao's First Five-Year Plan
1954	Geneva Conference
1956	Hungarian revolution

1957	USSR launches Sputnik
1958–1961	Great Leap Forward (Mao's second Five-Year Plan)
1959	Cuban Revolution China occupies Tibet
1961	Construction of the Berlin Wall
1962	Cuban Missile Crisis
1966	Cultural Revolution in China
1968	Communist invasion of Czechoslovakia
1972	SALT I Treaty
1973	U.S. forces leave Vietnam
1975	North Vietnamese take South Vietnam
1975–1979	Khmer Rouge Killing Fields Helsinki Accords
1978–1989	Vietnamese occupation of Cambodia
1979	Sandinistas overthrow Somoza Ayatollah Khomeini assumes power in Iran Seizure of U.S. embassy and hostages in Iran SALT II Treaty Soviets invade Afghanistan
1980–1988	Iran-Iraq War
1983	Strategic Defense Initiative
1989	Tiananmen Square Incident

IMPORTANT PEOPLE, PLACES, EVENTS, AND CONCEPTS

Yalta Conference*
United Nations
General Assembly
Security Council
satellite nation*
Potsdam Conference*
iron curtain
containment*
Truman Doctrine*
Marshall Plan*
Great Leap Forward*
commune*
Red Guards
Cultural Revolution*
Zhou Enlai
Kim Il Sung
Kim Jong Il
domino theory*
French Indochina
Ho Chi Minh
Third World*
Fulgencio Batista
Bay of Pigs invasion
Sandinistas
Daniel Ortega
Contras
Violeta Chamorro
Mohammed Reza Pahlavi
ayatollah*
Ayatollah Ruholla Khomeini

Berlin Airlift
NATO (North Atlantic Treaty Organization)*
Warsaw Pact*
H-bomb
brinkmanship*
intercontinental ballistic missile*
Francis Gary Powers
Dwight D. Eisenhower
Nikita Khruschev
Dalai Lama

Vietminh
Dien Bien Phu
Geneva Conference*
Ngo Dinh Diem
Vietcong
Gulf of Tonkin Resolution*
Vietnamization*
Khmer Rouge
Pol Pot

Saddam Hussein
destalinization*
Imre Nagy
Leonid Brezhnev
Alexander Dubceck
détente*
Richard M. Nixon
Helsinki Accords*
Strategic Defense Initiative*

MANAGING THE PEACE

Even before the conclusion of World War II, plans for peace in the postwar world were underway. In February 1945, the leaders of the United States, Great Britain, and the Soviet Union met at **Yalta,** a resort city on the Black Sea. There they agreed to divide postwar Germany into zones of occupation controlled by the Allied military. Germany would be forced to make payments to the Soviet Union as compensation for the loss of life and property, and Stalin pledged to conduct free elections in East Europe. In return for these concessions, Stalin agreed to join in the war against Japan. As part of the Yalta agreement, the USSR also gained Sakhalin and the Kurile Islands, two warm-water ports, and railroad rights in the territory of Manchuria.

The United Nations

In April 1945, another peace initiative was undertaken when the United States, the Soviet Union, and 48 other countries drafted a charter for the **United Nations**. The United Nations, which would be headquartered in New York, was organized to protect its members against aggression and future wars.

The United Nations charter set up a large body called the **General Assembly**, in which each member could vote on a wide range of issues. An 11-member body called the UN **Security Council** possessed actual power to settle disputes; today the number of Security Council members has been expanded to 15. Five members of the Security Council were permanent: Great Britain, China, the United States, France, and the Soviet Union. Each nation could veto any decision of the Security Council, preventing any nations from voting as a bloc.

During the Cold War, when international conflicts became increasingly difficult to resolve or prevent, the United Nations redefined its role to one of peacekeeping. Peacekeeping involves the prevention of fighting and the maintenance of order. Creating buffer zones or overseeing a cease-fire are also among its objectives.

THE USSR ACQUIRES SATELLITE NATIONS

As World War II drew to a close, the Soviet Union occupied a belt of countries along its western border. Disregarding the agreement made at Yalta, Stalin helped to establish communist governments in Albania, Yugoslavia, Poland, Bulgaria, Hungary, Romania, and Czechoslovakia. At a conference in **Potsdam**, Germany, in July 1945, President Truman and Prime Minister Churchill met with Stalin in an attempt to persuade him to abandon his policy toward the Soviet **satellite countries**. Stalin refused to comply.

The Yalta Conference had also provided for the division of postwar Germany. The Soviet Union controlled the eastern part of Germany, while Great Britain, France, and the United States jointly occupied western Germany. The capital city of Berlin, which lay within the Soviet zone of occupation, was similarly divided, with the Soviets controlling the eastern portion. The Communist government of East Germany was named the German Democratic Republic, while in 1947, the western zones became the Federal Republic of Germany. In the words of Winston Churchill, an "**iron curtain**" had fallen across Europe.

The United States Reacts to Soviet Policies

The United States responded to the Soviets' desire to spread communism by adopting a policy of **containment**. Containment meant forging alliances to assist vulnerable countries in resisting the spread of communism. In 1947, as part of the containment policy, President Truman issued a statement requesting support for the struggles of Greece and Turkey against communist encroachment upon their territories. His position became known as the **Truman Doctrine**.

The United States Congress eventually authorized military and economic assistance for the beleaguered countries of Greece and Turkey. This was not the only incidence of postwar aid: The **Marshall Plan**, proposed by U.S. Secretary of State George Marshall and passed by Congress in 1948, provided the opportunity for European nations to apply for economic aid to rebuild after the war. The Marshall Plan was especially successful in Yugoslavia and Western Europe.

Showdown Over Berlin

In 1949, France, Great Britain, and the United States withdrew their occupation forces from West Germany, resulting in the formation of the Federal Republic of Germany in May 1949. In October 1949, the German Democratic Republic was formed from the Soviet zone of occupation. The Soviet Union responded to the rebuilding of West Germany by blockading all traffic into the western portion of Berlin. The Allies broke the blockade by airlifting food and supplies into West Berlin. The **Berlin Airlift** lasted almost 11 months until the Soviet Union, recognizing its defeat, lifted the blockade in May 1949.

In 1961, the Soviet Union faced a problem because of the large flow of refugees from East Germany through West Berlin. As a result, the government of East Germany began building a concrete and barbed wire wall to separate West Berlin from East Berlin. The Berlin Wall became the symbol of the ideological separation between the two superpowers.

THE COLD WAR

The relationship between the USSR and the United States had quickly developed into a Cold War—one fought with propaganda, diplomacy, and clandestine strategies. In 1949, after the threat posed by the Berlin blockade, the nations of Western Europe joined the United States and Canada to form a defensive military alliance called **NATO** (The North Atlantic Treaty Organization). The Soviets countered with their own alliance, the **Warsaw Pact** in 1955, which counted among its member nations the Soviet Union, East Germany, Poland, Czechoslovakia, Romania, Hungary, Bulgaria, and Albania.

Other alliances arose to stem the tide of Soviet aggression. The Central Treaty Organization (CENTO), joined by Turkey, Iran, Iraq, Pakistan, the United States, and Great Britain, was formed to prevent Soviet expansion into the territory of its neighbors in Southwest Asia. Prevention of Soviet intrusion into the Far East was the goal of the Southeast Asia Treaty Organization (SEATO). Members of SEATO included the United States, Great Britain, France, Thailand, the Philippines, Pakistan, New Zealand, and Australia.

Nuclear Power

In 1949, the Soviet Union developed its own atomic bomb. President Truman, determined to stay ahead of the USSR in the race for nuclear armaments, authorized work on the production of a hydrogen bomb. The **H-bomb**, a thermonuclear weapon produced by nuclear fusion, was first tested by the United States in November 1952. Within nine months, the Soviets also possessed thermonuclear power.

Since nuclear devastation was now within the capabilities of the two superpowers, the Cold War took on a new focus. The superpowers developed a policy of **brinkmanship**, or the willingness to defend their interests, even to the point of war. Both the United States and the Soviet Union began stockpiling huge collections of nuclear bombs.

Sputnik and the U-2 Incident

In 1957, the first unmanned satellite, called Sputnik I, was launched by the Soviet Union. The Soviets and the United States had already made technological history by developing an ICBM, or **intercontinental ballistic missile**, which was a rocket that would be used to launch Sputnik I. In January 1958, the United States would successfully launch its own satellite.

Tensions between the superpowers escalated in 1960, when an American U-2 spy plane piloted by **Francis Gary Powers** was shot down over the Soviet Union. The U-2 Incident heightened Cold War tensions, leading to the cancellation of a summit meeting between President **Eisenhower** and Soviet Premier **Nikita Khruschev** to discuss the arms buildup of both nations.

COMMUNISTS TAKE OVER CHINA

World War II had produced vast devastation in Chinese cities. During the war the Nationalists and Communists had temporarily put aside their differences in order to fight the Japanese. The United States had supported the Nationalist Chinese in an effort to have them form a coalition government with the Communists. Instead, Jiang Jieshi used U.S. aid to prepare for civil war.

After World War II, the Communists and Nationalists resumed their struggle for power in China. As the Chinese civil war continued, the Communists under Mao Zedong controlled northwestern China, while the Nationalists under Jiang Jieshi were headquartered in southwestern China. The United States continued to aid the Nationalists during the Chinese civil war, which lasted from 1946 to 1949. At first, the Nationalists outnumbered the Communist Chinese in troop strength. But then the Nationalists, who did little to pledge future support to Chinese peasants, began experiencing massive desertions of their soldiers to the ranks of Mao Zedong's army. By October 1949, Mao, who had promised land reform to the peasants, won control of China, renaming it the People's Republic of China. Jiang and his Nationalist followers fled to the island of Taiwan (named Formosa by Portuguese explorers). In February 1950, the Chinese and the Soviets signed a friendship pact, creating new fears of Communist expansion among the nations of the free world.

Two Chinas

Jiang's government on Taiwan, now named the Republic of China, continued to receive U.S. support. Meanwhile, the USSR lent military and financial assistance to the People's Republic of China. The two countries also formed a mutual defense pact. The United States responded to the existence of two Chinas by attempting to increase its influence in Asia. Continuing differences between the United States and the Communist world would result in the division of Korea into two countries. North Korea would receive support from the Soviet Union, and South Korea would receive support from the United States.

Chinese Communist Expansion

Shortly after solidifying its hold over China, Mao's government extended itself into Inner Mongolia and Tibet. In 1950 and 1951, after promising self-rule to the Tibetans, the Chinese strengthened their control over the area. The Tibetans were unified under the leadership of their religious leader, the **Dalai Lama**. Further Chinese control prompted the Dalai Lama to flee to India in 1959.

When the Tibetans' revolt against the Chinese failed in 1959, Tibet fell to Chinese control and Buddhism was repressed. India received not only the Dalai Lama but also other Tibetan refugees. Consequently, friction grew between China and India, particularly after a 1962 border dispute between the two nations.

The Government of Communist China

The Chinese Communists followed the example of the Soviet Union in setting up a Communist Party organization alongside the national government. Mao Zedong would rule as head of both until 1959. Shortly after assuming power, Mao initiated a policy of land reform. In the Agrarian Land Reform Law of 1950, Mao seized the property of the large landholders and distributed it among the peasants. Landlords who resisted the policy were executed. Between 1952 and 1957, Mao continued his policy by forcing the peasants to work on collective farms. Women were granted equality in the home and the workplace, and state-sponsored child care was provided.

Mao also brought all businesses and industry under government ownership and, in 1953, imposed a five-year plan modeled after the Soviet Union's. The plan produced immediate results in increasing industrial production.

The Great Leap Forward

In 1958, Mao, wanting to compete with the industrial production of developed nations, launched the **Great Leap Forward**. This program proposed the establishment of **communes**, or large collective farms. The communes were composed of several villages with up to 25,000 people working the thousands of acres of land assigned to each farm. Industries and businesses were managed collectively, and production quotas were established. Peasants lived in communal housing and had no private possessions. As a result of the Great Leap Forward, workers lost their initiative and produced low-quality products. A series of poor harvests produced a famine in which as many as 30 million Chinese died. Inefficient planning contributed to the disaster of the Great Leap Forward, and the program was discontinued in 1961.

Rift with the Soviet Union

In 1960, differences between China and the Soviet Union over leadership in the Communist world led to the Soviet removal of economic aid to China and to a split between the two Communist giants. After the failure of the Great Leap Forward and the Sino-Soviet rift, Mao somewhat reduced his role in the government. Other Chinese Communist leaders stepped in and allowed the Chinese to own their own houses and small parcels of land and to profit from the sale of their farm produce. Mao reacted to the capitalist principles of these leaders by creating the **Red Guards** in 1966. The Red Guards was an organization of high school and college students whose purpose was to continue the Communist revolution.

The Cultural Revolution

The Red Guards led a campaign called the **Cultural Revolution.** Its goal was to set up a society of equal workers. Because any intellectual or artistic pursuit was deemed a threat, the Red Guard closed schools and universities. People who resisted the Cultural Revolution were exiled to hard labor camps, jailed, or executed. Student brigades openly ridiculed Mao's political rivals; Deng Xiaoping was imprisoned, **Zhou Enlai** was forced to retreat into seclusion, and other political bureaucrats were driven from their positions.

The progress of the Cultural Revolution threatened to return China to a period of chaos. When its excesses interfered with industrial and agricultural production, the Chinese began to turn against the revolution. In 1976, Mao Zedong died. Deng Xiaoping gained control of the radicals and brought the Cultural Revolution to an end.

CONFLICT IN KOREA

The Korean conflict brought the Cold War to Asia. In 1949, most of the American and Soviet troops had been withdrawn from Korea. The Soviets, however, continued to supply money and military equipment to North Korea. On June 25, 1950, the North Koreans crossed the 38th parallel into South Korea. South Korea petitioned the United Nations for assistance. The Soviet Union was not present in the Security Council session that addressed the Korean situation, having walked out earlier to boycott the seating of the Republic of China rather than the People's Republic of China. The Security Council, therefore, was free of the threat of Soviet veto and voted to send an international force under General Dwight D. Eisenhower to Korea to stop the Communist invasion.

In October 1950, the Chinese entered the Korean conflict in an attempt to turn back U.S. troops approaching the Chinese–North Korean border. Hundreds of thousands of Chinese troops entered North Korea and pushed UN forces back beyond the 38th parallel. In July 1953, North Korea and the UN forces signed a ceasefire agreement that set the border between North and South Korea near the 38th parallel. A demilitarized zone was established on either side of the truce line.

The Koreas After the War

North Korea continued to evolve under communism. Its dictator, **Kim Il Sung**, encouraged heavy industry, set up collective farms, and strengthened the military. In 1994, his son **Kim Jong Il** came to power while the country was grappling with serious economic problems and energy and food shortages.

In contrast, South Korea, aided by the United States and other nations, has continued to prosper since the Korean conflict. Its success is largely owed to its emphasis on industry and global trade. At first ruled by dictators, South Korea established free elections in 1987.

Since the Korean Conflict, there have been efforts to reunite the two Koreas, particularly evident in the early twenty-first century. The government of North Korea, however, continues to show its power. In 1996, North Korea sent troops into the demilitarized zone (DMZ) between the two Koreas. North Korea has also developed its own nuclear weapons. The United States continues to maintain troops in South Korea. In 1999, North Korea agreed to allow U.S. inspection teams into a suspected nuclear development site, and in June 2000, the North Korean and South Korean heads of state met for peace and unification talks.

THE VIETNAM CONFLICT

A major fear of the United States after World War II was the spread of communism throughout Southeast Asia, particularly after the French lost control over Vietnam. President Eisenhower referred to this threat as the **domino theory**; the fall of one Southeast Asian nation would lead to the fall of neighboring countries. As a result, in 1955 the United States began providing financial aid and advisors to Vietnam, formerly part of the colony of French Indochina.

Communist influence over Vietnam went back to the period between the world wars. In the 1930s, independence movements began to stir in **French Indochina**. In Vietnam, a young nationalist named **Ho Chi Minh** sought aid from the Communists and led several revolts against the French. After the French imposed a death sentence upon him, he fled Vietnam. Returning in 1941, **Ho Chi Minh** became a founder of the **Vietminh**. During World War II, Vietnam came under the control of Japan. After the Vietminh defeated the Japanese in 1945, Ho Chi Minh proclaimed the independence of the Democratic Republic of Vietnam. In 1946, the French tried to regain their colony.

War with the French

The Communist Vietnamese Nationalists united against the French. In 1954, when the French were dealt a major defeat at **Dien Bien Phu**, they surrendered to Ho. At the **Geneva Conference** held in 1954, Vietnam was divided at the 17th parallel. Ho Chi Minh and the Communists would rule the north, while the United States and France would set up an anti-Communist government under **Ngo Dinh Diem**.

Ho Chi Minh's land redistribution program garnered popular support in the north, while Diem's dictatorial rule made him unpopular in the south. Realizing that an election would likely place Ho Chi Minh in power over the whole country, the South Vietnamese, with U.S. support, disregarded the Geneva Agreements and cancelled plans for an election.

The unpopularity of Diem's government led to the formation of the **Vietcong**, or Communist guerrillas, in South Vietnam. In 1963, a group of South Vietnamese generals backed by the United States staged a coup in which they assassinated Diem.

The United States Increases its Involvement

As a takeover of the Vietcong seemed increasingly possible, the United States began to escalate its involvement in Vietnam, sending not only more advisers, but also military equipment, planes, and tanks. In August 1964, after President Johnson claimed U.S. ships were under attack, the U.S. Congress passed the **Gulf of Tonkin Resolution**, which authorized the president to send troops into Vietnam. At the end of 1965, U.S. soldiers were fighting in Vietnam, and American planes had begun to bomb North Vietnam. In addition, North Vietnam, the Soviet Union, and China were sending troops and weapons to the Vietcong. When the Americans turned to air strikes to destroy enemy hiding places, peasants in South Vietnam became more opposed to their government.

U.S. Withdrawal from Vietnam

The unpopularity of the Vietnam conflict in the United States caused President Richard Nixon to begin a policy called **Vietnamization**. This plan called for the gradual withdrawal of U.S. troops from Vietnam while at the same time increasing the combat responsibilities of the South Vietnamese. Nixon also authorized massive bombings against North Vietnamese bases and supply lines and Vietcong hideouts in Laos and Cambodia. In 1973, the last U.S. forces left Vietnam. The North Vietnamese then capitalized on the weakness of the South Vietnamese and overran the country in 1975.

Southeast Asia After the Vietnam Conflict

After winning control of Vietnam, the North Vietnamese placed businesses and industries under government control. Over a million people fled Vietnam, many heading for the United States and Canada. In 1994, the United States lifted its trade embargo against Vietnam. Today the Communist government of Vietnam is seeking foreign investment and welcomes tourism.

Cambodia continued to suffer after the Vietnamese conflict. In 1975, Communists known as the **Khmer Rouge** set up a government in Cambodia under the leadership of **Pol Pot**. Pol Pot's effort to transform Cambodia into an agricultural society resulted in the killing of one to two million people. In 1978, the Vietnamese overthrew the Khmer Rouge and dominated Cambodia until 1989. Although Pol Pot died in 1998, the Khmer Rouge continues to participate in the coalition government of Cambodia. In 1993, UN representatives supervised Cambodia as it adopted a constitution and held its first election. UN peacekeeping troops remain in Cambodia.

RIVALRIES IN THE THIRD WORLD

Conflicts between Communist and free nations extended to the developing nations of the **Third World**. Once controlled by imperialist powers, the developing nations of Asia, Africa, and Latin America were characterized by unstable governments and extreme poverty among their citizens. Often boundaries of the developing nations had been drawn without regard for ethnic groupings, and native peoples had not been trained in the use of technology. Third World nations desperately needed a model for their government and economy. Both the United States and the USSR would vie for that role, sometimes instigating revolutionary wars. The United States also provided military aid and educational programs and sent volunteer workers such as the Peace Corps to developing nations. The USSR offered technical and military assistance. Some nations, such as India and Indonesia, remained nonaligned, independent of either the United States or the Soviet Union.

Cold War in Latin America

In Latin America, the ever-present gap between the wealthy and the poor, as well as government instability, led nations to seek assistance from the USSR or the United States. One of the hot spots of the postwar era was Cuba. After World War II, the United States supported the leadership of Cuban dictator **Fulgencio Batista**. In January 1959, Fidel Castro overthrew Batista. While at first he made improvements in the economy, healthcare, and conditions for women, Castro later showed himself a dictator who cancelled elections, imposed censorship, and imprisoned or executed his opponents. He then nationalized the economy and seized American-owned sugar refineries. When President Eisenhower imposed a trade embargo on Cuba, Castro turned to the USSR for aid. In April 1961, the United States backed an invasion by anti-Castro Cuban exiles in Florida. But when the United States failed to provide air support for the operation, the invaders were easily countered by Castro's forces. The **Bay of Pigs invasion** resulted in major embarrassment and loss of prestige for the United States under President John F. Kennedy.

The Cuban Missile Crisis

A missile crisis in Cuba provided a dramatic example of brinkmanship at work. In 1962, Soviet Premier Khruschev began to secretly construct missile sites in Cuba. When their presence was noted by American U-2 planes, Kennedy and Khruschev faced a showdown. After Kennedy imposed a blockade of Cuba to prevent the installation of more missiles, Khruschev eventually agreed to remove the missiles in return for a U.S. pledge not to invade Cuba.

After the missile crisis, Cuba depended upon Soviet support. Cuba showed its appreciation to the Soviets by sending 50,000 soldiers to fight against colonialism in Angola in the 1970s. Cuban troops were not evacuated from Angola until 1988. When the Soviet Union broke up in 1991, aid to Cuba ended, dealing a severe blow to the Cuban economy.

Unrest in Nicaragua

In 1933, the United States had begun supporting the dictatorship of Nicaraguan Anastasio Somoza and his son. In 1979, Communist rebels called **Sandinistas** overthrew the dictatorship of Somoza's son. At first, both the USSR and the United States gave assistance to the Sandinista leader, **Daniel Ortega**. When the United States discovered that the Sandinistas had assisted socialist rebels in El Salvador, the United States backed Nicaraguan anti-Communist rebels called **Contras**, supporting them with both legal and illegal funds supplied by the administration of President Ronald Reagan. In 1990, the Nicaraguan civil war ended when President Ortega agreed to hold free elections. He was defeated by **Violeta Chamorro**, who ruled until the 1997 election of José Lacayo.

Southwest Asia

In Southwest Asia, tensions arose between the forces of modernization and those of traditional Muslim values. The oil-rich countries of Southwest Asia captured the interest of both the United States and the Soviet Union. In Iran, Shah **Mohammed Reza Pahlavi** allied himself with Western governments and oil companies. In 1953, the United States supported the shah during a revolt in which he was nearly deposed. The shah westernized Iran, but at the same time maintained secret police and did little to alleviate the poverty of millions of his people. When the shah de-emphasized the role of Islam in political affairs, Iran's **ayatollahs**, or conservative Islamic leaders, opposed him. In 1978, riots erupted throughout Iran, causing the shah to flee the country in 1979. An exiled conservative leader, **Ayatollah Ruholla Khomeini**, returned to Iran. Banning Western influences, Khomeini restored traditional Islamic values and law.

When the United States allowed the deposed shah to enter its borders for medical treatment in 1979, Iranians retaliated by seizing the U.S. embassy in Tehran and taking 69 hostages. Fifty-five of the hostages would remain in captivity until their release in 1981.

In 1980, Khomeini, from the Shi'a sect of Islam, became embroiled in a war with Iraq's leader **Saddam Hussein**, of the Sunni sect. Hussein's military machine was taking advantage of the internal turmoil in Iran to expect a quick victory that might place Hussein in control of the Arab Islamic world. During the war, in an effort to gain release of its hostages, the United States secretly sold arms to Iran. By 1988 the Iran-Iraq war had wound down, with no real claim of victory on either side.

Soviet Invasion of Afghanistan

In 1979, when the Communist government of Afghanistan was on the verge of collapse from a Muslim revolt, the Soviets invaded Afghanistan. The United States responded by placing an embargo on grain shipments to the Soviet Union and by boycotting the 1980 summer Olympic games in Moscow. The United States, Pakistan, and Saudi Arabia also equipped and trained the Afghan rebels. After a ten-year occupation, the Soviet forces withdrew.

COLD WAR TENSIONS EASE

In the 1950s and 1960s, stirrings of independence arose in the satellite countries of the Soviet Union. When Stalin died in March 1953, Nikita Khruschev became the new leader of the Soviet Union. Khruschev denounced the brutal policies of Stalin, and adopted a policy of "**destalinization**," or ridding the country of the memory of Stalin's rule.

The Cold War in Eastern Europe

Destalinization did not alleviate the animosity in some of the satellite countries. In October 1956, Hungarians overthrew their Soviet-dominated government. A more liberal Hungarian Communist named **Imre Nagy** formed a new government that provided free elections. In response, in November 1956, Soviet tanks rolled into Hungary and overpowered the Hungarians. Pro-Soviet leaders were again installed in Hungary, and Nagy was executed.

Because of the outcome of the Cuban Missile Crisis, Khruschev lost favor with the Communist party leaders and, in 1964, was removed from power. His successor, **Leonid Brezhnev**, clamped down on basic human rights and upon those who opposed him. In 1968, when Czech leader **Alexander Dubcek** relaxed censorship laws, the Warsaw Pact nations invaded Czechoslovakia, demonstrating once again that the Soviet Union felt it had the right to intervene if its satellites failed to uphold communist principles.

Efforts Toward Détente

After the Soviet Union strengthened its hold on Eastern Europe, communism began to show areas of strain around the globe. As the Chinese carried their version of communism among Third World nations, Khruschev punished their self-reliance by not sharing secret information concerning nuclear weapons. In 1960, the USSR ended technological aid to China; later border skirmishes occurred along the Sino-Soviet border.

While tensions increased between the two major Communist powers, the United States and the Soviet Union attempted to coexist more peacefully in order to prevent the possibility of nuclear war. After the U.S. withdrawal from the Vietnam conflict, the two superpowers replaced the policy of brinkmanship with one of **détente**, or a cooling of Cold War tensions. The new spirit of détente, which began during the administration of President **Richard Nixon**, was manifested in his state visit to the People's Republic of China in 1972. Later that same year, Nixon paid a state visit to the Soviet Union, during which he and Brezhnev signed the SALT I (Strategic Arms Limitation Talks) Treaty. The five-year pact limited each country to its 1972 levels of intercontinental ballistic and submarine-launched missiles. In 1975, 35 nations, including the United States and the Soviet Union, signed the **Helsinki Accords**, a pledge to practice détente. The Helsinki Accords also dealt with the freedom of movement as well as the freedom to publish and share information, and called for cooperation in humanitarian endeavors.

The End of Détente

President Gerald Ford continued the policy of détente. In June 1979, in spite of President Jimmy Carter's protest against the Soviet Union's human rights policies, Carter and Brezhnev signed a SALT II agreement. The treaty was not ratified by the U.S. Congress, however, because of the Soviet invasion of Afghanistan in December 1979. Meanwhile, more countries in Europe and Asia (including India, Pakistan, and China) began stockpiling nuclear weapons.

The policy of détente eroded further when President Ronald Reagan took office in 1981. In 1983, Reagan initiated a program called the **Strategic Defense Initiative** (SDI) to protect the United States against incoming enemy missiles. The program, nicknamed "Star Wars," was never activated, but remained a threat to the Communist nations.

THINGS TO REMEMBER

- Shortly after World War II, the Soviet Union installed satellite communist governments in Albania, Yugoslavia, Poland, Bulgaria, Hungary, Romania, Czechoslovakia, and East Germany.
- The United States practiced the Truman Doctrine of "containment" of communism.
- China came under communist rule in 1949, when Mao Zedong's forces triumphed over the Nationalists.
- The Cold War between the U.S. and Soviet Union was fought in various Third World nations, via diplomacy, and via the stockpiling of nuclear weapons as a deterrent against actual war.
- Brinksmanship (constant preparation for war) gave way by the late 1960s to a warmer relationship between the superpowers. Part of this was due to the split between China and the Soviet Union in 1960.
- After the 1979 Soviet invasion of Afghanistan, and with nuclear technology spreading, the United States initiated the development of a defense system against nuclear attack (SDI or "Star Wars").

REVIEW QUESTIONS

1. All of the following are true of the conflict between the Chinese Communists and the Nationalists EXCEPT
   (A) it began after World War II.
   (B) it saw superpower intervention.
   (C) it had its roots in the period immediately following the fall of the Qing dynasty.
   (D) it came to a halt during World War II in favor of national interests.
   (E) it became a major concern to free nations after the signing of the 1950 Sino-Soviet friendship pact.

2. China under the rule of Mao Zedong
   (A) revitalized the Chinese economy by implementing collectivization.
   (B) denied women equality in either home or workplace.
   (C) allowed some elements of the market economy to boost the Chinese economy.
   (D) increased industrial production after bringing factories under government control.
   (E) split with the Soviet Union over Mao's policies during the Cultural Revolution.

3. Latin America during the Cold War era
   (A) was an example of the the superpowers' use of the Third World as an ideological battleground.
   (B) was noted for the political stability of its governments.
   (C) had narrowed the gap between wealthy and poor classes.
   (D) received humanitarian aid rather than military assistance from the superpowers.
   (E) saw the intervention of capitalist nations other than the United States.

4. During the Cold War period, Southwest Asia displayed all of the following conflicts EXCEPT
   (A) a conflict between traditional values and modernization.
   (B) a conflict between the Shia and Sunni sects of Islam.
   (C) a conflict between the superpowers.
   (D) a conflict between Communism and fascism.
   (E) a conflict between tolerance of the West and traditional Islamic values.

5. The period of détente
   (A) was caused in part by rivalries between China and the Soviet Union.
   (B) was confined to relations between the superpowers.
   (C) was hindered by the withdrawal of the United States from Vietnam.
   (D) restored the policy of brinkmanship.
   (E) was strengthened in the decade preceding the end of the Soviet Union.

ANSWERS AND EXPLANATIONS

1. (A)

The conflict between the Chinese Communists and Nationalists halted during World War II in order to allow both to struggle against their common enemy, the Japanese (D). It had begun, however, not after World War II, but after the fall of the Qing dynasty in 1911–1912 (C). The Nationalists received support from the United States (B). The Sino-Soviet pact of 1950 further illustrated the crucial role of the Chinese struggle in the Cold War (E).

2. (D)

Mao's First Five-Year Plan, launched in 1953, brought industry under government control and increased production. Collectivization curbed initiative and brought disappointing results in agricultural productivity (A). Women in the People's Republic were deemed as important as men to the welfare of China (B). Mao reacted to the implementation of capitalist principles in China by creating the Red Guard (C). The Sino-Soviet split, which occurred prior to the Cultural Revolution, was caused by differences over leadership in the Communist world.

3. (A)

Latin American nations sought assistance from either superpower in order to alleviate the huge gap between poor and wealthy (C) and to assist their unstable government (B). Although other capitalist nations did not step in to assist the Latin Americans (E), the United States gave both military and humanitarian aid. The Soviet Union offered technical and military assistance (D).

4. (D)

Fascism was not part of the politics of Southwest Asia. The struggles between modernization and traditional values (A) and between Western and non-Western cultures (E) were illustrated in the Iranian revolution. Differences between the Shia and Sunni sects of Islam were apparent in the Iran-Iraq War (B). Both superpowers had an interest in this oil-rich area (C).

5. (A)

The rift in 1960 between the Soviets and the Chinese somewhat eased tensions between the Soviet Union and the United States. Détente also carried over into U.S.-China relations after U.S. President Nixon's visit to China in 1972 (B). The U.S. withdrawal from Vietnam eased the way toward détente (C). The easing of tensions brought the end of brinkmanship, or the state of always being on the brink of war (D). In the 1980s, détente was eroded after the Soviet invasion of Afghanistan and the initiation of Star Wars (E).

CHAPTER 29

Global Independence Movements

TIMELINE

1910	Independence of South Africa
1912	Formation of the African National Congress
1917	Balfour Declaration
1919	Amritsar Massacre
1940	Lahore Conference
1945	Founding of the Pan-African Congress
1946	Great Calcutta Killing The Philippine Islands are granted independence Juan Perón elected president of Argentina
1947	British House of Commons partitions Indian subcontinent India is granted independence
1948	Assassination of Gandhi Burma gains its independence Beginnings of apartheid in South Africa Creation of the state of Israel First Arab-Israeli war Marshall Tito expelled from Soviet bloc
1949	War begins between India and Pakistan Indonesia is granted independence

1952	Nasser overthrows King Farouk of Egypt
1956	Independence of Morocco and Tunisia Nasser nationalizes the Suez Canal
1957	Creation of the Federation of Malaya Ghana becomes independent
1960	Nigeria wins independence Belgian Congo gains its independence Independence of French colonies in west and equatorial Africa Sharpeville Massacre
1960s	Rebellion in Angola
1962	Independence of Algeria
1963	Creation of the Organization of African Unity Kenya gains its independence
1964	Creation of the Palestine Liberation Organization
1965	Singapore becomes a separate city-state Formation of the Federation of Malaysia Suharto seizes power in Indonesia Mobutu takes power in the Congo
1966	Marcos becomes president of the Philippines
1967	Biafra secedes from Nigeria Six-Day War
1970	Nigeria is reunited
1971	The United States table tennis team tours China America promotes UN membership for the People's Republic of China
1972	President Nixon visits China
1973	The October (Yom Kippur) War
1975	Portugal withdraws its troops from Angola
1976	Suharto annexes East Timor Riots in Soweto, South Africa
1977	Murder of Steve Biko in South Africa
1978	Selection of Pope John Paul II
1979	Jerry Rawlings takes power in Ghana Signing of the Camp David Accords The United States and China establish diplomatic relations

1980	Solidarity strike in Gdansk, Poland
1981	Assassination of Benigno Aquino Assassination of Anwar Sadat
1982	Gorbachev comes to power in the USSR
1983	Hausa-Fulani coup in Nigeria
1984	Assassination of Indira Gandhi
1985	Revival of Islamic-based government in Algeria *Glasnost* and *perestroika*
1986	Corazón Aquino is elected president of the Philippines
1987	INF Treaty
1988	Cuban troops leave Angola
1989	de Klerk becomes president of South Africa Walesa elected president in Poland's first free election Communist Party dissolved in Hungary Fall of the Berlin Wall End of Communism in Czechoslovakia and Romania Protests in Tiananmen Square
1990	de Klerk releases Nelson Mandela from prison Beginning of repeal of apartheid laws in South Africa Reunification of Germany Lithuania declares its independence
1990s	Rebellions in the Chiapas district of Mexico
1991	Assassination of Rajiv Gandhi The United States gives up its military bases in the Philippines Yeltsin elected president of the Russian Republic Remaining Soviet republics declare their independence Formation of the Commonwealth of Independent States Yugoslavia invades Croatia and Slovenia
1992	Bosnia-Herzegovina declares its independence
1992–1995	Bosnian War
1993	Declaration of Principles Creation of Slovakia and the Czech Republic
1994	Nelson Mandela elected president of South Africa
1995	Assassination of Yitzhak Rabin

1997	Mobutu is overthrown by Kabila Partial Israeli withdrawal from Hebron Jiang Zemin assumes power in China Hong Kong is transferred to China
1998	Rebellion in the Democratic Republic of Congo
2000	UN peace-keeping troops enter the Congo Vicente Fox elected president of Mexico

IMPORTANT PEOPLE, PLACES, EVENTS, AND CONCEPTS

Congress Party
Muslim League
Muhammad Ali Jinnah
Clement Atlee
Jawaharlal Nehru
British Commonwealth*
Indira Gandhi
green revolution*
Rajiv Gandhi
Benazir Bhutto
Nawaz Sharif
Tamils*
Sukarno
Suharto
Bell Act*
Ferdinand Marcos
Benigno Aquino
Corazón Aquino
Fidel Ramos
Négritude
Kwame Nkrumah
Marcus Garvey
Jerry Rawlings
Jomo Kenyatta
Mau Mau*
Daniel arap Moi
Patrice Lumumba
Moise Tshombe
apartheid*
homeland*
African National Congress*
Sharpeville Massacre
Nelson Mandela
Desmond Tutu
F.W. de Klerk
Zionism*
Theodor Herzl
Alfred Dreyfus
pogrom*
Balfour Declaration*
kibbutzim*
David Ben Gurion
West Bank
Gaza Strip
Gamal Abdel Nasser
Suez Canal
Aswan Dam
Gulf of Aqaba
Six-Day War
Sinai Peninsula
Golan Heights
Anwar Sadat
Yom Kippur*
Golda Meir
Jimmy Carter
Menachem Begin
Yitzhak Rabin
Benjamin Netanyahu
Leonid Brezhnev
Politburo*
Mikhail Gorbachev
glasnost*
perestroika*
democratization*
INF Treaty
Pope John Paul II
Lech Walesa
Solidarity
Aleksandr Kwasniewski
Erich Honecker
Egon Krenz
Helmut Kohl
Milos Jakes
Vaclav Havel
Nicolae Ceausescu
Boris Yeltsin
CIS
Josip Broz (Marshall Tito)
Slobodan Milosevic
ethnic cleansing*
genocide*
Zhou Enlai
Deng Xiaoping
Four Modernizations*

Joseph Mobutu	Camp David Accords	Jiang Zemin
Laurent Kabila	Hosni Mubarak	Lázaro Cárdenas
Hutu tribe	Palestine Liberation Organization*	PRI
Tutsi tribe	Yasir Arafat	Vicente Fox
Ahmed Ben Bella	intifada*	Juan Perón
Afrikaner*	Declaration of Principles	Eva Perón
nonalignment*		

INDEPENDENCE FOR SOUTH ASIA

More than any other event, the Amritsar Massacre in 1919 had caused the Indians to initiate an independence movement. Each of the two leading organizations promoting Indian independence had its own aim: While the Hindu-dominated **Congress Party** (the Indian National Congress) claimed to represent all the people of India, the purpose of the **Muslim League** was to protect Muslim interests. The leader of the Muslim League, **Muhammad Ali Jinnah**, had once been a member of the Congress Party. When he became leader of the Muslim League, he proclaimed that India would not become independent if independence meant rule by the Congress Party.

At the Lahore Conference in 1940, the Muslim League proposed that a separate nation be provided for the Muslims, who lived in the northeastern and northwestern areas of South Asia. The British encouraged the rift between Muslims and Hindus in the hope that it would prevent a strong independence movement. In 1946, a riot between Muslims and Hindus known as the Great Calcutta Killing resulted in the deaths of about six thousand people.

On July 16, 1947, the British House of Commons partitioned the Indian subcontinent into two nations: India, primarily Hindu, and Pakistan, primarily Muslim. Massacres continued as Muslims, Hindus, and Sikhs now found themselves located in areas where they were minorities. Gandhi undertook a number of hunger strikes in an attempt to halt the violence between Hindus and Muslims. When Gandhi traveled to Delhi in January 1948 to campaign for fair treatment for Muslims, he was assassinated by a Hindu extremist.

Indian Independence

When India was granted its independence on August 15, 1947, it became the largest democracy in the world. Its first prime minister, **Jawaharlal Nehru**, was devoted to the modernization of his country. In 1949, war broke out between India and Pakistan over control of Kashmir. China then seized a portion of Kashmir in 1962. Conflict between India and Pakistan over the control of Kashmir continues today.

When they became independent, India and Pakistan became Dominion members in the **British Commonwealth** and adopted English as their official language. Nehru led India to enlist the support of other newly independent nations in an alliance independent of the United States or the Soviet Union. Hostilities between India and Pakistan, however, made both susceptible to influence by the superpowers. India accepted military assistance from the Soviet Union, while Pakistan sought alliance with the United States. Nehru also encouraged industrialization and promoted social reforms such as women's rights and an elevation in status for members of the lower castes.

The Rule of Indira Gandhi and Rajiv Gandhi

Upon Nehru's death in 1964, his daughter, **Indira Gandhi**, became prime minister. Under her rule, agricultural production increased after the implementation of the "**green revolution**." However, wealthier farmers tended to reap the benefits while peasant farmers continued to sink deeper in poverty. India also faced the problems of overpopulation in addition to conflicts between religious groups. When Indira Gandhi suspended the democratic process and imposed strict national birth control policies, she was voted out of office in 1977. After she returned to power in 1980, violence between the Indian army and Sikh extremists marred her administration. The Sikhs were involved in acts of violence in their efforts to become an independent state. In June 1984, two of Indira Gandhi's Sikh bodyguards assassinated her in retaliation for her ordering an attack against a Sikh temple.

Indira Gandhi was succeeded by her son, **Rajiv Gandhi**, in 1984. After his party was accused of corruption, however, he lost leadership of the Indian government in 1989. In 1991, Rajiv was killed by a bomb supplied by a female terrorist who belonged to a group of Tamil terrorists from Sri Lanka.

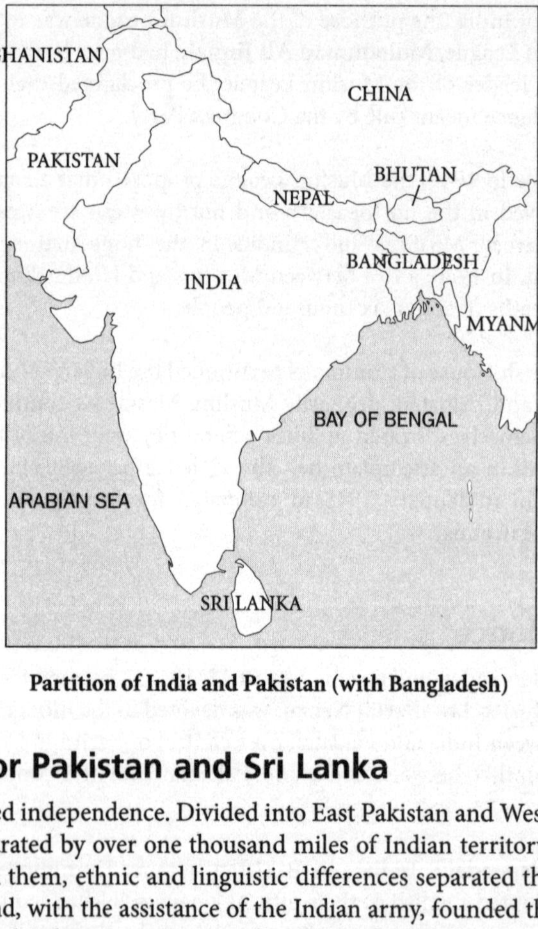

Partition of India and Pakistan (with Bangladesh)

Independence for Pakistan and Sri Lanka

In 1947, Pakistan achieved independence. Divided into East Pakistan and West Pakistan, the two parts of the country were separated by over one thousand miles of Indian territory. While Islam served as a unifying force between them, ethnic and linguistic differences separated them. In December 1971, East Pakistan revolted and, with the assistance of the Indian army, founded the nation of Bangladesh. West Pakistan, now called Pakistan, saw wave after wave of military coups. Among the numerous Pakistani leaders was a woman prime minister, **Benazir Bhutto**. Removed from office in 1996, she was eventually succeeded by **Nawaz Sharif** in 1997.

Sri Lanka's modern history has also proven tumultuous. While the majority of the people of Sri Lanka are Buddhists, its population also includes a group of Hindus known as **Tamils**, some of whom desire an independent nation. Throughout the 1980s and 1990s, the two religious groups were engaged in guerrilla warfare. As a result, a 1983 agreement allowed Indian troops to enter Sri Lanka to disarm the rebels. This proved unsuccessful, and the Indian troops withdrew in 1990.

INDEPENDENCE MOVEMENTS IN SOUTHEAST ASIA

Independence for South Asia inspired similar movements throughout Asia and Africa. India's independence was a turning point, after which the British proceeded to relinquish their colonies in Southeast Asia. Other countries eventually followed Great Britain's example.

Independence Among the British Colonies

Burma (which changed its name to Myanmar in 1989) had long petitioned Great Britain for independence. Becoming a self-governing republic in 1948, it chose not to seek membership in the British Commonwealth. The postwar years witnessed a continuous struggle between military dictatorship and pro-democratic forces. Ethnic animosities and conflicts among Communists hurt the nation throughout the twentieth century.

After World War II, the British attempted to organize Malaysia into a single nation. A Communist uprising and ethnic resistance hampered their efforts. While Malays constituted the majority on the peninsula, the Chinese were the dominant ethnic group in Singapore. The creation of the Federation of Malaya in 1957 united Malaya, Sarawak, Sabah, and Singapore. In 1965, when Singapore separated from the federation to become a separate city-state, the other three territories formed the Federation of Malaysia. Singapore, an extremely wealthy banking and trade center, became one of the busiest seaports in the world, enjoying a standard of living well above that of the other countries of southeast Asia.

Indonesian Independence

Throughout their colonial rule of Indonesia, Dutch officials had settled permanently in the East Indies and had prevented Indonesians from participating in higher education or entering government service. During World War II, Indonesia had been occupied by the Japanese. After the war, an Indonesian named **Sukarno** rose to lead the Indonesian independence movement and assembled a guerrilla army. In 1949, the Dutch agreed to grant Indonesia its independence.

Ethnically diverse, Indonesia became one of the world's most populous nations and the nation with the world's largest Islamic population. Sukarno failed in his attempt to create a parliamentary democracy. In 1965, a general named **Suharto** put down a coup, only to subsequently seize power for himself. With Suharto blaming the coup on Indonesian Communists, the violence that followed resulted in the deaths of perhaps a million Indonesians, many of them Communists.

Suharto, appointed president in 1967, converted Indonesia to a police state characterized by bribery and corruption, discrimination against Chinese inhabitants, and the persecution of Christians. In 1976, Suharto annexed East Timor, and later was criticized for human rights violations. Social stratification led to unequal distribution of the wealth that had resulted from an improved economy.

The United States Grants Philippine Independence

On July 4, 1946, the United States granted independence to the Philippines—giving the Philippines the distinction of being the first of the world's colonies to achieve independence after World War II. However, the United States continued to display some control over its former colony. The **Bell Act**, reluctantly approved by the Filipinos, granted them war damages in exchange for the establishment of free trade between the Philippines and the United States for eight years. After that period, tariffs would gradually increase.

To protect its Asian interests from both the Soviet Union and China, the United States insisted on a 99-year lease on its military bases in the Philippines. Since the Filipinos perceived the existence of these bases as a sign of American imperialism, they eventually negotiated other agreements with the United States to shorten the term of the leases. In 1991, the United States gave up both of its Philippine bases.

From 1966 to 1986, **Ferdinand Marcos** was president of the Philippines. His administration imposed authoritarian rule and stole millions of dollars from the nation's treasury. From 1972 to 1981, he imposed marital law upon the Philippines. In 1981, with the promise of future elections, the opponent of Marcos, **Benigno Aquino**, was assassinated as he returned to the Philippines from the United States.

In the 1986 elections, the widow of Benigno Aquino, **Corazón Aquino**, ran against Marcos and won. Marcos was exiled to Hawaii, where he later died. When Corazón Aquino was succeeded by **Fidel Ramos** in 1992, his presidency was restricted to a single six-year term so that the abuses of the twenty-year Marcos regime would never be repeated.

THE DECOLONIZATION OF AFRICA

The countries of Africa were also caught up in the postwar surge for independence. The Africans faced additional obstacles, however, because the imperialist nations had carved up Africa without regard for ethnic groups, failed to prepare the Africans for political or economic independence, and interrupted self-sufficient village agricultural systems in favor of large cash-crop plantations. The boundaries of the newly independent nations remained the same as those of the colonial period, giving rise to ethnic tensions.

While European imperialist countries began to question the economic feasibility of maintaining their African possessions, there arose in Africa a middle class that had been educated in the Western world and was now intent upon creating a new era for the African continent. Following the example of pan-African movements that had emerged in the Caribbean and the United States, these African intellectuals, especially active in the French colonies of western Africa, promoted a movement called ***Négritude***, or the celebration of the black race and its accomplishments.

Independence for the British Colonies

Ghana

The people of the British colony of the Gold Coast were led in their efforts toward independence by **Kwame Nkrumah**, who had studied in the United States. A leftist who had won the support of the Soviet Union, his organization of boycotts and strikes was successful in winning self-rule for his country. In

1957 the Gold Coast, taking the name Ghana, became the first African colony in sub-Saharan Africa to gain independence. As its president, Nkrumah instituted healthcare policies, educational improvements, and improved roads that, although needed, also crippled the economy of the new nation.

Nkrumah also became involved in a pan-African movement influenced by the Jamaican-born **Marcus Garvey**. The movement, whose goal was the creation of an Africa ruled by Africans, resulted in the founding of the Pan-African Congress in 1945. The efforts of Nkrumah also led to the creation of the Organization of African Unity (OAU) in 1963. In 1966, while Nkrumah was in China, the military and police force of Ghana revolted against Nkrumah's dictatorial rule and seized power. Since that time, Ghana has changed several times between civilian and military rule and has suffered significant economic problems. In 1979 and 1981, **Jerry Rawlings**, an Air Force pilot, took over power in Ghana.

Nigeria

Nigeria gained its independence from Great Britain in 1960. The most populous and prosperous country in Africa, Nigeria was also ethnically diverse, a situation that led to war. After independence, Nigeria adopted a federal system and set up a state for each of its ethnic groups—the Muslim Hausa-Fulani, and the Christian and animist Yoruba and Igbo. To complicate matters even further, the Yoruba were accustomed to rule by a monarch, while the Igbo preferred democratic elements.

In 1963, non-Yoruba minorities in the Yoruba homeland tried to break away. In 1966, fighting erupted, which led the Eastern Region to secede from Nigeria in 1967 and to rename itself Biafra. A subsequent civil war lasted for three years and ended with Biafra's surrender in 1970 and the ultimate reunification of Nigeria. Throughout the civil war, several million Igbo died from warfare and starvation.

After the end of the civil war, Nigerians attempted to rebuild and modernize their country, becoming one of the world's largest oil producers and a member of OPEC. In 1983, however, the Hausa-Fulani staged a coup and formed a government that discriminated against other ethnic groups. For the next 16 years, Nigeria would be ruled by the military. In 1999, however, a new constitution was adopted, and civilian government was restored.

Kenya

In Kenya, independence from British rule was realized through the efforts of the Kenyan nationalist **Jomo Kenyatta**, educated in Great Britain, as well as the efforts of the **Mau Mau**, a secret organization composed primarily of Kikuyu farmers who had been driven out of the rich farmland of the northern highlands by the British. The British were able to get the United States on their side by classifying the Mau Mau as communist-inspired. When the British granted Kenya its independence in 1963, Kenyatta became its president. Under his rule, the capital city of Nairobi became a modern, major business center in East Africa, and efforts were made to unite the various ethnic groups of Kenya.

Kenyatta's death in 1978 was followed by the administration of **Daniel arap Moi**, who faced demonstrations in favor of a more democratic government. At the close of the twentieth century, economic reversals and ethnic strife plagued the country of Kenya.

Independence for the Congo

The Belgian Congo had suffered greatly under imperialist rule. Rubber and copper resources had been drained from the country, and no programs had been set up to either assist the Congolese during colonization or prepare them for eventual independence. When the Belgian Congo received its independence in 1960, **Patrice Lumumba** became its first prime minister. The new country, however, was not united: In the southeastern province of Katanga, which was rich in copper mines, a local leader named **Moise Tshombe** declared the region's independence.

Tshombe was backed by Belgians who were interested in the mineral wealth of the Congo, while Lumumba had communist leanings. When Lumumba's appeal to the United Nations did not bring him the desired assistance, he appealed to the Soviet Union. A coup, led by an army officer named **Joseph Mobutu**, overthrew Lumumba and turned him over to Tshombe. Since Lumumba had Marxist leanings, the U.S. Central Intelligence Agency was sympathetic to Mobutu's coup. European democracies joined the United States in supporting Mobutu in the hopes of averting a communist takeover in the Congo. Shortly after the coup, Lumumba was murdered. Tshombe ruled the Congo briefly before his overthrow by Mobutu in 1965.

Upon coming to power, Mobutu renamed his country Zaire. For the next 32 years, Mobutu would subject his country to authoritarian one-party rule, amassing huge sums of money for himself and his family in the process. In 1997, Mobutu was overthrown by **Laurent Kabila**, who initially ruled as an autocrat, but who promised free elections by 1999. Kabila changed the country's name from Zaire to the Democratic Republic of Congo. In 1998, his government was attacked by Congolese rebels who were supported by the governments of Rwanda and Uganda. Drawn into the Congolese civil war were the ethnic conflicts between the **Hutu tribe** (pro-Kabila) and the **Tutsi tribe** (anti-Kabila). Some consider this conflict, which eventually involved most of Central Africa, to be Africa's first world war. In February 2000, the United Nations sent peacekeeping troops into the Congo, and in August a cease-fire was arranged.

Algerian Independence

France's main colony was Algeria, situated in North Africa. Since thousands of French colonists had lived in Algeria for decades, France attempted to mollify the Algerian desire for independence by claiming to offer full citizenship to its subject peoples. In actuality, the colonial powers remained in control over the Algerians. Conflicts between French and Algerian peoples erupted in a violent demonstration in 1945. In 1954, the Algerian National Liberation Front (FLN) declared its goal of achieving independence for Algeria; the French responded by sending troops into Algeria.

When Charles de Gaulle returned to power in France in 1958, he freed most French possessions in Africa out of fear that the Algerian rebellion would spread. France had already granted independence to Morocco and Tunisia in 1956, and the year 1960 saw the independence of French colonies in west and equatorial Africa. In July 1962, France granted Algeria its independence, with **Ahmed Ben Bella** as its first prime minister (and later its first president). Although Ben Bella improved education and initiated land redistribution, he was overthrown in 1965. When the price of oil fell in 1985, economic and political problems led to rioting and a revival of Islamic-based government.

Independence for Angola

Like other imperialist powers, Portugal had not prepared the people in its colony of Angola for independence. After World War II, Angola offered its people inferior education and health care, and trade was almost nonexistent. By the 1960s, three Angolan revolutionary groups had emerged. When the Portuguese sent in large numbers of troops to squelch the rebellions, discontent over the resulting expenses to Portugal caused the overthrow of the government in Lisbon.

When the Portuguese withdrew their troops from Angola in 1975, the Communist-controlled Popular Movement for the Liberation of Angola (MPLA) seized the capital at Luanda. The takeover resulted in a civil war, with each side backed by foreign powers. Cuba and the Soviet Union came to the aid of the MPLA, while the National Front for the Liberation of Angola (FNLA) was supported by Zaire and the United States. Another organization involved in the conflict was the National Union for the Total Independence of Angola (UNITA), aided by the United States and South Africa. In 1988, under the leadership of the United States, the various organizations reached a settlement, and Cuban troops left Angola. As the twentieth century closed, all three groups were planning to achieve mutual representation in the Angolan government.

SOUTH AFRICA

The story of South Africa unfolded differently from that of the remainder of sub-Saharan Africa. From colonial times, South Africa had consisted of a small white minority who governed a substantial black majority. The seventeenth-century Dutch way station of Cape Town at the tip of Africa had been captured by the British during the Napoleonic Wars and was annexed to the British empire in 1815. The resulting conflict between the British and the Dutch, or Boers, was especially heated over the subject of slavery, which was abolished in the British empire in 1833.

As a result of their conflicts with the British, the Boers began fleeing the Cape Colony for the flat grasslands, or *veld*, of the South African interior. Throughout the course of their Great Trek, the Boers frequently clashed with Bantu tribes such as the Zulus. In the 1850s, the Boers founded two republics in the interior of South Africa: the Orange Free State and the Transvaal. After diamonds and gold were discovered in South Africa in the late nineteenth century, more and more Europeans arrived, among them Cecil Rhodes of Great Britain. By 1889, Rhodes had created a monopoly over global diamond production. The following year he became prime minister of the British Cape Colony and served in that capacity until 1896.

The arrival of more and more British migrants and entrepreneurs into South Africa further strained relationships between the Boers and the British. Mounting tensions between the two groups resulted in the Boer War (1899–1902). During the war, European settlers began to leave South Africa. The Boers who remained began to exert a dominance over the Africans that would lead to the development of apartheid.

In 1910, South Africa gained its independence as a dominion of the British Empire, and in 1931, it became an independent member of the British Commonwealth. Its constitution gave the white minority power over the black majority. At the same time, industrialization offered new employment opportunities to blacks, creating the possibility of a change in their economic and social status.

Apartheid

In 1948, the National Party came to power in South Africa and immediately promoted Dutch South African, or **Afrikaner**, prominence. It also initiated a policy of separation of the races called **apartheid**. Non-whites were classified by a variety of ethnic designations, including colored or biracial peoples, Indians, and Bantu, a category further defined by division into various tribal groups. By 1959, the white minority had established **homelands**, or segregated areas, for black South Africans, keeping the largest and best land areas for the whites.

In 1912, black South Africans had formed the **African National Congress** (ANC) to try to win their rights. Because the goals of the ANC were in conflict with white rule, the South African government dubbed it a communist-controlled organization and increased its overt opposition to black activism. Demonstrations such as the 1960 **Sharpeville Massacre** took the lives of protestors. The incident led to the arrest and imprisonment of the ANC leader, **Nelson Mandela**, and to increased radical activism. In 1976, riots over school policies erupted in the black township of Soweto. In 1977, Steve Biko, a prominent protest leader, was beaten to death while he was in custody, prompting a global outcry against the policy of apartheid.

Pressure for Change

By the 1980s, pressure for South Africa to initiate change was mounting from other world nations. Many imposed trade restrictions against South Africa in response to a call from a South African bishop, **Desmond Tutu**. South Africa had also been barred from participation in the Olympic Games since the 1960s.

In 1989, white South Africans elected a new president, **F.W. de Klerk**. In February 1990, de Klerk legalized the African National Congress and released Nelson Mandela from prison. The South African Parliament then proceeded to repeal apartheid laws, causing other nations to begin relaxing their economic restrictions against South Africa. President de Klerk agreed that in April, 1994, South Africa would hold its first elections in which all races could vote.

A New Era for South Africa

The election of 1994 resulted in the election of Nelson Mandela as president and a majority for the African National Congress in the National Assembly, the larger house of the South African Parliament. In 1996, South Africa wrote a new constitution that guaranteed equal rights for all citizens and included a bill of rights modeled on that of the United States. The South African bill of rights provides for social and economic rights, the right for all people to travel freely, and protection for the rights of minorities and children. Other societies have looked to South Africa as a model for the future of human rights worldwide.

MOVEMENTS FOR SELF-RULE IN SOUTHWEST ASIA

In the late nineteenth and early twentieth centuries, Zionists had begun to settle in Palestine. **Zionism** was a movement that had begun in the 1890s under the leadership of **Theodor Herzl** in response to several anti-Semitic incidents. One of these incidents was the Dreyfus Affair in France in 1894, in which **Alfred Dreyfus**, a captain in the French army, was falsely accused of selling military secrets to Germany. Another was the frequency of Russian **pogroms**, or violent campaigns against Jewish settlements, which prompted emigration from Russia to the United States and other countries. The history of persecutions of the Jews prompted some to work toward the establishment of their own homeland in Palestine.

When Zionists first began moving into Palestine, the territory was still part of the Ottoman empire. After the defeat of the Ottoman empire during World War I, the League of Nations requested that Great Britain oversee Palestine until it was prepared for independence. In 1917, Great Britain issued the **Balfour Declaration**, which favored the establishment of a separate homeland for the Jews in Palestine, but at the same time protected the rights of non-Jews already living in Palestine. When the Balfour Declaration proved too vague to provide a workable solution to the claims of both Jews and Arabs to Palestine, the British made plans to divide Palestine. Conflicts between Arabs and Jews had already arisen in Palestine. The Jews arriving in Palestine were of primarily European descent, and many Arabs felt threatened when they set up **kibbutzim**, or communal agricultural settlements. Meanwhile, the persecution of Jews in Nazi Germany promoted more and more Jewish immigration to Palestine. This increasing Jewish population further disturbed the Arabs because it threatened to surpass the number of Arabs in Palestine.

The Creation of Palestine

At the conclusion of World War II, Great Britain submitted the issue of Palestine to the United Nations. Over the objections of Palestinians and the Islamic world in general, the United Nations partitioned Palestine into a Jewish state and a Palestinian state. Jerusalem was to be an international city controlled by neither side.

The Jews favored the proposal, which granted them 55 percent of Palestine, even though at the time the Jews made up only 34 percent of the population of Palestine. The state of Israel was formed on May 14, 1948, under the leadership of **David Ben Gurion**.

Crises Between Arabs and Jews

Hostilities between Arabs and Jews began the day after Israeli independence, when the Arab states of Egypt, Iraq, Jordan, Syria, Saudi Arabia, and Lebanon invaded Israel. Israel, supported by the United States, won the war. Further wars erupted in 1956, 1967, and 1973. The Palestinian state provided by the United Nations declaration did not materialize because of partitions during the initial Arab-Israeli conflict in 1948. Israel took half the proposed Palestinian land, while Jordan annexed the **West Bank**, and Egypt took the **Gaza Strip**. Thousands of Palestinians fled from Jewish-controlled areas to refugee camps that bordered their former homeland.

The Suez Crisis

In 1952, King Farouk of Egypt was overthrown by **Gamal Abdel Nasser**. Adopting a neutral position in international politics, Nasser initiated policies designed to modernize Egypt militarily and economically, with the goal of making it the leader in a pan-Arab movement.

French and British commercial interests continued to control the **Suez Canal** until Nasser seized the canal in 1956. Nasser, who was angered by his loss of British and American financial support to construct the **Aswan Dam**, planned to use the money collected from his nationalization of the Suez Canal to offset the cost of building the dam. While Britain and France provided air support, the Israelis advanced toward the canal, routing the Egyptians. Pressure from the United States, the Soviet Union, and other nations caused the Israelis to withdraw from Egypt, leaving the canal in the hands of the Egyptians.

The Six-Day War

In 1967, another conflict arose when Nasser closed off the **Gulf of Aqaba**, Israel's only outlet to the Red Sea. The Israelis then attacked airfields in Syria, Egypt, Iran, and Jordan. The war concluded in six days with devastating loss of life for the Arabs. After the **Six-Day War**, Israel occupied Jerusalem, the **Sinai Peninsula**, the West Bank, and the **Golan Heights**. Palestinians living in Jerusalem were given a choice of Israeli or Jordanian citizenship; those residing in other areas became stateless.

The October War

In October 1973, Nasser's successor, **Anwar Sadat**, attacked the Israelis on the most sacred of Jewish holidays, **Yom Kippur**. Caught by surprise, the Israelis lost some of the territory gained during the Six-Day War and also suffered severe casualties. The Israeli prime minister, **Golda Meir**, then launched a counterattack in which the Israelis regained most of the territory they had lost.

The Camp David Accords

In November 1977, Anwar Sadat made a peace initiative in which, in exchange for his offer of peace, the Israelis would recognize Palestinian rights and would withdraw from the territory taken in 1967 from Egypt, Jordan, and Syria. In 1978, U.S. President **Jimmy Carter** offered to oversee the peace talks between Sadat and the Israeli leader **Menachem Begin** at Camp David, the presidential retreat in Maryland. Their negotiations resulted in the **Camp David Accords**, in which Egypt recognized the legitimacy of Israel and Israel agreed to return the Sinai Peninsula to Egypt. Signed in 1979, the accords were the first signed agreement between an Arab country and Israel. In 1981, Sadat was assassinated by Islamic extremists. Egypt's new ruler, **Hosni Mubarak**, pledged to continue the peace between Egypt and Israel.

Demands for Palestinian Independence

In spite of peace accords, the Israelis began to build settlements along the West Bank and the Gaza Strip. Meanwhile, the Palestinians began to depend on the leadership of the **Palestine Liberation Organization**, or the PLO, founded in 1964 under the leadership of **Yasir Arafat**. In 1987, the Palestinians began to use the ***intifada*** to make known their sentiments. A series of demonstrations, boycotts, and violent attacks, the intifada attracted the attention of the world and pressured Israel to engage in peace talks in October 1991.

The Declaration of Principles

In 1993, secret talks in Oslo, Norway, produced a document known as the **Declaration of Principles**. According to its provisions, Israel, led by Prime Minister **Yitzhak Rabin**, conceded to Palestinian self-rule in the Gaza Strip and the West Bank. Arafat and Rabin signed the agreement at the White House in September 1993. In 1995, Rabin was assassinated by a Jewish extremist who opposed the provisions of the declaration. Rabin was succeeded by **Benjamin Netanyahu**, who attempted to uphold the agreement. In 1997, Netanyahu and Arafat planned a partial Israeli withdrawal from Hebron on the West Bank. In 2005, Israel withdrew from the Gaza Strip, evacuating all Jewish settlements. In spite of the Declaration of Principles, violence between Arabs and Jews continues to the present.

A NEW ERA FOR THE SOVIET UNION

Under the leadership of **Leonid Brezhnev**, the **Politburo**, which served as the governing committee of the Communist Party, suppressed disagreement to Soviet political policy. The Soviet people lived in a world of censorship and denial of the freedoms of speech and of worship. When Brezhnev died in 1982, he was succeeded by **Mikhail Gorbachev**, who favored policies that would bring reforms to the Soviet Union.

Glasnost and Perestroika

Gorbachev was aware that the economic and social future of the Soviet Union depended upon the exchange of ideas. In 1985, therefore, he announced a new policy called ***glasnost***, or openness. Glasnost encouraged the Soviet people to share their opinions about ways to improve their society. Churches were opened once again, and previously banned books were published. Political prisoners were released, and the press was allowed to speak out against public officials. One of the chief areas people complained about was the Soviet Union's command economy. Soviet central planning had restricted production so that little human initiative remained to increase productivity. Supplies were limited, and Soviet citizens often had to stand in long lines to purchase common household items or food products.

In 1985, Gorbachev introduced another new concept to the Soviet people, ***perestroika***, or the restructuring of the economy. In order to make communism more productive, Gorbachev permitted the Soviet people to own their own small businesses, and managers gained more local and personal control over farms and factories.

Changes in the Political System and Foreign Policy

In 1987, Gorbachev initiated even more reform when he announced a moderation of the political system, which he termed ***democratization***. New elections allowed voters to choose from a slate of candidates rather than from a limited number chosen by the Communist Party. The elections resulted in the selection of some candidates who favored further reforms for the Soviet Union.

Gorbachev's new foreign policy favored arms control. In December 1987, he and U.S. President Ronald Reagan signed the Intermediate-Range Nuclear Forces **(INF) Treaty**, which placed a ban on nuclear missiles with ranges of 300 to 3,400 miles. Gorbachev also encouraged the Communist rulers of Eastern Europe to reform their own economic and social systems.

REFORM IN POLAND AND HUNGARY

Among the first countries to heed Gorbachev's call for reform were Poland and Hungary. Poland had already experienced movements toward reform, beginning in 1978 with the elevation of a Polish archbishop to the papacy as **Pope John Paul II**. The new pope supported the anticommunist movement in his native land. In 1980, workers in the shipyard of the city of Gdansk, led by **Lech Walesa**, went on strike in order to demand government recognition of **Solidarity**, their labor union. Although the Polish government initially agreed to the union's demands, the following year it reversed its policy and imposed martial law on the country.

Further social unrest and strikes by Solidarity led to an agreement in April 1989 which permitted Poland's first free election since the communist takeover. In elections held in 1989 and 1990, the Polish people elected Lech Walesa president and chose Solidarity over communist candidates. Communism had ended as a political force in Poland.

Walesa remained in power until 1995, when Poles unhappy with the slow pace of economic improvement voted him out of office in favor of a former communist, **Aleksandr Kwasniewski**. Kwasniewski favored a combination of government social programs and free enterprise.

Hungary followed Poland's example, urging some private enterprise and permitting a small stock market. A new constitution allowed free elections. In October 1989, radical reformers took over the Communist Party of Hungary, deposing party leaders and dissolving the party. National elections in 1990 placed a non-communist government in power. In 1994, a coalition between a socialist and a democratic party ruled Hungary, and was forced to raise taxes in order to improve economic conditions.

THE FALL OF COMMUNISM IN EAST GERMANY

Communism in East Germany was challenged in 1989 when Hungary allowed East German tourists to cross its border into Austria. From Austria they could cross into West Germany and, in this manner, escape from East Germany. East Germany responded to this new escape route by closing the borders of East Germany. Demonstrations broke out in October 1989, with protestors demanding free travel and free elections. East Germany's communist leader, **Erich Honecker**, was unable to control the demonstrators; he resigned and was replaced by **Egon Krenz**. Hoping to restore order by allowing people to leave East Germany, Krenz opened the Berlin Wall on November 9, 1989. Thousands of East Germans poured into the city of West Berlin. Krenz and other officials were later charged with corruption and removed from office; by the end of 1989, the Communist Party of East Germany no longer existed.

German Reunification

After the fall of communism in East Germany, Germans began to consider the reunification of Germany. Many world leaders feared that reunification would lead to a Germany that would want to dominate Europe once again. West German Chancellor **Helmut Kohl** assured the other nations of the world that Germany was now committed to a democratic government. With the eventual support of many of the world's nations, Germany was reunified on October 3, 1990.

The most serious problem facing a unified Germany was absorbing the severe economic problems of East Germany. To finance the eastern portion's economic deficits, Kohl raised taxes. In 1994, Kohl was re-elected, and by the mid-1990s the German economy began to slowly improve. Germany also began to resume its interest in its global position in international affairs.

CZECHOSLOVAKIA AND ROMANIA

The example of East Germany prompted demonstrations in Czechoslovakia in 1989. In each case, police brutally attacked the demonstrators. Protestors continued to demand an end to communist rule. On November 24, 1989, Communist Party leader **Milos Jakes** and his advisers resigned and were replaced by **Vaclav Havel**, a government critic.

Rapid economic reforms in Czechoslovakia produced widespread unemployment, which especially affected Slovakia, the eastern third of Czechoslovakia. Disagreements over economic policies caused a rift between the two sections of Czechoslovakia. On January 1, 1993, the country divided into two nations: Slovakia and the Czech Republic.

In 1989, Romania was under the harsh rule of **Nicolae Ceausescu**, who used secret police to carry out his brutality. A government massacre of protestors in December 1989 led to an uprising against Ceausescu. Within days, the army joined the Romanian people, causing Ceausescu and his wife to attempt to flee the country. They were captured, however, and were tried and executed on Christmas Day, 1989. After elections were held in 1990 and 1992, the Romanian government introduced some aspects of capitalism to institute economic reforms.

THE COLLAPSE OF SOVIET COMMUNISM

As the nations of Eastern Europe gradually ended communism within their borders, ethnic unrest began to stir in the Soviet Union. The first nations to launch a protest against Soviet Communism were the Baltic states of Latvia, Lithuania, and Estonia, all of which had been annexed by the Soviet Union in 1940. In March 1990, Lithuania declared its independence, causing Gorbachev to order a blockade in an attempt to force it back into the Soviet Union. In January 1991, Soviet troops attacked civilians in the capital of Lithuania.

The Lithuanian attack and the failure of Gorbachev to bring real economic improvement to the USSR prompted the Soviet people to favor the leadership of **Boris Yeltsin**, the former mayor of Moscow and a member of the parliament. In June 1991, voters elected Yeltsin as the first elected president of the Russian Republic.

Hard-line Communist officials who opposed reform now decided to overthrow Gorbachev and demanded his resignation. On August 20, 1991, they ordered troops to attack the Soviet parliament, but the soldiers refused. Gorbachev resigned as head of the Communist Party, and the parliament voted to stop all activities of the party, effectively ending the power of the Communist Party in the Soviet Union. Estonia and Latvia declared their independence and were shortly followed by the other Soviet republics.

Yeltsin and most of the former Soviet republics agreed to form the Commonwealth of Independent States, or **CIS**. A loose federation of former Soviet republics, it was joined by all the former Soviet territories except for Georgia and the Baltic republics. On Christmas Day, 1991, Gorbachev resigned as president of the Soviet Union.

Yeltsin embarked on an immediate program to reform the Russian economy. He lowered trade restrictions, ended subsidies to government-controlled industries, and ended price controls. His efforts resulted in widespread inflation, and thousands of Russian workers lost their jobs.

A particularly troubled spot was Chechnya, an area in southwestern Russia populated largely by Muslims. In 1991, Chechnya declared its independence, but Yeltsin ordered Russian troops into the republic to prevent it from seceding. The troops demolished the capital city of Grozny. When the Russian people voiced their disapproval of Yeltsin's policies, he negotiated a peace treaty with Chechnya in August 1996.

THE DIVISION OF YUGOSLAVIA

Yugoslavia continued to be plagued by problems relating to its extreme ethnic diversity. After World War II, Yugoslavia had become a federation of six republics, each of which was ethnically mixed. Yugoslavia managed to hold together under **Josip Broz**, known as **Marshall Tito** (1945–1980). Tito's policy of resistance to Soviet dominance resulted in his expulsion from the Soviet bloc by Stalin in 1948. His foreign policy included maintaining peaceful relations with communist states of eastern Europe as well as establishing ties with nonaligned nations.

After Tito's death, Serbian leader **Slobodan Milosevic** claimed Serbian leadership over Yugoslavia. The republics of Slovenia and Croatia then declared their independence. In June 1991, the Yugoslav army, led by Serbs, invaded both Croatia and Slovenia. While the Slovenians quickly ousted the Serbs, the Croatians did not. Croatia was populated by a large Serbian minority who resented Croatian rule. All-out war erupted, and thousands of lives were lost. In January 1992, the United Nations arranged a ceasefire.

Warfare in Bosnia

In February 1992, Bosnia-Herzegovina declared its independence. Bosnia's population was composed of three major groups: Muslims, Serbs, and Croats. Bosnian Serbs opposed independence and, supported by Serbia, began a war in March 1992. Approximately 200,000 people were killed, and more than half of the population of Bosnia left the country. Serbian policy involved **ethnic cleansing**, or the systematic elimination of a particular ethnic group—in this case, the murder of Bosnian Muslims living in lands held by the Serbs. United Nations troops were sent to Bosnia to keep the peace and alleviate suffering. In December 1995, the leaders of the Muslims, Serbs, and Croats signed a peace treaty, and in September 1996, Bosnians elected a presidency composed of one leader from each of the three groups.

CHINA STRENGTHENS ITS COMMUNIST REGIME

Through the 1960s, China had kept itself largely isolated from world affairs. It had recently broken with the Soviet Union and was continuing its animosity toward the United States because of U.S. support for the government on Taiwan. In 1971, Premiere **Zhou Enlai** began reversing this isolation by inviting a U.S. table tennis team to tour China.

A new period in Chinese-American relations now began. In 1971, the United States reversed its previous policy and promoted membership in the United Nations for the People's Republic of China. When President Nixon made a state visit to China in 1972, he made arrangements with Mao and Zhou for cultural exchanges and the beginning of some trade. The United States and the People's Republic of China established diplomatic relations in 1979.

The Rule of Deng Xiaoping

When both Mao and Zhou died in 1976, they were succeeded in 1978 by **Deng Xiaoping**, a moderate. His goals were called the **Four Modernizations**, a program for changes in industry, agriculture, defense, and science and technology. Communes were abolished, and farmland was leased to farmers, who could then sell their own produce for profit. Private businesses were permitted, and a limited amount of foreign investment was encouraged in special economic zones (SEZs).

As a result of Deng's efforts to integrate China into international financial and trade networks, families purchased more appliances and Chinese youth became interested in Western fashions and music, while foreign tourism increased markedly. Deng also sent tens of thousands of Chinese students to universities in other countries to educate them in academic subjects and managerial programs necessary to his vision of a modern China.

Tiananmen Square

As Western customs and ideals became more familiar to the Chinese, students in particular began to question the restrictive policies of their government. In April 1989, more than 100,000 students occupied Tiananmen Square in Beijing, calling for democratic reforms and an end to governmental corruption and economic inflation. Deng responded by imposing martial law and sending in troops to surround Beijing. On June 4, 1989, army tanks ploughed through the square, killing hundreds of demonstrators.

China After Deng Xiaoping

Deng's economic policies brought increasing prosperity to China. When he died in 1997, **Jiang Zemin** assumed power. The same year Jiang paid a state visit to the United States in which he refused to promise any changes in Chinese policies on human rights. For years the United States had pressured China to release political prisoners, but the Chinese continued on the road of repression of policies that were pro-democratic. The Chinese people, however, continued their quest for freedom.

Hong Kong

The future status of Hong Kong is another issue the Chinese will have to deal with in the twenty-first century. For 155 years, Hong Kong had been a colony of Great Britain. On July 1, 1997, the prosperous business and trade center was returned to China. As part of the transfer agreement, China pledged to continue Hong Kong's economic and political system for another 50 years. The world waits to see the style of rule that China will impose upon Hong Kong at the end of the 50-year period.

MODERN LATIN AMERICA

Twentieth-century Latin America continued to grapple with issues of land redistribution, foreign investments, and dictatorial rule. By the mid twentieth century, Latin America had somewhat reversed its economic dependency on foreign nations and was exporting manufactured goods as well as foodstuffs and minerals. The global depression of the 1970s and 1980s, however, was devastating to Latin America. Debt payments to technological nations provided the developed world with increased opportunities for influence on Latin American countries. By the closing years of the twentieth century, however, the economies of the nations of Latin America were sufficiently strong to combat dependency on foreign nations.

Mexico

During the presidency of **Lázaro Cárdenas** (1934–1940), the monopoly that wealthy Mexican citizens held over the land and its resources was ended. Cárdenas made the Mexican government return land to the peasants, and made foreign investors return control over Mexico's oil wells.

Traditional, conservative Mexican governments backed by **PRI**, or the Institutional Revolutionary Party, vacillated between allowing or disallowing dependence on foreign investments. In the 1990s, PRI was often criticized for its harsh policies, as peasants in the Chiapas district of Mexico rebelled against political oppression. The later years of the twentieth century saw opposition parties rise to exercise increasing influence over Mexican voters. In 2000, **Vicente Fox** of PAN (Partido Acción Nacional) was elected president in PRI's first defeat since 1929.

Argentina

During World War II, Argentina saw military leaders gain power in the government. **Juan Perón**, an army colonel, was elected president in 1946 and established a "popular dictatorship." His wife, **Eva Perón**, became a popular, charismatic first lady of Argentina. Perón's program called for industrialization, support for the working class, and resistance to foreign control of the country's economy; however, he also placed severe limits on civil liberties. Although removed from power in 1955, Perón's brief return in the 1970s was only a short respite before the return of military dictators. In 1982, after the war with Great Britain in the Falklands, Argentina started moving toward a representative democracy.

THINGS TO REMEMBER

- The post-World War II era saw the former European colonies of Africa and Asia gain their independence.
    - Nearly all of the independence movements involved protracted struggles and unrest.
    - Weakened by the war, Europe's imperialist powers could no longer afford to maintain their colonies.
    - Independence brought social problems.
        - Many of the new countries had arbitrary borders drawn by colonizers, without respect for ethnic and linguistic groups.
        - Imperialist countries did not prepare subject peoples for the social and economic issues of independence. They had failed to share technology and invest in infrastructure.
    - In 1947, India was partitioned into two states, one for Hindus and one for Muslims. India and Pakistan have been at war or on the brink of war ever since.
    - Zionist dreams of a Jewish homeland in Palestine were realized with the establishment of Israel in 1948. Palestinian resistance has caused numerous wars and domestic strife.
    - The fall of communism in the Soviet Union and its Eastern European satellites (circa 1989), as well as the crumbling of the USSR itself (1991), created new economic and ethnic problems.

    - East and West Germany overcame the difficulties of reunification.
    - Yugoslavia fragmented into smaller states with horrible ethnic violence.
- Under Deng Ziaoping, China moved towards limited capitalism. But it did not allow its citizens any political rights, as underscored by the massacre of student protesters in Tiananmen Square (1989).

REVIEW QUESTIONS

1. During the period of their newly acquired independence, the former European colonies

   (A) were generally well prepared for independence.
   (B) were finally able to resolve issues among ethnic groups.
   (C) lacked native leaders capable of directing their people.
   (D) broke off all ties with former imperialist powers.
   (E) faced the question of alignment with the United States or the Soviet Union.

2. "We are the finest race in the world and the more of the world we inhabit, the better it is for the human race."

   The speaker of these words was
   (A) F.W. de Klerk.
   (B) Nelson Mandela.
   (C) Cecil Rhodes.
   (D) Kwame Nkrumah.
   (E) Desmond Tutu.

3. The African National Congress

   (A) was formed after the age of the new imperialism.
   (B) was accused of Communist leanings by the South African government.
   (C) prompted the South African government to decrease its opposition to black activism.
   (D) decreased its activism after the Sharpeville Massacre.
   (E) had difficulty gaining support from other nations.

4. The regime of Mikhail Gorbachev differed from that of Brezhnev in that

   (A) Gorbachev closed churches in the Soviet Union.
   (B) Gorbachev prevented the private ownership of business.
   (C) Gorbachev imposed strict censorship.
   (D) Gorbachev strengthened the Soviet command economy.
   (E) Gorbachev allowed some elements of a market economy.

5. Under Deng Xiaoping,
   (A) the productivity of communal farms was increased.
   (B) all Western influences were discouraged.
   (C) foreign investment was discouraged.
   (D) small private businesses were allowed.
   (E) foreign tourism decreased.

ANSWERS AND EXPLANATIONS

1. (E)

Upon acquiring independence, many of the former colonies faced the question of alignment with a superpower or nonalignment. A few leaders of subject peoples had been well educated and possessed the skills necessary to lead their people (C). Some subject peoples continued ties with former imperialist powers, such as the membership of India in the British Commonwealth (D).

2. (C)

Cecil Rhodes, the author of these words, was a strong believer in the superiority of the British people and felt they had a responsibility to establish colonies to spread their culture.

3. (B)

The South African government accused the ANC of communist leanings in order to win the support of other nations against the Congress. The ANC was founded in 1909 (A). The ANC prompted the South African government to increase its opposition (C). The organization increased its activism after the Sharpeville Massacre (D), and was supported by many of the nations of the world (E).

4. (E)

Under perestroika, Gorbachev allowed some elements of the market economy in order to strengthen the Soviet economy. The other choices all represent policies of Brezhnev, not Gorbachev.

5. (D)

Deng Xiaoping allowed some small private businesses to operate. Collective farms were abolished because of their lack of productivity (A). Western products were introduced through trade and tourism (B, E). Some foreign investment was allowed in special economic zones (C).

CHAPTER 30

Global Interdependence

TIMELINE

1947	General Agreement on Tariffs and Trade
1948	Universal Declaration of Human Rights
1950	Chinese marriage law
1950s	Green revolution begins
1950s and 1960s	U.S. civil rights movement
1958	European Economic Community
1960	Introduction of the birth control pill Formation of Organization of Petroleum Exporting Countries
1967	Association of Southeast Asian Nations founded
1968	Nuclear Non-Proliferation Treaty signed
1970s	Strategic Arms Limitation Talks
1973	OPEC oil embargo
1975	Docking of the *Apollo* and the *Soyuz* UN begins international conferences on women
1979	Mother Teresa wins the Nobel Peace Prize
1980	U.S. Equal Rights Amendment fails to achieve ratification
1988	Burma's National League for Democracy is formed Daw Aung San Suu Kyi becomes General Secretary of Burma

1989	Fall of the Berlin Wall
1990	Iraq invades Kuwait Construction of the Hubble Telescope
1990s	The Internet
1991	Gulf War
1994	North American Free Trade Agreement Chandrika Bandaranaike Kumaratanga president of Sri Lanka
1995	Formation of the World Trade Organization
1997	The United States lands the *Pathfinder* on Mars Taliban win control of Afghanistan
2001	Terrorist attack on the United States
2002	Introduction of the euro
2001	Terrorist attack on the United States
2003	War in Iraq

IMPORTANT PEOPLE, PLACES, EVENTS, AND CONCEPTS

robotics*
Four Tigers*
GATT
World Trade Organization*
European Economic Community
European Union*
euro*
NAFTA
LAFTA
ASEAN
OPEC*
Gulf War
Operation Desert Storm
chlorofluorocarbons*
Apollo
Soyuz
space shuttle*
space station*
space probe*
Pathfinder
Hubble Telescope
green revolution*
human cloning*
stem cell research*
consumerism*
McDonaldization*
Civil Rights Act
Osama Bin Laden
World Trade Center*
al Qaeda
Taliban*
*burqa**
Universal Declaration of Human Rights*
multinational corporation*
civil rights movement*
Martin Luther King
internal migration*
external migration*
push-pull factors*
guest workers*
World Health Organization*
UN Fund for Population Activities
Nuclear Non-Proliferation Treaty*
Equal Rights Amendment
one-child policy*
dowry death*
Mother Teresa
global village*

TOWARD A GLOBAL COMMUNITY

The second half of the twentieth century—and the beginnings of the twenty-first—witnessed an increasing interdependency among the nations of the world. In spite of economic and political differences, the modern era has reflected strong global links in trade, technology, human rights issues, and mass culture. The worldwide connections established in the early modern era have come full circle as people are increasingly drawn into the common experiences of a global culture.

REVOLUTIONS IN WORLD ECONOMIC DEVELOPMENT

The postwar period throughout the West and in Asia saw economic growth through advances in technology, such as the production of plastics and the use of robotics to automate industry. Advances in the communications and computer industries made possible new global connections through the rapid processing and transmission of information. As a result of more sophisticated technology, industrialization became more widespread in the developing nations.

After World War II, the Japanese imported and developed the best advances of Western technology, becoming a leader in electronics and automobile production. Japan had a large labor force that was generally willing to handle working conditions and wages at a much lower standard than the organized labor of the United States and western Europe. In addition, the use of **robotics** and a team approach in industry initially left Japan with a competitive advantage over other industrialized nations. By the early 1990s, however, trade imbalances and speculation led to the collapse of the Japanese economy.

Four areas of the Pacific Rim—Taiwan, Singapore, Hong Kong, and South Korea—have achieved such notable strides in electronics and finances that they have been dubbed the **Four Tigers**. In the 1990s, Malaysia and China also reached a level competitive with other nations of the Pacific Rim. The integration of Hong Kong into the Chinese economy has increased China's impact on global trade.

THE GROWTH OF WORLD TRADE

With the increasing links among the nations of the world in both technology and information transfer, a number of multinational corporations have arisen. These are corporations who construct factories in several countries in order to capitalize upon inexpensive raw materials, inexpensive labor, and markets in those countries. Some examples of multinational corporations are Exxon, IBM, Volvo, and Mitsubishi.

Trade Agreements

The breakdown of national barriers in trade has promoted the concept of free trade among the nations of the world. Several organizations have arisen to further the breakdown of tariffs among nations, including the 1947 General Agreement on Tariffs and Trade **(GATT)**. In 1995, the **World Trade Organization** was set up to manage free trade. **The European Economic Community** (EEC), which grew out of the European Common Market, was established in 1958 to eliminate tariffs among member nations. The EEC, currently called the **European Union** (EU), has been joined by the following European countries: Austria, Belgium, Denmark, Finland, France, Germany, Greece, Ireland, Italy, Luxembourg, the Netherlands, Portugal, Spain, Sweden, and the United Kingdom. On May 1, 2004, the following nations became EEC/EU members: Cyprus, Czech Republic, Estonia, Hungary, Latvia, Lithuania, Malta, Poland, Slovakia, and Slovenia. In January 2002, the introduction of a common currency, the **euro**, was accepted by most of the European countries, excluding the United Kingdom and Denmark.

The success of the European free trade organizations inspired the creation of other trade agreements. The North American Free Trade Agreement (**NAFTA**) was established in 1994 to eliminate tariff and trade restrictions among Mexico, Canada, and the United States. The Latin American Free Trade Agreement (**LAFTA**) was formed in 1961 to promote trade between Argentina, Belgium, Brazil, Colombia, Ecuador, Mexico, Paraguay, Uruguay, and Venezuela; replaced in 1981 by the Latin American Integration Association, it also worked to decrease dependence on nations with more advanced economies.

Another regional trade alliance is the Association of Southeast Asian Nations (**ASEAN**). Founded in 1967 by Thailand, Singapore, Malaysia, Indonesia, and the Philippines, its primary purposes were to further economic stability and progress in southeast Asia. ASEAN increased its influence after signing cooperative trade agreements with Japan in 1977 and with the European Community in 1980. In 1992, its members voted to establish free trade and to cut tariffs on manufactured goods over a period of 15 years.

Energy Sources and the Global Community

The worldwide growth of manufacturing has steadily increased the importance of an adequate supply of oil as a source of energy. Nations possessing large reserves of oil and natural gas are in a position to exert control over the nations of the world. In 1960, the Organization of Petroleum Exporting Countries (**OPEC**) was established by the oil-producing countries of Iran, Iraq, Kuwait, Saudi Arabia, and Venezuela. The organization was later joined by Libya, Qatar, Indonesia, Algeria, Nigeria, Abu Dhabi, Ecuador, and Gabon.

During the Arab-Israeli War of 1973, OPEC ordered an embargo on oil shipments to the United States (Israel's ally) and also raised prices fourfold within a period of only two years. Japan, which also imported most of its oil from Southwest Asia, was affected as well. The petroleum price increase precipitated global economic decline. By the 1980s, the influence of OPEC had declined because of overproduction and disagreements among its members over the Iran-Iraq War and the Gulf War.

The Gulf War

An example of the control exerted by the oil-producing nations was clearly illustrated in 1990, when Iraq invaded Kuwait, threatening to cut off oil supplies from Kuwait and the remainder of Southwest Asia. This threat was potentially serious—especially for the United States, Europe, and Japan, which imported the majority of their oil. Members of the United Nations came together to wage war on Iraq. The **Gulf War**, also termed **Operation Desert Storm**, was waged during January and February of 1991 and resulted in the acceptance of a cease-fire by Iraq and in the liberation of Kuwait. Another impact of the Gulf War was environmental damage; during the course of the conflict, the Iraquis set fire to many of Kuwait's oil wells and dumped more than two million gallons of Kuwait's oil into the Persian Gulf.

Environmental Threats

Accompanying industrialization is the threat of air pollution and acid rain caused by the burning of coal and oil as energy sources. The earth's ozone layer, the primary protection against harmful ultraviolet rays, has been steadily eroded by the release of chemicals known as **chlorofluorocarbons** used not only in industry but also in air conditioners and refrigerators. An increase in ultraviolet radiation has produced a rise in skin cancer in various parts of the world and may also be damaging plants at the lowest levels of the food chain.

Economic and industrial development has often resulted in deterioration of the land. Depletion of the world's rain forests has contributed to global warming. Land development often destroys the natural habitats of wildlife, threatening the extinction of many species and the possible destruction of the balance of life-sustaining processes.

SCIENCE AND TECHNOLOGY STRIVE TO IMPROVE THE GLOBAL OUTLOOK

The Space Race

One of the defining features of technological growth in the years after World War II was the space race. From the 1950s through the 1970s, the United States and the Soviet Union developed both unmanned and manned space programs. In 1972, the space race became a cooperative venture between the two superpowers when the United States and the Soviet Union signed an agreement with the goal of docking the American ***Apollo*** and the Soviet ***Soyuz*** crafts in space; the docking finally occurred on July 17, 1975.

During the late twentieth century, the superpowers devoted their efforts to the development of **space shuttles** that could return to earth under their own power and to **space stations** that served as orbiting scientific laboratories. Both superpowers assembled international teams to fly special invitational missions on their respective space shuttles.

The planets of the solar system became the subjects of study by the American and Soviet **space probes** that transmitted to earth photographs of and information about the planets. In 1997, the United States landed the ***Pathfinder*** space probe on Mars. European and United States space agencies also cooperated to construct the **Hubble Telescope** in 1990, a device that transmits information about remote areas in space.

Communications Technology

Global communications were transformed in the 1960s with the launch of artificial satellites. The use of silicon chips resulted in the reduction in the size of computers, an improvement that not only made practical the personal computer but also revolutionized the operational features of automobiles and everyday home and office machines and appliances. The personal and corporate use of the Internet since the 1990s has revolutionized the transmission of information and linked individuals to the global village on a daily basis.

The Green Revolution

The **green revolution** was an effort begun in the 1950s to increase food sources worldwide. Especially implemented in areas such as India and other Asian regions as well as in South America, the green revolution involved the use of fertilizers and pesticides as well as improved hybrid crops to increase crop yield rather than merely increasing the amount of crop land. The increased production of rice, wheat, and maize ended famine in some parts of Asia and South America. The accomplishments of the green revolution, however, were helpful only in those regions whose governments permitted the proper distribution of food supplies. The tendency of the green revolution toward commercial use did not always improve the diets of individual inhabitants. Also, the benefits of the program were often offset by its expense for the average farmer and by the health dangers inherent in the use of fertilizers and pesticides. Requiring the use of irrigation, the green revolution has increased the salinity of soils and has decreased ground water supplies.

Medical Breakthroughs

Since World War II, the medical field has achieved notable advances in areas such as ultrasound and laser surgery. CAT scans and MRIs provide three-dimensional views of the human body. Genetic engineering has produced stronger, more resilient crops while at the same time generating debate concerning the safety of genetically engineered food supplies. In the late twentieth and early twenty-first centuries, **human cloning** and **stem cell research** have shown promise in providing possible cures for debilitating diseases, but they also raise moral issues regarding the value of human life.

The postwar use of antibiotics, vaccines, and insecticides, as well as improved water supplies, have combined to produce a significant decline in global death rates, resulting in marked population increases. Concerns about the capacity of the planet to support its rapidly growing population have prompted many nations to enact birth control programs. The United Nations and two of its agencies, the **World Health Organization** (WHO) and the **UN Fund for Population Activities**, have assisted countries in promoting family-planning programs.

THREATS TO GLOBAL SECURITY

The threat of nuclear warfare during the aftermath of World War II prompted efforts on the part of nations worldwide to deter nuclear buildup. In 1968, a number of nations signed the **Nuclear Non-Proliferation Treaty**, in which the signers pledged to help prevent the spread of nuclear weapons. The Strategic Arms Limitation Treaties signed by the United States and the Soviet Union in the 1970s resulted in the deactivation of some of the weapons in their respective nuclear arsenals. New threats arose in 1998 when both India and Pakistan tested their own nuclear weapons; neither country has yet signed the non-proliferation treaty.

Terrorist Threats

Terrorist activity was by no means new to the twentieth century, but the twentieth century and the opening months of the twenty-first saw the increase of terrorist attacks worldwide. Terrorism is being implemented not only as hate crimes but also as a method of undermining the authority of established governments. Terrorists have gained further notoriety through television news coverage of their violent attacks. Palestinian groups opposed to the existence of the Israeli state carried out hijackings of airplanes in 1968, while their murder of 11 members of the Israeli Olympic team at the 1972 Munich Olympics gained them further media coverage.

Acts of terrorism have not been confined to Palestinian groups. Bombings have been carried out in the British Isles by the Irish Republican Army (IRA), whose goal is to unite Northern Ireland and the Irish Republic. In 1983, 241 U.S. sailors and Marines were killed when a Lebanese terrorist blew up U.S. barracks in Beirut, Lebanon. A March 1995 attack by the members of a Japanese cult released nerve gas in a Tokyo subway, resulting in 12 deaths and thousands of injuries. Beginning in late 1996, a group of hostages were held for over three months at the Japanese embassy in Lima, Peru, by a group of Japanese terrorists. The 1998 bombings of U.S. embassies in Kenya and Tanzania, attributed by the United States to Osama Bin Laden of Afghanistan, further demonstrated the power of terrorist activity.

The September 11 Attack on the United States

Terrorism took on an even more devastating impact on September 11, 2001, when a group of Islamic terrorists under the leadership of **Osama Bin Laden** attacked the United States. Targeting Washington, D.C. and New York City, the terrorists boarded planes and then sent them crashing into the Pentagon in the District of Columbia and into the **World Trade Center** in New York City. Another hijacking, aborted by passengers, culminated in a plane crash in Pennsylvania. The attack took the lives of nearly 3,000 people and plunged the United States into a war with Afghanistan in an effort to locate Bin Laden and his supporters, members of a terrorist organization called **al Qaeda**.

In 1997, the Islamic fundamental movement called the **Taliban** had won control of Afghanistan after years of civil war. Imposing harsh Islamic laws upon Afghanistan, the Taliban especially repressed women, requiring them to wear the ***burqa***, a head-to-toe garment with a mesh-like panel covering the face. By the end of 2001, United States troops and aircraft had driven the Taliban from Afghanistan and had installed a provisional government in its place.

Ethnic Cleansing

The years of the late twentieth century saw the horrors of ethnic cleansing, or the systematic elimination of ethnic minorities, among the peoples of the former Yugoslavia. The African country of Rwanda witnessed the slaughter of the Tutsi minority by the Hutu majority. The Kurds, a nomadic group from Southwest Asia who occupy territory in Turkey, Iran, and Iraq, have repeatedly been the victims of persecution from members of all three nations; in the 1980s, about 5,000 Kurds were killed when Iraqis subjected them to poison gas.

MOVEMENTS FOR HUMAN RIGHTS

A chief proponent of human rights has been the United Nations, which, in 1948, issued the **Universal Declaration of Human Rights**. The declaration listed the basic universal human rights as "life, liberty, and security of person." The civil rights movement of the 1950s and 1960s in the United States focused on changing laws to eliminate segregation for African Americans. Dr. **Martin Luther King**, one of many leaders of the civil rights movement, based his nonviolent philosophy for change on the teachings of Gandhi. From the civil rights movement came other efforts to achieve rights for women, Hispanics, Native Americans, and the disabled.

During the late twentieth century, the issue of human rights became an increasingly important issue in global politics. However, some governments view any criticism of their human rights policies as an interference with their sovereignty, while some religious groups perceive the issue of human rights as an intrusion into their traditions.

Human rights proponents often operate through international associations known as nongovernmental organizations (NGOs). One example is Amnesty International, founded in 1961 to secure release for those imprisoned illegally. Nongovernmental organizations often center their activities around issues that transcend geographical and political boundaries, such as famine relief and aid to refugees.

MIGRATION

The twentieth century has seen numerous waves of migration as some flee their homelands to escape religious, political, or ethnic persecution. Internal migration involves the movement of people from rural to urban areas, while external migration describes the relocation of people across long distances or international borders. Migration is governed by ***push-pull factors***—those conditions that push individuals to leave their country such as natural disaster, economic distress, or persecution, and those that pull individuals to another location, such as economic opportunity and freedom of religion.

A common form of mass migration in the latter half of the twentieth century was the movement of people from developing countries to industrialized countries. Since the 1960s, millions of **guest workers** from southern Europe, Turkey, and northern Africa have migrated to western Europe to take advantage of employment opportunities and have then remained as permanent residents. Some of the refugees came from former colonies of European nations, as in the case of North Africans from Algeria, Tunisia, and Morocco who migrated to France. The attitudes of the citizens of host countries have often prevented the guest workers from acquiring citizenship, however. Once welcome because of a need to alleviate labor shortages in Europe, by the 1980s the guest workers often became the victims of anti-foreign sentiment after the slowing of the European economy in the 1980s. The United States has admitted millions of permanent residents, especially from Mexico, as well as from other Latin American countries and from Asia. Japan also admitted laborers from other Asian countries.

Another common form of migration is from rural to urban areas, often as a result of the desire to escape rural poverty. This pattern is becoming increasingly common in Latin America and South Asia and, to a lesser extent, Africa. Millions of people live in poverty-stricken settlements surrounding cities such as Mexico City and Calcutta. In developed countries, however, migration is often in a reverse direction, as city residents migrate to the country.

Still another migratory pattern is flight from war-torn areas or from political oppression. After the 1947 partition of the Indian subcontinent, millions of Hindus fled Pakistan for India, while millions of Muslims left India for Pakistan. In the 1980s, refugees from Afghanistan fled their war-ravaged country for Europe, Iran, and Pakistan. In 1980, Cubans expelled by Fidel Castro fled to the United States. As a result of the plight of refugees, the United Nations and other international organizations set up refugee camps. After the 1947 partition of Palestine, approximately seven million displaced Palestinians found refuge in camps in Syria, Jordan, the Gaza Strip, and Lebanon. Refugee camps have been set up in Pakistan to shelter the refugees from Afghanistan and in the Congo to provide for escapees from the ethnic cleansing of warring tribes from Rwanda. The Albanians have provided camps for refugees from the 1999 Kosovo crisis who fled to Macedonia and were then sent by the Macedonians to the Albanians.

Increased economic opportunities even draw citizens from technologically advanced countries to other lands. Today more than half the laborers of the oil-producing countries of Southwest Asia are foreigners. Sometimes migration is only temporary, as in the case of tourism, a form of migration that serves to link global cultures.

A GLOBAL MASS CULTURE

In a world culture that shares not only television, radio, and movies but also Internet connections and cellular phones, global communication and awareness have created a global culture. Although Mandarin Chinese is the most commonly spoken native language, in the latter half of the twentieth century English emerged as the international language of trade and commerce, science and medicine. The influence of the English language is a primary factor in the emergence of a global culture. In spite of these global links, however, not everyone has found a home in the **global village**, where residence requires capital and technological knowledge.

Non-Western influences are making a more noticeable impact on the Western culture as well. Particularly important are philosophical and religious traditions emanating from the East. Islam has become the world's fastest-growing religion. Elements of the Daoist philosophy of China have become popular in the Western culture, such as the use of the yin/yang symbols in jewelry and common language and the popularity of the art of feng shui.

The defining characteristic of the global culture is **consumerism**. Industrialization and ever-rising standards of living have produced a culture in which goods and services satisfy our wants rather than our needs. Some have called the new global culture the "McWorld," or the **"McDonaldization"** of the world. The power of advertising has certainly promoted the marketing of a global mass culture in which companies such as McDonald's, Pizza Hut, and Coca-Cola are found throughout the world.

WOMEN IN THE GLOBAL VILLAGE

In the twentieth century, women in the United States, Europe, the Soviet Union, and China achieved greater equality with men, although they still do not enjoy full political, economic, or social equality. In all countries, women earn less than men for the same work and are usually restricted from entering the highest paid professional positions.

Western Women

In the United States, the civil rights movement of the 1960s served as the springboard for the advancement of women's rights. The U.S. **Civil Rights Act** of 1964 banned discrimination on the basis of race and sex. Traditional roles of American women were altered by the introduction of the birth control pill in 1960 and by the legalization of abortion in the 1970s. Another measure that would have provided gender equality, the **Equal Rights Amendment** (ERA), failed to achieve ratification before its 1982 deadline.

In other Western countries, new laws made abortions more accessible, particularly in the Scandinavian countries and in Great Britain. Mediterranean countries such as Italy and Greece began to see a marked decline in birth rates as more and more women chose employment outside the home rather than a life devoted to the rearing of children. Increasingly, European children have been placed in day care centers sponsored by the governments of their respective countries.

Women in the Non-Western World

In China, the marriage law of 1950 abolished patriarchal practices such as the betrothal of children and promoted equal rights for both men and women in employment, inheritance, and property ownership. In rural villages, however, traditional Confucian ideas perpetuate the concept of female subordination. China's **one-child policy** has sometimes resulted in the abandonment and infanticide of baby girls in favor of future attempts to produce a male child. Chinese school records show that, in some families, female infants have been placed with grandparents and other relatives to afford families the opportunity to have a boy child.

In the Arab world, women often face a life of illiteracy, although this situation is beginning to change somewhat as more women have been given educational opportunities in the last years of the twentieth century.

Many Indian women continue to live in patriarchal families. In India, **dowry deaths** are reportedly becoming more frequent as men who are disappointed with the amount of their wife's dowry or with the wife herself follow the practice of dousing her with kerosene and setting her on fire; according to UNICEF estimates, about 5,000 Indian women are the victims of dowry deaths each year.

The twentieth century saw more women attaining the right to vote and participating more fully in politics. Indira Gandhi of India, while criticized for her censorship of the press, was also noted for providing land redistribution and economical housing for the poor as well as the extension of suffrage. In 1994, Chandrika Bandaranaike Kumaratunga became the first woman president of Sri Lanka. Daw Aung San Suu Kyi became the leader of the democratic movement in Burma in 1988; placed under house arrest from 1989 to 1995 and again in 2000, she was awarded the Nobel Peace Prize in 1991. In the Nicaraguan elections of 1990, which ended the control of the Sandanistas, Violeta Chamorro was elected president.

In 1975, the United Nations hosted the first of many international conferences on the status of women throughout the world. Included in the themes discussed at the conferences were the prevention of violence against women and efforts to encourage women to assume more involved leadership roles. Among the participants at the United Nations fourth women's conference in Beijing in 1995 was **Mother Teresa**, an Albanian missionary working among the orphans and the homeless of Calcutta, India. She was awarded the Nobel Peace Prize in 1979 for her efforts to help the poor and sick. Although Mother Teresa died in 1997, her legacy continues to the present.

THINGS TO REMEMBER

- Technological advances in communications and advertising have created a global culture.
    - Television, movies, radio, and the Internet connect people around the world.
    - Complaints of "McDonaldization" of world culture have arisen, due to the power of American-based advertising and consumerism.
- Global commerce and free-trade agreements have become the norm.
    - General Agreement on Tariffs and Trade (GATT), 1947
    - World Trade Organization (1995)
    - European Union (grew out of European Economic Community, 1958)
    - North American Free Trade Agreement (NAFTA), 1994
    - Latin American Free Trade Agreement (LAFTA), 1961, later Latin American Integration Association
    - Association of Southeast Asian Nations (ASEAN)
- Migration for political or economic reasons has contributed to the global culture.
- The status of women has improved in Western and non-Western nations (working outside the home, female world leaders), but practices like infanticide (China) and "dowry deaths" (India) indicate much progress remains to be made.
- Challenges facing the world today include terrorism, population pressure, ethnic strife, preservation of the environment, and promotion of human rights.

REVIEW QUESTIONS

1. One problem resulting from internal migration would be

    (A) anti-foreign sentiment against immigrants.
    (B) impoverished settlements near major Latin American cities.
    (C) the control of disease in UN-sponsored refugee camps.
    (D) loss of ethnic identity attributed to globalism.
    (E) difficulties on the part of immigrants in acquiring citizenship.

2. In the modern world,

    (A) women in India have emerged from patriarchal control.
    (B) literacy for women of the Islamic world has increased markedly.
    (C) European governments have cooperated with women in careers.
    (D) women in all parts of China have equal rights with men.
    (E) women world leaders have been confined to Western nations.

3. All of the following conflicts resulted from religious issues EXCEPT

    (A) the conflict between India and Pakistan over Kashmir.
    (B) the Iran-Iraq War.
    (C) the Taliban takeover in Afghanistan.
    (D) the Persian Gulf War.
    (E) the Iranian Revolution.

4. In the twentieth century, Japan

    (A) experienced continuous economic depression in the years following World War II.
    (B) returned to its isolationist policy regarding Western technology.
    (C) saw speculation lead to a downward economic spiral in the 1990s.
    (D) saw the use of robotics decrease worker initiative.
    (E) suffered from a limited labor force.

5. "We, the people of South Africa, feel fulfilled that humanity has taken us back into its bosom, that we, who were outlaws not so long ago, have today been given the rare privilege to be host to the nations of the world on our own soil… The time for healing of wounds has come. The moment to bridge the chasms that divide us has come." (Nelson Mandela)

    The occasion of these words was

    (A) the establishment of homelands for the South African blacks.
    (B) the election of Mandela as president of South Africa.
    (C) South Africa's hosting of the international women's conference.
    (D) the lifting of economic sanctions imposed against South Africa because of apartheid.
    (E) the treaty ending the Boer War.

ANSWERS AND EXPLANATIONS

1. (B)

Internal migration involves the movement from rural to urban areas, which often results in the rise of poor shantytowns surrounding major cities. The other answer choices are problems associated with external migration, or the movement of people across long distances or international borders. Choice (A) and choice (E) are situations typically encountered by guest workers. Choice (C) is a problem found in external migration resulting from warfare. Choice (D) is a phenomenon common to the shrinking of the globe through trade or long-distance migration.

2. (C)

European governments have often set up day care centers for children of working mothers. Indian women often live in patriarchal families (A). Although in some areas Muslim women have been offered increased educational opportunities, they often remain illiterate (B). Women in rural areas of China often remain subject to Confucian values of female subordination (D). Women leaders have risen in Sri Lanka and Burma (E).

3. (D)

The Persian Gulf War was an effort by Iraq to assert control over the Western world and Japan by cutting off oil supplies. The conflict over Kashmir involves the tensions between Hindus and Muslims in South Asia (A). The Iran-Iraq War was a conflict between Shi'ite and Sunni Muslims (B). The Taliban takeover and the Iranian Revolution involved Islamic extremism (C, D).

4. (C)

In the early 1990s, trade imbalances and speculation led to the collapse of the Japanese economy. Japan saw marked recovery and economic progress after World War II (A). It imported and developed the best of Western technology (B), and successfully used robotics in their factories (D). The Japanese have a large labor force (E).

5. (B)

These words, spoken at Mandela's election to the presidency of South Africa, reflect the unity of an election in which South Africans of all races were allowed to participate. Homelands were the segregated areas under apartheid (A). The passage talks of opportunities, not restrictions (D). The Boer War (E) preceded the career of Mandela.

Section Four

PRACTICE TESTS

HOW TO TAKE THE PRACTICE TESTS

Before taking a practice test, find a quiet room where you can work uninterrupted for one hour. Make sure you have several No. 2 pencils with erasers.

Use the answer grid provided to record your answers. Guidelines for scoring your test appear on the reverse side of the answer grid. Time yourself. Spend no more than one hour on the 95 questions. Once you start the practice test, don't stop until you've reached the one-hour time limit. You'll find an answer key and complete answer explanations following the test. Be sure to read the explanations for all questions, even those you answered correctly.

Good luck!

HOW TO CALCULATE YOUR SCORE

Step 1: Figure out your raw score. Use the answer key to count the number of questions you answered correctly and the number of questions you answered incorrectly. (Do not count any questions you left blank.) Multiply the number wrong by 0.25 and subtract the result from the number correct. Round the result to the nearest whole number. This is your raw score.

SAT Subject Test: World History Practice Test 1

Number right		Number wrong		Raw score
□	–	(0.25 × □)	=	□

Step 2: Find your scaled score. In the Score Conversion Table below, find your raw score (rounded to the nearest whole number) in one of the columns to the left. The score directly to the right of that number will be your scaled score.

A note on your practice test scores: Don't take these scores too literally. Practice test conditions cannot precisely mirror real test conditions. Your actual SAT Subject Test: World History score will almost certainly vary from your practice test scores. However, your scores on the practice tests will give you a rough idea of your range on the actual exam.

Conversion Table

Raw	Scaled	Raw	Scaled	Raw	Scaled	Raw	Scaled	Raw	Scaled	Raw	Scaled
95	800	75	760	55	650	35	530	15	420	−5	300
94	800	74	760	54	640	34	530	14	410	−6	290
93	800	73	750	53	640	33	520	13	410	−7	280
92	800	72	740	52	630	32	520	12	400	−8	280
91	800	71	740	51	630	31	510	11	400	−9	270
90	800	70	730	50	620	30	500	10	390	−10	260
89	800	69	730	49	620	29	500	9	380	−11	260
88	800	68	720	48	610	28	490	8	380	−12	250
87	800	67	720	47	600	27	490	7	370	−13	250
86	800	66	710	46	600	26	480	6	370	−14	240
85	800	65	700	45	590	25	480	5	360	−15	240
84	800	64	700	44	590	24	470	4	360	−16	230
83	800	63	690	43	580	23	460	3	350	−17	220
82	800	62	690	42	580	22	460	2	340	−18	220
81	800	61	680	41	570	21	450	1	340	−19	210
80	800	60	680	40	560	20	450	0	330	−20	210
79	790	59	670	39	560	19	440	−1	320	−21	200
78	780	58	670	38	550	18	440	−2	320	−22	200
77	780	57	660	37	550	17	430	−3	310	−23	200
76	770	56	660	36	540	16	420	−4	300	−24	200

Answer Grid
Practice Test 1

1. (A) (B) (C) (D) (E)
2. (A) (B) (C) (D) (E)
3. (A) (B) (C) (D) (E)
4. (A) (B) (C) (D) (E)
5. (A) (B) (C) (D) (E)
6. (A) (B) (C) (D) (E)
7. (A) (B) (C) (D) (E)
8. (A) (B) (C) (D) (E)
9. (A) (B) (C) (D) (E)
10. (A) (B) (C) (D) (E)
11. (A) (B) (C) (D) (E)
12. (A) (B) (C) (D) (E)
13. (A) (B) (C) (D) (E)
14. (A) (B) (C) (D) (E)
15. (A) (B) (C) (D) (E)
16. (A) (B) (C) (D) (E)
17. (A) (B) (C) (D) (E)
18. (A) (B) (C) (D) (E)
19. (A) (B) (C) (D) (E)
20. (A) (B) (C) (D) (E)
21. (A) (B) (C) (D) (E)
22. (A) (B) (C) (D) (E)
23. (A) (B) (C) (D) (E)
24. (A) (B) (C) (D) (E)
25. (A) (B) (C) (D) (E)
26. (A) (B) (C) (D) (E)
27. (A) (B) (C) (D) (E)
28. (A) (B) (C) (D) (E)
29. (A) (B) (C) (D) (E)
30. (A) (B) (C) (D) (E)
31. (A) (B) (C) (D) (E)
32. (A) (B) (C) (D) (E)
33. (A) (B) (C) (D) (E)
34. (A) (B) (C) (D) (E)
35. (A) (B) (C) (D) (E)
36. (A) (B) (C) (D) (E)
37. (A) (B) (C) (D) (E)
38. (A) (B) (C) (D) (E)
39. (A) (B) (C) (D) (E)
40. (A) (B) (C) (D) (E)
41. (A) (B) (C) (D) (E)
42. (A) (B) (C) (D) (E)
43. (A) (B) (C) (D) (E)
44. (A) (B) (C) (D) (E)
45. (A) (B) (C) (D) (E)
46. (A) (B) (C) (D) (E)
47. (A) (B) (C) (D) (E)
48. (A) (B) (C) (D) (E)
49. (A) (B) (C) (D) (E)
50. (A) (B) (C) (D) (E)
51. (A) (B) (C) (D) (E)
52. (A) (B) (C) (D) (E)
53. (A) (B) (C) (D) (E)
54. (A) (B) (C) (D) (E)
55. (A) (B) (C) (D) (E)
56. (A) (B) (C) (D) (E)
57. (A) (B) (C) (D) (E)
58. (A) (B) (C) (D) (E)
59. (A) (B) (C) (D) (E)
60. (A) (B) (C) (D) (E)
61. (A) (B) (C) (D) (E)
62. (A) (B) (C) (D) (E)
63. (A) (B) (C) (D) (E)
64. (A) (B) (C) (D) (E)
65. (A) (B) (C) (D) (E)
66. (A) (B) (C) (D) (E)
67. (A) (B) (C) (D) (E)
68. (A) (B) (C) (D) (E)
69. (A) (B) (C) (D) (E)
70. (A) (B) (C) (D) (E)
71. (A) (B) (C) (D) (E)
72. (A) (B) (C) (D) (E)
73. (A) (B) (C) (D) (E)
74. (A) (B) (C) (D) (E)
75. (A) (B) (C) (D) (E)
76. (A) (B) (C) (D) (E)
77. (A) (B) (C) (D) (E)
78. (A) (B) (C) (D) (E)
79. (A) (B) (C) (D) (E)
80. (A) (B) (C) (D) (E)
81. (A) (B) (C) (D) (E)
82. (A) (B) (C) (D) (E)
83. (A) (B) (C) (D) (E)
84. (A) (B) (C) (D) (E)
85. (A) (B) (C) (D) (E)
86. (A) (B) (C) (D) (E)
87. (A) (B) (C) (D) (E)
88. (A) (B) (C) (D) (E)
89. (A) (B) (C) (D) (E)
90. (A) (B) (C) (D) (E)
91. (A) (B) (C) (D) (E)
92. (A) (B) (C) (D) (E)
93. (A) (B) (C) (D) (E)
94. (A) (B) (C) (D) (E)
95. (A) (B) (C) (D) (E)

Practice Test 1

Directions: Each question or incomplete statement is followed by five suggested answers or completions. Select the best answer and fill in the corresponding oval on the answer sheet.

1. Which of the following empires was LEAST likely to display a tolerant attitude toward subject peoples?

   (A) Ottomans
   (B) Incas
   (C) Persians
   (D) Assyrians
   (E) Romans

2. Accounts of religious activity in the Mediterranean world of the first century CE are found in the

   (A) Upanishads.
   (B) Code of Hammurabi.
   (C) Torah.
   (D) New Testament.
   (E) Qur'an.

3. The immediate cause for the fall of Rome was

   (A) poor harvests.
   (B) the vastness of the empire.
   (C) barbarian members of the army.
   (D) inefficient leadership.
   (E) the movement of Germanic tribes into the empire.

4. Greek colonization accomplished all of the following EXCEPT

   (A) increasing communication among Mediterranean peoples.
   (B) facilitating trade among the *poleis.*
   (C) building a centralized state.
   (D) spreading the Greek language and culture.
   (E) heightening social life in Anatolia.

5. Which of the following civilizations did NOT develop a system of writing?

   (A) Egyptian
   (B) Sumerian
   (C) Incan
   (D) Mayan
   (E) Indus Valley

6. Which of the following artifacts is likely to have been found from the neolithic period?

   (A) Glyphs
   (B) An iron plow
   (C) A representation of a goddess of vegetation
   (D) A codex
   (E) An aqueduct

GO ON TO THE NEXT PAGE

7. Which of the ancient civilizations was situated near the Persian Gulf?
   (A) Sumer
   (B) Egypt
   (C) Yellow River Valley
   (D) Nubian
   (E) Indus Valley

8. Japanese society in 1200 was most similar to which other thirteenth-century society?
   (A) India
   (B) Vietnam
   (C) Byzantium
   (D) Western Europe
   (E) China

9. Tensions between Eastern and Western Christianity
   (A) were resolved by the sixteenth century.
   (B) revolved in part around the iconoclastic controversy.
   (C) resulted in reconciliation between popes and patriarchs in 1054.
   (D) involved only practical, not doctrinal, differences.
   (E) were eased by the political unity existing between the two portions of the Roman empire.

10. Monasticism was
   (A) confined to practitioners of the Christian faith.
   (B) limited to men.
   (C) common to the Buddhist faith.
   (D) a complete withdrawal of religious from the secular community.
   (E) opposed to education as a deterrent to religious faith.

11. In classical times, long-distance trade
   (A) seriously hampered local economies.
   (B) spread epidemic disease in the Roman and Han empires.
   (C) involved the exchange of raw materials rather than manufactured goods.
   (D) was assisted by the cooperation of Parthian merchants.
   (E) required most merchants to undertake extremely long journeys.

12. Women in dar al-Islam
   (A) enjoyed fewer rights than women in many other lands.
   (B) were barred from participation in business activities.
   (C) were considered property.
   (D) were unique in that theirs was not a patriarchal society.
   (E) adopted the use of the veil after encounters with Byzantines and Persians.

13. Which of the following is the proper sequence of Chinese dynasties?
   (A) Tang, Zhou, Shang, Ming, Han
   (B) Shang, Zhou, Han, Tang, Ming
   (C) Han, Shang, Song, Tang, Ming
   (D) Shang, Han, Zhou, Tang, Ming
   (E) Zhou, Tang, Shang, Ming, Han

14. All of the following are true concerning the development of India EXCEPT:
   (A) The Gupta empire embraced the northern portion of the subcontinent.
   (B) Southern India was a maritime-based economy.
   (C) India and Rome were trading partners.
   (D) The Tamils in southern India were not conquered by the Mauryans.
   (E) Central India became the key agricultural center of the country.

GO ON TO THE NEXT PAGE

15. All of the following innovations were attributed to dar al-Islam EXCEPT
    (A) checks.
    (B) caravanserais.
    (C) Arabic numerals.
    (D) camel saddles.
    (E) improvements in Chinese paper.

16. During the Tang and Song dynasties,
    (A) the Chinese failed in their attempts to establish tributary relationships with Korea and Vietnam.
    (B) the cultural traditions of Korea, Vietnam, and Japan became absorbed into those of China.
    (C) China extended its governmental techniques to Korea, Japan, and Vietnam.
    (D) the Viets welcomed the presence of the Chinese in their land.
    (E) Vietnamese women had fewer rights than Chinese women.

17. When Islam first came to East Africa,
    (A) it was eagerly embraced by most Africans.
    (B) the lower classes were the earliest converts.
    (C) African women were accustomed to enjoying more rights than Islamic women.
    (D) elite rulers were the most resistant to the new religion.
    (E) it was especially strong in the central portion of the continent.

18. Which of the following structures is paired correctly with its location?
    (A) Dome of the Rock—Byzantium
    (B) Angkor Wat—Khmer Cambodia
    (C) Taj Mahal—Arabia
    (D) Ka'aba—Palestine
    (E) Hagia Sophia—India

19. The artwork shown on the buildings in the above picture owes its distinctive appearance to
    (A) the influence of the Far East upon Arabic designs.
    (B) the alteration of Arabic art by its contact with Spanish artwork during the Arabic occupation of Spain.
    (C) the desire of Arabic artists to represent Arabic advances in mathematics.
    (D) the blend of Persian art with Islamic tradition.
    (E) the Islamic perception of the artistic representation of the human form as idolatry.

20. Which of the following is NOT an example of a trade organization?
    (A) ASEAN
    (B) SEATO
    (C) LAFTA
    (D) EU
    (E) NAFTA

GO ON TO THE NEXT PAGE

21. Which of the following is true about the empire of Charlemagne and the Holy Roman Empire?
    (A) The Holy Roman Empire was of shorter duration.
    (B) Neither provided a centralized administration for Europe.
    (C) The dissolution of both led to the further fragmentation of government in Europe.
    (D) France and Spain were included in both empires.
    (E) In contrast to the empire of Charlemagne, the Holy Roman Empire brought about the beginnings of a regional state in Germany.

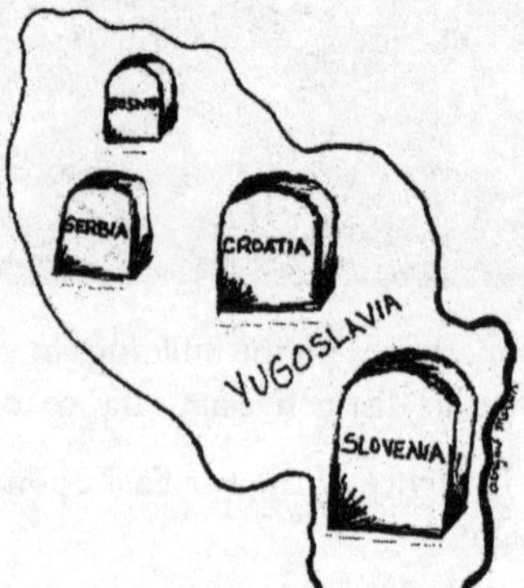

22. The cartoon above expresses the political situation in the Balkans
    (A) under Ottoman rule.
    (B) after the peace agreements of World War I.
    (C) during the Bosnian conflict.
    (D) after the dissolution of communism in Yugoslavia.
    (E) during World War I.

23. All of the following periods saw significant population increases EXCEPT
    (A) the world of 8000 BCE
    (B) mid-fourteenth-century Europe and China.
    (C) western Europe in 1000 CE.
    (D) Europe, Asia, and Africa in the seventeenth century.
    (E) China in the nineteenth century.

24. The first truly global war was
    (A) the Seven Years' War.
    (B) the Hundred Years' War.
    (C) World War II.
    (D) the Thirty Years' War.
    (E) the Crimean War.

25. Which of the following has NOT experienced ethnic cleansing and/or genocide in the twentieth century?
    (A) Bosnia
    (B) Rwanda
    (C) Tibet
    (D) Turkey
    (E) Venezuela

26. Nomadic peoples
    (A) did not participate in long-distance trade networks.
    (B) often organized and led caravans across central Asia.
    (C) had no military organization.
    (D) had rigidly stratified societies.
    (E) remained isolated from settled peoples.

27. Under Ottoman rule,
    (A) slavery was not practiced.
    (B) Christians and Jews were denied freedom of worship.
    (C) only Turks could serve as janissaries in the Ottoman empire.
    (D) the practice of millets led to ethnic separation that exists to the present in the Balkans.
    (E) Buddhists and Hindus were honored as "people of the book."

GO ON TO THE NEXT PAGE

28. Which of the following revolutions was an independence movement?
    (A) The Haitian Revolution
    (B) The French Revolution
    (C) The Mexican Revolution
    (D) The Russian Revolution
    (E) The Chinese Revolution of 1911–1912

29. Which of the following is correctly paired with his philosophy?
    (A) Marx—laissez faire
    (B) Nietzsche—existentialism
    (C) Owen—utilitarianism
    (D) Smith—socialism
    (E) Bentham—communism

30. The Crusades
    (A) decreased the volume of Eurasian trade.
    (B) were a long-term cause leading to the end of the Middle Ages.
    (C) ended with Jerusalem in Christian hands.
    (D) decreased the power of monarchies.
    (E) decreased the power of the Church.

31. All of the following were true of women in Bantu society EXCEPT:
    (A) They were respected as sources of life.
    (B) They could engage in military combat.
    (C) They were prohibited from positions of power.
    (D) They participated in long-distance trade.
    (E) They participated with men in the harvesting of crops.

32. "Whatever silver the merchants may carry with them as far as Cathay, the lord of Cathay will take from them and put into his treasury. And to merchants who thus bring silver they give that paper money of theirs in exchange… and with this money you can readily buy silk and all other merchandise that you have a desire to buy."

    The above words were written about
    (A) Korea.
    (B) Russia.
    (C) Prussia.
    (D) China.
    (E) Mexico.

33. The bubonic plague
    (A) had little effect on the European work force.
    (B) increased reliance on the Catholic Church.
    (C) was especially devastating in India.
    (D) died out after the seventeenth-century London epidemic.
    (E) led to the collapse of the Yuan dynasty in China.

34. The late sixteenth century saw all of the following EXCEPT
    (A) trade in human beings.
    (B) global networks linking the Americas, Africa, Asia, and Australia.
    (C) Manila galleons acting as agents in the trade of Mexican silver for Chinese luxury goods.
    (D) sugar and tobacco going to Europe.
    (E) European guns and manufactures going to Africa.

GO ON TO THE NEXT PAGE

Year	European Population
1500	81,000,000
1600	100,000,000
1700	120,000,000
1800	180,000,000

35. What event or process did NOT contribute to the pattern of population growth shown in the above chart?
    (A) The agricultural revolution
    (B) The devastation of the Hundred Years' War
    (C) New food introduced by the Columbian Exchange
    (D) The end of widespread outbreaks of the bubonic plague
    (E) Population losses during the Thirty Years' War

36. The policy of Nasser toward the relation of his country with the superpowers was most similar to that of
    (A) Kim Il Sung.
    (B) Ho Chi Minh.
    (C) Jawaharlal Nehru.
    (D) Fidel Castro.
    (E) Patrice Lumumba.

37. All of the following were true of the settlement of Australia EXCEPT
    (A) Europeans sailing the Pacific in the sixteenth century had no interest in settling Australia.
    (B) Captain James Cook proclaimed eastern Australia fit for settlement.
    (C) Eastern Australia was more suited for settlement than the western section.
    (D) the native peoples of Oceania were resistant to European diseases.
    (E) the colony was established as a penal colony.

38. The kingdoms and empires of West Africa
    (A) resisted European efforts to carry on the slave trade.
    (B) were part of the global trade in silver.
    (C) became centers of Christianity in Africa.
    (D) did not enslave human beings in their own societies.
    (E) saw themselves as centers of Islamic culture.

39. Trade routes in Africa included all of the following EXCEPT
    (A) ninth-century routes from North Africa to the Mediterranean.
    (B) fifteenth-century routes from Swahili port cities to the Caribbean.
    (C) sixteenth-century routes from central Africa across the Indian Ocean.
    (D) eighteenth-century routes from West Africa to Brazil.
    (E) sixteenth-century routes from central Africa to Jamaica.

40. The Congo
    (A) was an example of nonalignment.
    (B) was subject to dictatorial rule in the 1970s.
    (C) saw democratic rule in the 1960s.
    (D) is linguistically homogeneous.
    (E) began as a French colony.

41. A modern example of the Shia and Sunni divisions in the Muslim world was evident in the
    (A) Gulf War.
    (B) Arab-Israeli War of 1973.
    (C) Iran-Iraq War.
    (D) bombing of the U.S. Marine barracks in Lebanon.
    (E) 2001 attack on the World Trade Center.

GO ON TO THE NEXT PAGE

42. In 1644, the Ming dynasty was overthrown by the Manchu, a foreign people who maintained Chinese tradition by

(A) encouraging intermarriage between the Chinese and the Manchu people.
(B) delegating the maintenance of irrigation and flood-control projects to local authorities.
(C) requiring men to wear their hair in a queue.
(D) requiring those with an audience before the emperor to perform the kowtow.
(E) preserving the Chinese civil service system.

43. Because of their common history of feudalism, both Japan and the nations of western Europe have a tradition of

(A) industrialism.
(B) militarism.
(C) centralized government.
(D) imperialism.
(E) a strong executive.

44. "Most of the inhabitants of India are infidels, called Hindus, believing mainly in the transmigration of souls… They have no harmony nor proportion in their arts and crafts… no advanced educational institutions."

The writer of these words was most probably

(A) a Mughal conqueror of India.
(B) a member of the Jainist religion.
(C) a Hun invader of India.
(D) an Aryan conqueror of India.
(E) a member of the elite class in Harappan society.

45. The Mongols and Ottomans shared all of the following EXCEPT

(A) autocratic authority.
(B) an interest in long-distance trade.
(C) steppe diplomacy.
(D) administrative expertise.
(E) gunpowder technology.

46. In which era and location did women enjoy the greatest opportunities?

(A) Western Europe during the Middle Ages
(B) China under Mao Zedong
(C) Iran under the Ayatollah Khomeini
(D) China under the Song dynasty
(E) Western Europe during the sixteenth century

47. "The just shall live by faith."

The reformer who would have agreed LEAST with this statement would have been

(A) John Knox.
(B) John Huss.
(C) Martin Luther.
(D) Ignatius of Loyola.
(E) John Wycliffe.

48. The French Revolution

(A) gave women the right to vote.
(B) gave France a permanent republican government.
(C) permanently ended autocratic rule in France.
(D) was successful in meeting all its goals.
(E) awakened republican goals among French commoners.

49. A smaller-scale representation of the themes involved in World War II was carried out during the

(A) Spanish Civil War.
(B) invasion of Manchuria.
(C) invasion of the Sudetenland.
(D) annexation of Austria.
(E) invasion of Poland.

50. Which of the following works was a product of the Enlightenment?

(A) *The Communist Manifesto*
(B) *The Gulag Archipelago*
(C) *The Declaration of the Rights of Women*
(D) *Code Napoleon*
(E) *The Origin of Species*

GO ON TO THE NEXT PAGE

Questions 51–53 refer to the areas in the map below.

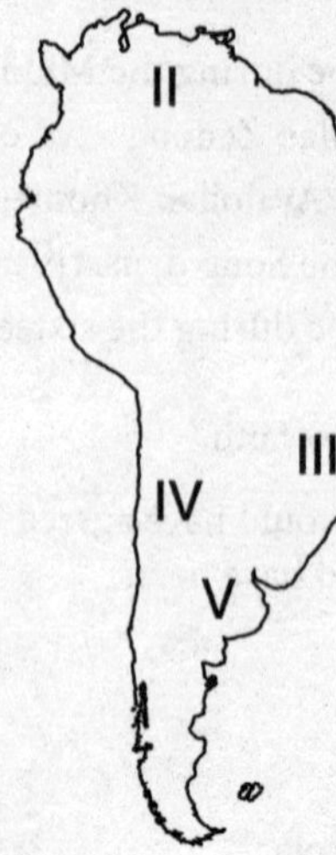

51. Which of the following areas won its independence without a rebellion?

(A) I
(B) II
(C) III
(D) IV
(E) V

52. Which country experienced a general strike of its population in 2001 as a result of the country's economic plight?

(A) I
(B) II
(C) III
(D) IV
(E) V

53. Which area was included in the Gran Colombia envisioned by Bolívar?

(A) I
(B) II
(C) III
(D) IV
(E) V

54. The Romantic movement

(A) was a return to the classical civilizations of Greece and Rome.
(B) celebrated the achievements of man over the wonders of nature.
(C) idealized the role of elite classes.
(D) was tied to the nationalist movement.
(E) emphasized reason over emotion.

55. In the early twentieth century, Russia

(A) lagged behind most nations in steel production.
(B) emerged victorious in the Russo-Japanese War.
(C) remained a backward nation because of serfdom.
(D) led a pan-Slavic movement in the Balkans.
(E) gained new territory from the Ottomans.

56. All of the following are true about the unification movements of Italy and Germany EXCEPT:

(A) Unification had been delayed by their inclusion in the Holy Roman Empire.
(B) Both resulted from entering into military conflicts with other nations.
(C) Both led to weak states susceptible to dominance by their neighbors.
(D) Both were accomplished through skilled diplomacy.
(E) They were the last western European states to unite.

57. As industrialization progressed, all of the following occurred EXCEPT

(A) the emergence of a middle class.
(B) the abolition of slavery in industrialized lands.
(C) decreased political power of the working classes.
(D) decreased interdependence among the members of nuclear families.
(E) a sharp distinction between work and family life.

GO ON TO THE NEXT PAGE

58. By the twentieth century, which country remained an exporter of primary products?

(A) Germany
(B) Argentina
(C) Japan
(D) France
(E) Great Britain

59. The railroad was LEAST vital to the modernization of

(A) Spain.
(B) Canada.
(C) Japan.
(D) Russia.
(E) the United States.

60. Under the rule of Porfirio Díaz, Mexico experienced

(A) declining foreign investment.
(B) a reduction in the power of wealthy landowners.
(C) continuing industrial development.
(D) shorter working hours.
(E) economic independence.

61. By the late seventeenth century, the Ottoman empire

(A) was a leader in technological advances in warfare.
(B) extended its empire at the expense of Russia.
(C) remained an exporter of raw materials.
(D) carried on active trade with Europe.
(E) had a strong central government.

62. Primary sources for the study of the background of World War II would include all of the following EXCEPT

(A) *Mein Kampf.*
(B) The Treaty of Versailles.
(C) *All Quiet on the Western Front.*
(D) a photograph of a German family during the Great Depression.
(E) a felt Star of David worn by a German Jewish citizen.

63. Which of the following is the correct sequence of events leading to World War II?

(A) Japanese invasion of China; Sudetenland annexation; German reoccupation of the Rhineland; Munich Conference
(B) German reoccupation of the Rhineland; Japanese invasion of China; Sudetenland annexation; Munich Conference
(C) Sudetenland annexation; Japanese invasion of China; German reoccupation of the Rhineland; Munich Conference
(D) Munich Conference; Sudetenland annexation; Japanese invasion of China; German reoccupation of the Rhineland
(E) German reoccupation of the Rhineland; Sudetenland annexation; Munich Conference; Japanese invasion of China

64. The twentieth-century leader who considered the United States to be "the Great Satan" was

(A) Helmut Kohl.
(B) Mikhail Gorbachev.
(C) Mahatma Gandhi.
(D) Ayatollah Khomeini.
(E) Anwar Sadat.

65. The immediate cause of World War II in Europe was

(A) the signing of the non-aggression pact between Germany and the USSR.
(B) worldwide depression.
(C) the invasion of Poland.
(D) the provisions of the Versailles Treaty.
(E) the remilitarization of the Rhineland.

GO ON TO THE NEXT PAGE

66. The Buddhas in the photograph above are typical of the portrayal of the Buddha in a sect that

(A) was more strict than traditional Buddhism.
(B) rejected salvation for all.
(C) emphasized individual discipline.
(D) became the most popular form of Indian Buddhism.
(E) permitted popular worship.

67. Marx and Engels considered ______ the "opiate of the people."

(A) religion
(B) democracy
(C) industrialization
(D) education
(E) socialism

68. Post-World War I territorial changes

(A) rewarded Russia with territorial gains.
(B) punished Germany with minor European territorial losses.
(C) united Austria and Hungary.
(D) created the Polish Corridor from German territory.
(E) strengthened the Ottoman empire.

69. The Balkans and the African colonies shared in common

(A) a lack of nationalist aspirations.
(B) divisive religious differences.
(C) a lack of intervention by the United States.
(D) political boundaries drawn without regard for the location of ethnic groups.
(E) ethnic unity.

70. Which of the following is the correct pairing of colony and imperialist nation in 1914?

(A) Hong Kong—United States
(B) Taiwan—Japan
(C) Indochina—Great Britain
(D) Philippine Islands—Great Britain
(E) Burma—France

71. As a general rule, during the era of imperialism

(A) European powers did not attempt to Christianize subject peoples.
(B) colonizing powers retained village agricultural structures.
(C) because of the fear of rebellion, colonists did not fight in the armies of imperial nations.
(D) railroads and utilities were established for the benefit of the colonizing nations.
(E) colonists were well schooled in technology in preparation for eventual independence.

GO ON TO THE NEXT PAGE

72. Both the modernization of Japan and of Russia resulted in the

(A) centralization of political power.
(B) removal of the structures of feudalism.
(C) restoration of monarchical rule.
(D) decrease in taxes imposed on peasants.
(E) development of a representative government.

73. Archeologists studying which culture would discover iron tools and terra cotta figures with hairdos arranged in six buns?

(A) Masai
(B) Kushite
(C) Fulani
(D) Swahili
(E) Nok

74. All the following languages reflect linguistic blending EXCEPT

(A) Ge'ez.
(B) Greek.
(C) Swahili.
(D) Urdu.
(E) English.

75. "No Japanese ships may leave for foreign countries... No Japanese may go abroad secretly."

These requirements were most likely made during

(A) the Russo-Japanese War.
(B) the American occupation after World War II.
(C) the Meiji Restoration.
(D) Tokugawa Japan.
(E) World War II.

76. The kingdom of Aksum can be described by all of the following statements EXCEPT:

(A) It saw a religious controversy that led to the rise of Coptic Christianity.
(B) It was the first sub-Saharan state to mint its own coins.
(C) It fell to the Bantu-speaking peoples.
(D) It was an international trading center.
(E) It was one of the few ancient African kingdoms with a written language.

77. A person's good or evil deeds on earth explain the meaning of

(A) the Aryan *brahmin.*
(B) the Way of Daoism.
(C) the Buddhist *dharma.*
(D) the Buddhist *nirvana.*
(E) the Hindu *karma.*

78. Dr. Sun Yixian

(A) believed in the dictatorship of the proletariat.
(B) proclaimed a republic for China in 1912.
(C) encouraged foreign investment in China after the 1911 revolution.
(D) followed a policy of non-alignment with the superpowers.
(E) had been a strong supporter of the Qing dynasty.

79. Which country changed allegiances between World War I and World War II?

(A) Russia
(B) Japan
(C) Belgium
(D) China
(E) Spain

GO ON TO THE NEXT PAGE

80. Gothic cathedrals differed from Romanesque cathedrals in that the Gothic style featured

(A) flying buttresses.
(B) smaller windows.
(C) simpler columns.
(D) low walls.
(E) rounded arches.

81. Which portion of the former Roman empire did Justinian regain for the Byzantine empire?

(A) northern Gaul
(B) southern Spain
(C) Britain
(D) Asia Minor
(E) Greece

82. During the High Middle Ages, the political unit most likely to create political stability was

(A) the southern Italian states.
(B) England.
(C) the Holy Roman Empire.
(D) France.
(E) Spain.

83. Which school of philosophy best reflects the sentiment of the Hellenistic age?

(A) Utilitarianism
(B) Epicureanism
(C) Stoicism
(D) Liberalism
(E) Cynicism

84. Ashoka accomplished all of the following under his rule EXCEPT

(A) encouraging vegetarianism to reduce the killing of animals.
(B) increasing the power of the brahmins.
(C) embracing Buddhism.
(D) improving the status of Indian women.
(E) sending missionaries to Ceylon.

85. All of the statements listed below are true of the Etruscans EXCEPT:

(A) They were traders and artisans.
(B) They are believed to have migrated from Anatolia.
(C) They transmitted the alphabet through the Greeks to Rome.
(D) They contributed the concept of republican government to Rome.
(E) They transferred many of their religious beliefs to Rome.

86. A future historian examining the nature of the present-day global village would find

(A) the use of French as the international language of trade and diplomacy.
(B) the interconnection of all peoples to the global culture.
(C) an entire world centered around the adoption of U.S. products.
(D) the lessening of national interests in favor of a global culture.
(E) animosity toward the role of the United States in global mass culture.

87. Knowledge of monsoon winds would have been most valuable to

(A) the voyages of Paul of Tarsus.
(B) the Viking voyages.
(C) the expedition of Columbus.
(D) Mongol invaders of Japan.
(E) the voyages of the Malay mariners.

88. The *hijra* resulted in

(A) Muhammad writing the Qur'an.
(B) the birth of Islam.
(C) a campaign against Christians and Jews.
(D) a belief in the divinity of Muhammad.
(E) the end of resistance to Muhammad's followers.

GO ON TO THE NEXT PAGE

89. During the High Middle Ages,

(A) merchants tended to oppose the rule of monarchs.
(B) nationalism declined in western Europe.
(C) the government of France became further fragmented.
(D) elements of parliamentary government began in Great Britain.
(E) the Catholic Church gained wider support.

90. Medieval towns saw the following activities EXCEPT for

(A) markets and fairs.
(B) Christians engaged in usury.
(C) the rise of a market economy.
(D) entertainment.
(E) guild-sponsored apprentices.

91. Kievan Rus

(A) embraced the Byzantine form of Christianity.
(B) successfully repelled Mongol invasions.
(C) increased in power as Byzantium declined.
(D) rejected the use of icons in religious worship.
(E) was isolated from main trade routes.

92. During the European Renaissance,

(A) human reason was de-emphasized.
(B) women were expected to be well-rounded in academic areas.
(C) men and women relied more than ever on the teachings of the Church.
(D) women enjoyed more privileges than during medieval times.
(E) Greco-Roman civilization was admired as a model.

93. Trans-Saharan trade rose markedly during the third century CE with

(A) the mining of salt in the Sahara.
(B) the use of the camel by the Berbers.
(C) the discovery of gold in West Africa.
(D) the arrival of Islam in West Africa.
(E) the rise of powerful empires in West Africa.

94. During their occupation of China, the Mongols

(A) destroyed the Grand Canal.
(B) adopted the Chinese art of footbinding.
(C) failed in their efforts to conquer Korea.
(D) persecuted Christians and Muslims.
(E) set up a tribute empire.

95. "It doesn't matter whether a cat is black or white, so long as it catches mice."

The above quote, spoken by Deng Xiaoping, illustrates his belief that

(A) hardline communism must be maintained in China.
(B) foreign influence should be limited in China.
(C) policies that produced results were more important than Communist doctrines.
(D) the Cultural Revolution was an effective Chinese policy.
(E) racial equality was a major concern of the Communist Chinese society.

STOP!

If you finish before time is up, you may check your work.

Answer Key
Practice Test 1

1. D	25. E	49. A	73. E
2. D	26. B	50. C	74. B
3. E	27. D	51. A	75. D
4. C	28. A	52. E	76. C
5. C	29. B	53. B	77. E
6. C	30. B	54. D	78. B
7. A	31. C	55. D	79. B
8. D	32. D	56. C	80. A
9. B	33. E	57. C	81. B
10. C	34. B	58. B	82. C
11. B	35. B	59. A	83. C
12. E	36. C	60. C	84. B
13. B	37. D	61. C	85. D
14. E	38. E	62. C	86. E
15. C	39. B	63. B	87. E
16. C	40. B	64. D	88. B
17. C	41. C	65. C	89. D
18. B	42. E	66. E	90. B
19. E	43. B	67. A	91. A
20. B	44. A	68. D	92. E
21. E	45. D	69. D	93. B
22. B	46. B	70. B	94. E
23. B	47. D	71. D	95. C
24. A	48. E	72. B	

ANSWERS AND EXPLANATIONS

1. **(D)** The Assyrians adopted the practice of not only killing or enslaving their captives but dispersing them throughout their empire so that the captives would lose their cultural identity. The Incas (B) and the Persians (C) treated their subjects with relative tolerance as long as they did not disobey their laws. Although captive Christian boys were enslaved as janissaries and girls as household slaves, millets gave subject peoples some voice before the sultan (A). The Romans allowed conquered peoples to attain status as citizens or allies (E).

2. **(D)** The New Testament chronicles the missionary efforts of the followers of Jesus throughout the Mediterranean basin in the first century, including the missionary journeys of Paul of Tarsus. The Upanishads (A) were Hindu dialogues between a student and teacher. The Code of Hammurabi (B) was a Babylonian legal code. The Torah (C) deals with the religious history and beliefs of the Jews before the first century. The Qur'an (E) is the holy book of the Muslims, a religion which did not have its beginnings until the seventh century CE.

3. **(E)** The other responses are underlying causes of the fall of the empire; choice (E) was the factor that precipitated the actual takeover of the Roman throne.

4. **(C)** Greece remained a number of disunified city-states, even after colonization spread its borders and culture. Colonization spread the Greek language (D) throughout the Mediterranean world, increasing communication (A); this communication facilitated trade (B). The Greek colonies brought a level of culture to Anatolia that heightened social life (E).

5. **(C)** The Incas did not possess a system of writing but used a system of record-keeping known as the *quipu*, which was a collection of cords of different colors upon which were knots of different sizes and shapes, each representing a different aspect of Incan life and government. The Egyptians used hieroglyphics (A); the Sumerians, cuneiform (B); the Mayas, glyphs (D). The language of the Indus Valley consisted of pictographs that today are undecipherable (E).

6. **(C)** The neolithic period is characterized by an emphasis on fertility; the other responses include items not yet discovered or developed in the neolithic period. Glyphs (A) were developed in the river valley civilizations and in civilizations of the Americas. Iron tools were developed by the Hittites and iron plows specifically were used in the European Middle Ages (B). A codex was a Mayan book (D), and aqueducts were typical of the Roman civilization (E).

7. **(A)** Sumer, in present-day Iraq, was situated to the north of the Persian Gulf. Egypt was located on the Mediterranean (B); the Yellow River Valley civilization was found in China (C). The Nubian civilization was close to the Red Sea (D), while the Indus Valley civilization was near the Arabian Sea (E).

8. **(D)** Both Western Europe and Japan underwent a feudal period of organization. The other societies mentioned did not depend on feudal relationships, which involved a grant of land in exchange for military and/or agricultural services.

9. **(B)** The use of icons, or two-dimensional religious images, in public worship was a highly divisive issue between the Eastern and Western branches of Christianity. In 1054, the eastern and western branches of the Christian Church split (C) permanently (A). The propriety of icons was both a doctrinal and a practical issue (D). By the eleventh century, the Roman empire had already fallen, and the Eastern portion of the empire remained (E).

10. **(C)** Both monks and nuns were found in Buddhist monasteries; they were especially instrumental in the spread of Buddhism in India in the years immediately following its founding. Buddhist monasteries often served as lodging for travelers; Christian monks and nuns often worked among the poor and needy of their respective communities (D). Christian monks copied books by hand during the medieval period in Western Europe (E).

11. **(B)** Both the Roman and Han empires were weakened by disease spread along the Silk Roads. Long-distance trade tended to boost regional economies (A). Both raw materials and manufactured goods were exchanged over long distances (C). Parthian merchants often attempted to keep trade competition out of their area (D). Most merchants did not travel long distances over the trade routes, but rather used middlemen to carry their goods part of the way (E).

12. **(E)** The use of the veil by Muslim women was customary only after the exposure of the Arabic culture to that of the Persians and Byzantines. Initially, Islamic women enjoyed more rights than those of other lands (A) and were allowed to engage in business activities (B). Although subject to their husband (D), Islamic women were not considered property (C).

13. **(B)** Shang (1766–1122 BCE); Zhou (1122–256 BCE); Han (206 BCE–220 CE); Tang (618–907 CE); Ming (1368–1644 CE).

14. **(E)** The key agricultural area of India was the northern part of the country, watered by the Indus and Ganges rivers. The central part was devoted to the Deccan Plateau, the most arid area of the subcontinent. The Guptas conquered the northern half of India (A). The people of southern India, whose land was unsuitable for farming, traded in the Indian Ocean and also through the Arabian Sea with Sumer (B). Roman coins have been found in southern India (C). The Mauryas did not extend their empire to southern India (D).

15. **(C)** Arabic numerals were an Indian invention; they acquired their name because of their transmission to the western world via Arabic caravans. Arabic *sakhs* were the forerunners of checks (A). *Caravanserais* were inns in the Saharan trade in an area dominated by Muslim merchants (B). Camel saddles were introduced to the Sahara by Muslims (D), and the Muslims refined Chinese paper (E).

16. **(C)** While Japan, Korea, and Vietnam retained their own cultural traditions, they did adopt some of the organization of the Chinese government. The Chinese established tributary relationships with Korea and Vietnam (A); the cultural traditions of China influenced those of Korea, Vietnam, and Japan (B). The Viets revolted and won their independence from the Tang (D), and Vietnamese women carried on a more active role in trade than Chinese women (E).

17. **(C)** African women found that they generally enjoyed more gender equality within their own society. Most Africans preferred to cling to their native religion (A). The elite classes tended to be the earliest converts (B, D). Islam was especially strong in North Africa and West Africa and, to a lesser extent, East Africa; it was not commonly embraced in central Africa (E).

18. **(B)** The correct pairs are: Dome of the Rock—Palestine; Taj Mahal—India; Ka'aba—Arabia; Hagia Sophia—Byzantium.

19. **(E)** The Islamic prohibition against portraying human images led to the characteristic geometric designs of Arabic art as well as to the use of calligraphy.

20. **(B)** SEATO, the Southeast Asia Treaty Organization, is a mutual defense agreement, not a trade agreement. ASEAN, the Association of Southeast Asia, was formed to further economic progress and promote political stability in Southeast Asia (A); LAFTA is the Latin American Free Trade Agreement (C); the European Union (EU) is a trade agreement of European countries (D); and NAFTA stands for the North American Free Trade Agreement, which includes Canada, the United States, and Mexico (E).

21. **(E)** While the empire of Charlemagne did not endure much beyond his death, the Holy Roman Empire brought organization to the Germanic states that proved the nucleus of a regional state upon its dissolution. The empire of Charlemagne (768–843) temporarily provided a centralized administration for Europe, but the Holy Roman Empire embraced only Germany and the northern portion of Italy (B). Spain was excluded from Charlemagne's empire; France and Spain were excluded from the Holy Roman Empire (D).

22. **(B)** The peace treaties after World War I created a Yugoslavia that embraced various ethnic groups with different linguistic and religious backgrounds, disallowing the various cultures to enjoy self-rule. Under Ottoman rule, the Balkans peoples were organized in millets within the empire (A). The Bosnian conflict (C), which occurred after the dissolution of communism in Yugoslavia (D), occurred between the various nations that were once included within the country of Yugoslavia, but are currently separate countries. During World War I, the current countries of the former Yugoslavia were divided between Austria-Hungary and the Ottoman empire (E).

23. **(B)** The bubonic plague decimated the populations of Europe and China during the mid-fourteenth century. The world of 8000 BCE saw agriculture spread throughout many locations in the world (A). New

crops and agricultural methods increased populations in western Europe in 1000 CE (C). The Columbian Exchange had added new nutrients to the diets of Europeans, Africans, and Asians in the seventeenth century (D). China in the nineteenth century used high-yield rice crops that increased population (E).

24. **(A)** The Seven Years' War (1756–1763) involved both European nations and their colonies, making it a conflict of global impact. The Hundred Years' War of the fourteenth and fifteenth centuries was confined to France and England (B). World War II followed the Seven Years' War (C). The Thirty Years' War was a European conflict (D), and the Crimean War was a Eurasian conflict (E).

25. **(E)** Bosnia (A) has seen ethnic conflict between Muslims and Christians, Serbs and Croatians; Rwanda (B) between Hutu and Tutsi tribe members; Tibet experienced ethnic cleansing from the Chinese; and Turkey has violated the human rights of the Kurds.

26. **(B)** Assistance in leading caravans was common among pastoral nomads in central Asia. Nomadic peoples often traded with those who traveled along the trade routes (A). They were usually organized along tribal or kinship lines (C) and had societies of elites and commoners (D). They frequently traded with settled peoples (E).

27. **(D)** Millets caused ethnic peoples in the Ottoman empire to communicate directly with the sultan rather than forging relationships with other ethnic groups within the empire, thus setting up a lack of relationships among ethnic and cultural groups that endures to the present. The janissaries were slaves from conquered Christian peoples who were used in the military (A, C). Christians and Jews were given freedom of worship and special privileges as "people of the book" (B, E).

28. **(A)** The Haitian Revolution was a movement of independence against the French. The French Revolution struggled against absolute monarchs and denial of political privileges (B). The Mexican Revolution was one demanding liberal reforms (C). The Russian Revolution arose from a desire to rid Russia of czarist rule (D). The Chinese Revolution was a reaction to rid China of foreign influence and to modernize the country (E).

29. **(B)** Marx (A) is associated with communism; Owen (C) with socialism; Smith (D) with laissez-faire; and Bentham (E) with utilitarianism.

30. **(B)** The Crusades not only furthered the development of cities, which led to the demise of feudalism, but also to the rise in the power of monarchs, which led to the end of feudalism and the formation of nation-states. Knowledge of new products from East Asia and Southwest Asia increased the volume of Eurasian trade (A). Only the First Crusade ended with Jerusalem in Christian hands (C). The power of the Christian Church increased because of the religious fervor of the Crusades (E).

31. **(C)** Bantu women were sometimes placed in positions of authority. Sometimes women participated in all-female combat units (B). They participated in long-distance and local trade (D) and worked alongside men in farming (E).

32. **(D)** The key words in this passage indicating its reference to China are *Cathay* (an ancient name for China), *silver* (the basis of the Chinese currency), and *silk* (a traditional product of China).

33. **(E)** The Yuan (Mongol) dynasty weakened as a result of population losses caused by the plague. The plague especially affected the European serfs (A). It was weaker in India than elsewhere (C). Although not active after the seventeenth-century epidemic, the plague bacillus remains dormant to the present (D).

34. **(B)** Australia was not part of the global trade network. The Manila galleons sailed between Mexico and China from the 1500s to the 1800s (C). Sugar and tobacco were part of the triangular trade (D), while European guns and manufactures were traded for African slaves (A, E).

35. **(B)** The Hundred Years' War preceded this period. The agricultural revolution of the 1600s and early 1700s produced new nutrients (A), as did the Columbian Exchange (C). Population growth was countered, however, by the Thirty Years' War (E). The end of widespread plague episodes also aided in population growth from the 1700s onward (D).

36. **(C)** Nehru and Nasser both believed in nonalignment. The others were all aligned with the Soviet Union.

37. **(D)** The native peoples of Oceania died readily from their lack of immunity to European diseases. Europeans sailing the Pacific in the sixteenth century saw mostly the dry, western side of Australia (A, C). Captain Cook explored the wetter eastern side, proving it suitable for settlement (B). Australia, when opened to settlement, became a colony for prisoners (E).

38. **(E)** The Islamic areas of West Africa were centers of learning respected by the world around them; of particular note was the city of Timbuktu as a cultural center. They cooperated with Europeans in the slave trade (A), were part of the gold trade (B), became centers of Islam (C), and enslaved human beings within their society (D).

39. **(B)** Swahili ports were located in eastern Africa; therefore, they did not connect with routes to the Caribbean. Slaves were transported along this route to Southwest Asia. The slave trade, as well as the exchange of gold, ivory, ebony, and animal skins, crossed the Indian Ocean (C). Choices (D) and (E) were part of the trans-Atlantic slave trade.

40. **(B)** Under Mobutu, the Congo (renamed Zaire) was subjected to a harsh dictatorial rule. The Congo under Lumumba (C) aligned itself with the Soviet Union and received support from the United States under Mobutu (A). The Congo was once a Belgian colony (E) and has seen linguistic disunity (D).

41. **(C)** Iraq is primarily a Sunni nation; while Iran is dominated by the Shia division of Islam. The events in the other answer choices, although all dealing with Islam, did not relate to the Shia/Sunni split.

42. **(E)** The Chinese civil service system was a tradition in place long before the beginning of the Manchu dynasty. The Manchu discouraged intermarriage (A). Chinese tradition delegated the care of irrigation and flood-control projects to the central government (B). Choices (C) and (D) are both incorrect because, although they were requirements of the Manchu dynasty, they were not traditional Chinese practices.

43. **(B)** Militarism linked the feudal traditions of Japan and western Europe. Japan's political tradition was of rule by families or clans with the emperor as a figurehead (E).

44. **(A)** The negative reference to Hinduism reflects the traditional conflict between Muslims and Hindus in India, while the mention of educational institutions indicates a society, such as that of the Mughals, where education is valued.

45. **(D)** The Mongols were known for being ineffective administrators. The Ottomans traded with a number of peoples until the final years of the empire; the Mongols were trade facilitators in the Eurasian sphere (B). Both were knowledgeable of the power structure of peoples of the steppe (C).

46. **(B)** Under Mao, women enjoyed rights similar to those of men. During the European Middle Ages, women enjoyed few opportunities (A), and their status declined during the sixteenth century. Under Iranian Islamic fundamentalism, women were subjected to the rule of men (C), and China during the Song dynasty saw the widespread use of foot-binding (D).

47. **(D)** The quotation is a passage from the Book of Romans in the Christian New Testament which prompted Martin Luther to debate faith v. good works as the key to heaven. As a Roman Catholic reformer, Loyola (D) would have emphasized the importance of good works and Church traditions as necessary to salvation. Knox, Huss, and Wycliffe were all reformers who, like Luther, believed in faith in Jesus Christ as the key to salvation: Knox (A) founded the Presbyterian Church; Huss (B) taught that Biblical authority was above that of the pope; Wycliffe (E) proclaimed that the true head of the Church was Jesus Christ, not the pope.

48. **(E)** Although the French Revolution failed to permanently realize its goals (D), the common people of France would carry on its message into the nineteenth century.

49. **(A)** The Spanish Civil War was a conflict between fascism and republicanism, much like that of World War II. The remaining responses deal with Germany or Japan's annexation or seizure of territory prior to, or at the onset of, World War II.

50. **(C)** Choice (C) was a document reflecting the Enlightenment thinking of the French Revolution. *The Communist Manifesto* (A), written in 1848, describes the ideas of Karl Marx and Friedrich Engels regarding the future of capitalism and the rise of communism. Aleksandr Solzhenitsyn's *The Gulag Archipelago* (B), published in 1974, describes the impact of communist Russia between the revolution of 1917 and the end of Stalin's regime. *Code Napoleon* (D) was a code of laws established in 1804. The code stabilized French society, but limited individual rights in favor of the establishment of political order. Charles Darwin's *The Origin of Species* (E), published in 1859, proposed the theory of natural selection.

51. **(A)** In 1822, Brazil won its independence without fighting when Brazilian creoles demanded independence from Portugal. Venezuela (B) was liberated in 1819 under the leadership of the revolutionary Simón Bolívar. Paraguay (C) won its independence through revolt against Spain in 1811. Chile (D) achieved its independence in 1818 through the military efforts of San Martín and O'Higgins, while Argentina (E) won independence from Spain in 1816 under San Martín's leadership.

52. **(E)** Argentina experienced reactions against its economic decline in 2001. The other countries designated on the map are: Brazil (I), Venezuela (II), Paraguay (colonial boundaries, III), and Chile (IV).

53. **(B)** The northern part of South America, which eventually became Colombia, Ecuador, and Venezuela, was included in Gran Colombia. The remaining areas marked on the map—Brazil (I), Paraguay (III), Chile (IV), and Argentina (V)—were outside the unified region envisioned by Bolívar.

54. **(D)** The emotion of the nationalist movement was reflected in the Romantic movement. The Romantic movement did not emphasize classical themes (A), but rather celebrated the wonders of nature (B), stressed emotion over reason (E), and idealized the role of commoners.

55. **(D)** Russia and Serbia were allied through a pan-Slavic movement. Russia was one of the leaders in steel production (A), but had lost the Russo-Japanese War (B). Serfdom had ended in 1861 (C).

56. **(C)** Both Italy and Germany emerged as strong states after their unification. The Holy Roman Empire embraced German states and those of northern Italy (A). Cavour of Italy and Bismarck of Prussia used diplomacy to unify their respective areas (D). Bismarck engaged in military conflicts with Austria and France to accomplish unification, while Cavour provoked war with Austria (B).

57. **(C)** Through unions the political power of working classes increased. As family members entered the work force, the intimacy of the nuclear family was often eroded (D). Work, now done outside the home, was distinct from family life (E). Mechanization lessened the need for forced labor (B).

58. **(B)** Argentina continued to rely more on exports of raw materials rather than manufactured goods. The other four choices were industrialized nations by the twentieth century.

59. **(A)** Spain, with its mountainous terrain, did not rely on the railroad so heavily or so early as did the other nations included.

60. **(C)** Díaz promoted industry for Mexico. Dependence on foreign investment grew, the wealthy acquired more and more land, and working conditions were poor.

61. **(C)** The Ottomans were unable to keep pace with European industrial development. By this time, the Ottomans were declining (B, E), and they traded with Europe only when Europeans took the intitiative (D).

62. **(C)** Choice (C) is a novel of World War I and a secondary source. The other choices are primary sources. Hitler's *Mein Kampf* (A), written in 1923 while he was in jail, outlined his beliefs in Aryan superiority and his vision for Germany. The Treaty of Versailles (B), which humiliated Germany, paved the way for Germany's future rearmament and aggression. Visuals such as photographs (D) are also primary sources. In this case, the setting of the photograph in depression-era Germany is significant since the shortages of the Great Depression counted among the factors that led that country into World War II. Artifacts such as the Star of David (E) also serve as primary sources. In this example, the treatment of the Jews is significant to the understanding of the course of World War II.

63. **(B)** German reoccupation of the Rhineland (1936), Japanese invasion of China (1937), Sudetenland annexation (September 1938), and the Munich Conference, a reaction to the Sudetenland annexation (September 9, 1938).

64. **(D)** Ayatollah Khomeini strongly opposed modernization and Western influences upon the Iranian people. Helmut Kohl (A) was chancellor of West Germany, an ally of the United States, and was later elected chancellor of a united Germany. Mikhail Gorbachev (B) was the leader of the Soviet Union until the end of communism in that country in 1991. Mahatma Gandhi (C) was the leader of the Indian independence movement against Great Britain. Anwar Sadat (E) was the Egyptian president in the late twentieth century and a signer of the Camp David Accords negotiated by U.S. President Jimmy Carter.

65. **(C)** The invasion of Poland was the aggressive act that initiated World War II. The other answer choices were underlying causes of World War II.

66. **(E)** Mahayana Buddhism, suggested by the ornate Buddhas in the picture, permitted popular worship. It was less strict than the traditional Indian form, or Theravada Buddhism (A). It offered salvation for the faithful (B), was less insistent on discipline (C), and became the most popular form of Buddhism in East Asia and Southeast Asia (D).

67. **(A)** According to Marx and Engels, religion stifled the revolutionary zeal of the people, since people are more likely to accept the status quo if they believe they will be rewarded in the afterlife.

68. **(D)** The Polish Corridor was created to provide the restored nation of Poland a window on the sea. Russia lost territory (A), while Germany's loss of European territory was the greatest (B). Austria and Hungary became two nations (C), and the Ottoman Empire was confined to Turkey (E).

69. **(D)** Both experienced national lines drawn without concern for ethnic and cultural boundaries. Both aspired to independence, while the Balkans experienced religious divisions that produced conflict in the 1990s (B). Both experienced U.S. intervention (C) and ethnic diversity (E).

70. **(B)** The imperialist nation for Hong Kong (A) was Great Britain; for Indochina (C), France; for the Philippines (D), the United States; and Burma (E), Great Britain.

71. **(D)** Railroads were used primarily to transport raw materials, then passengers, for the colonizing nations. Although eventually subject peoples benefited from railroads and utilities, they were constructed initially for the colonizing nations. The spread of Christianity was part of the role of the imperialist nations (A). Village agricultural structures were replaced by cash-crop plantations (B). Colonists fought in the armies of the imperialist powers (C). On the whole, technology transfer was inadequate to train subject peoples for independence (E).

72. **(B)** Both nations had to rid themselves of the feudal structures—in the case of Japan, the shogunate, and in the case of Russia, serfdom. Russian power was already centralized (A) and under monarchist rule (C) which hindered its progress. Neither resulted in a decrease in taxes (D) nor the development of representative government (E).

73. **(E)** Terra cotta figures were common to the Nok culture, and the distinctive hairstyle, which is still worn by some people of Nigeria, was specific to the Nok culture. Iron smelting was also known to the people of early Nigeria, the location of the Nok culture. The Masai (A) were cattle herders in eastern Africa. The Kushite (B) and Swahili (D) cultures of East Africa, although knowledgeable of the process of iron smelting, were not known for the specific terra cotta figures addressed. The Fulani (E) were pastoral people of West Africa.

74. **(B)** Greek did not develop from a blend of diverse languages as did the others. Ge'ez (A) is a Semitic language using Arabic characters and the language of Aksum (present-day Ethiopia). Swahili (C) developed from Bantu. Urdu (D) developed from Hindi and Arabic. English (E) developed from Norman French and Anglo-Saxon.

75. **(D)** Tokugawa Japan was noted for strict isolationist policies. The events in the other answer choices occurred after Japan emerged from isolationism, modernized, and became a world power.

76. **(C)** Aksum fell to the influx of Arabic peoples. In 451, Aksum saw a religious controversy over the nature of Christ that led to the formation of the Coptic Church (A). It traded in the Red Sea, Mediterranean Sea, and the Indian Ocean (D). Its written language was Ge'ez (E).

77. **(E)** *Karma* determines whether a person is reincarnated to a higher or lower caste. The Way of Daosim refers to the way of nature (B), while *brahmin* was an Aryan caste (A). The Buddhist *dharma* consists of the Four Noble Truths and the Eightfold Path (C). *Nirvana* is the Buddhist state of peace reached as the result of several reincarnations (D).

78. **(B)** Sun Yixian attempted to create a republic for China after the revolution. Choice (A) is incorrect since it reflects communist doctrine; Sun Yixian favored democracy. He also believed in nationalism, or the end of foreign influence in China (C). He had participated in the revolution against the Qing (E), and attempted to align the republic with the Western democracies (D).

79. **(B)** Japan fought on the side of the Allies in World War I and of the Axis Powers in World War II. Russia (A) and China (D) fought on the side of the Allies in both world wars. Spain (E) and neutral Belgium (C) were noncombatants in both wars.

80. **(A)** Flying buttresses were a support system characteristic of Gothic cathedrals. Gothic cathedrals featured large stained-glass windows (B). The Gothic style used tall, pointed spires (C) and higher walls (D) than that of the Romanesque style. Pointed arches (E) were employed in the Gothic style.

81. **(B)** Southern Spain was regained by Justinian. Greece and Asia Minor (Anatolia) were already parts of the empire (D, E).

82. **(C)** The Holy Roman Empire had created a new state by uniting the small states of Germany with some of the city-states of Italy. The southern Italian states were disunited (A). France and England were involved in the Hundred Years' War (B, D), and Spain was under the Reconquest (E).

83. **(C)** The ethics of Stoicism appealed to people of many cultural backgrounds, making it more attractive than the other Hellenistic philosophies of Epicureanism and Cynicism (B, E). Liberalism (D) was an eighteenth-century philosophy, and utilitarianism (A) was a nineteenth-century school of thought.

84. **(B)** Ashoka was opposed to the caste system and decreased the power of the brahmins. His emphasis on preserving the lives of animals was a factor in the establishment of reverence for cattle in the Indian culture (A).

85. **(D)** The Etruscans were governed by a king. They had learned of the alphabet through trade with the Phoenicians (C). Among the beliefs they transferred to Rome was the concept of household gods, the *lares* and *penates* (E).

86. **(E)** Although the global village has seen the use of many products from the United States (C), they have not been widely adopted by areas such as China and the fundamentalist Islamic world. English is the international language (A). Many developing nations have yet to connect to the global culture (B). National interests and products are still appreciated in the global village (D).

87. **(E)** The Malay mariners were active traders in the Indian Ocean, where monsoon winds were present. Paul traveled the Mediterranean (A), the Vikings traveled the Atlantic and Baltic (B), Columbus sailed the Atlantic (C), and the Mongols navigated the Sea of Japan (D).

88. **(B)** The *hijra* refers to Muhammad's flight to Medina, where his teachings were more widely accepted. The Qur'an was written after Muhammad's death (A). Muhammad was not worshipped as a divinity but was revered as a prophet (D).

89. **(D)** The Great Council met several times during the thirteenth century, and the Model Parliament was convened in 1295. Merchants favored the law and order that monarchs could provide (A). Nationalism grew in western Europe (B). The French government strengthened after the Hundred Years' War (C), and the Catholic Church and its doctrines began to be questioned after the Black Death (E).

90. **(B)** Christians were forbidden from charging usury, or interest.

91. **(A)** Vladimir chose the Byzantine form of Christianity for his subjects. Situated on major trade routes (E), Kievan Rus decreased in prominence with the rise of Byzantium (C), was unable to repel Mongol rule (B), and used icons (D).

92. **(E)** The Renaissance was a return to classical forms. Women were not encouraged to be interested in learning and probably had fewer privileges than medieval women (B, D). People started to rely on reason rather than the faith of the Church (C).

93. **(B)** Although some trans-Saharan trade had occurred prior to the third century, it was heightened by the use of camels. After the benefits of the camel became more widely known, the lucrative trans-Saharan trade in gold and salt escalated. Salt was mined in the Sahara (A) and gold was discovered in West Africa (C) before the widespread use of the camel. Islam did not arrive in West Africa until the tenth century (D), about the time that powerful empires arose in that region (E).

94. **(E)** Tribute empires were characteristic of the Mongols. They refused to promote foot-binding (B), failed in their efforts to conquer Japan (C), and accepted both Christians and Muslims (D).

95. **(C)** Deng Xiaoping was more interested in using alternatives, such as some elements of the market economy, to bolster the Chinese economy rather than relying on pure communist practices that did not produce results. The Cultural Revolution was no longer in effect during this time (D). Deng was not opposed to allowing foreign influence to improve the Chinese economy (B).

HOW TO CALCULATE YOUR SCORE

Step 1: Figure out your raw score. Use the answer key to count the number of questions you answered correctly and the number of questions you answered incorrectly. (Do not count any questions you left blank.) Multiply the number wrong by 0.25 and subtract the result from the number correct. Round the result to the nearest whole number. This is your raw score.

SAT Subject Test: World History Practice Test 2

Number right		Number wrong		Raw score
□	−	(0.25 × □)	=	□

Step 2: Find your scaled score. In the Score Conversion Table below, find your raw score (rounded to the nearest whole number) in one of the columns to the left. The score directly to the right of that number will be your scaled score.

A note on your practice test scores: Don't take these scores too literally. Practice test conditions cannot precisely mirror real test conditions. Your actual SAT Subject Test: World History score will almost certainly vary from your practice test scores. However, your scores on the practice tests will give you a rough idea of your range on the actual exam.

Conversion Table

Raw	Scaled	Raw	Scaled	Raw	Scaled	Raw	Scaled	Raw	Scaled	Raw	Scaled
95	800	75	760	55	650	35	530	15	420	−5	300
94	800	74	760	54	640	34	530	14	410	−6	290
93	800	73	750	53	640	33	520	13	410	−7	280
92	800	72	740	52	630	32	520	12	400	−8	280
91	800	71	740	51	630	31	510	11	400	−9	270
90	800	70	730	50	620	30	500	10	390	−10	260
89	800	69	730	49	620	29	500	9	380	−11	260
88	800	68	720	48	610	28	490	8	380	−12	250
87	800	67	720	47	600	27	490	7	370	−13	250
86	800	66	710	46	600	26	480	6	370	−14	240
85	800	65	700	45	590	25	480	5	360	−15	240
84	800	64	700	44	590	24	470	4	360	−16	230
83	800	63	690	43	580	23	460	3	350	−17	220
82	800	62	690	42	580	22	460	2	340	−18	220
81	800	61	680	41	570	21	450	1	340	−19	210
80	800	60	680	40	560	20	450	0	330	−20	210
79	790	59	670	39	560	19	440	−1	320	−21	200
78	780	58	670	38	550	18	440	−2	320	−22	200
77	780	57	660	37	550	17	430	−3	310	−23	200
76	770	56	660	36	540	16	420	−4	300	−24	200

Answer Grid
Practice Test 2

1. (A) (B) (C) (D) (E)
2. (A) (B) (C) (D) (E)
3. (A) (B) (C) (D) (E)
4. (A) (B) (C) (D) (E)
5. (A) (B) (C) (D) (E)
6. (A) (B) (C) (D) (E)
7. (A) (B) (C) (D) (E)
8. (A) (B) (C) (D) (E)
9. (A) (B) (C) (D) (E)
10. (A) (B) (C) (D) (E)
11. (A) (B) (C) (D) (E)
12. (A) (B) (C) (D) (E)
13. (A) (B) (C) (D) (E)
14. (A) (B) (C) (D) (E)
15. (A) (B) (C) (D) (E)
16. (A) (B) (C) (D) (E)
17. (A) (B) (C) (D) (E)
18. (A) (B) (C) (D) (E)
19. (A) (B) (C) (D) (E)
20. (A) (B) (C) (D) (E)
21. (A) (B) (C) (D) (E)
22. (A) (B) (C) (D) (E)
23. (A) (B) (C) (D) (E)
24. (A) (B) (C) (D) (E)
25. (A) (B) (C) (D) (E)
26. (A) (B) (C) (D) (E)
27. (A) (B) (C) (D) (E)
28. (A) (B) (C) (D) (E)
29. (A) (B) (C) (D) (E)
30. (A) (B) (C) (D) (E)
31. (A) (B) (C) (D) (E)
32. (A) (B) (C) (D) (E)
33. (A) (B) (C) (D) (E)
34. (A) (B) (C) (D) (E)
35. (A) (B) (C) (D) (E)
36. (A) (B) (C) (D) (E)
37. (A) (B) (C) (D) (E)
38. (A) (B) (C) (D) (E)
39. (A) (B) (C) (D) (E)
40. (A) (B) (C) (D) (E)
41. (A) (B) (C) (D) (E)
42. (A) (B) (C) (D) (E)
43. (A) (B) (C) (D) (E)
44. (A) (B) (C) (D) (E)
45. (A) (B) (C) (D) (E)
46. (A) (B) (C) (D) (E)
47. (A) (B) (C) (D) (E)
48. (A) (B) (C) (D) (E)
49. (A) (B) (C) (D) (E)
50. (A) (B) (C) (D) (E)
51. (A) (B) (C) (D) (E)
52. (A) (B) (C) (D) (E)
53. (A) (B) (C) (D) (E)
54. (A) (B) (C) (D) (E)
55. (A) (B) (C) (D) (E)
56. (A) (B) (C) (D) (E)
57. (A) (B) (C) (D) (E)
58. (A) (B) (C) (D) (E)
59. (A) (B) (C) (D) (E)
60. (A) (B) (C) (D) (E)
61. (A) (B) (C) (D) (E)
62. (A) (B) (C) (D) (E)
63. (A) (B) (C) (D) (E)
64. (A) (B) (C) (D) (E)
65. (A) (B) (C) (D) (E)
66. (A) (B) (C) (D) (E)
67. (A) (B) (C) (D) (E)
68. (A) (B) (C) (D) (E)
69. (A) (B) (C) (D) (E)
70. (A) (B) (C) (D) (E)
71. (A) (B) (C) (D) (E)
72. (A) (B) (C) (D) (E)
73. (A) (B) (C) (D) (E)
74. (A) (B) (C) (D) (E)
75. (A) (B) (C) (D) (E)
76. (A) (B) (C) (D) (E)
77. (A) (B) (C) (D) (E)
78. (A) (B) (C) (D) (E)
79. (A) (B) (C) (D) (E)
80. (A) (B) (C) (D) (E)
81. (A) (B) (C) (D) (E)
82. (A) (B) (C) (D) (E)
83. (A) (B) (C) (D) (E)
84. (A) (B) (C) (D) (E)
85. (A) (B) (C) (D) (E)
86. (A) (B) (C) (D) (E)
87. (A) (B) (C) (D) (E)
88. (A) (B) (C) (D) (E)
89. (A) (B) (C) (D) (E)
90. (A) (B) (C) (D) (E)
91. (A) (B) (C) (D) (E)
92. (A) (B) (C) (D) (E)
93. (A) (B) (C) (D) (E)
94. (A) (B) (C) (D) (E)
95. (A) (B) (C) (D) (E)

Practice Test 2

Directions: Each question or incomplete statement is followed by five suggested answers or completions. Select the best answer and fill in the corresponding oval on the answer sheet.

1. In African societies before 1000 CE,
   (A) slavery was not practiced.
   (B) wealth was determined by private property.
   (C) district chiefs imposed law and order among their people.
   (D) political allegiances centered around kingdoms and empires.
   (E) age grades provided a key form of social organization.

2. The abolition of slavery arose in the early nineteenth century for all the reasons below EXCEPT:
   (A) The slave trade was no longer profitable for Africans.
   (B) Sugar prices were declining.
   (C) Europeans began to concentrate on industry.
   (D) It was no longer as profitable for Europeans as in the previous century.
   (E) There was a threat of slave rebellions.

3. The Russians explored and traded during the eighteenth and nineteenth centuries in all of the following areas EXCEPT
   (A) the Hawaiian Islands.
   (B) Alaska.
   (C) Indonesia.
   (D) California.
   (E) Canada.

4. Which of the following would be difficult to prove or disprove through historical research?
   (A) The Russian culture embraced some elements of the Byzantine culture.
   (B) The Jews had a greater claim to Palestine than the Arabs.
   (C) The Northern Renaissance occurred after the Italian Renaissance.
   (D) The variety of food introduced to the eastern hemisphere by the Columbian Exchange produced population increases.
   (E) The Black Death was confined to European populations.

GO ON TO THE NEXT PAGE

5. The Russo-Japanese War of 1904–1905
   (A) gave Russia a hold over Korea.
   (B) made Japan a world power.
   (C) strengthened national pride in Russia.
   (D) increased the power of the Russian czars.
   (E) resulted in a loss of territory for Japan.

Questions 6 and 7 refer to the following cartoon.

6. The cartoon above reflects the alliances some Africans made with either superpower
   (A) during the era of colonialism.
   (B) during and following their struggles for independence.
   (C) immediately after the Berlin Conference.
   (D) before the founding of the African National Congress.
   (E) after the election of Nelson Mandela.

7. Another geographical area which could replace Africa in the cartoon above would be
   (A) China during the Opium War.
   (B) Indonesia under Sukarno.
   (C) the Indian subcontinent after its partition.
   (D) Iran during the Iran-Iraq War.
   (E) Egypt under Nasser.

8. In the twentieth and early twenty-first centuries, Cairo, Calcutta, and Mexico City have experienced which of the following patterns of migration?
   (A) Migrants fleeing the ravages of ethnic cleansing
   (B) Migrants living in shantytowns in the environs of each city
   (C) Flight from the central cities to the countryside
   (D) Thousands of migrants fleeing to UN-sponsored refugee camps
   (E) The influx of workers from developed nations

9. The concept of yin and yang
   (A) became an integral part of the Buddhist faith.
   (B) balanced male assertiveness and female submission.
   (C) was unique to Confucianism.
   (D) explained reincarnation.
   (E) was a key belief of Manichaeism.

10. The covenant relationship was central to the teachings of
   (A) Islam.
   (B) Buddhism.
   (C) Zoroastrianism.
   (D) Judaism.
   (E) Hinduism.

11. "All who die by the way, whether by land or by sea, or in battle against the pagans, shall have immediate remission of sins."

   These words were a call to
   (A) defend Jerusalem from the Christians.
   (B) rescue Judah from the Babylonians.
   (C) participate in the intifada.
   (D) participate in a crusade to recapture the Holy Land.
   (E) establish Islam in eastern Africa.

GO ON TO THE NEXT PAGE

12. Under Roman law,

    (A) women could not own property.
    (B) patricians enjoyed greater privileges than plebeians.
    (C) accused persons were guaranteed legal protection.
    (D) the accused was guilty until found innocent by a court of law.
    (E) women had few protections.

13. "And in one Lord Jesus Christ, the only-begotten Son of God—being of one substance with the Father, by whom all things were made; who for us men and for our salvation… was made man."

    These words from the Nicene Creed were written by early Christians to emphasize their belief that

    (A) Jesus was a creation of God.
    (B) Jesus' human nature should be stressed.
    (C) Coptic Christians were correct in accepting only Christ's divinity.
    (D) Jesus was at the same time fully human and fully divine.
    (E) Jesus came into existence after the creation of the world.

14. Which exchange on the Silk Roads most influenced the society of the European Middle Ages?

    (A) Wine
    (B) The stirrup
    (C) Grain
    (D) Olive oil
    (E) Christianity

15. In the Soviet Union under Stalin,

    (A) women were prevented from enjoying as many educational opportunities as men.
    (B) women were expected to fully devote themselves to childrearing.
    (C) universities were closed.
    (D) teachers were not allowed academic freedoms.
    (E) technical training was abolished.

16. Wearing the "royal purple" was possible because of the trade of the

    (A) Minoans.
    (B) Egyptians.
    (C) Malaysians.
    (D) Phoenicians.
    (E) Parthians.

17. World War I

    (A) strengthened ties between the Australians and Canadians and the British empire.
    (B) delayed the fall of czarist rule in Russia.
    (C) extended the amount of German colonial territory in Africa.
    (D) saw the strengthening of the Ottoman empire.
    (E) witnessed the active involvement of subject nations of the British empire.

18. The Norman invasion of England

    (A) imposed a brand of feudalism similar to that of other European regions.
    (B) provided the cultural blend that would define the English people.
    (C) retarded the rise of centralized government in England.
    (D) resulted in the loss of territory after William's death.
    (E) was England's first invasion by a foreign power.

19. After the Crusades,

    (A) animosity between East and West temporarily halted trade.
    (B) a middle class developed.
    (C) the power of monarchs decreased.
    (D) banking and manufacturing were interrupted.
    (E) Russians repelled Viking traders.

GO ON TO THE NEXT PAGE

20. "Now the French are come, with their powerful weapons of war to cause dissension among us. We are weak against them; our commanders and our soldiers have been vanquished. Each battle adds to our misery... The French have immense warships, filled with soldiers and armed with huge cannons."

The above words were written by a citizen of

(A) Vietnam.
(B) Singapore.
(C) Burma.
(D) the Philippines.
(E) Siam.

21. "It stopped the fire raids and the strangling blockade; it ended the ghastly specter of a clash of great land armies."

The writer of this passage is referring to

(A) the detonation of the first hydrogen bomb.
(B) the bombing of London.
(C) the bombing of Hiroshima and Nagasaki.
(D) the blockade of Cuba during the Missile Crisis.
(E) the U.S. 2001 bombing of Afghanistan.

22. Japan's quest for empire was fueled by

(A) the need for mineral resources.
(B) a desire to retain its traditional values.
(C) the need for food resources to increase its population.
(D) its desire to establish diplomatic relations with western European nations.
(E) its disdain of Western technology.

Founding Dates of European Universities

Cambridge	1209
Naples	1224
Salamanca	1242
Rome	1303
Prague	1347
Florence	1349
Vienna	1365
Heidelberg	1385
Leipzig	1409
Poitiers	1431
Barcelona	1450
Glasgow	1451
Nantes	1460

23. The chart above illustrates that

(A) the Muslim occupation of Spain delayed the establishment of Spanish universities.
(B) European universities had little impact on the Renaissance.
(C) Western Europe already showed signs of the revival of learning during the High Middle Ages.
(D) the earliest universities were confined to the Iberian Peninsula.
(E) universities tended to develop in northern Europe before they did in the southern part of the continent.

GO ON TO THE NEXT PAGE

24. The structure pictured above

(A) was a monument along the Silk Roads.
(B) was a ceremonial site of the Aryans.
(C) served as a calendar among ancient Mesoamericans.
(D) was a religious site in Neolithic Britain.
(E) marked the ruins of an Incan settlement.

25. "Take up the White Man's Burden—
Send for the best ye breed—
Go bind your sons to exile
To serve your captives' need."

Kipling's poem can best serve to analyze

(A) point of view.
(B) cause and effect.
(C) primary v. secondary sources.
(D) continuity and change.
(E) encounter and exchange.

26. A lasting effect of Charlemagne's reign was

(A) the unification of Italy.
(B) the Reconquest of Spain.
(C) the establishment of Christianity as the foremost religious tradition of western Europe.
(D) bringing unity to the European continent.
(E) the breakdown of education during the Middle Ages.

27. Which area was NOT a part of the Ottoman empire in the sixteenth century?

(A) Istanbul
(B) Baghdad
(C) Vienna
(D) Cairo
(E) Belgrade

28. All of the following applied to the Tang and Song dynasties EXCEPT

(A) foot-binding.
(B) the construction of the Great Wall.
(C) gunpowder technology.
(D) printing with moveable type.
(E) the magnetic compass.

29. "All sorts of merchants come here from the land of Babylon, from the land of Shinar, from Persia, Media, and all the sovereignty of the land of Egypt, from the land of Canaan, and the empire of Russia, from Hungary, and the land of Lombardy and Spain... In ______ is the church of Hagia Sophia, and the seat of the pope of the Greeks, since Greeks do not obey the pope of Rome."

These words describe the city of

(A) Kiev.
(B) Constantinople.
(C) Athens.
(D) Cairo.
(E) Carthage.

30. The Silk Roads included the following routes EXCEPT

(A) Korea through the South China Sea to Malaya.
(B) India through the Arabian Sea and Red Sea to the Nile.
(C) across northern Iran to the Persian Gulf.
(D) China around the Taklamakan Desert to Persia.
(E) China through the Straits of Malacca to India.

GO ON TO THE NEXT PAGE

31. The following contributed to Sumer's contacts with other peoples EXCEPT
    (A) long-distance trade.
    (B) few natural boundaries.
    (C) its fertile land.
    (D) the use of city walls.
    (E) regional trade.

32. The early Mesoamerican societies had in common
    (A) monotheistic religion.
    (B) long-distance trade networks.
    (C) the legend of Quetzalcoatl.
    (D) the cultivation of sweet potatoes.
    (E) the use of pack animals.

33. The Pax Mongolica and the Pax Romana had in common
    (A) a high volume of trade connected with the Silk Roads.
    (B) a common language.
    (C) common religious beliefs.
    (D) a common currency.
    (E) interruption of trade routes by pastoral nomads.

34. The Qur'an
    (A) is considered a holy book in all languages.
    (B) helped to spread the Arabic language.
    (C) proclaims the divinity of Muhammad.
    (D) allowed polytheistic worship.
    (E) contains no similarities to the Old Testament.

35. The most significant cause of the fall of the Aztec empire was
    (A) Spanish weaponry.
    (B) the assistance of Malinche.
    (C) the aid of conquered native peoples to the Spanish army.
    (D) exposure of the Aztecs to smallpox.
    (E) the size of the Spanish forces.

www.earlyoak.co.uk

36. The Delft vase pictured above shows evidence of cultural borrowing between western Europe and
    (A) Meiji Japan.
    (B) Khmer Cambodia.
    (C) Ming China.
    (D) Kievan Rus.
    (E) Safavid Persia.

37. "The revolution will triumph in America and throughout the world, but it is not for revolutionaries to sit in the doorways of their houses waiting for the corpse of imperialism to pass by."

    With these words, Fidel Castro
    (A) demonstrated his belief in the traditional goals of communism.
    (B) supported foreign intervention in the Cuban economy.
    (C) shared his hopes for a gradual, rather than an abrupt, change for Cuba.
    (D) supported the principles of the Monroe Doctrine.
    (E) stated that imperialism in Cuba was already dead.

GO ON TO THE NEXT PAGE

38. Around 1500 CE, the balance of global power
    (A) was dominated by the technological knowledge of China.
    (B) was controlled by the expansion of the Islamic empire.
    (C) centered around Byzantium.
    (D) shifted to the Americas.
    (E) shifted to the technologically advanced Europeans.

39. Indian Ocean trade in the early fifteenth century
    (A) saw the active presence of China's Ming dynasty.
    (B) witnessed the dominance of Portugal.
    (C) was a prominent focus of Japanese trade.
    (D) proved a source of rivalry between England and the Netherlands.
    (E) was overshadowed by trans-Atlantic trade.

40. In their use of natural resources, the Bantu people were most similar to the
    (A) Aryans.
    (B) Mongols.
    (C) Persians.
    (D) Hittites.
    (E) Egyptians.

41. Herodotus's statement, "Neither snow nor rain nor heat nor gloom of night stays these couriers from the swift completion of their appointed rounds," refers to the communication network of the
    (A) Hellenistic empire of Alexander.
    (B) Byzantine empire of Justinian.
    (C) Mongol Peace.
    (D) Incas.
    (E) Royal Road of Achaemenid Persia.

42. All of the religions listed below were spread through missionary endeavor EXCEPT
    (A) Christianity.
    (B) Buddhism.
    (C) Islam.
    (D) Manichaeism.
    (E) Judaism.

43. Which process would contribute most widely to the growth of civilization in Mesoamerica?
    (A) The rise of centralized government
    (B) The cultivation of maize
    (C) The domestication of animals
    (D) The use of iron tools
    (E) The use of the wheel

44. The European Renaissance owed its beginnings to
    (A) the revival of learning in northern Europe.
    (B) the unification of Italy.
    (C) the trade network of the Hanseatic League.
    (D) the stability of Charlemagne's empire.
    (E) the Islamic Golden Age.

45. As a result of the Protestant Reformation,
    (A) Europe was united on religious issues.
    (B) the power of the papacy increased.
    (C) education was de-emphasized.
    (D) the Roman Catholic Church altered its basic beliefs.
    (E) national political units were strengthened.

46. The majority of the labor force that flocked to the eighteenth-century factories of England came from
    (A) southern Europe.
    (B) the tenements of London.
    (C) areas where farmers were forced off their land by the enclosure movement.
    (D) Asia.
    (E) farms in eastern Europe.

47. In the seventeenth and eighteenth centuries, Europeans and Africans had in common the following EXCEPT for
    (A) engagement in the slave trade.
    (B) the rise of autocratic rulers in regional states.
    (C) an appreciation of European technology.
    (D) a general decline in their respective populations.
    (E) participation in the triangular trade.

GO ON TO THE NEXT PAGE

48. Which of the following scientists is correctly matched with his or her discovery or invention?

(A) Edison—radio
(B) Pierre and Marie Curie—germ theory of disease
(C) Ford—the assembly line
(D) Pasteur—radioactivity
(E) Marconi—phonograph

49. British democracy in the eighteenth century included all of the following EXCEPT

(A) the secret ballot.
(B) increased power for the House of Commons.
(C) universal manhood suffrage.
(D) increased power for the monarch.
(E) the end of property requirements to enter Parliament.

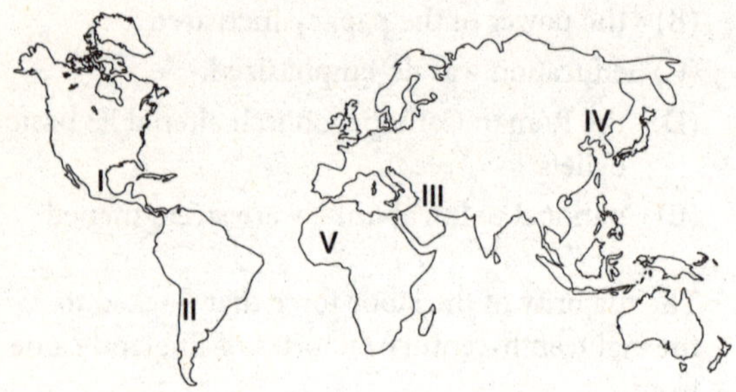

50. Prior to 1000 CE, the areas marked on the above map were all sites of

(A) iron-smelting.
(B) major religious monuments.
(C) discoveries of early humans.
(D) early agriculture.
(E) principal trade cities.

51. "What is the sound of one hand clapping?" is a riddle typical of

(A) Confucianism.
(B) Legalism.
(C) Stoicism.
(D) Zen Buddhism.
(E) Shintoism.

52. During the age of exploration,

(A) Western nations remained aloof from contacts with the East.
(B) the Japanese and Chinese welcomed Christian missionaries.
(C) China abandoned its voyages of exploration in the fifteenth century.
(D) China made efforts to enter global trade after the defeat of the Mongols.
(E) Japan opened its doors to foreign trade.

53. The development of what crop most greatly influenced the growth of slavery in the Americas?

(A) Cotton
(B) Tea
(C) Rice
(D) Sugar
(E) Indigo

54. "The ordinary means therefore to increase our wealth and treasure is by foreign trade, wherein we must ever observe this rule: to sell more to strangers yearly than we consume of theirs in value."

These words would most likely have been written by a supporter of

(A) joint-stock companies.
(B) utopianism.
(C) mercantilism.
(D) socialism.
(E) utilitarianism.

55. The African diaspora involved all of the following areas EXCEPT

(A) the Caribbean.
(B) South America.
(C) North America.
(D) Europe.
(E) Australia.

GO ON TO THE NEXT PAGE

56. The new political order in Europe following the Napoleonic Age led to
    (A) the return of liberal governments to power.
    (B) colonial Latin American governments declaring their independence.
    (C) France's power.
    (D) the decrease in the power of Great Britain and Prussia.
    (E) an imbalance in political power.

57. As a result of the Opium War,
    (A) Great Britain was denied extraterritoriality in China.
    (B) Great Britain received control of Singapore.
    (C) foreign contact was welcomed by the Chinese.
    (D) the United States proposed equal trading rights for all nations in China.
    (E) the number of cities open to foreign inhabitants was decreased.

58. By the eighteenth century, a key difference between the regions of India and China and that of early modern Europe was that
    (A) while China and India developed as small regional states, Europe unified under a centralized government.
    (B) while Mughal India and China were centralized political entities, Europe developed as an area of independent states.
    (C) while India and China became fragmented by religious differences, Europe was not.
    (D) both China and India remained relatively isolated from global trade, while Europe embraced trade.
    (E) the populations of India and China were decreasing, while European populations were increasing.

59. Reforms that accompanied the industrial revolution in the 1800s included all of the following EXCEPT
    (A) collective bargaining.
    (B) child labor laws.
    (C) women's suffrage.
    (D) minority rights.
    (E) free public education.

60. The regimes of Peter the Great and Nicholas II were alike in that they
    (A) upheld serfdom.
    (B) experienced difficulties in maintaining a large army.
    (C) allowed the Duma to participate in policyholding.
    (D) upheld the autocratic powers of the czar.
    (E) sought to westernize Russia.

61. The principles of the scientific revolution
    (A) can be expressed by the words of Descartes: "I think, therefore I am."
    (B) relied more completely on the teachings of the Church.
    (C) implemented observation and experimentation.
    (D) relied on common sense.
    (E) were based on the findings of ancient scientists and mathematicians.

62. In the Pacific during the new imperialism,
    (A) Japanese migrants became a majority in Malaysia.
    (B) the Dutch ruled Indonesia indirectly from Amsterdam.
    (C) European imperialists were conscious of preserving the botanical environment of the areas they dominated.
    (D) Siam came under the control of Belgium.
    (E) the welfare of sugar planters dominated U.S./Hawaiian relations.

GO ON TO THE NEXT PAGE

63. Population trends at the beginning of the twenty-first century show that
    (A) the birth rate in Mediterranean Europe is steadily increasing.
    (B) industrialized nations are experiencing a large influx of older workers.
    (C) developing nations must deal with the problems of an increasingly older population.
    (D) Japan's population is becoming increasingly younger.
    (E) in spite of famine and disease, the population of Africa continues to increase.

64. The revolutions of 1848
    (A) permanently replaced conservatives.
    (B) succeeded in providing a more democratic Europe.
    (C) upheld the policies of Metternich.
    (D) failed to achieve their goals.
    (E) proved the end of the ideals of the French Revolution.

65. The Europeans were assisted in their efforts to colonize Africa by all EXCEPT
    (A) superior technology.
    (B) the discovery of quinine.
    (C) the invention of the steam engine.
    (D) African unity.
    (E) cable communications.

66. The term "economic imperialism" best describes the case of
    (A) Kenya.
    (B) the Congo.
    (C) Latin America.
    (D) India.
    (E) Angola.

67. Feudalism was dealt a blow in the High Middle Ages by all EXCEPT
    (A) the Black Death.
    (B) the Hundred Years' War.
    (C) the rise of cities.
    (D) the agricultural revolution.
    (E) the increase in the number of Huguenots.

68. The end of World War I saw all of the following EXCEPT
    (A) the re-emergence of Poland on the map of Europe.
    (B) independent former Ottoman lands in Southwest Asia.
    (C) an influenza epidemic.
    (D) new attitudes concerning the role of women.
    (E) the breakup of the Austro-Hungarian empire.

69. The Russian empire was brought down by
    (A) rapid industrialization.
    (B) czarist embrace of nationalistic sentiment.
    (C) revolts of ethnic minorities.
    (D) the lack of bread and fuel.
    (E) the liberal rule of the czars.

70. A totalitarian state is characterized by all EXCEPT
    (A) one-party rule.
    (B) state control of all aspects of public and private life.
    (C) the use of force to crush opposition.
    (D) relegation of the needs of the individual to those of the state.
    (E) religious persecution.

GO ON TO THE NEXT PAGE

71. Lenin and Stalin differed in their rule in that only
    (A) Lenin allowed a degree of the market economy in the USSR.
    (B) Lenin's regime sponsored technical schools.
    (C) Lenin placed all power in the Communist Party.
    (D) Lenin created a command economy for the USSR.
    (E) Lenin placed communication under government control.

72. Under Gupta India,
    (A) the caste system was more loosely defined.
    (B) infanticide and *sati* were outlawed.
    (C) women's position in society improved.
    (D) government became more centralized than under the Mauryans.
    (E) arranged marriages were the custom.

73. The Russian Revolution of March 1917 and the Chinese Revolution of 1911–12 were alike in that they
    (A) were able to provide strong central governments.
    (B) resulted in temporary democratic governments.
    (C) led to the long-term establishment of self-governing republics.
    (D) produced a second revolution.
    (E) were strongly supported by the Western democracies.

74. After the breakup of the Ottoman empire,
    (A) both Turkey and Persia overthrew Western powers in their midst.
    (B) Turkey instituted a republic based on Western law.
    (C) the new country of Iran strictly limited the rights of women.
    (D) Saudi Arabia overthrew Western control.
    (E) Turkey and Saudi Arabia promoted industry more than Persia did.

75. The period between World War I and World War II saw all EXCEPT
    (A) the influence of African and Asian styles in Western art.
    (B) novels reflecting the optimism of the era.
    (C) the rise of the science of psychoanalysis.
    (D) non-traditional styles of music.
    (E) the formulation of the theory of relativity.

76. Existentialism is to philosophy as stream of consciousness is to
    (A) music.
    (B) theater.
    (C) architecture.
    (D) literature.
    (E) art.

77. The concept of "form follows function" would have been implemented by
    (A) Jean Paul Sartre.
    (B) Igor Stravinsky.
    (C) Pablo Picasso.
    (D) Franz Kafka.
    (E) Frank Lloyd Wright.

78. After World War I, European governments
    (A) saw coalitions bring stability.
    (B) witnessed the strengthening of imperial rule.
    (C) saw the strengthening of democracies.
    (D) were able to recover economically from World War I.
    (E) prompted some Europeans to want the stability of totalitarianism.

79. Fascism differed from communism in that fascism
    (A) upheld loyalty to the state as its highest goal.
    (B) permitted multi-party rule.
    (C) focused on the nationalist goals of a single country.
    (D) sought a classless society.
    (E) sought worldwide revolution.

GO ON TO THE NEXT PAGE

80. "It is a grandiose idea to think of consolidating the New World into a single nation, united by pacts into a single land."

These world were written by

(A) Benito Júarez.
(B) Juan Perón.
(C) Porfirio Díaz.
(D) Simón Bolívar.
(E) Vicente Fox.

81. The weakness of the League of Nations between the world wars was shown in all BUT

(A) Hitler's annexation of Austria.
(B) the Italian invasion of Ethiopia.
(C) the Japanese invasion of Manchuria.
(D) Hitler's movement into Russia.
(E) Hitler's rearmament of Germany.

82. "Dialogue is God's style" was an idea embraced by

(A) Nicolae Ceausescu.
(B) Lech Walesa.
(C) F.W. de Klerk.
(D) V.I. Lenin.
(E) Fidel Castro.

83. The dispute over Kashmir has involved all of the following issues EXCEPT

(A) terrorist activity in the twenty-first century.
(B) conflict between Muslims and Buddhists in South Asia.
(C) global concern over the dispute because of the nuclear potential of India and Pakistan.
(D) Chinese occupation of a portion of its territory.
(E) its independence movements in the twenty-first century.

84. After World War II, Japan

(A) unlike Germany, was not occupied by Allied powers.
(B) became a representative democracy.
(C) retained control over its Pacific island colonies.
(D) was allowed to keep its emperor as head of state.
(E) would endure a long road to economic recovery.

85. Both world wars

(A) contributed to the end of European global hegemony.
(B) saw the decline of Japanese power.
(C) contributed to the Russian domination of Europe.
(D) saw the rise of new totalitarian states in their aftermath.
(E) led to the creation of superpowers.

86. Global depression between the world wars

(A) was the result of a steady postwar decline in European prosperity.
(B) was in part caused by reparations imposed after World War I.
(C) occurred despite U.S. efforts to pour continued capital into Europe.
(D) produced no effect on colonial economies.
(E) strengthened Germany's Weimar Republic.

87. "... our Celestial Empire possesses all things in prolific abundance and lacks no product within its own borders. There was therefore no need to import the manufactures of outside barbarians in exchange for our own produce."

These words were written by a citizen of

(A) Japan.
(B) China.
(C) Indonesia.
(D) Mughal India.
(E) Korea.

GO ON TO THE NEXT PAGE

88. "Freeman and slave, patrician and plebeian, lord and serf, guild-master and journeyman, in a word, oppressor and oppressed, stood in constant opposition to one another, carried on an uninterrupted, now hidden, now open fight, a fight that each time ended, either in a revolutionary reconstitution of society at large, or in the common ruin of the contributing classes."

These words describe the philosophy behind

(A) fascism.
(B) capitalism.
(C) mercantilism.
(D) feudalism.
(E) communism.

89. The Seljuk Turks

(A) used their knowledge of gunpowder to overpower the Ottoman Turks.
(B) successfully resisted Mongol invasion into their territory.
(C) assimilated into the Persian culture.
(D) were defeated by the Byzantines at Manzikert.
(E) were efficient administrators of their empire.

90. The Mongols

(A) caused the Chinese to adopt their traditions.
(B) were no longer a threat to Chinese borders after the fall of the Yuan dynasty.
(C) although forced by Stalin to move from the Crimea in the twentieth century, remained a presence in central Asia.
(D) had one of the longest-lasting empires in history.
(E) were untouched by the Black Death.

91. Which of these waterways was a major trade route in early Russia?

(A) the Oder
(B) the Aegean Sea
(C) the Elbe
(D) the Dnieper
(E) the Danube

92. "In serving his parents, a filial son renders utmost respect to them at home; he supports them with joy; he gives them tender care in sickness; he grieves at their death; he sacrifices to them with solemnity."

The above words would describe the goals of

(A) Daoism.
(B) Hinduism.
(C) Buddhism.
(D) Confucianism.
(E) Legalism.

93. "Listen to the voice of the people in all that they say to you; for they have not rejected you, but they have rejected me from being king over them. Just as they have done to me from the day I brought them out of Egypt, to this day forsaking me and serving other gods, so also they are doing to you."

These words are a passage from

(A) the New Testament.
(B) the Qur'an.
(C) the Vedas.
(D) Dao De Ching.
(E) the Old Testament.

94. During the late twentieth century, the government of Argentina moved toward

(A) representative democracy.
(B) socialism.
(C) fascism.
(D) communism.
(E) monarchism.

95. "He who studies how things originated and came into being… will achieve the clearest view of them," were words spoken by

(A) Aristotle.
(B) Ptolemy.
(C) Virgil.
(D) Alexander the Great.
(E) Herodotus.

STOP!

If you finish before time is up, you may check your work.

Answer Key
Practice Test 2

1. E
2. A
3. C
4. B
5. B
6. B
7. C
8. B
9. B
10. D
11. D
12. C
13. D
14. B
15. D
16. D
17. E
18. B
19. B
20. A
21. C
22. A
23. C
24. D
25. A
26. C
27. C
28. B
29. B
30. A
31. D
32. C
33. A
34. B
35. D
36. C
37. A
38. E
39. A
40. D
41. E
42. E
43. B
44. E
45. E
46. C
47. D
48. C
49. D
50. D
51. D
52. C
53. D
54. C
55. E
56. B
57. D
58. B
59. C
60. D
61. C
62. E
63. E
64. D
65. D
66. C
67. E
68. B
69. D
70. E
71. A
72. E
73. B
74. B
75. B
76. D
77. E
78. E
79. C
80. D
81. D
82. C
83. B
84. B
85. A
86. B
87. B
88. E
89. C
90. C
91. D
92. D
93. E
94. A
95. A

ANSWERS AND EXPLANATIONS

1. **(E)** Age grades were groups of villagers from the same age group who passed through life experiences and responsibilities at the same time. African societies took slaves in battle (A). Wealth was determined by the number of slaves a person owned (B). African slavery caused conflicts among chiefs (C). Political allegiances centered around kinship groups (D).

2. **(A)** While in the early nineteenth century the slave trade was no longer as profitable for Europeans as it had been previously, it continued to be a profitable source of income for Africans. Most slaves were used on the sugar plantations (B), while industry did not need slave labor (C, D).

3. **(C)** The Russians did not become involved in Indian Ocean trade, but they did explore the other areas listed and claimed Alaska in the 1800s (B).

4. **(B)** Choice (B) is an opinion rather than a fact that can be proven or refuted.

5. **(B)** Japan, a third-rate power, was victorious over the major power of Russia during the war. Japan would dominate Korea (A) and receive control of the Liaodong Peninsula and the southern half of Sakhalin Island (E). Russia was humiliated (C), and the power of the czars decreased (D).

6. **(B)** An example is the political situation in the Congo after independence. New African countries had to make the decision of aligning with a superpower or remaining nonaligned. During colonialism, they were linked with their European power (A), as they were after the Berlin Conference (C), and before the founding of the African National Congress (D). By the election of Mandela, the Cold War had ended and alignment was no longer an issue (E).

7. **(C)** After independence, when Pakistan lost its battle over Kashmir, it sought an alliance with the United States, while India received military aid from the Soviet Union.

8. **(B)** Migrants from rural areas have been seen around all three cities—a form of internal migration. Choice (C) is another example of internal migration. Choices (A), (D), and (E) illustrate external migration, which occurs over long distances or across political boundaries.

9. **(B)** Gender distinctions were inherent in the balance of nature represented by yin and yang. Yin and yang became an integral part of Daoism (A, C, E). The concepts explained ancient Chinese beliefs of the balance in nature (D).

10. **(D)** Judaism was based on a covenant, or agreement, between God and man. Islam is based on following the Five Pillars, while Buddhism is based on the Four Noble Truths and the Eightfold Path. Zoroastrian belief reflects a battle between good and evil, while Hinduism relies on a person's *karma*, or good and evil deeds, to determine his or her fate.

11. **(D)** The Roman Catholic Church promised those who undertook a crusade the immediate forgiveness of their sins. Key words are *battle* and *remission of sins*, a concept that would be contrary to the beliefs of those in (C) and (E).

12. **(C)** The accused were offered full protection under Roman law. All persons were equal before the law (B, E). Roman women were allowed to own property (A).

13. **(D)** The Council of Nicea was convened to reaffirm the belief of the Church in the human and divine natures of Christ. Christianity believes that Jesus is God from eternity (A, E).

14. **(B)** The stirrup contributed to knighthood in the European Middle Ages. The other answer choices, although all exchanges along the Silk Road, did not directly affect the development of feudal society as the stirrup did.

15. **(D)** Teachers who criticized the Soviet government in any way were subject to punishment by the state. Women were considered important to the welfare of the state and often worked in industry (A, B).

16. **(D)** The rare purple dye was obtained from the murex shell off the coast of Phoenicia. The limited amounts of the dye made purple a color that only the very elite could afford to procure.

17. **(E)** Subject nations served in the British army during World War I. Their participation in the war caused these areas to loosen their ties with Britain and desire independence (A). World War I deprivations hastened the fall of czarist rule in Russia (B). After World War I, Germany lost its colonial territories in Africa (C), and the Ottoman empire was limited to Turkey (D).

18. **(B)** The Norman and Anglo-Saxon blends would provide the basis for English language and culture. The Norman version of feudalism established a direct relationship between a vassal and the monarch (A), which promoted the rise of centralized government in England (C). It was the last successful invasion of England by a foreign power (E).

19. **(B)** The middle class, comprised of merchants, bankers, and traders, strengthened after the increased trade accompanying the Crusades. Trade increased between Europe and Asia (A), the power of monarchs increased because of the support of merchants (C), and the increase in trade promoted the strengthening of banking and manufacturing interests (D). By the time of the Crusades, Viking traders were an integral part of Russian society (E).

20. **(A)** Vietnam was colonized by France. Burma and Singapore were ruled by the British, and the Philippines by the United States. Siam was not controlled by a foreign power.

21. **(C)** The United States felt that the atomic bomb was an alternative to a massive land invasion of Japan. Japan had previously been subjected to Allied fire raids, also referenced in the quotation. The detonation of the first hydrogen bomb occurred in 1952 (A). London was not subjected to fire raids during World War II (B), nor was Cuba during the 1962 Missile Crisis (D). Afghanistan was the target of neither fire raids or blockade during the conflict against the Taliban (E).

22. **(A)** Japan possessed few resources to operate its factories. Japan needed food resources because of its large population (C). After World War II, Japan would adopt some Western technology, especially in its factories (E).

23. **(C)** By the 1200s, the beginnings of universities demonstrated that learning had already shown signs of strong renewal in Europe. Universities were already established in the Spanish cities of Salamanca and Barcelona during the Muslim occupation (A). There is insufficient information in the chart to respond to (B). Only one of the earliest universities was found on the Iberian Peninsula (D). Early universities were scattered through the European continent (E).

24. **(D)** Stonehenge was a religious site in England. Its structure appears to have been constructed to mark the changing of the seasons, an important concept in Neolithic religion.

25. **(A)** Kipling's poem reveals his satirical treatment of the "mission" of imperialist nations toward subject peoples.

26. **(C)** Under Charlemagne, Christianity became the primary unifying force in Europe. Italian unification might have been a result if Charlemagne's empire had endured longer, but its division after his death placed Italy within the domain of Lothar, which also included part of Germany (A). Spain was not a part of Charlemagne's empire (B). His reign did not last long enough to bring lasting unity to the continent (D). Charlemagne fostered education by setting up palace and monastery schools (E).

27. **(C)** Vienna was outside the domain of the Ottomans. Istanbul (A) in Anatolia; Baghdad (B) in Iraq at the eastern extreme of the empire; Cairo (D) in Egypt; and Belgrade (E) in the Balkans were all located within the Ottoman borders in the sixteenth century.

28. **(B)** The Great Wall as it appears today is a restructuring of China's defensive walls that had arisen under the Qin and Han empires. Gunpowder, moveable type, and the magnetic compass were invented during the Tang and Song dynasties (C, D, E). The practice of foot-binding began during this period (A).

29. **(B)** Key words that refer to Constantinople are *Hagia Sophia* and *the pope of the Greeks.* The varied origins of the merchants also indicate an area with a high volume of trade. Kiev in Russia (A) and Cairo in Egypt (D) are incorrect answers because the passage mentions traders coming from Russia and from Egypt. Although the passage refers to the Greeks, Athens (C) is an incorrect answer

because of the reference to the pope of the Greeks, or the patriarch of the Eastern Orthodox Church, who resided in Constantinople. Carthage (E), a Phoenician colony in North Africa, would not have seen traders from Russia nor the presence of the Orthodox faith.

30. **(A)** The Silk Roads did not run through Korea. The other land and sea routes mentioned were parts of the Silk Roads.

31. **(D)** Sumerian cities were walled because of the lack of natural boundaries (B) to keep invaders from overrunning its fertile land (C). Sumer traded locally and also over long-distances, most notably with the peoples of the Indus Valley (A, E).

32. **(C)** The legend of Quetzalcoatl was passed from one society to another in Mesoamerica. All the early Mesoamerican societies were polytheistic (A). Some, such as the Toltecs, engaged in long-distance trade (B). Sweet potatoes were cultivated in the lowlands of the Andes Mountains (D), while the use of pack animals was confined to the societies of South America (E).

33. **(A)** The Mongols protected trade along the Silk Roads, while Roman roads connected with the routes of the Silk Roads. During the Pax Mongolica and the Pax Romana, trade routes were secure (E). While the Romans had a common language, the Mongols did not (B). Christianity was a major Roman religion, but there were many Romans who did not adhere to its beliefs; the Mongols did not share a common religion (C). Neither had a common currency (D).

34. **(B)** Since the Arabic version of the Qur'an was considered the only true one, the desire to read it prompted the spead of Arabic. The Qur'an does not proclaim the divinity of Muhammad (C), and it allowed the worship of only one god, Allah (D). Some of the passages in the Qur'an are similar to those in the Old Testament (E).

35. **(D)** Without any immunity to smallpox, the Aztec people, once exposed to the disease, died by the thousands. Spanish weaponry eased the conquest of a much larger army (A, E), while the assistance of Malinche as interpreter facilitated the entry of the Spanish into the Aztec empire (B). Conquered peoples joined the Spanish army out of animosity toward the Aztecs (C). Still, its was the devastation of disease that most effectively brought down the Aztec empire.

36. **(C)** The production of Delft China was initiated in response to the beauty of Ming porcelain and also to the relative unavailability of Ming porcelain after China became increasingly isolated from world trade.

37. **(A)** The reference to revolution indicates Castro's acceptance of a traditional goal of communism. The fact that Castro refers to foreign intervention as imperialism indicates that he does not support the Monroe Doctrine, which constituted a "hands-off" policy toward European imperialism, but not to influence on the part of the United States.

38. **(E)** After 1500, European technology had far surpassed that of the Eastern cultures. From that time until the world wars, European hegemony was a reality. Both Islamic cultures and the culture of China would lose interest in technological advancement in favor of the preservation of their traditional cultures (A, B). In 1500, technological development in the Americas was far behind that of the Europeans as well (D).

39. **(A)** In the first few years of the fifteenth century, the Chinese sent out massive voyages of reconnaissance into the Indian Ocean. Portugal would not enter the Indian Ocean trade until the voyage of Da Gama in 1498 (B). The Japanese were not interested in Indian Ocean trade at that time (C). England and the Netherlands had not yet entered the Indian Ocean trade (D), and the trans-Atlantic trade was also not a reality until the voyages of Columbus (E).

40. **(D)** Both the Bantu and the Hittites possessed and spread the knowledge of iron smelting as they migrated throughout sub-Saharan Africa and Central Asia, respectively. Historians credit the Hittites as the originators of the process; some historians also believe that the Bantu people may also have developed iron smelting independently. The Aryans (A), who were largely pastoral nomads, learned the use of iron from other peoples. The Mongols (B) who, unlike the Hittites and Bantu people, were not engaged in agriculture, learned of iron tools and weapons from other Central Asians. The Persians (C) also did not develop iron

working independently, but learned the process from others, as did the Egyptians (E), who used the iron works of Meroë to the south of Egypt as their source.

41. **(E)** The Royal Road was equipped with way stations to refresh messengers traveling its length. The Inca empire (D) also enjoyed similar characteristics in their system of roads, but the life of Herodotus, a Greek, predated the roads of the Incas of the fifteenth and sixteenth centuries.

42. **(E)** Judaism did not rely on missionary efforts to spread its doctrines; its ideas were made known to the world through the diaspora communities in Europe and Asia. Christianity was spread through missionary endeavor, especially that of Paul of Tarsus in the first century CE, and also along the Silk Roads, during the time of the new imperialism, and extending to the present (A). Buddhism spread through the messages of traders, but also through monks and nuns (B). The Sufi carried Islam throughout the Asian world (C), and Manichaeism spread through missionary efforts along the Silk Roads (D).

43. **(B)** The cultivation of maize provided a crop that dramatically increased population growth in Mesoamerica. Centralized government was not a reality in ancient Mesoamerica (A), nor was the use of iron tools (D), nor the wheel (E). Domestication of large animals in Mesoamerica was unknown (C).

44. **(E)** Islamic culture had preserved Greco-Roman culture and extended the learning of the Islamic world to Europe. The revival of learning occurred first in southern Europe (A). Italy was not unified at the time of the Renaissance (B). The Hanseatic League operated in northern Europe (C). Charlemagne's empire had eroded by the end of the ninth century, long before the Renaissance occurred (D).

45. **(E)** As the power of the papacy decreased (B) after the Protestant Reformation, the power of monarchs and nations rose in Europe. Europe was divided into religious factions because of the Protestant Reformation (A). Education was key to both the Protestant and the Catholic Reformations (C). The Roman Catholic Church altered some of its practices at the Council of Trent, but reaffirmed its beliefs (D).

46. **(C)** Displaced farmers from southeastern England sought employment in the factories of the northwest and constituted the bulk of the labor force in the early English factories. The availability of a large labor force was a contributing factor to the success of the Industrial Revolution in England. While England was taking the lead in industrialization, the inhabitants of southern Europe (A) and eastern Europe (E) continued their primarily agrarian lifestyle. The tenements of London (B) were largely a by-product of the Industrial Revolution as the factory system spread from its early location in northwestern England. Asia (D) was essentially isolated from the Western world during the early Industrial Revolution.

47. **(D)** Both European and African populations grew during this time period. Both were involved in the slave trade (A). Western Africa saw the rise of regional autocratic rulers who controlled the slave trade in their area; Europe saw the rise of absolute monarchs (B). Both Europeans and Africans were dependent upon European technology (C), and both participated in the triangular trade (E).

48. **(C)** Edison (A) invented the phonograph; the Curies (B) discovered radioactivity; Pasteur (D) came up with the germ theory of disease; and Marconi (E) invented the radio.

49. **(D)** The power of the monarch decreased as it was limited by Parliament. The use of the secret ballot in Parliament meant the end of pressure put upon members to vote a certain way (A). Power shifted to the elected House of Commons (B). After 1884, most adult males in Britain had the right to vote. The end of property requirements to serve in Parliament meant that men of all walks of life could participate (E).

50. **(D)** The map indicates sites of the independent origins of agriculture. Locations indicated on the map are: Mesoamerica (I), maize, squash, and beans; South America (II), potatoes and maize; Southwest Asia (III), wheat and barley; East Asia (IV), rice, millet, wheat, barley, and sorghum; West Africa (V), sorghum and yams. The Americas were not sites of early iron smelting (A). Neither South America nor West Africa were noted for major religious monuments (B). Discoveries of early humans (C) were concentrated in East Africa and Asia.

Prior to 1000 CE, the Americas were regional trade centers only (E).

51. **(D)** Zen Buddhism is a more mystical branch of Buddhism typified by questions such as this. Confucianism (A) was a philosophy concerned with reverence for the family, effective government, and quality education. Legalism (B) was a Chinese philosophy that advocated strong governmental authority. Stoicism (C), a Hellenistic philosophy, stressed duty and virtue. Shintoism (E), an ancient Japanese faith, centered around reverence for one's ancestors.

52. **(C)** Shortly after exploring the Indian Ocean, China retreated into isolation after further threats from Mongols along its borders. The age of exploration saw European nations exhibit a renewed interest in the East, particularly through Indian Ocean trade (A). Throughout most of the period of exploration, the Chinese and Japanese included Christian missionaries among foreigners whom they mistrusted (B). The defeat of the Mongols caused the Chinese to retreat from global trade in favor of promoting its national interests (D). Except for allowing the Netherlands access to the port of Nagasaki, Japan would not open its doors to foreign trade until the 1850s (E).

53. **(D)** The sugar plantations, with their need for huge amounts of laborers, produced the tremendous growth of slavery in the Americas. Only about five percent of slaves went to the cotton-, rice-, and indigo-producing areas of North America (A, C, E). Tea (B) was not grown in the Americas.

54. **(C)** Mercantilism was based on the principle that nations needed to amass as much wealth as possible through a favorable balance of trade. Joint-stock companies were the forerunners of early corporations (A). Utopianism was a belief in the equality of all people (B). Socialism (D) advocates the governmental management of the means of production. Utilitarianism was the belief that government actions were good only if they produced the greatest benefit for the greatest number of people. (E)

55. **(E)** The Caribbean and South America were the two areas that saw the greatest influx of Africans (A, B), while North America received about five percent of the slave trade (C). Europe received a small percentage of slaves as household workers (D).

56. **(B)** In the early nineteenth century, the Latin American nations no longer felt an allegiance to the new political order of Europe. Monarchical government were returned to power (A), and the power of France declined after Napoleon (C). Great Britain and Prussia would gradually increase in power as the power of France decreased (D), producing a relative balance of power in Europe (E).

57. **(D)** The Open Door Policy was proposed by the United States after the treaties following the Opium War. Great Britain was granted extraterritoriality and the port of Hong Kong (A, B). Foreign contact was resented by the Chinese (C), and the number of cities open to foreigners was increased (E).

58. **(B)** The various ethnic and cultural groups of Europe caused its division into independent states rather than organization as a unified political order on the European continent (A). Europe saw the practice of a number of religious faiths (C). India was actively involved in Indian Ocean trade (D). Populations in all three areas were increasing (E).

59. **(C)** Women's suffrage would not be achieved until the early twentieth century. Labor would begin to address its grievances through collective bargaining (A). Child labor laws would limit working hours of children (B) and free public education would be extended (E). Abolitionism would ride the tide of the general reform movement in the 1800s (D).

60. **(D)** Although the two czars differed in their approach to relations with the West, both upheld the Russian tradition of an autocratic monarch. Serfdom had been abolished by the time of Nicholas (A). Both maintained large armies (B). Nicholas would not allow the newly created Duma to exercise real power (C). Only Peter the Great sought to westernize Russia (E).

61. **(C)** The scientific revolution relied on proof through experimentation rather than on traditional ways of thinking. The teachings of the Church were called into question by the scientific revolution (B). Common sense was not deemed so important as proof through scientific investigation (D). Ancient scientists and

mathematicians were not revered because of their lack of experimentation (E).

62. **(E)** U.S./Hawaiian relations were based on economic imperialism, especially with regard to sugar planters. Chinese migrants became a majority in Malaysia (A). The Dutch ruled Indonesia through settlers (B). Europeans exploited the land at will (C). Siam did not come under control of any foreign power (D).

63. **(E)** The African birth rate more than compensates for the death rate from famine and disease. The birth rate in Mediterranean Europe is decreasing as women limit families in order to work outside the home (A). Industrialized nations are experiencing an influx of younger workers (B). The populations of developing nations are not aging because of poor health care (C). Japan's population is becoming increasingly older (D).

64. **(D)** The revolutions of 1848 failed to bring permanent liberal government to Europe. The ideals of the French Revolution would not die with the failed revolutions of 1848 (E), even though the revolutions did not provide greater democracy for Europe (B). Metternich's conservative policies were attacked by the revolutionaries (A, C).

65. **(D)** African disunity promoted the ease of European imperialism. Quinine eliminated the European fears of contracting malaria (B), while steam engines allowed ships to navigate the cataracts common in African rivers (C). Cable increased communications throughout colonial areas and Europe (E).

66. **(C)** Economic imperialism is the dominance of an area by businesses rather than governments. Latin America was dominated by U.S. businesses, while the other answer choices were influenced politically by other nations.

67. **(E)** Huguenots were Protestants, and the Protestant Reformation took place after the High Middle Ages. The Black Death decimated serf populations (A), while the Hundred Years' War contributed to the rise of nations (B). The rise of towns gave opportunity for serfs to flee to urban areas from the manors (C), and the agricultural revolution provided chances for some serfs to work off the manor (D).

68. **(B)** Former Ottoman lands became the targets of imperialist interests. Poland was replaced on the map of Europe and granted the Polish Corridor (A). The Spanish flu raged through military camps and became a devastating epidemic (C). Women assumed new roles after they filled in for men in industry during the war (D). Austria-Hungary was broken up into a number of states (E).

69. **(D)** The lack of basic needs prompted the rebellion of the Russian people. Industry advanced slowly (A), and the czar was more interested in personal power than in the nation (B, E). Ethnic minorities were not an issue in Russia before the revolution (C).

70. **(E)** Totalitarianism sometimes permits the practice of religious beliefs. The other answer choices are aspects of totalitarianism.

71. **(A)** Lenin's policies allowed a measure of the market economy and some private ownership to shore up the Soviet economy. Lenin began technical schools under the NEP; Stalin also provided state-sponsored technical schools (B). Under Lenin's regime a constitution for the USSR was written; however, actual power resided in the Communist Party. Stalin created a totalitarian state in which he also controlled the Communist Party (C). Although Lenin's vision was for a command economy, the NEP broke slightly with that goal. Stalin, on the other hand, created a command economy for the Soviet Union (D). Both Lenin and Stalin placed communication under government control (E).

72. **(E)** Gupta society favored arranged marriages. The caste system was made more restrictive under the Gupta (A), and the position of women deteriorated (C) as female infanticide and *sati* were practiced (B). The Gupta empire did not achieve the central control of the Mauryans (D).

73. **(B)** While Sun Yat-Sen initially attempted to institute democratic government in China, the Russian Revolution immediately resulted in the democratic-based government of Kerensky. Only the March Revolution produced a second revolution (D). Neither was strongly supported by the Western democracies (E).

74. **(B)** The new Turkish government subordinated Islamic law to the laws of the secular government and used Western governments as a model. Neither overthrew Western powers (A). Saudi Arabia was subjected to the threat of Western control in its oil fields, but did not act to overthrow that control (D).

75. **(B)** Novels tended to reflect the pessimism of the era. Between the world wars, a number of schools of art arose that reflected African and Asian influences; some of the cubist works of Picasso are examples (A). Sigmund Freud pioneered the science of psychoanalysis (C). Musical forms featured irregular rhythms; examples are jazz, the Charleston, and Stravinsky's *Rite of Spring* (D). Einstein's theory of relativity broke with the laws set forth by Isaac Newton (E).

76. **(D)** While existentialism is a form of philosophy, stream of consciousness is a style of writing.

77. **(E)** Frank Lloyd Wright was a pioneer of the architectural style known as functionalism. Sartre and Kafka were philosophers, Stravinsky was a musician, and Picasso was an artist.

78. **(E)** The instability of coalition governments caused some Europeans to prefer the stability of totalitarian government (A). Europe saw the end of empire (B) and the rise of dictators (C). Europe was devastated economically by the war (D).

79. **(C)** Fascism was concerned with the nationalist goals of a single country rather than a struggle for worldwide dominance. Both upheld loyalty to the state as their highest goal (A). Both permitted only one-party rule (B). Only communism sought a classless society (D) and worldwide revolution (E).

80. **(D)** A Gran Colombia was the goal of Bolívar after Latin American independence had been achieved. Juárez (A) was Mexico's president in the 1860s. Perón (B) was the dictator of Argentina in the mid-twentieth century. Díaz (C) was Mexico's president before that country's revolution in 1910. Fox (E) was elected president of Mexico in 2000.

81. **(D)** Hitler's movement into Russia did not occur until the war was underway. In all the other incidents mentioned, the League was unable to act to prevent further aggression.

82. **(C)** This quotation of de Klerk demonstrated his willingness to dialogue with the black African majority in South Africa. Ceausescu (A) was the brutally oppressive leader of Communist Romania. Walesa (B), former president of Poland, was also the leader of Solidarity, a labor-backed movement which led to political and social revolution in Poland. Lenin (D) was the first ruler of the Soviet Union, and Castro (E) the revolutionary Communist leader of Cuba.

83. **(B)** The conflict in Kashmir is between Muslims and Hindus. China has occupied a section of northern Kashmir (D).

84. **(B)** Japan developed a democracy with a constitution modeled on that of the United States. Both Japan and Germany were occupied by Allied powers (A). Japan lost its colonial empire (C); its emperor was reduced to a figurehead (D). Economic recovery would come quickly to Japan (E).

85. **(A)** Europe would be so weakened by the wars that her world dominance would be terminated. Only World War II contributed to the Soviet domination of Eastern Europe (C) and saw the creation of the superpowers (E).

86. **(B)** Economic decline was precipitated by the inability of nations such as Germany to repay its reparations. The U.S. contributed to the European depression when it withdrew capital from Europe (C). Colonial raw materials brought lower prices (D), and the Weimar Republic was weakened by its inability to handle the depression (E).

87. **(B)** The Chinese considered the cultures and products of other nations barbaric in relationship to their own. The term *Celestial Empire* is also a key to identifying this passage since this was a term the Chinese used for themselves.

88. **(E)** This quotation from *The Communist Manifesto* illustrates that communism saw all history as the result

of a class struggle. Fascism (A) does not seek worldwide revolution. Capitalism (B) is an economic system which supports private property and the opportunity for profits, both concepts which are opposed by communism. Mercantilism (C) was an economic policy which held that there was a limited amount of wealth worldwide, and that nations should amass wealth by selling more commodities than they were buying. Although the quotation refers to lord and serf, both elements of European feudalism, the author was referring to the feudalistic relationship as an example of class struggle (D).

89. **(C)** The Seljuks appreciated the Persian culture, even adopting the title of *shah* for their rulers. The Seljuks were overpowered by the gunpowder empire of the Ottoman Turks (A). They defeated the Byzantines at Manzikert (D). The Seljuks were not noted for their administrative skills (E). They were defeated by a Mongol invasion in 1258 (B).

90. **(C)** The Mongols helped to unify Russia by forcing all its principalities to pay them tribute. While controlling China, the Mongols adopted some of the Chinese traditions (A). They remained a threat to the northwestern border of China after the fall of the Yuan dynasty (B). Their empire lasted only a few generations because of their poor administrative ability (D). They were not only highly affected by the Black Death, but they had inadvertently brought the plague bacillus from the steppes to China (E).

91. **(D)** The Dnieper River was a major area of trade in Russia. The Oder is in Poland, the Aegean Sea is off the coast of Greece, the Elbe is in Germany, and the Danube is in Eastern Europe.

92. **(D)** Confucianism was based on reverence for ancestors and the family. Daoism (A) is a philosophy concerned with creating balance, but it does not deal specifically with the filial piety important to Confucianism. Legalism (E), another Chinese philosophy, advocated order achieved through authoritarian government. Hinduism (B) views religion as a vehicle for freeing the soul from the disillusionment of everyday life. Buddhism (C) is based upon adherence to the Four Noble Truths, which entails following the Eightfold Path of right living.

93. **(E)** These words are an Old Testament account of the selection of Saul as the first king of Israel. The key words in this passage are *brought them out of Egypt*, a reference to the Hebrew Exodus.

94. **(A)** After decades of political upheaval, Argentina moved toward a representative democracy after the war with Great Britain in the Falklands in 1982. Socialism (B) is an economic system based on government control of the major means of production. Fascism (C) is a one-party rule that promotes nationalism. Upon coming to power in 1946, Argentine dictator Juan Perón attempted to establish a government like that of Europe's fascists, but his government did not reach that level of total control. Communism (D) is an economic system in which the state controls the means of production. Monarchism (E) is rule by a king or queen.

95. **(A)** Aristotle was consumed with a passion for a broad-based knowledge and examined the mysteries of the universe. Ptolemy was an astronomer, Virgil was a poet, Alexander the Great was an empire builder, and Herodotus was a historian.

Glossary

abolition
the termination of slavery

absolute monarch
a monarch who claimed the right of complete authority over the government and the lives of his/her people

African National Congress
organization founded in 1912 by black Africans to campaign for their rights

Afrikaner
South African inhabitant of Dutch ancestry

age grade
a cohort group in which tribal members of a common age range shared experiences and responsibilities appropriate to that age group

Allah
the Muslim name for God

Anabaptists
a Protestant Church that stressed adult baptism and the separation of church and state

animism
a belief that spirits inhabit the features of the natural world

anthropology
the study of humans as a species

apartheid
a South African policy in which the races were separated by law

apostle
a follower of Jesus who helped spread his teachings

appeasement
offering concessions to an aggressive ruler or nation in order to avoid conflict and/or war

apprenticeship
a guild-sponsored system of training craftsmen

archeology
the study of cultures through examination of their artifacts

aristocracy
government in the hands of the wealthy or the nobility

armistice
a ceasefire agreement

artifact
an object shaped by humans

astrolabe
an instrument that allowed mariners to determine latitude by measuring the position of the stars

Atlantic Charter
a declaration advocating free trade and self-determination resulting from the August 1941 meeting of U.S. President Franklin Roosevelt and British Prime Minister Winston Churchill to plan for the peace after World War II; includes the idea of peace with territorial expansion or secret agreements

Australopithecenes
"southern apes"; hominids who emerged about four million years ago in southern and eastern Africa and were the first to make stone tools

ayatollah
religious title of a conservative Islamic leader in Iran

balance of power
a policy of assuring that no one nation becomes powerful enough to threaten the status of another

Balfour Declaration
a 1917 proclamation of Great Britain supporting the establishment of a separate homeland for the Jews in Palestine while protecting the rights of non-Jews already residing in Palestine

Balkans
a region in southeastern Europe currently composed of the republics of the former Yugoslavia, the European portion of Turkey, Greece, Albania, and Bulgaria

Bell Act
agreement between the United States and the Philippines that granted the Filipinos war damages in exchange for the establishment of free trade between the Philippines and the United States

benefice
in medieval Europe, a privilege granted to a vassal in exchange for military service or agricultural labor

blitzkrieg
a "lightning war" in which initial rapid surprise attacks by aircraft are followed by massive attacks of ground forces, as in the 1939 German invasion of Poland

Boers
South Africans of Dutch descent who were farmers

Bolsheviks
Russian Marxist group who desired radical change carried out by a small group of extremely committed revolutionaries

Bosporus Strait
the strategic narrow body of water between the Black Sea and the Sea of Marmara

bourgeoisie
according to Marx and Engels, the middle class; in pre-revolutionary France, a portion of the Third Estate comprised of a middle class of artisans and merchants

brahmin
a member of the priestly class in Aryan society

brinkmanship
the willingness of a country to go to the point of war to defend its interests

British Commonwealth
currently known as the Commonwealth of Nations, an association of nations whose members accept the British monarch as a symbolic head; most member nations were at one time associated with the British empire or with another current member nation

burgess
a member of the middle class in medieval England

burgher
a member of the middle class in medieval Germany

burqa
head-to-toe garment with a mesh-like panel covering the face; required attire for women under the Taliban regime in Afghanistan and by other Islamic societies

bushi
warrior leaders in feudal Japan

bushido
code of conduct of the samurai class in feudal Japan that stressed self-discipline, bravery, and simple living

capital
money, equipment, and materials used to produce more wealth through investments in businesses and factories

capitalism
an economic system based on private ownership in order to produce profits; prices are based on supply and demand

caravanserais
inns that provided lodging for caravan travelers across the Sahara Desert

caravel
a small ship with triangular and rectangular sails as well as a sternpost rudder that permitted greater control in steering the vessel

caste
one of the four classes of society in Aryan India

Catholic Reformation
also called the Counter-Reformation, a period of renewal within the Roman Catholic Church as a response to the Protestant Reformation

caudillo
a Latin American military dictator

checks and balances
the concept of Enlightenment philosopher Montesquieu that each branch of government be granted distinct powers that served to limit those of the other branches of the government

chinampa
a floating plot of land created by the Aztecs to expand the agricultural capacity of Tenochtitlán

chivalry
the code of conduct required of a knight in feudal Europe

chlorofluorocarbons
a family of chemicals used in industry, air conditioning, refrigeration, and consumer products; one of the chief destroyers of the earth's ozone layer

city-state
a city and its surrounding territory under the rule of a single government

civil disobedience
the use of passive resistance, or public refusal to obey a law that is perceived to be unjust

civilization
a culture characterized by advanced cities, specialized workers, complex institutions, a system of writing or alternate form of record keeping, and advanced technology

civil rights movement
a movement of the 1950s and 1960s in the United States to alter laws in order to eliminate segregation for African Americans and to assure them the right to vote

civil service system
a series of examinations given to determine qualifications for government-related jobs

coalition
a temporary alliance of a number of small political parties

Code of Hammurabi
Babylonian legal code that established governmental responsibility for criminal justice

collective bargaining
negotiations between employees and employers for higher salaries and improved working conditions

collective farming
large farms owned by the government in which profits are shared by all farmers

colony
a territory under the direct control of a stronger country

Columbian Exchange
beginning in the fifteenth century, the exchange of plants, livestock, diseases, and slaves between the eastern and western hemispheres

comedy
form of drama developed by the Greeks that often satirized a society

command economy
economic system in which decisions are in the hands of the government rather than the consumer

commercial agriculture
agriculture carried out on a large scale to produce crops for sale to competitive global markets

Commercial Revolution
business practices—including capitalism, joint-stock companies, and mercantilism—that characterized Europe during the sixteenth and seventeenth centuries

commune
large collective farm

communism
economic system in which the means of production are owned by all the people in common, goods and services are shared equally by all, and private property is nonexistent

concession
a form of imperialism under which land and mineral rights were granted to private businesses with investments in colonial territories

conservative
an advocate of gradual political change

constitutional monarchy
a government in which the monarch's power is limited by law

consul
one of two leaders elected by the patrician assembly who held executive authority under the Roman republic

consumerism
characteristic of a culture in which the consumption of goods and services has reached a level where it satisfies wants rather than needs only

containment
U.S. post-World War II policy of forging alliances to assist vulnerable countries in their resistance against communism

Council of Trent
a Roman Catholic council convened in 1545 to examine the Church's teachings; the outcome of the meeting was a reaffirmation of the teachings of the Roman Catholic Church and an effort to end abuses in the Church

covenant
an agreement; in the Hebrew religion, the relationship between the people and their God

creole
a term used to denote those of European descent who were born in French or Spanish colonies in the Americas

cubism
a school of art in which the normal shapes of objects or persons are changed into geometric forms

Cultural Revolution
campaign carried out by the Chinese Red Guards between 1966 and 1976, with the goal of revitalizing the Chinese Communist Party and consolidating Mao's leadership

cuneiform
Sumerian system of writing formed by pressing a wedge-shaped stylus into wet clay

Cynicism
Hellenistic philosophy calling for a return to simplicity and a rejection of materialism

Cyrillic alphabet
the alphabet of the Russian and other Slavic languages

czar (tsar)
Russian emperor

Dadaism
an artistic movement in the early twentieth century that produced works that were meaningless and whimsical

daimyo
a Japanese feudal lord who had a private army of samurai serving under him

Dar al-Islam
Arabic word meaning "house of Islam," referring to lands under the rule of Islam

Deism
a belief that maintained that, although there was a God, the role of the deity was simply to set natural laws in motion

democratization
Soviet reform initiated in 1987 by Mikhail Gorbachev by which the political system was moderated to allow voters to choose from a slate of candidates

destalinization
policy of Soviet Premier Nikita Khruschev to eliminate the memory of Josef Stalin and his policies in the Soviet Union

détente
a cooling of Cold War tensions, initiated during the administrations of U.S. President Nixon and Soviet Premier Brezhnev

devshirme
a policy under which the army of the Ottomans' sultan removed Christian boys from their families, educated them in the principles of Islam, and trained them for military service

dharma
in Hinduism, the rules of one's caste; in Buddhism, the doctrines of the faith

diaspora
the scattering of specific ethnic groups throughout various parts of the world

dictator
a sole ruler with absolute power

diocese
an administration of a group of local Christian churches

direct democracy
a government in which voters decide on issues themselves rather than through representatives

dissident
one who disagrees; a dissenter

divine right of kings
the belief of absolute monarchs that they were granted their right to rule from God

DNA dating
a method of dating artifacts by determining the rate of change in DNA

domestic system
the production of manufactured goods in the homes of workers

domino theory
idea prevalent during the Cold War period that, if one nation fell to communism, neighboring nations would likewise fall

dowry death
the killing of unwanted wives in India by which the husband douses the wife with kerosene, sets her on fire, and then reports the incident as a cooking accident

Duma
Russian Parliament

dynasty
members of the same ruling family maintaining control of their country's government for several generations

economic imperialism
control of a region by business interests rather than by an outside government

Edict of Nantes
a 1598 decree that granted religious freedom to the Huguenots

Eightfold Path
keys to right living in the Buddhist faith

emir
a Muslim ruler

empire
a government unit in which several countries or peoples are under the authority of one ruler

enclosure movement
a movement in the 1700s in England in which wealthy landowners purchased the lands of smaller farmers or took control of common areas and then fenced off their larger land holdings

encomienda
a grant of land in the Spanish American colonies that carried with it the right to exploit the Native Americans living on the land

enlightened despot
an Enlightenment-era monarch who embraced reform and ruled with the welfare of his or her subjects in mind

Enlightenment
a European intellectual movement of the seventeenth and eighteenth centuries stating that human beings were basically good and could be further improved through education, and upholding reason as the key to truth

entrepreneurship
the ability to organize and utilize the factors of production to realize profits

Epicureanism
Hellenistic philosophy that sought inner peace and pleasure, defined as the avoidance of pain

estate
a social class in medieval and pre-revolutionary France

Estates-General
the French assembly (1200s–1789) made up of clergy, nobles, and the common people

ethnic cleansing
policy of murder and other violent acts directed against a particular ethnic group by another; initially applied to the killing of Bosnian Muslims by Serbia after the breakup of Yugoslavia

euro
a common European currency introduced in January 2002 by the European Union

European Union
an organization of European countries to promote free trade among its members

existentialism
philosophy that holds that life in itself has no meaning and that each person decides the meaning of life for himself or herself

expressionism
a school of art featuring the use of bold colors and the distortion of forms

external migration
the relocation of people across long distances or international borders

extraterritorial rights
a privilege that exempts foreign residents from the laws of the nation in which they are residing

factors of production
those factors essential to industrialization: land, labor, capital, and entrepreneurship

fascism
a political movement that emphasizes extreme nationalism and loyalty to the state and features one-party rule by an authoritarian ruler

feminist
a woman who holds to the belief in equal rights and opportunities for both men and women

feudalism
a political system in which a monarch or noble granted land to other nobles in exchange for military services, protection, and loyalty

fief
a grant of land in medieval Europe

Final Solution
Hitler's systematic elimination of the Jews and other populations he considered inferior

Five Pillars
the five duties required of all Muslims: faith, prayer, alms, fasting during Ramadan, and the hajj

Five-Year Plans
economic plans to increase industrial and agricultural productivity in the Soviet Union, China, and India

foraging
hunting and gathering

Forbidden City
a lavish community of the rulers of Ming China, forbidden to commoners

Four Modernizations
goals issued by China's Deng Xiaoping that included changes in industry, agriculture, defense, and science and technology

Four Noble Truths
a philosophy of life's struggles according to the Buddhist faith: everything in life is suffering; the cause of all suffering is people's desire; suffering can be ended by ending all desires; desires may be overcome by following the Eightfold Path

Fourteen Points
peace plan for the post-World War I world proposed by President Woodrow Wilson; its major points included the principle of self-determination and the establishment of an association of nations

Four Tigers
the four economically successful areas of Hong Kong, Singapore, South Korea, and Taiwan

fresco
a painting done on wet plaster that was typical of the art of the Greeks and Romans and of the European Renaissance

functionalism
an architectural school of the twentieth century which held that buildings should be constructed so that their design reflected their function

Geneva Conference
conference held in 1954 which divided Vietnam at the seventeenth parallel

genocide
the organized elimination of an entire population group

geocentric theory
the theory of the Greek astronomer Ptolemy, stating that the earth was the center of the universe

ghazi
a warrior for Islam

ghetto
segregated community (e.g., Jewish community in Poland)

glasnost
a Soviet policy introduced in 1985 by Mikhail Gorbachev emphasizing openness in the sharing of information and ideas

global village
the view of the earth as one human community in which people of all cultures share common needs, wants, and experiences

glyph
a symbol used as part of a writing system

golden mean
Greek ideal of balance, moderation, and proportion

Gospel
one of the first four books of the Christian New Testament

Greater East Asia Co-Prosperity Sphere
Japanese name for the areas it occupied during World War II

Great Leap Forward
a five-year plan launched by Mao Zedong in China in 1958 to increase industrial and agricultural output under which he set up communes in China

green revolution
an effort begun in the twentieth century to increase the global food supply by the use of pesticides, fertilizers, and developments in disease-resistant crops

griot
an African storyteller who passed on oral traditions

guest workers
workers who have migrated from developing countries to industrialized ones to take advantage of employment opportunities and ultimately to stay as permanent residents

guild
in medieval Europe, a merchant organization founded to regulate production standards and prices within specific trades

Gulf of Tonkin Resolution
resolution passed by the U.S. Congress to authorize President Lyndon Johnson to send U.S. troops into Vietnam

Guomindang
Nationalist party founded in China by Sun Yixian; after 1925, headed by Jiang Jieshi

Hagia Sophia
magnificent Eastern Orthodox Church constructed in Constantinople by the emperor Justinian

hajj
a pilgrimage to Mecca required once during the lifetime of a follower of Islam

harem
the wives and concubines of households in Africa, Arabia, or Southwest Asia

Hellenistic culture
a blend of eastern and western culture characteristics (Greek, Egyptian, Persian, and Indian) in the period between the reign of Alexander the Great and the Roman occupation of Greece

helot
agricultural laborer in ancient Sparta

Helsinki Accords
a 1975 pledge to practice détente and promote human rights that was signed by the Soviet Union, the United States, and 33 other nations

hieroglyphics
ancient Egyptian picture writing

hijra
the flight of Muhammad from Mecca to Medina in 622 CE, and the first year of the Muslim calendar

Holocaust
the mass extermination of Jews and other civilians in Nazi Germany

homeland
reserved territory in the least desirable areas of South Africa set aside for black residents

hominid
a humanlike creature that walks upright

Homo sapiens
thinking man; the species to which modern humans belong

hubris
a fatal flaw of overconfidence, often displayed by the main character in a Greek tragedy

Huguenots
French Protestants

human cloning
copying a human DNA sequence to create a new human being

humanism
an intellectual movement of the Renaissance period which emphasized reason and concerned itself with everyday human problems

Huns
a nomadic group from central Asia who undertook a mass migration toward the Roman empire in the 400s CE

icon
two-dimensional religious images used by Eastern Christians in their celebrations and devotions

iconoclastic controversy
a conflict between papal and secular authority sparked by the use of icons in the Eastern Orthodox Church

illuminated manuscript
a manuscript copied by hand by medieval monks, who enhanced its beauty with elaborate lettering and detailed pictures

imperialism
the political, economic, or social domination of a strong country over another

impressionism
a mid-nineteenth century artistic movement that reacted against realism by portraying subjects as they appeared to the artist at a given moment in time

indulgence
in the sixteenth-century Roman Catholic Church, a paper whose purchase guaranteed the buyer the forgiveness of sins

Inquisition
a Roman Catholic Church court especially powerful in Spain and Italy during the Counter-Reformation

intercontinental ballistic missile (ICBM)
a ballistic missile with the capacity to travel from one continent to another

internal migration
the movement of people from rural to urban areas

intifada
a series of demonstrations, boycotts, and violent attacks employed by Palestinians from 1987 onward to attract world attention to their desire for a Palestinian homeland

island-hopping
U.S. World War II strategy of seizing control of key islands of strategic importance around Japanese strongholds in the Pacific

janissary
slave boy taken by the Ottoman Turks from conquered Christian territories

jazz
a twentieth-century style of music developed primarily by African-American musicians

joint-stock company
a business that was a forerunner of the modern corporation in which investors pooled their resources and shared in the profits

Junkers
landowning classes in eighteenth-century Russia, used as officers in the Prussian army

justification by faith
the belief that persons receive eternal salvation through their faith in Jesus Christ as the savior of the world

Justinian Code
a compilation of Roman laws, legal treatises, and Byzantine laws passed after 534 that were codified by the Emperor Justinian

Ka'aba
a shrine which contained the Black Stone, a relic of the polytheistic beliefs of the early Arabs and later the destination of the Muslim hajj

kaiser
a German emperor

kamikaze
World War II Japanese suicide pilots who flew their bomb-loaded planes into American ships; the Japanese name for a "divine wind" that drove back Mongol invasions of the Japanese islands in the thirteenth century

karma
in Hinduism, a person's good or evil deeds while on earth

Kellogg-Briand Pact
a 1928 agreement to outlaw war that was signed by most countries

kibbutzim
Israeli communal agricultural settlements

kinship group
a group of families that formed the basis of villages in some parts of Africa

kowtow
a ritualistic bow required of all visitors to the Chinese court

laissez-faire
economic theory proposed by Adam Smith which argued that government should not interfere with the natural laws of supply and demand

lateen sail
triangular sail that permitted greater control of ships

latifundia
large estate in ancient Rome

League of Nations
an association of world nations created by the Treaty of Versailles after World War I

lebensraum
the German word for "living space," a goal Hitler wished to attain by conquering Eastern Europe and Russia

legion
in ancient Rome, a military unit of 5,000 to 6,000 infantry

legitimacy
the right of a dynasty to rule

Lend-Lease Act
a policy passed by the U.S. Congress in 1941 to allow President Roosevelt to lend or lease arms and other supplies to any nation considered vital to the security of the United States

liberal
in the early nineteenth century, a term referring to those Europeans who favored granting increased power to elected assemblies

loess
fine, yellow, windblown silt

Luftwaffe
the German air force

macadam road
a road developed by Scottish engineer John McAdam in which a pavement was created of small stones compacted together into layers

Magna Carta
document signed by England's King John in 1215 that limited the power of the king and protected the rights of nobles

Magyars
a nomadic people from central Asia who eventually settled in modern Hungary

major domo
the major of the palace; the most powerful person in Gaul by the early eighth century

mameluke
military slave who fought in the armies of the Abbasids

mandate
a former colonial territory that is supervised by another country during its transition to an independent nation

mandate of heaven
divine approval used to grant authority to Chinese dynasties

Manhattan Project
the U.S. plan to develop an atomic bomb

Manichaeism
a blend of some of the beliefs of Zoroastrianism, Buddhism, and Christianity which held that life was a struggle between good and evil

manor
a self-sufficient estate in feudal Europe

marathon
a twenty-six mile race

Marshall Plan
a U.S. program of economic assistance to European nations to aid them in restoring their economies and societies after World War II

Mau Mau
in Kenya, a secret organization of primarily Kikuyu farmers driven out of the farmland of the northern highlands by the British

McDonaldization
the global culture inspired and promoted by U.S. advertising

Mensheviks
early twentieth-century Marxist group in Russia that wanted to engage popular support for revolution in Russia

mercantilism
an economic system in which nations attempted to amass as much wealth as possible by exporting more than they imported; central to mercantilism was the acquisition of colonies

Messiah
Hebrew word meaning "the anointed"; in Judaism, the promised deliverer of the Jews; in Christianity, a term referring to Jesus

mestizo
person in colonial Spanish America who was of mixed European and Native American heritage

Middle Passage
the trans-Atlantic route of slaves from Africa to the Americas

militarism
a policy of advocating military power and maintaining a standing army

millet
ethnically homogenous nations under the Ottoman empire who were allowed a representative to serve as a voice before the sultan

missi dominici
imperial officials under Charlemagne's empire who had the duty of overseeing the records of the counts, or local rulers

mobilization
movement of a military force to an area in conflict

moderate
term referring to those in the French Legislative Assembly whose stand on political issues was neither radical nor conservative

Mongol Peace
the period between 1250 and 1350, in which the Mongols restored the security of trade over the Silk Roads between Europe and Asia

monotheism
the belief in one god

monsoon
seasonal wind used by mariners to navigate the Indian Ocean

multinational corporation
a corporation which constructs factories in a number of countries in order to capitalize upon inexpensive raw materials and cheap labor in those countries

mystery religion
a Hellenistic religion that involved faith in Eastern deities and the promise of eternal life to believers

nationalism
a deep sense of pride in one's nation

nation-state
an independent state whose citizens are bound by a common cultural identity

NATO (North Atlantic Treaty Organization)
a 1949 defense alliance initiated by the United States, Canada, and ten nations of Western Europe

natural selection
according to Darwin's theory of evolution, the concept that those organisms best adapted to their environment would be the most likely to survive in succeeding generations (i.e., "survival of the fittest")

Neo-Confucianism
a blend of Confucianism and Buddhism that emphasized traditional Chinese values of self-discipline, family loyalty, and obedience to authority

Neolithic Age
the period between 8000 BCE and approximately 3000 BCE; also known as the New Stone Age

Neolithic Revolution
the change from hunting and gathering to agriculture

New Deal
a reform program initiated by U.S. President Franklin Roosevelt to restore the U.S. economy during the Great Depression

New Economic Policy (NEP)
Lenin's policy to improve the Soviet economy by permitting small private businesses

Nicene Creed
a statement of the Christian faith issued in 325 CE stating that Jesus was at the same time fully human and fully divine

nirvana
in Buddhism, a state of perfect peace

nonalignment
neutrality of developing nations during the Cold War

nongovernmental organization
international organization dedicated to investigating human rights violations and providing humanitarian aid

Nuclear Non-Proliferation Treaty
an agreement signed in 1968 by several nations who pledged to help prevent the spread of nuclear weapons

Nuremberg Trials
post-World War II trials held in Nuremberg, Germany, to try Nazi leaders charged with war crimes

oracle bone
a bone or shell used by the Chinese to determine the will of the gods

one-child policy
a policy adopted in the 1980s in the People's Republic of China stating that a couple is allowed only one child

OPEC (Organization of Petroleum Exporting Countries)
an organization established in 1960 by several of the world's oil-producing countries to regulate prices and production

Operation Barbarossa
Hitler's 1941 invasion of the Soviet Union

Operation Overlord
the Allied invasion of Normandy in northwestern France on June 6, 1944

Operation Sea Lion
Hitler's plan against Great Britain, which began with the bombing of Britain in the summer of 1940

Palestine Liberation Organization (PLO)
an organization whose chief aim is the establishment of an independent Palestinian state in Southwest Asia

Paleolithic Age
the period from 2,500,000 to about 8000 BCE; also called the Old Stone Age

paleontologist
a scientist who studies fossilized remains

Papal States
territory under the dominion of the papacy

parallel descent
a pattern of inheritance in which daughters inherit from their mother and sons from their father

pariah
an untouchable, or a person whose status is below that of the Hindu castes

parliament
a national legislative assembly

pasteurization
developed by Louis Pasteur, the process of destroying bacteria in milk and other liquids

pastoral nomadism
periodic migration in order to locate grazing lands for domesticated herds

patriarch
leading bishop of the Eastern Orthodox Church

patriarchal
describes a male-dominated society

patrician
member of the elite class in ancient Rome

Peace Corps
program begun under the administration of U.S. President John Kennedy to send volunteer workers to developing nations to assist them in improving education, agricultural methods, sanitation, and other areas of need

peninsular
member of the elite social class of colonial Spanish America, composed of persons who had been born in Spain

people of the book
term used by Muslims to refer to Christians and Jews, whom the Muslims respected for possessing a scripture

perestroika
Soviet policy introduced in 1985 by Mikhail Gorbachev in which the Soviet people were permitted to own small private businesses

philosopher
one who pursues the meaning of truth

plebeian
a member of the class in ancient Rome that included farmers, artisans, and merchants, and comprised the majority of the population

pogrom
a campaign of violence against Jewish settlements in Russia in the late nineteenth century

polis
a Greek city-state

Politburo
the governing committee of the Communist Party in the USSR

polygamy
marriage to more than one wife

polytheism
the worship of many gods

Potsdam Conference
a 1945 conference held at Potsdam, Germany, in which Truman and Churchill met with Stalin to attempt to persuade him to abandon his policy of domination of the Soviet satellite nations

predestination
according to John Calvin, the concept that God, before the beginning of the world, had chosen some people for heaven and others for hell

proletariat
according to Marx and Engels, the members of the working class

propaganda
the dissemination of materials or messages to promote one's own cause or diminish the cause of an adversary

protectorate
a region that is controlled by an outside power but is allowed to maintain its own government

Protestant Reformation
the sixteenth-century reform movement in the Christian Church that emphasized salvation through faith in Jesus Christ alone

psychoanalysis
science developed by Sigmund Freud that focused on psychological rather than physiological causes of mental disorders

purdah
in India, public isolation of women from non-family members

push-pull factors
those conditions that compel individuals to leave their country and those that pull persons to another location

qanat
ancient underground irrigation system used in Southwest Asia and China

quinine
an antimalaria drug

quipu
an Incan record keeping device that consisted of a cord from which were suspended a number of cords, each containing a variety of knots of various sizes, shapes, and colors

radical
a member of the French Legislative Assembly who wanted immediate, drastic change in the French government

radiocarbon dating
a method of measuring the amount of radiocarbon in fossilized material

reactionary
a person in favor of returning to the status quo

realism
a mid-nineteenth-century movement in art and literature that focused on the ills of industrialization

realpolitik
the politics of reality put into practice by Otto von Bismarck

Reconquest (Reconquista)
the process, lasting from about 1000 to 1492, by which Christians drove the Muslims from Spain

Renaissance
the period in European history from about 1300 to 1600 (though some historians prefer the dates 1100 to 1600) in which a return to classical themes dominated art, literature, and education

reparations
payments for war damages imposed upon losing nations

repartamiento
a replacement for the *encomienda* system which allowed for the payment of wages to Native American workers in the Spanish American colonies

republic
government in which citizens are ruled by elected representatives

robotics
the technology associated with the application of robots

romanticism
artistic and literary movement of the early nineteenth century that reflected an admiration for nature and an emphasis on individual thought and feelings

rotten borough
in nineteenth-century England, a voting district without residents

Royal Road
a 1,600-mile communication route in ancient Persia

sakk
letter of credit issued by Islamic banks; forerunner of modern checks

samurai
armies of soldiers in feudal Japan

satellite nation
a nation that is under the political domination of another, as in the domination of the USSR of the nations along its western border

sati
practice in some areas of India in which widows threw themselves onto the burning funeral pyre of their husband

satrap
provincial governor in the Persian empire

Scientific Revolution
a change in scientific thought beginning in the mid-sixteenth century in which scientific knowledge was based on experimentation and research rather than the acceptance of traditional beliefs

scorched-earth policy
a tactic of burning everything in the path of an invading army

Senate
the patrician assembly that approved all major decisions in republican Rome

separation of powers
idea proposed by the Enlightenment philosopher Montesquieu in which the powers of government are divided among different branches

sepoys
Indian soldiers serving under the command of British army officers

seppuku
a custom of disembowelment carried out by the samurai as an honorable alternative to the acceptance of defeat

serf
in feudal Europe, a peasant bound to the lord's land

shah
a Persian king

shariah
Muslim social and ethical law

shi
ancient Chinese class of scholars

Shia
a traditional form of Islam that supported the election of only the family members of Muhammad

Shinto
ancient Japanese religion centered around the veneration of ancestors and spirits of nature

Shiva
Hindu god portrayed as both creator and destroyer

shogun
in feudal Japan, a superior military leader who ruled in the name of the emperor

Sikhs
a people whose religious philosophy blended Hinduism, Buddhism, and Sufism

Silk Roads
ancient and medieval trade routes that linked China to the Mediterranean world

social contract
the Enlightenment concept that government is based upon an agreement in which the people relinquish their rights to a ruler in order to receive the protection offered by law and order

Social Darwinism
the nineteenth- and early twentieth-century application of the theories of Charles Darwin to social science in an effort to create the notion that some races were superior to others

socialism
an economic system in which the means of production belong to the public and are operated for the common welfare

Society of Jesus
also called the Jesuits, an organization founded in 1534 by Ignatius of Loyola to promote education, establish missions, and stop the spread of Protestantism

soviet
local council of peasants, laborers, and soldiers organized by Russian revolutionaries

space probe
a spacecraft that carries instruments capable of transmitting to earth photographs and information about the planets

space shuttle
spacecraft with the capacity to return to earth under its own power

space station
spacecraft that serves as an orbiting scientific laboratory

specialization of labor
the development of and use of skills in a specific type of work

sphere of influence
area that granted investment or trading privileges to another country

stateless society
a society ruled by a number of equal kinship groups rather than by a central government

stele
stone pillar that was the characteristic architectural structure of Aksum

stem cell research
the study of cells that have the capacity to divide in a culture and produce specialized cells

steppe
an almost treeless flat grassland stretching across central Asia and eastern Europe

Stoicism
the most popular of the Hellenistic philosophies, the belief that individuals had a responsibility to aid others and lead virtuous lives

Strategic Defense Initiative (SDI)
also called Star Wars, a 1983 program launched by President Ronald Reagan to protect the United States against incoming enemy missiles

stream of consciousness
a literary technique influenced by psychoanalysis that reveals the character's thoughts and feelings at the moment in which they occur

stupa
great shrines of stone constructed to house relics of the Buddha

suffrage
the right to the vote

Sunni
the branch of Islam that supported the authority of the earliest caliphs

Surrealism
an artistic movement in which paintings are characterized by a dreamlike quality

Swahili
a widely spoken language among East Africans which is a blend of Arabic and the Bantu languages

Taliban
an Islamic fundamentalist group that gained control of Afghanistan in 1997

Tamils
the people of southern India who speak the Tamil language

terra cotta
hard, reddish-brown clay used in pottery

theocracy
government controlled by religious rulers or by a ruler considered divine

theory of evolution
theory proposed by English biologist Charles Darwin which held that biological change is affected by the process of natural selection

theory of relativity
a theory proposed by Albert Einstein which stated that the measurement of motion varies relative to a specific observer and that a small amount of mass can be converted into a vast amount of energy

thermoluminescence dating
a method of dating flint and clay objects by measuring the amount of electrons released when the subject is heated

Third Reich
the Third Empire of Germany established in the 1930s by Adolph Hitler

Third World
a Cold War term referring to developing nations nonaligned with either the Soviet Union or the United States

Time of Troubles
a period of violence in Russia between 1598 and the choice of Mikhail Romanov as czar in 1613

Torah
the scripture that contains the history of the ancient Jewish people and their covenant with their God

totalitarian state
a government characterized by the rule of only one party whose beliefs support the welfare of the state above all else

tragedy
serious Greek drama dealing with the downfall of the main character

Treaty of Tordesillas
a 1494 treaty that divided the lands in the Americas between Portugal and Spain

Treaty of Versailles
peace treaty ending World War I between the Allied Powers and Germany; included in the treaty were clauses placing the blame for the war on Germany and requiring Germany to pay heavy reparations

tree-ring dating
also called dendrochronology, the study of the chronological order of the annual growth rings in trees

trench warfare
a form of warfare in which opposing armies dig parallel trenches from which they engage in combat; used in World War I

triangular trade
a trans-Atlantic trade route from Europe to Africa, then to the Americas, and then returning to Europe

tribune
an elected representative of the plebians, who sat as a member of the Tribal Assembly in republican Rome

Triple Alliance
pre-World War I military pact among Germany, Austria-Hungary, and Italy

Triple Entente
pre-World War I pact among Great Britain, France, and Russia

triumvirate
a government of three rulers

Truman Doctrine
a policy announced by U.S. President Truman in 1947 to offer military and economic aid to free nations threatened by communism

truncated pyramid
a trapezoid-shaped pyramid typical of the architecture of pre-Columbian Mesoamerica and South America as well as early Polynesian societies

tyrant
in ancient Greece, a ruler who seized power and ruled with sole authority

U-boats
German submarines, or *Unterseeboten*

umma
the Muslim community of the faithful

Universal Declaration of Human Rights
statement issued in 1948 by the United Nations which defined basic universal human rights as "life, liberty, and security of person"

Urdu
a linguistic blend of Arabic and Hindi which is currently the official language of Pakistan

usury
in medieval Europe, the practice of charging interest

utopian socialist
in the first half of the nineteenth century, an intellectual who believed in human equality and in practicing cooperation in industry

utilitarian
an advocate of a philosophy which held that government actions and policies were useful only when they promoted the common good

vassal
in feudal Europe, a person who received from his lord a grant of land in exchange for loyalty and military or agricultural services

veto
the power to prevent the execution of a law

Vietnamization
President Richard Nixon's plan for the gradual withdrawal of U.S. troops from Vietnam while at the same time increasing the combat responsibilities of the South Vietnamese

Warsaw Pact
a 1955 defense alliance organized by the Soviet Union, Czechoslovakia, Hungary, East Germany, Poland, Albania, Bulgaria, and Romania

World Health Organization (WHO)
a United Nations-sponsored agency whose goals are to improve world health and assist countries in promoting family-planning programs

World Trade Center
a New York building complex housing numerous companies and organizations dealing with global trade; a target of the 2001 terrorist attack on the United States

World Trade Organization
an organization established in 1995 to supervise free trade

Yahweh
the Hebrew name for God

Yalta Conference
a 1945 conference attended by the leaders of the United States, Great Britain, and the Soviet Union in the city of Yalta on the Black Sea; its goal was to divide postwar Germany into zones of occupation

yin and yang
Chinese concept of balance in nature represented by male assertiveness and female submission

Yom Kippur
the Jewish Day of Atonement

Zen Buddhism
a blend of Buddhism with some of the teachings of Daoism to form a faith dependent upon meditation and enlightenment

ziggurat
a multitiered pyramid that served as a temple in Sumer

Zionism
movement beginning in the 1890s, its main focus was the establishment of a Jewish homeland in Palestine

NOTE FOR INTERNATIONAL STUDENTS

If you are an international student considering attending an American university, you are not alone. Over 586,323 international students pursued academic degrees at the undergraduate, graduate, or professional school level at U.S. universities during the 2002–2003 academic year, according to the Institute of International Education's *Open Doors* report. Almost half of these students were studying for a bachelor's or first university degree. This number of international students pursuing higher education in the United States is expected to continue to grow. Business, management, engineering, and the physical and life sciences are particularly popular majors for students coming to the United States from other countries.

If you are not a U.S. citizen and you are interested in attending college or university in the United States, here is what you'll need to get started.

- If English is not your first language, you'll probably need to take the TOEFL® (Test of English as a Foreign Language) or provide some other evidence that you are proficient in English in order to complete an academic degree program. Colleges and universities in the United States will differ on what they consider to be an acceptable TOEFL score. Because American undergraduate programs require all students to take a certain number of general education courses, all students—even math and computer science students—need to be able to communicate well in spoken and written English.
- You may also need to take the SAT® or the ACT®. Many undergraduate institutions in the United States require both the SAT and TOEFL of international students.
- There are over 3,400 accredited colleges and universities in the United States, so selecting the correct undergraduate school can be a confusing task for anyone. You will need to get help from a good advisor or at least a good college guide that gives you detailed information on the different schools available. Since admission to many undergraduate programs is quite competitive, you may want to select three or four colleges and complete applications for each school.
- You should begin the application process at least one year in advance. An increasing number of schools accept applications throughout the year. In any case, learn the application deadlines and plan accordingly. Although September (the fall semester) is the traditional time to begin university study in the United States, you can begin your studies at many schools in January (the spring semester).

In addition, you will need to obtain an I-20 Certificate of Eligibility from the school you plan to attend if you intend to apply for an F-1 Student Visa to study in the United States.

KAPLAN ENGLISH PROGRAMS

If you need more help with the complex process of university admissions, assistance preparing for the SAT, ACT, or TOEFL, or help building your English language skills in general, you may be interested in Kaplan's programs for international students.

Kaplan English Programs were designed to help students and professionals from outside the United States meet their educational and career goals. At locations throughout the United States, international students take advantage of Kaplan's programs to help them improve their academic and conversational English skills, raise their scores on the TOEFL, SAT, ACT, and other standardized exams, and gain admission to the schools of their choice. Our staff and instructors give international students the individualized attention they need to succeed. Here is a brief description of some of Kaplan's programs for international students:

General Intensive English

Kaplan's General Intensive English classes are designed to help you improve your skills in all areas of English and to increase your fluency in spoken and written English. Classes are available for beginning to advanced students, and the average class size is 12 students.

General English Self-Study

For students needing a flexible schedule, this course helps improve general fluency skills. Kaplan's General English Self-Study course employs the communicative approach and focuses on vocabulary building, reading and writing. You will receive books, audio and video materials as well as three hours of instructor contact per week.

TOEFL and Academic English

Kaplan has updated its world-famous TOEFL course to prepare students for the new TOEFL iBT. Designed for high-intermediate to advanced-level English speakers, our new course focuses on the academic English skills you will need to succeed on the new test. The course includes TOEFL-focused reading, writing, listening and speaking instruction, and hundreds of practice items similar to those on the exam. Kaplan's expert instructors help you prepare for the four sections of the TOEFL iBT, including the new Speaking Section. Our new simulated online TOEFL tests help you monitor your progress and provide you with feedback on areas where you require improvement. We will teach you how to get a higher score!

SAT Test Preparation Course

The SAT is an important admission criterion for U.S. colleges and universities. A high score can help you stand out from other applicants. This course includes the skills you need to succeed on each section of the SAT, as well as access to Kaplan's exclusive practice materials.

Other Kaplan Programs

Since 1938, more than 3 million students have come to Kaplan to advance their studies, prepare for entry to American universities, and further their careers. In addition to the above programs, Kaplan offers courses to prepare for the ACT, GMAT, GRE, MCAT, DAT, USMLE, NCLEX-RN® exam, and other standardized exams at locations throughout the United States.

Applying to Kaplan International Programs

To get more information, or to apply for admission to any of Kaplan's programs for international students and professionals, contact us at:

Kaplan International Programs
700 South Flower, Suite 2900
Los Angeles, CA 90017, USA
Phone (if calling from within the United States): 800-818-9128
Phone (if calling from outside the United States): 213-452-5800
Fax: 213-892-1364

Email: world@kaplan.com
Web: www.kaplanenglish.com

Kaplan is authorized under federal law to enroll nonimmigrant alien students. Kaplan is accredited by ACCET (Accrediting Council for Continuing Education and Training).

Test names are registered trademarks of their respective owners.